THE TROJAN HORSE AND OTHER STORIES

What makes us human? What, if anything, sets us apart from all other creatures? Ever since Charles Darwin's theory of evolution, the answer to these questions has pointed to our own intrinsic animal nature. Yet the idea that, in one way or another, our humanity is entangled with the non-human has a much longer and more venerable history. In the West, it goes all the way back to classical antiquity. This grippingly written and provocative book boldly reveals how the ancient world mobilized concepts of 'the animal' and 'animality' to conceive of the human in a variety of illuminating ways. Through ten stories about marvellous mythical beings – from the Trojan Horse to the Cyclops, and from Androcles' lion to the Minotaur – Julia Kindt unlocks fresh ways of thinking about humanity that extend from antiquity to the present and that ultimately challenge our understanding of who we really are.

Julia Kindt is Professor of Ancient History at the University of Sydney, a Future Fellow of the Australian Research Council (2018–22), a member of the Sydney Environment Institute, and Fellow of the Australian Academy of the Humanities. She is a senior editor of the *Oxford Research Encyclopedia of Religions* (*ORE*), and a member of the editorial boards of the *Journal of Ancient History* and *Antichthon.* She is also a contributor to the *Times Literary Supplement,* the *Australian Book Review, Meanjin, The Conversation,* and other periodicals. Her previous, highly regarded, books include *Rethinking Greek Religion* (Cambridge University Press, 2013) and *Revisiting Delphi: Religion and Storytelling in Ancient Greece* (Cambridge University Press, 2016).

'In this beautifully written and timely book, Julia Kindt provides a fascinating account of how humans use real and imaginary animals to think about what it means to be human, and an eloquent defence of the power of storytelling. With each of its chapters comparing classical and modern sources in innovative, accessible, and engaging ways, *The Trojan Horse and Other Stories* is sure to start an important conversation about how the ancient world foreshadows our contemporary consideration of the human–animal relation.'
- Chris Danta, Professor of English, Australian National University

'Julia Kindt has found a miraculous new lens through which to scrutinize our oldest, most loved stories and find in them colours, shapes, and qualities that we have never really seen before. Humankind's relationship with animals has been examined through archaeology, history, and art, but never before, to my knowledge, through myth, legend, and story. The insights that this absorbing and imaginative approach reveal are enthralling and profound. The stories are told with wit, imagination, and sparkle; the animals who star in them brought wondrously to life.'
- Stephen Fry

'The stories from ancient Greece are foundational for all our imaginations – and they are some of the best and most long-lasting stories we have! Julia Kindt is a wonderful guide to what they are, what they mean, and how they have influenced us.'
- Simon Goldhill, Professor of Greek Literature and Culture, University of Cambridge

'Kindt's wide-ranging volume tackles a question seldom addressed in the ever-expanding literature of ancient animal studies: how do non-human animals make us human? Investigating this question through an examination of ten animals and animal types that appear in classical mythology and history and live on in recent literature and art, she offers fresh insights on issues central to ancient animal studies, including the nature of animal intellect and emotion, the ethical obligations of human beings towards other species, and the significance of hybridity and metamorphosis. Kindt's scrupulously researched yet highly readable text will prove informative and stimulating to classical scholars and non-specialists alike.'
- Stephen T. Newmyer, Professor Emeritus of Classics, Duquesne University

THE TROJAN HORSE AND OTHER STORIES

Ten Ancient Creatures That Make Us Human

Julia Kindt

The University of Sydney

Shaftesbury Road, Cambridge CB2 8EA, United Kingdom

One Liberty Plaza, 20th Floor, New York, NY 10006, USA

477 Williamstown Road, Port Melbourne, VIC 3207, Australia

314–321, 3rd Floor, Plot 3, Splendor Forum, Jasola District Centre, New Delhi – 110025, India

103 Penang Road, #05–06/07, Visioncrest Commercial, Singapore 238467

Cambridge University Press is part of Cambridge University Press & Assessment, a department of the University of Cambridge.

We share the University's mission to contribute to society through the pursuit of education, learning and research at the highest international levels of excellence.

www.cambridge.org
Information on this title: www.cambridge.org/9781009411387

DOI: 10.1017/9781009411332

First published 2024

Printed in the United Kingdom by TJ Books Limited, Padstow Cornwall

A catalogue record for this publication is available from the British Library

A Cataloging-in-Publication data record for this book is available from the Library of Congress

ISBN 978-1-009-41138-7 Hardback

Contents

Figures

Preface

What makes us human? What, if anything, sets us apart from all other creatures? As far as questions go, they hardly get bigger and more fundamental than these. Moreover, these questions matter. They have a direct impact on how we relate to each other and to the world we inhabit.

Ever since Charles Darwin's theory of evolution, the answer to these questions has pointed us to our own animal nature. And yet, the idea that, in one way or another, our humanity is entangled with the non-human has a very long history. In the West, it goes all the way back to classical antiquity (and probably beyond).

This book seeks to speak to and engage all those with an interest in the question of the human in its relation to the non-human – or, in the words of David Abraham (an ecologist and philosopher) 'more than human'. More specifically, it illustrates how the ancient world mobilised concepts of 'the animal' and 'animality' to conceive of the human in various ways.

The ancient Greeks and Romans held the idea that there is an intrinsic quality to members of the human species and set out to explore it from the earliest times onwards. The major genres of Greco-Roman thought and literature – epic, history, tragedy and comedy, medicine and philosophy (to mention just a few) – all, in one way or the other, investigate the human condition. And all of them, in various ways, do so in reference to the animal.

By investigating ancient views of the human and the non-human animal, this book is part of a larger endeavour to reveal some of the foundations on which Western humanism rests. It aims to show how ancient conceptions have shaped and continue to shape the present, and to make visible some of the assumptions on which they are based – including those assumptions which today appear problematic or discriminatory. To this end, it offers ten essayistic interventions into ways of 'thinking the human' that connect antiquity with the present. Each strand is focused through the lens of an iconic creature and the sometimes amusing, sometimes disturbing, but always deeply engaging stories that sustain it.

In order to make the chapters that follow accessible to a wider group of readers, this book deviates from the standard classical book in a number of ways. It includes brief explanations of concepts and terms that would not need explaining if the book was only addressed to the classical reader. The book also features the dates of ancient authors and their texts whenever relevant and provides information on the disciplinary background of scholars mentioned in the text if they are from fields other than classical studies. References are kept to a minimum and relegated to the end of the book. They are mainly there for the academic reader who may be interested in following up on the ancient texts and the modern scholarly debates to which they relate. It is absolutely possible to read through the book without consulting them.

With the general reader in mind, I have resisted the urge to include long quotations from the sources in the original ancient Greek and Latin. Instead, I have included Latin and transliterated Greek only when it clarifies a particular point and matters to the larger argument. All translations from the ancient languages are grounded in those of the Loeb Classical Library except when otherwise noted. I have made adjustments where I felt the translation suggested did not sufficiently reflect the meaning of the original and when this mattered to the argument. Finally, even though I sometimes use the term 'animals' instead of the somewhat formulaic 'non-human creatures', or 'non-human animals', I do so for variation and not to imply a fundamental distinction between us and them.

Acknowledgements

I enjoyed writing every single one of my books, but this one has been special. Researching it took me to many new places, even though most of the time I was stuck at home due to the pandemic. I thank the Australian Research Council (ARC) for awarding me a four-year research fellowship (Future Fellowship) to write this book and Colin and Mary McCann for supporting Classics at Sydney (and this project) for many years. To be able to dedicate such an extended period of time to thinking, reading, and writing in the middle of my career has been a deeply transformative experience. It allowed me to move beyond my disciplinary comfort zone, to forge a plethora of new connections and collaborations, to engage in new conversations – as well as continuing on in existing ones – and to read much more thoroughly and widely than otherwise possible. Working on this project made me see the presence of non-human animals in the lives of the human animal (past and present) much more clearly than previously the case.

It made me look at the world with different eyes.

I thank my husband Daniel and my daughter Sophie for putting up with me during intense periods of writing. I thank Tanja Latty for allowing me to attend her introduction to biology lectures (BIOL 1006, *Life and Evolution*) in semester 1, 2018, and for answering my relentless questions about honeybees and other insects. I thank the Sydney Environment Institute (SEI) for making me a member and including me in a group of truly inspiring and engaging scholars. I thank Thom van Dooren and Peter Wilson for discussing aspects of this project with me. I thank Rick Benitez, Tristan Bradshaw, Danielle Celermajer, Bob Cowan, Richard Gordon, Kitty Hauser, Brooke Holmes, Stephen

Newmyer, Robin Osborne, and Anne Rogerson for reading and commenting on individual chapter drafts and Jan Bremmer for reading through the whole manuscript. Paul Cartledge for answering my questions on Socrates and ostracism. Early drafts of several chapters were improved by my academic writing group convened by Barbara Caine and Glenda Sluga. Individual chapters were presented to audiences at the University of Sydney, the Greek Festival of Sydney, and in Tokyo and Kyoto, and I thank Noboru Sato for inviting me to visit Japan.

I would like to thank Billy Griffith for helping me find a title for the book. I thank Maria Merkeling and Edward Armstrong for proofreading and editing, and Rebecca Georgiades, Brennan Nicholson, and Louise Pryke for their help with other aspects of the typescript. Thanks also to Candace Richards and Craig Barker for helping me with some of the images.

Finally, I thank the anonymous peer reviewers of Cambridge University Press for the care and diligence with which they read my manuscript and for making invaluable suggestions for further improvement.

Introduction

WHEN, AFTER AN ABSENCE THAT LASTED THE BETTER PART of two decades, Odysseus finally finds his way home to Ithaca and his wife Penelope, he discovers an unruly bunch of aristocrats squatting in his palace. They are, quite literally, feasting off his assets, wining and dining as they please. They are seeking to win his wife, Penelope, and power over Ithaca. With the help of the goddess Athena, the cunning hero first checks out the situation disguised as an old beggar, draped in animal hides.

On approaching his palace, he encounters his old dog Argos ('the swift'), a puppy when Odysseus departed for Troy some twenty years before (Figure 0.1).

Odysseus is immediately struck by its presence: 'And a dog that lay there raised his head and pricked up his ears, Argos, steadfast Odysseus' dog, whom of old he had himself bred, but had no joy of him, for before that he went to sacred Ilium.'[1] Even though the old and neglected dog is in poor shape, it does not take him long to recognize his old master: 'There lay the dog Argos, full of dog ticks. But now, when he became aware that Odysseus was near, he wagged his tail and dropped both ears, but nearer to his master he had no longer strength to move.'[2] The whole scene stirs deep sentiments in the returning hero: 'Then Odysseus looked aside and wiped away a tear.'[3]

Argos does not live to see his master's final return to Ithaca. While Odysseus eventually confronts the suitors, reinstalls himself at Ithaca, and reunites with Penelope, the dog's life comes to a sudden end. Almost as soon as man and dog lock eyes, the animal passes away.[4] Argos' death is

0.1 Louis Frederic Schutzenberger, *Retour d'Ulysse* (1884).

the ultimate token of devotion to Odysseus, and a final, endearing twist in the story of their encounter.

In the figure of Argos, Homer has created the archetypal member of a species that, unlike any other, lends itself to associations of domesticity and belonging. Argos provides a strong example of the quality most often associated with dogs in the ancient and the modern worlds: unconditional and unquestioning loyalty.[5] Dogs, this scene shows, in particular companion dogs, have always counted among man's closest and most beloved non-human friends.

But is there more? Is there anything in this scene beyond the touching and endearing? Can this tale ever be more than a trivial footnote to what some may well regard as the more serious objects of historical, cultural, and literary inquiry? After all, we may wonder: why should we care about Argos, an animal, when we have Odysseus, Achilles, and Hector – not to mention the ever-inscrutable Penelope – in all their *human* complexity to consider?

And yet, to dismiss the presence of Argos as of little consequence would be to suggest that animals cannot be worthy objects of critical inquiry in their own right: they already are. More importantly, perhaps, it would disregard what is at stake in this particular story and how it relates to the larger one of which it is part. The final encounter between Argos and Odysseus is not tangential to the broader themes of the *Odyssey*; rather, it goes right to the core of the questions and problems raised by Odysseus' return to Ithaca.[6]

Odysseus' encounter with the dog conjures memories of youthfulness and vitality: 'In days past the young men were accustomed to take the dog to hunt the wild goats, and deer, and hares; but now he lay neglected, his master gone, in the deep dung of mules and cattle.'[7] These memories bring out just how much time has passed since Odysseus left Ithaca. The passing of time becomes tangible in the gap between the here and now and the long ago. Referring to the dog, the swineherd Eumaios tells the beggar (Odysseus): 'If he were but in form and action such as he was when Odysseus left him and went to Troy, you would soon be amazed at seeing his speed and his strength.'[8] The once-swift Argos is no longer agile, just as Odysseus himself has aged since he left Ithaca. In the image of the frail canine, Odysseus faces the time that has passed since he left home – time now irrevocably gone in all but memory.

It matters that Argos is not just any kind of dog, but a hunting dog.[9] In the ancient Greek and Roman worlds, dogs played important roles in tracking down and trapping wild animals, such as deer, hares, and wild boars. The ancient literature on hunting gives strong evidence of the close and intimate bonds between hunters and their dogs.[10] Through Argos' presence, the *Odyssey* mobilizes the image of the hunt as an important initiatory stage in a young man's life. Like a hunter, young Odysseus once left Ithaca in order to prove himself out in 'the wild'. And like a successful hunter he is now returning home to reclaim his rightful place at its core.

But unlike a hunter, Odysseus had set out on his momentous journey without his dog. He has proven himself not side by side with loyal Argos, but side by side with his human comrades at Troy. Argos has been left behind to guard the threshold of the house and to greet Odysseus upon his return. His presence thus marks the real and symbolic boundary that

Odysseus is about to cross.[11] It helps to depict Odysseus' return as the momentous transition that it is: back from battlefields and the twisty journey that followed into the *oikos* ('house', 'home') and the adoption of his rightful place at its core.

And yet, despite their long separation there is a deep sympathy between Argos and Odysseus in the literal sense of the ancient Greek *sympathein* ('to suffer together', 'to share in one's suffering'). Like Odysseus, Argos is displaced, barred from his rightful place at the master's hearth. And dog and master both are deprived of the privileges they once enjoyed.[12] In the moment of recognition, the conditions of human and animal align, one referencing the other in a 'metonymic relationship'.[13] And the recognition is mutual and does not rely on tokens or persuasion.[14] Indeed, Argos here features as a 'faithful *philos*' ('friend'), in analogy, perhaps, to Eumaios himself and in contrast to other figures including the unfaithful servants and Odysseus' son Telemachus, who will need convincing that Odysseus has indeed returned.[15]

In order to bring out such correspondences, the dog is humanized. In the *Odyssey* as a text not poor in dogs and dog-references, he is the only one which is named in the text, his death is referred to as *moira* ('fate'), and he is attributed with a *demas* ('body', 'frame') – a word that elsewhere in the *Odyssey* is reserved for the human body only.[16] All this helps to align the condition of Argos and his owner. The dog reflects the situation and identity of Odysseus at this particular point in the story.

Moreover, the juxtaposition of human and non-human does not stop with Odysseus and Argos. The dog's extraordinary loyalty implicitly raises the question of the loyalty and capacity of another figure close to the returning hero: his wife Penelope. While the dog recognizes Odysseus instantly, the reunion of husband and wife is postponed until the hero and the reader alike have entertained the possibility that she may, after all, have given up. Odysseus cannot be certain whether Penelope is still waiting for his return or whether she has submitted to the suitors' demands. Ultimately, she too will prove to be loyal. But when Odysseus first arrives at Ithaca, it is not clear what exactly awaits.

So, the focus on the dog does not take away from the human protagonists in the story. Rather, human identities, sentiments, and relations are at centre stage in the moment of Argos' recognition of Odysseus.

***

By attributing to Argos such a powerful role, Homer acknowledges the fact that our humanity is invariably bound up with non-human creatures. With Darwin's theory of evolution, the animality of the human took centre stage.[17] But, in many ways, Darwin's account of our descent from other animals merely placed on a scientific footing an observation that had long dominated thinking about the question of the human: that in order to understand who we really are, we have always looked to non-human creatures. It is through the way we relate to animals – not merely by comparing and contrasting ourselves with them but also by addressing, conversing with, and appropriating them in multiple ways – that we grapple with different aspects of our humanity, even those that we would rather keep concealed under a layer of deceptive animal clothing. In a nutshell: it is impossible to understand humanity's view of itself without acknowledging and appreciating the way the human animal defines itself in and against the animal realm.

This book sheds light on the ancient history of a conversation that revolves around various attempts to answer the question of what it means to be human. This conversation started in Greek and Roman antiquity (if not before) but is still going strong today. It involves the Greek and Roman philosophers who variously defined the human in relation to the animal, and, in doing so, anticipated many of the positions that are still evoked today; but it does not remain restricted to them. Over time the conversation came to feature numerous ancient voices that spoke to the question in a range of registers and pitches. Most notably, it drew on stories and the practice of storytelling to raise fundamental questions about our own humanity and animality – without necessarily always providing an answer to them.

TEN CREATURES THAT MAKE US HUMAN

The ten essayistic interventions that follow focus on ten ancient creatures which, like Argos, have an unnerving capacity to expose the kind of humans we really are. Some are domesticated, tame, and endearing; others are wild and ferocious. Some are noticeably Greek in origin; others are distinctly Roman. Most defy an easy attribution to a particular time and place. They roam the real and imaginary landscapes of the ancient world more widely, crossing, migrating, travelling among them. Some are – or at least could be – real; most are obviously imaginary. Many, but not all, come from the realm of mythology. Some (also) inhabit ancient observations about the natural world. At least one – the infamous Socratic gadfly – is merely a figure of speech.

All these creatures come together in drawing on ideas of human and animal, embodying them, combining them, and stretching out between them in different ways. And yet, they do so by representing fundamentally different categories: the Socratic gadfly serves as a metaphor. The Trojan horse embodies the idea of a device that serves a certain purpose. The Sphinx, the Cyclops, and the Minotaur represent or relate to the category of the monstrous. Different notions and conceptions of the human become tangible within or between these categories.

In particular, the animal -natures of the creatures featured in this book matter in this respect. They represent different ways in which humans categorize non-human animals, between the domestic and wild, edible and inedible, notions of the sacred, the ferocious, and the disgusting (to mention just a few). So, by representing these and other categories, the creatures populating this book embody different ways in which human and animal, humanity and animality come together. Their role as 'type specimens' – prototypes that biologists use as points of reference for the description and identification of further members of their species – is acknowledged by the fact that they have been attributed with Latin binominals in their respective chapter headings.

Again, Argos, Odysseus' dog, leads the pack here. Even though there is no doubt that he is fully a member of the canine species, he enacts values, experiences, and concerns that are ultimately human. He is thus a prototypical member of yet another category we have created for certain kinds of animals – that of the companion animal or pet – and the whole ratbag of human/animal intimacies that come with it. Throughout this book we join Argos in seeking to peer through all deceptive clothing and to sniff out the human within.

HUMANITIES PAST AND PRESENT

The main focus is on Greek and Roman antiquity, but in each chapter, we track down and pursue the creature's trail into the present. This takes the form of a sustained discussion of individual strands of their reception. Or it comes in the form of brief comments on the persistence of the larger theme the creature in question represents in modern conceptions of the human. This is why we follow the Sphinx from Sophoclean drama into the works of Sigmund Freud, the Socratic gadfly from Plato into the writing of the modern political theorist Hannah Arendt, and the Minotaur from Greco-Roman mythology into the works of Pablo Picasso.

To take such a broader view is important because explaining the way in which the ancient creatures resonate in the here and now matters. It is this bigger picture which allows the ancient and modern worlds to converse. Freud, Arendt, and Picasso articulate modern conceptions of the human. But they do so in conversation with the ancient world through their adaptation and interpretation of these figures. Comprehensiveness is nowhere claimed or achieved. We merely illuminate strands in 'thinking the human' that reach from the ancient into the modern world.

But who is the 'we' speaking here? And to whom?

Throughout this book I offer a critical appreciation of certain moments in the history of ideas as they evolve in and out of Greco-Roman thought and literature. The 'we' addressed here includes – but is not limited to – all those who have their intellectual homes within this tradition. The purpose is to show the ancient dimension in Western thinking about human and non-human animals that all too frequently go unexplored.

Of course, the use of the animal for the sake of human self-definition is hardly specific to the West. Non-Western conceptions of the human also frequently draw on non-human creatures.[18] Indeed, one of the central premises of this book – that it is impossible to understand conceptions of the human animal without understanding conceptions of the non-human animal – applies to numerous cultures, both past and present. Different worlds articulate themselves in parallel ways – all equally valuable, equally real, and equally true to themselves. Various cultural traditions draw on animals in thinking the human in ways that are both equally fascinating and fundamentally different from the material considered in this book. And while some of them also relate to categories such as the bestial that feature prominently in the Western tradition, they frequently conceive of them in radically different ways.[19]

The conception of the human under investigation here has proved invariably powerful. Not so long ago, many considered it superior to others. These days its claims to universality and dominance no longer stand unchallenged. Indeed, most recently, the study of the ancient world and its reception in the modern have been at the core of a much larger critical reckoning with Western colonialism and dominance and the intellectual traditions in which they are based. And yet, some of the ideas associated with the traditional Western conception of the human still prevail. The idea that humans differ from animals through the presence of *logos*, for example, still informs our thoughts, actions, and attitudes in many ways.

This is because the idea of human exceptionalism was further energized by Christianity which propagated the idea that man was made in the image of god and the human the pinnacle of creation.[20] Even though the anthropomorphism of the Greco-Roman gods also made a connection between the human and the divine, it was Christianity that further disseminated the idea of a fundamental gulf that separated humans from other animals. The particulars of this development are beyond the scope of this book. Suffice it to say here that this link not only explains how the anthropocentric perspective came to prevail in Western thinking but also accounts for why Darwin's theory of evolution received such an adverse response from some Christians: his insistence of a continuity between humans and animals fundamentally challenged the Christian account of creation and the idea that humans were fundamentally different from animals.

As this book will show, the Western concept of the human and the non-human as it emerged out of classical antiquity comes at a certain price which is not always evident and taken into account. And this price is paid not only by animals but by certain humans too. The point is that the very forces that came to separate the human from the animal in Greco-Roman antiquity have also led to the suppression of women, slaves, and foreigners. So, this book follows the current interest in grappling with the difficult legacies of this tradition and the way in which the classical past has been put to use in it.

We will return to the larger implications of the way in which the ancient world resonates in the modern in the conclusion to this book. At this point we merely reiterate that the 'we' imagined here is not meant to be exclusive. In its most general sense, it can also be taken to refer to me (as the author) and you (the reader) as human animals whose understanding of ourselves emerges through our interactions with and appropriations of non-human creatures.

THE HUMAN, THE HUMANITIES, AND THE ANIMAL

Over the last thirty-odd years, there has been a new wave of interest in the study of animals. There is now a sizeable interdisciplinary group of people who share a common interest in how humans relate to animals in a variety of ways as well as the motivations, values, and cultural assumptions underpinning these relations.[21] The study of the ancient world has not been impartial to this trend even though it fully took off here later than in many other disciplines.[22] In particular since the turn of the millennium, there has been a sharp rise in works that throw light on the manifold ways in which the ancient Greeks and Romans related to animals in a number of texts and contexts, historical, philosophical, literary, and material.[23]

This interest has generated invaluable knowledge about the ways in which human and animal lives intersect in the ancient world. And yet, this knowledge has so far not been incorporated into the larger picture. *If* the modern debate references the ancient world at all, it mostly points to Aristotle. The reason for this is that people working on the ancient material do not always flag what is interesting about their material to other disciplines.[24] At the same time, the contemporary conversation is still heavily driven by philosophical perspectives on the question of the human and so is naturally drawn to the origins of their own discipline in classical antiquity.

Separating the human from the non-human animal was a major concern of the Greco-Roman philosophers. The notion that humans are separated from animals by a deep gulf gave rise to a line of reasoning that came to be known as 'the man-only-*topos*': the view that humans stand apart from all other animals through one or more distinctive features, capacities, or habits.[25] Among the Greek and Roman philosophers, this idea was fleshed out in ever new formulations: the human alone among all animals has reason, thought, or intellect (*logos, dianoia*).[26] The human alone among all animals has speech.[27] The human alone among all animals can sit comfortably on his hipbones.[28] And, more curiously: the human alone has the capacity to mourn.[29] The human alone has hands that allow the building of altars to the gods and the crafting of their statues.[30] The human alone has the capacity to mate throughout the year and into old age.[31] In order to prove that humans stand out, the ancient Greek philosophers drew on a range of observations that reach from the banal to the outlandish and absurd (to say nothing about their veracity).[32] Throughout classical antiquity, some of the ancient philosophers sought to establish – or refute – the existence of an essential and irrevocable difference between the human and non-human animal.[33]

We will return to the philosophical debate throughout this book. Suffice to say here that the quest to separate the human from all other animals extended well beyond the confines of the philosophical debate and into the realm of storytelling. There is much ancient evidence that relates directly to the conversation beyond the works of the major Greek and Roman philosophers. Thinking about the nature of the human (and the animal) started much earlier than the philosophical debate, with the first written texts and material evidence that have come down to us from classical antiquity. This evidence includes some of the most famous works of classical literature, such as Homer's *Iliad* and *Odyssey*, Virgil's *Aeneid*, and Ovid's *Metamorphoses*, but it does not remain confined to them. The question of what makes us human implicitly plays into *all* genres of Greek and Roman literature: it informs mythography, animal lore, natural history, didactic poetry, and ancient fables. It has a major place in ancient drama (tragedy, comedy) as well as in ancient stories told in material form (such as paintings on pottery), to mention just a few examples. Unfortunately, this evidence is not always known beyond those with an explicit interest in the ancient world. It is brought together here for the first time in a broad account that puts the ancient and modern in conversation with each together and that transcends the disciplinary boundaries of history, literature, and philosophy as well as ancient and modern accounts of the question of the human and the animal.

HUMAN/ANIMAL 'ENTANGLEMENTS'

This book does not tell a traditional history grounded in a chronological account. Rather, it seeks to capture certain strands in the history of ideas in a more thematic fashion. Each of the creatures included in this book represents a particular way, a particular theme in which our humanity comes into focus through what I will refer to as our 'entanglement' with non-human animals.[34] By 'entanglement' I mean the myriad ways in which human and non-human identities remain bound up with each other. Each creature inhabiting this book illuminates a particular dimension of this 'entanglement' by throwing light on the paradoxes that emerge in our relationships to animals in different areas of life.

To present just two examples that feature in some detail later in this book: who would have thought that the inclination to endow honeybees with political qualities in general and monarchical tendencies in particular (as implied in the idea of a queen bee) can already be found in the ancient world? It goes all the way back to the Greek philosopher Aristotle, if not before. Given that the power of what we today call the queen bee is strictly limited to her reproductive function, we may wonder: why do we project our political culture onto honeybees? Why do accounts of honeybees touch upon politics? And why does politics need the honeybee, starting from its initial conception in the ancient world? The answer, as we will see, leads straight to the way that human political identities are crafted.

Likewise, who would have thought that some ancient thinkers already invoked ethical arguments for vegetarianism in much the same way we do today? In doing so, they opted out of the link between certain kinds of masculinity and meat-eating that revealed itself, for example, in the ostentatious consumption of meat at Roman dinner parties and the no less flamboyant digestive accomplishments of ancient Greek athletes. It might seem curious that, in this sense, the association between manliness and power has not changed in fundamental ways since the days when the four-horse chariot was the vehicle of choice for those wishing to compensate for their vulnerable masculinities. Yet its stubborn persistence points to the fact that there is indeed something unwaveringly human on show here, transcending differences of time and place.

The notion of 'entanglement' helps to characterize these relationships: it allows us to make sense of how our humanity veers between relationships of likeness and difference to non-human animals without ever committing fully to either side. 'Entanglement' brings out the ways in which our humanity is inextricably bound up with our own animality: the more we try to get away from it by trying to define ourselves as different, the more we become ensnared.

***

The medium best suited to explore this entanglement is that of narrative and storytelling. It is here that we find attempts to push back on the idea of human exceptionalism and to imagine alternate worlds in which humans and animals come together in different ways.[35] This strand of the conversation does not follow the vain (and ultimately futile) goal of establishing an abstract philosophical case for human exceptionalism – even though it continues to refer to such attempts in its own storylines. Instead, it shows how humans, in their interactions with non-human creatures, continue to grapple with the ambiguity at the heart of the human condition: we *are* indeed animals, but animals that like to think of ourselves as different. The resulting paradoxes haunt us up to this day. They are fundamental to the human/animal story as the medium perhaps best suited to explore the shifting ground of our humanity: between the wish to be different from all other creatures inhabiting this planet – and the ultimate realization that we are not.

The ancient world generated a particularly rich and iconic set of human/animal stories. Myth, fables, the wonder literature, and nature writing (to mention just a few examples) all draw on narrative and storytelling to explore the ways in which humans and animals relate. It is about time that we take them seriously, that we listen to what they tell us, and that we bring them to the attention of all those interested in what it means to be human.

And on this note, we move straight on to the first one.

CHAPTER 1

Chapter 1 introduces the human as a question. It revolves around the figure of the Theban Sphinx and her interaction with Oedipus. More specifically, it invokes the Sphinx as a presence that both prompts and challenges the way we think the human. Oedipus' troubled humanity emerges at the intersection between his success in solving the Sphinx's riddle and his apparent failure to understand how her words apply to his own existence. The story of his encounter with the hybrid beast introduces us to the idea of *logos* (reason) as a force that is frequently invoked in favour of human exceptionalism. The Sphinx' intervention at Thebes exposes a deep-seated vulnerability at the core of the human condition – a vulnerability springing from the fact that while the riddle of the human can be solved with the powers of reasoning, the human as a riddle remains enigmatic and beyond the application of *logos.*

1.1. The Theban Sphinx (detail), Attic red-figure lekythos (ca 460 BCE).

The Sphinx (*Sphinx aenigmatica*)

According to a famous myth, the city of Thebes in the central Greek region of Boeotia once faced a peculiar situation: on a mountaintop outside of the city's gates a monstrous creature had taken up residence – a sphinx with wings, the body of a lion, and the head of a woman.[1] Yet it is not just the apparition that terrifies but her wit as well. According to Apollodorus (first/second century CE) who offered a detailed account of the story, the Sphinx stopped in their tracks anyone wishing to pass and challenged them with the following question:

> What is that which has one voice (*phōnē*) and yet becomes four-footed (*tetrapous*) and two-footed (*dipous*) and three-footed (*tripous*)?[2]

Solving the riddle is no idle pastime or amusing exercise. Rather, it is a matter of life and death. Those who fail to come up with the right answer are instantly devoured by the beast. The Thebans think hard what the solution to the riddle may be: 'They often met and discussed the answer, and when they could not find it, the Sphinx used to snatch away one of them and gobble him up.'[3] Numerous attempts at providing the answer fail and the resulting loss of life is great, according to some sources even comprising members of the Theban royal family.[4]

That is, until Oedipus comes along. He is the son of Laios, king of Thebes, but unaware of his lineage. As a baby, he was exposed in the wild and raised by foster parents in Corinth. Travelling to Thebes as a stranger, Oedipus, too, comes face to face with the Sphinx.

He ponders the question and – after careful reflection – provides an answer. The solution is as simple as it is perplexing: the creature in question is – you guessed it – the human! As a baby the human is crawling on all fours, later he is walking upright on two legs and, in old age, man is using a walking stick, appearing decisively 'three-footed'. The Sphinx's riddle describes the different stages of human life, from infancy to old age.

The reaction of the Sphinx to Oedipus' intervention is instantaneous, absolute, and final. Upon hearing Oedipus' response, the beast throws herself down a cliff to her death. Oedipus reaps the rewards of his success: as a prize for liberating the city from the monster's lethal grip, he ascends the throne of Thebes and marries the widowed queen, Jocasta.

The story could have ended here with king and queen living happily ever after, but this is not what happens. For all is not well in Thebes under Oedipus. Soon infertility, famine, and other calamities strike the city – sure (divine) signs that the humans in question have committed some sort of heinous outrage.[5]

What has gone wrong?

Didn't the Thebans choose an outstanding individual to be their king, one who had just distinguished himself through his mental agility and power of reasoning?

Oedipus tries to find the source of the defilement – without success. Only once it finally dawns on him that he himself is the reason for the calamities that have befallen the city is he ready to consider the truth and embrace its consequences. Oedipus learns that he is not the biological child of the Corinthian royal couple that raised him but the biological offspring of Laios of Thebes and his wife Jocasta. Right after birth he had been given to a shepherd to be exposed in the wild because, years before, an oracle had predicted his parents' offspring would kill his father and marry his mother. The shepherd, however, could not bring himself to follow orders. He passed baby Oedipus to one of his colleagues who, in turn, passed him on to the Corinthian royals who raised him as their own.

Not knowing his real identity, Oedipus inadvertently fulfilled the prophecy he tried so hard to prevent. By marrying his mother and killing his father, as the Oracle of Delphi had predicted years before, he committed unspeakable offence and incurred pollution. On realizing the defilement, he blinds himself and leaves Thebes – never to return. Later, at Colonus, he dies, having lost everything he once valued.[6]

***

This is, in broad brushstrokes, the core of the well-known story of Oedipus. Situated in a mythical time before the Trojan War, it concerns the ancient Greek city of Thebes and its royal family, the House of Labdacus (the so-called 'Labdacids'). But why start with this story? Why Oedipus and the Sphinx? What is this tale about and how does it relate to the larger themes of this book?

By turning the ancient figure into a 'complex' of the same name, Sigmund Freud maintained that we are all, in a way, Oedipus. Indeed, Freud's psychologizing reading of the myth – one of the famous instances of the reception of the ancient world in the modern – has turned the specific struggles of Oedipus into everyman's experience. We will see that this is by no means a coincidence: Freud could draw on an ancient story that already depicted Oedipus' humanity as exemplary of the human condition.

This chapter focuses on the figure of the Sphinx to tell the story of her role in defining both ancient and modern humanities. We will find that she is the perfect creature inhabiting the opening chapter of this book. This is because her presence at Thebes introduces the question of the human by posing the human as a question. And not just any kind of question but one of the highest importance – literally a matter of life and death. Her riddle itself and its solution through Oedipus anticipate the ancient philosophical debate on the question of the human – the core of the next chapter.

THE THEBAN SPHINX AND OTHER SPHINXES

First some background on the role and meaning of sphinxes in the ancient world. What exactly were these peculiar creatures? Where did they come from? And what did they represent?

The figure of the sphinx was originally not Greek but came to the Greco-Roman world from Egypt or Mesopotamia, where sphinxes both small and large – think of the famous monumental Sphinx at Giza – featured as early as the third millennium BCE.[7] Yet right from the start of their appropriation into the literary and artistic production of the Greco-Roman world, the ancient Greeks and Romans endowed these creatures with a special pedigree that integrated them into their own supernatural universe. At the same time, sphinxes always retained a particularly uncanny and inscrutable air due to their Egyptian origins.

The earliest reference in Greco-Roman literature comes from the seventh century BCE. In his *Theogony*, a grand account of the origins and structures of the divine pantheon, the ancient Greek poet Hesiod introduces the Sphinx as the monstrous offspring of two other no less monstrous figures: Orthos – a two-headed dog – and, in all likelihood, the Echidna, half woman, half snake.[8] And yet it would be wrong to make too much of this lineage. Not all Greco-Roman sphinxes looked the same. In terms of their physical appearances, they come in all sorts of shapes, forms, and sizes: while they always combine the body of an animal – most frequently a lion – and a human head, they differ in that the head could be either male or (more often) female. Some also had additional attributes such as wings or horns. In her hybrid body, the sphinx resembles numerous other monsters of Greco-Roman myth that also combine the parts of different creatures.[9]

The monstrous figure at the core of this chapter, the so-called Theban Sphinx, is thus the most famous specimen of a larger group of similar figures known to us from the ancient world. The Theban Sphinx stands out in the ancient record in that she is the only one with an extended literary life: while sphinxes were a prominent iconographic motif on Greco-Roman pots and are represented widely in monumental sculpture from the Minoan and Mycenean periods onwards, literary references to other sphinxes are rare and do not involve an extensive storyline.[10] Throughout classical literature, there is no other example of a sphinx challenging humans to solve a riddle.[11]

How (and why) this creature set up shop at Thebes is unclear.[12] The ancient authors attribute her deadly presence to the intervention of a deity. But which one? Various gods are named as responsible for her appearance but without a specific reason.[13] And even though he is not among them, her riddling, hybrid nature also points to the god Apollo, the god of prophecy, music, and healing, whose oracles are frequently just as riddling as her words. It seems clear that the Sphinx provides a reason for Oedipus' appointment to the highest office in Thebes.[14] This makes her an integral part of the story of Oedipus – so integral, indeed, that various ancient painters chose her facing Oedipus as the central image of the myth.[15]

SOPHOCLES' SPHINX AND THE FICKLENESS OF HUMAN FORTUNE

The figure of the Theban Sphinx is invariably linked to the humanity of a particular human: Oedipus. The figure of Oedipus, in turn, is intricately connected to the rendering of his story by a particular ancient author: that of the Athenian playwright Sophocles (ca 496–406 BCE). It is his telling of the story in his acclaimed tragedy *Oedipus the King* that set the ground for the reception of the ancient figure by Freud.

How did Sophocles represent the newly appointed head of Thebes? And what role does the Sphinx play in sketching out Oedipus' particular struggle?

On the face of it, merely a minor one. Despite the central role of the riddle in the story of Oedipus, it is strangely absent from Sophocles' telling. Contrary to what one may expect, the moment of Oedipus facing the Sphinx and the specific words of her riddle do not feature in *Oedipus the King* at all – hence the references to Apollodorus' version of the tale in the opening section of this chapter.[16] The play is set in a mythical time *after* Oedipus solved the riddle, following the demise of the Sphinx and Oedipus ascending to the throne of Thebes. It tells the story of Oedipus inquiring into the source of the pollution that has befallen the city, his gradual and belated understanding that *he himself* is its cause, and the suffering that springs from insight into his past transgressions and wrongdoing.

And yet despite this absence, the Sphinx's riddle has a distinct presence in the play. The ancient audiences would have been well familiar with the basic storyline of the myth, including the wording of the famous riddle. So, Sophocles' drama makes repeated reference to the Sphinx's enigma at key moments throughout the play without, however, spelling it out in detail. Moreover, the Sphinx is itself enigmatic. In *Oedipus the King*, she is called a 'prophesying maiden with hooked talons' a 'winged maiden', and a 'versifying hound' – thus pointing to her looks, her gender, her closeness to other articulations of the supernatural (see below), and her partial membership in the realm of animals.[17]

Direct pointers to the role of the Sphinx in the story of Oedipus then come in the form of a voice that speaks to us from within the drama: that of the Chorus of Theban elders. As a collective voice, such choruses always carry considerable weight. This particular chorus speaks with particular authority because it consists of older citizens. In *Oedipus the King*, they provide a commentary on the action. And they remind us more than once that the presence of the Sphinx is central not merely to the humanity of Oedipus but to the human condition more generally.

> Dwellers in our native land of Thebes, see to what a storm of cruel disaster has come Oedipus here, who knew the answer to the famous riddle and was a mighty man, on whose fortune every one among the citizens used to look with envy! So that one should wait to see the final day and should call none among mortals fortunate, till he has crossed the boundary of life without suffering grief.[18]

By pointing to the fact that the now fallen Oedipus was once the envy of the town, the Chorus here asserts a view that is also articulated elsewhere in ancient Greek thought and literature: that human life can only be deemed a success or failure towards the end of one's lifetime, once one has lived its full course.[19] This is because human fortune is fickle and subject to change sometimes due to divine intervention. As a result, it is impossible to know what the future will hold until it has actually become the present, and perhaps even the past.

Oedipus is a case in point. His success and fortune (in solving the riddle) are followed by loss and suffering later in life. In highlighting Oedipus' suffering and his futile attempts to get on top of the situation, Sophocles illustrates the reversal of fortune as a fundamental characteristic of the human condition. In the words of the Theban elders:

> Ah, generations of men, how close to nothingness I estimate your life to be! What man, what man wins more of happiness than enough to seem, and after seeming to decline? With your fate as my example, your fate, unhappy Oedipus, I say that nothing pertaining to mankind is enviable.[20]

So, Oedipus' humanity emerges between his success in solving the riddle and his failure in recognizing how it relates to his own life. And the resulting struggle is symptomatic of the human condition more broadly.

Incidentally, perhaps, the very same point, that human life is fickle and subject to dramatic shifts and changes is already anticipated in the Sphinx's riddle itself. By pointing to the different stages of the human life cycle – childhood, adulthood, and old age – it also takes a bird's-eye view of human life in its entirety. The Chorus' words point back to the Sphinx's riddle as the apparent apex of his success. It is in the tragic space between his capacity to solve the Sphinx's riddle and his failure to grasp his situation in the here and now that Oedipus' humanity is situated.

This humanity consists, to a significant extent, in the suffering springing from the need to navigate in the uncertain and shifting territory between fate, chance, and human moral responsibility – to find one's way in a world in which the gods intervene seemingly at random and in which even a man who strives to be righteous can find himself responsible for unspeakable wrongdoing.[21] In the myth, Oedipus' fall from grace is overdetermined – a consequence of fate (the result of a curse that was once cast on Oedipus' father Laios that affected the family over several generations) *and* his own actions. Oedipus is easily irritable, prone to resort to violence, and seems to have an unwavering trust in his own intellectual capacities.

And yet Oedipus' suffering is not just a personal tragedy; it is closely tied to his role as king of Thebes.[22] While there are many facets to Oedipus' humanity, the suffering springing from his increasingly futile attempts to uphold truth and justice – in a world where truth is hard to establish and justice ephemeral – looms prominently in a story in which his personal tragedy doubles as a collective crisis for the city.[23] When his mother Jocasta urges him to give up in his quest to find Laios' murderer, he insists: 'You will never persuade me not to find out the truth!'[24] But what if this truth shakes not just the fundamentals of the one who seeks it but the very foundations of society itself?

THE HUMAN AS RIDDLE

In highlighting the fickleness of human fortune and the cascading human uncertainties and suffering that result, the Chorus speaks to larger questions of knowing and not knowing which are central to Oedipus' tragic experience. Time and again Oedipus emphasizes his clever wit and his critical spirit, as evident in particular in his ability to solve the riddle. It is, for example, invoked when he reproaches the seer Tiresias for having been unable to free Thebes from the deadly clutches of the Sphinx:

> Why, come, tell me, how can you be a true prophet? Why when the versifying hound was here did not you speak some word that could release the citizens?

> Indeed, her riddle was not one for the first comer to explain! It required prophetic skill, and you were exposed as having no knowledge from the birds or from the gods. No, it was I that came, Oedipus who knew nothing, and put a stop to her; I hit the mark by native wit (*gnōmē kurēsas*), not by what I learned from birds.[25]

Oedipus here compares and contrasts the seer's supernatural knowledge as it informs his prophecies and predictions with his own critical ingenuity. Even though he has no special knowledge derived from the gods, he is quick to point out that it was he and not Tiresias who solved the Sphinx's riddle and released the Thebans from the monster's grip. The confidence on show here is also at work in Oedipus' subsequent attempts to find Laios' murderer and the reason for the pollution incurred by the city.

Yet despite his drive to get to the bottom of things, Oedipus has an astonishing capacity to overlook what is right there before his eyes. The poetics of seeing and blindness, both literally and metaphorically, evolve alongside – and as an articulation of – the poetics of knowing and not knowing mentioned above.[26] Indeed, the drama is full of puns on knowing, including extensive wordplay involving Oedipus' own name, one meaning of which alludes to the ancient Greek for 'I know' (*oida*).[27] His *logos* allows Oedipus to tackle some problems and challenges successfully. Full recognition and understanding, however, remains elusive. Oedipus may have successfully solved the riddle, but when it comes to himself, and his own identity, he has a considerable blind spot.

It is here that the Sphinx's epithet as a prophesying voice and Oedipus' insistence that the solution to her question requires 'prophetic skill' (*ek theōn ... gnōton*) matter.[28] In his reading of the riddle, Oedipus makes a typical mistake: Similar to numerous consultants at oracles like Delphi, he thinks he knows the answer to the riddle (the question) but does not really understand how the words of the Sphinx relate to his own life.[29] He may understand the human condition as an abstract idea, an intellectual concept – described by the Sphinx's words in the temporal arc from birth to death – but falls painfully short of realizing their deeper meaning for his own life.[30]

Oedipus' uncompromising drive to understand whilst turning a blind eye to what becomes more and more obvious carries the whiff of hubris.[31]

OEDIPUS' EXEMPLARY HUMANITY

That there is a fundamental correlation between Oedipus' humanity and that of man is not merely pointed out by the Chorus. It is also already evident in the Sphinx's riddle itself. First, its imagery of the 'footedness' of man points to Oedipus himself whose 'footedness' is itself an issue: his name reflects the fact that his ankles were swollen from being pierced as an infant when he was exposed (ancient Greek *oidein* is 'to swell' and *pous* means 'foot').[32] Second, Oedipus features in the myth as the one who knows (*oida*) the answer to the question of the foot – another link between the name and the riddle.[33] Third, *dipous* ('two-footed') is part of Oedipus' name. So, Oedipus as the riddle solver features within the imagery of the riddle itself.[34] When he comes upon the Sphinx, Oedipus is himself clearly in the two-footed stage of his life. As such, the riddle prompts him to place his own humanity within a larger understanding of the human condition.

The focus on the bipedal, upright Oedipus, however, is hardly an innocuous way of pointing to the human. The capacity to walk upright on two feet features prominently in the efforts of ancient Greek and Roman philosophers to distinguish the human from all other animals.[35] It is at the centre of the human look 'down' on animals, both literally (because many animals are smaller than humans and, as quadrupeds, look down towards the ground rather than up) and metaphorically (as creatures inhabiting a lower rung of existence than humans).[36] Incidentally, the most detailed variant of the Sphinx's riddle we have comes from the second-century CE Greek author Athenaeus who himself got it from a fourth-century source. It reverberates with similar efforts to present the human as a unique animal through its upright posture. In Athenaeus' account, the riddle reads like this:

> There is a creature upon the earth that has two feet and four, a single voice, and three feet as well; of all that moves on land, and through the air, and in

> the sea, it alone alters its nature. But when it makes its way propped on the largest number of feet, then the swiftness in its limbs is the weakest.[37]

The first part of this version of the riddle reads like the one in Apollodorus quoted at the beginning of this chapter. The second part, however, is new. It offers a biologizing description of the human that refers to the popular Greek differentiation between terrestrial, avian, and maritime animals. At the same time, it also resonates with the 'man-only *topos*' of Greek philosophy by insisting on man's uniqueness (see Chapter 2).[38] The human stands out from all other animals in that he changes his form of locomotion over his lifetime. Moreover, the human stands out in the apparent paradox that he is slowest when he walks on the greatest number of legs.

The Sphinx's riddle also resonates with the ancient conversation on what it means to be human in other ways. Its appeal to reason points to *logos* as a core distinguishing feature invoked by the philosophers to separate man from beast – as does its solution. Moreover, to describe man as a creature whose form of movement changes over time is to define man as an abstract concept. The capacity to derive abstract concepts, however, is another feature invoked by some ancient philosophers as specific to humans only.[39] By reminding us that man does not always walk upright, that human *logos* has its limits, and by juxtaposing an abstract conception of the human with its concrete manifestation in the humanity of Oedipus, the Sphinx's riddle challenges conceptions of the human without, however, itself offering a firm answer to the question of who and what is man. It is only when the blinded Oedipus finally leaves Thebes, hobbling away on a walking stick – himself now decisively *tripous* ('three-footed') – that the link between Oedipus' own story and the meaning of the riddle has become clear to him.[40] The figure of the Sphinx as a hybrid, liminal, and female creature seems uniquely suited to prompt this process of leaning. She speaks from the off, outside of the city, and outside of any other definite identity that would ground her message in a particular time and space, thus depriving it of its inherent ambiguities.

The insight into the meanings of the riddle (and thus the paradoxes and intricacies of the human condition) makes the figure of Oedipus the quintessential human. The world and the human place within it, as enacted by Sophocles, is characterized by a profound and pervasive ambiguity which makes it difficult to navigate.[41] This ambiguity is deeply inscribed in the figure of Oedipus himself. It articulates itself as a series of sudden reversals.[42] To mention just a few: the stranger from Corinth turns out to be a citizen of Thebes; Jocasta's husband is also her son; the savior of the city turns out to be a threat to its well-being; the figure praised and exalted for his intellect turns out to be blind to his own innermost secrets, and so forth.[43] Once these truths are out in the open, Oedipus gouges out his eyes and thereby trades one form of blindness for another. The inner defect has somatized: it has taken on physical form.[44]

Both Oedipus and the Sphinx, then, share a double nature, a hybridity or, indeed, ambiguity.[45] The moment of their encounter brings them, quite literally, face to face. This is the ultimate reason why their encounter – albeit not part of the events related to us by Sophocles – is central to the story: the Sphinx highlights the friction between knowing and not knowing and between our human and animal sides as essential to Oedipus' inner nature – and, more generally, the nature of the human as such. She is a part of Oedipus and indeed all of us who struggle to make sense of the world and the human place within it.[46]

ENTER FREUD: THE INNER SPHINX AND HUMAN PSYCHOLOGY

One person who pondered exactly these questions in the modern world is Sigmund Freud (1856–1939), whose interest in Greek mythology has yielded the term 'Oedipus complex'.[47] It is to the role of the Sphinx in his oeuvre that we now turn. We do so for two reasons: first, because Freud had a defining impact on modern ways of 'thinking the human'. Even though many of his concepts have now dated, he decisively shaped modern notions about the complex inner life of the human animal. Second, because Freud's interest in the Sphinx goes straight to the core of his conception of the human.

Freud's reading of the Oedipus myth is one of the famous and often invoked examples of classical reception. And yet while Freud's Oedipus has received plenty of scholarly attention, his references to the Theban Sphinx have not received the same level of scrutiny.[48] This is because, in contrast to some other modern thinkers (Georg Wilhelm Friedrich Hegel,

Vladimir Propp, Claude Lévi-Strauss), Freud does not grant the Sphinx a central place in his oeuvre.[49] The Sphinx appears only a handful of times in the course of his discussion of the Oedipus complex.[50]

And yet, the few times the Sphinx *does* make an appearance are invariably revealing. In Freud's writing, her presence is part of a larger attempt to generalize (and thus universalize) the observations he derived from work with his clients. At the same time, Freud's Sphinx speaks to us from inside the human psyche, thus expanding on Sophocles' representation of this figure in ways that are representative of a larger 'inward turn' in the reading of the Oedipus myth during the nineteenth and twentieth centuries.[51]

Before we explore the intricacies of Freud's Theban Sphinx, it is worth pointing out that Freud took a broad interest in ancient Greece, Rome, and Egypt and their various literary and material productions. Together with his brother, he had travelled to Greece and Rome and owned a sizeable collection of antiquities including several sphinxes, as well as an original Athenian red-figure *hydria* (an ancient Greek water jug used to store liquids) depicting Oedipus seated before the Sphinx.[52] Moreover, Freud was widely read in Greek and Roman literature and in parts of classical scholarship, as evident in numerous references throughout his oeuvre.[53] It is through this evidence that Freud engaged with the myth of Oedipus. And he did not read just for leisure; rather, as we will see, his engagement with the ancient world informed his views on human psychology. It is therefore no surprise that the infamous Oedipus complex is not the only condition he named after a mythical figure: another one, that of 'narcissism' got its name from the ancient figure of Narcissus, who fell in love with (the image of) himself.

Freud's interest in Oedipus remains focused on his parental relationships (patricide and incest) as they articulated themselves in the Oedipus complex. His work *The Interpretation of Dreams* (1899/1900) features the earliest published account of the complex.[54] Freud starts with a general description of it and highlights its potential to turn into a neurotic condition if not handled properly.

> In my experience, which is already extensive, the chief part in the mental lives of all children who later become psychoneurotics is played by their

> parents. Being in love with the one parent and hating the other are among the essential constituents of the stock of psychical impulses which is formed at that time and which is of such importance in determining the symptoms of later neurosis.[55]

So according to Freud, children in early infancy form a complex of desires revolving around the wish to possess the parent of the opposite sex and to eliminate the parent of the same sex – the classic Oedipus complex that played such an important role throughout Freud's writing.[56] According to Freud, this wish is present in all children. It is a normal developmental stage. It is only if it is not mastered (that is redirected, controlled, and thus managed) that this becomes a problem later in life.

However, Freud does not end with a description of the complex but extends it into a discussion of the ancient myth after which it is named:

> This discovery is confirmed by a legend that has come down to us from classical antiquity: a legend whose profound and universal power to move can only be understood if the hypothesis I have put forward in regard to the psychology of children has an equally universal validity. What I have in mind is the legend of King Oedipus and Sophocles' drama which bears his name.[57]

This reading of the story of Oedipus is grounded in Freud's broader understanding of myth as a repertoire of experiences so fundamental and universal that they manifest themselves in the form of timeless tales. Like dreams, myth provides insight into everyone's subconscious thoughts, fears, and desires. The myth of Oedipus is a case in point. The conflicts specific to his persona are not merely Greek but reveal something fundamental about the human condition. As Freud states in his essay *A Case of Hysteria* (referring back to his *The Interpretation of Dreams*):

> I have shown at length elsewhere at what an early age sexual attraction makes itself felt between parents and children, and I have explained that the legend of Oedipus is probably to be regarded as a poetical rendering of what is typical in these relations. Distinct traces are probably to be found in most people of an early partiality of this kind – on the part of a daughter for her father, or on the part of a son for his mother; but it must be assumed to

> be more intense from the very first in the case of those children whose constitution marks them down for a neurosis . . .[58]

In Freud's reading, the ancient story of Oedipus articulates a desire that he attributes if not to all of us so at least the male half of the population sometime in early childhood: the wish to slay our father and marry our mother. What makes the figure of Oedipus stand out, then, is that he actually acted upon it.

Oedipus' slow and painful (re)discovery of his true identity, then, is a way of coming to terms with this experience. Freud compares Sophocles' enactment of the myth and its focus on the long and painful process of Oedipus' self-discovery with the revelatory processes of psychoanalysis.[59] In the modern world, the tale of Oedipus has lost nothing of its dramatic appeal.

So Much for Oedipus in Freud's oeuvre: what about the Sphinx?

In contrast to the deadly hollows of the Oedipus complex, Freud's depiction of the Sphinx has a surprisingly uplifting touch that (for today's reader at least) may border on the comic. This is because to Freud, the Sphinx points to the first, biggest, and arguably most fundamental of all problems: the question of where babies come from. This point reappears formulaically whenever Freud mentions the ancient myth of Oedipus.[60] What triggers this question, according to Freud, is more often than not the arrival of a new sibling. So, in Freud's reading, the Sphinx's description of the different stages of human life – prominently on show in ancient representations of the Sphinx's riddle (see the first part of this chapter) – points to the question of its origins.

Various modern commentators have pointed out that this idea in effect establishes a link between the figure of the Sphinx and that dimension of the human psyche not usually accessible to critical reflection: the unconscious.[61] When children do not get a satisfying answer to the question of the origins of human life, the Sphinx's riddle keeps preoccupying their minds in less obvious, open, and psychologically productive ways (so Freud's theory).[62]

The Sphinx's affinity to Freud's conception of the unconscious brings us to a final dimension of her identity in his oeuvre: her femininity and, in particular, her sexuality. Intriguingly, perhaps, Freud's interest in this dimension seems to be linked not (just) to the myth itself but to its representation in the works of a painting of which a print was in his possession.

The renowned French painter Jean-Auguste-Dominique Ingres (1780–1867) provided several renderings of the myth, all focused on the same, sexualized scene of the encounter between Oedipus and the Sphinx.[63] In the version he completed in 1808 and extended in 1827 (Figure 1.2), the Sphinx's female attributes are – literally – the focus of attention. Sitting on a rocky ledge and surrounded by a mountain cave, she sports bare breasts, ostentatiously pointed towards the young, fully nude, and exceedingly handsome Oedipus. The breasts are directly in front of Oedipus' eyes – bringing her gender emphatically into focus. The artist's decision to illuminate them with natural light underlines this. Oedipus stretches out

1.2. Jean-Auguste-Dominique Ingres, *Oedipus and the Sphinx* (*Oedipe explique l'énigme du sphinx*, 1808/1827). Musée du Louvre, Paris. Photo © RMN-Grand Palais (Musée du Louvre) / Stéphane Maréchalle

a finger as if to touch the beast/the breasts. His other hand holds a spear and (inadvertently) points to himself – a gesture perhaps representing the solution to the Sphinx's riddle and the conception of the human as such. The Sphinx engages with her counterpart by staring Oedipus right in the eye and extending a front paw towards him. The whole scene carries seductive undertones in which the Sphinx, from her elevated position and with her direct stare, seems to play an active part.

Sexually suggestive as the encounter may be, it is not free from undertones of death and danger. The remnants of the Sphinx's previous victims – a foot, skull, and some bones – are clearly visible in the lower left of the picture. The creature's deadly powers thus quite literally underpin the moment, providing a counterpoint to the vitality of the two figures at its core. Another man flees towards the city, visible through a cleft in the rocks in the background. The whole scene raises a new series of questions: is the Sphinx's sexuality, and not her riddle, the real source of danger here? Or is her sexuality perhaps the riddle?

A print of this painting decorated Freud's consulting rooms at 19 Berggasse in Vienna.[64] It hung on the wall at the end of the couch on which his investigations into human psychology took place – clearly visible to all those having their lives examined. Of course, we cannot know what Freud saw in Ingres' painting. Did the way in which Ingres' Sphinx drew on conceptions of the oriental female appeal to his interest in ancient Egypt as a cultural tradition different from the prevailing Eurocentrism?[65] And, if so, did it reverberate with Freud's disillusionment with prevailing racist theories of Western superiority that increasingly gained public currency towards the end of his life? Whatever the answer may be, we will not be far off the mark if we assume that he was as enticed by the creatures' apparent sexuality as by Oedipus' response to it. Freud obviously identified with Oedipus as the solver of riddles.[66]

Owing to this association with the figure of Oedipus, Freud's conception of psychoanalysis took on a gendered dimension. Throughout his oeuvre, the analytic gaze is imagined as a distinctly male gaze focused on the unconscious imagined as female, seductive, and riddling.[67] The implications of this analogy are far-reaching and go beyond Freud's conception of the unconscious framed as female. The doctor assumes a fundamental primacy of the male over the female. The male body and male sexuality remain the constant point of reference for the description of the female psyche, without the obverse applying as well. Indeed, female concerns remained such a mystery to him that he (in)famously referred to female sexuality as a 'dark continent' and to women themselves as 'a riddle'.[68]

The implications of this view for Freud's reading of the myth are readily at hand. They have given rise to a sustained critical engagement with Freud and the principles and practices of psychotherapy more generally. In particular, feminist scholars have dismissed the overt androcentrism of Freud's view of the human. To some of them, Freud's work provides a powerful source with which to explore the structures of patriarchal society itself.[69]

But with these developments, we have reached the reception of Freud and developments that really took off in the 1960s and 1970s, long after his death. As far as his oeuvre is concerned, women appear as a force deeply at odds with society. Like the Sphinx, they remain outside the gates of the city – that space defined (in the ancient world) by the male pursuit of the cultural, social, and political. They remain a force ambiguous and capable of violent intervention into human life.

In *Civilisation and Its Discontents*, a late work from 1930, Freud writes:

> The work of civilisation has become increasingly the business of men, it confronts them with ever more difficult tasks and compels them to carry out instinctual sublimations of which women are little capable ... Thus the woman finds herself forced into the background by the claims of civilization and she adopts a hostile attitude towards it.[70]

The ancient city of Thebes, it seems, is never far away. The Sphinx's poisonous influence lives on in many ways, not least in the unfulfilled modern women who resist and resent their partner's roles in society. Or so Freud would have us believe ...

AND FINALLY ...

In psychologizing and universalizing the figures of both Oedipus and the Sphinx, Freud generalized the conception of the human he saw in play in Sophocles' telling of the story – and thus indirectly also that of the Sphinx, Oedipus' perennial sparring partner.[71] For this purpose, he focused on those aspects of the ancient story that seemed to confirm his theories of the human psyche while neglecting others. At the same time, he internalized the figure of the Sphinx, turning her into a representation of the unconscious while also elaborating on her female and threatening features. All this served Freud's larger purpose to name and describe parts of the human psyche that exist across time and space.

It might be tempting to see Freud's use of the ancient story as a misappropriation of the classical past. Yet that would be to misunderstand the nature of his interest in the ancient world. Freud never aimed at a faithful reading of Sophocles. Rather, he drew on myth as an articulation of the timeless nature of man, which helped him universalize his observations. Yet his use of the ancient story helped to ensure its enduring appeal in the present: it is thanks to Freud that the figure of Oedipus – and with it that of the Sphinx – have been popularized in the modern imagination. Even though the psychological profession has long moved on, many of Freud's concepts and theories endure in the modern cultural imagination. In the twenty-first century, Oedipus and his complex are a household name. And the idea that *logos* is a means of human self-definition, albeit one with its own weaknesses to be considered, is now more widely accepted than ever. In some ways, it seems, we are indeed all Oedipus.

In facilitating such considerations, the Theban Sphinx rightfully holds a place at the core of the opening chapter of this book. In both her ancient and modern renderings, she anticipates various themes and points of contestation that will feature in more detail in later chapters: by presenting the human as an enigma, her riddle raises the very questions of who and what is man. By offering a biologizing description of the human animal as different from all other creatures, the Sphinx's riddle also resonates with the idea of human exceptionalism as articulated most clearly in the 'man-only *topos*' of the philosophical debate. At the same time, the way in which Oedipus approaches the challenge – through the application and exercise of reason – anticipates the logocentric ways in which certain philosophers have sought to answer the question from the beginning of the debate in classical antiquity to the present.

And it is to this debate that we turn next.

CHAPTER 2

The second chapter touches more firmly on the philosophical debate and the arguments for human exceptionalism put forward over its course. The presence of *logos* (speech, reason) that was already a theme in the previous chapter is again at centre stage, as are a number of other arguments that evolved from the idea that it is the human capacity to speak and reason that makes the human stand out from all other creatures.

Xanthus, the speaking horse of the famous Greek fighter Achilles, leads the way here. In the pages that follow, he engages with other speaking animals, both ancient and modern, real and imaginary. Taken together, these creatures show that the figure of the speaking animal is central to Western conceptions of the human. In classical antiquity, it features in stories that confirm the vertical relationship between humans (at the top) and animals (below). And yet, at the same time, right from the start of the conversation in the ancient world, the apparent anthropomorphism of the speaking animal was also used to critique the very idea of human exceptionalism. There is a direct line between how some modern animal fables point to man's animal nature and the concept of the human explored in parts of the ancient evidence.

2.1. Henri Regnault, *Automedon with the Horses of Achilles* (1868). Museum of Fine Arts, Boston. 90.152. © Boston Museum of Fine Arts.

Xanthus, Achilles' Speaking Horse (*Equus eloquens*)

IF ANIMALS COULD TALK IN HUMAN LANGUAGE, WHAT WOULD they say?

Homer's *Iliad* provides us with an answer straight, as it were, from the horse's mouth.[1] In the figure of Xanthus ('the blond'), it features an animal that transcends the usual categories of being by addressing humans in their own voice. A long line of other speaking animals, both ancient and modern, have followed in his horseshoes.[2] Yet never again were their words so laden with foresight and so intricately connected to the fate of one man: Achilles, greatest of the Greek fighters at Troy, and the horse's proud owner.

For what the warhorse has to say is by no means trivial. Right there on the battlefield of Troy it speaks up for itself and for Balius, that other famous horse of the Greek hero. What it says is this:

> Still for this time we will save you mighty Achilles, though the day of doom is near you, nor will we be the cause of it, but a mighty god and overpowering Fate. For it was not through sloth or slackness of ours that the Trojans were able to strip the armour from the shoulders of Patroclus, but one, far the best of gods, he whom fair-haired Leto bore, slew him among the foremost fighters and gave glory to Hector. But for us two, we could run swift as the West Wind's blast, which, men say, is of all winds the fleetest; but for you yourself it is fated to be vanquished in fight by a god and a mortal.[3]

What the horse says in beautiful hexameters (faithfully rendered here into English prose) is that, due to their extraordinary swiftness, the two supernatural horses will bail Achilles out of his current troubles. But in the bigger picture there is no hope. Achilles will not survive the war and never set eyes on his hometown again. He is fated to die at Troy – just as his friend and protégé Patroclus did. The horse goes on to reject any responsibility for either hero's death, laying the blame squarely on divine intervention: it was Apollo ('he whom fair-haired Leto bore'), who killed Patroclus with a shot from Hector's bow. Achilles is destined to suffer a similar fate.

Even though this can hardly be good news, the Greek hero is unperturbed. He has learnt from his mother Thetis long ago that he has to make a choice: either to die a young but heroic death at Troy or to live an unremarkable life well into his old age in his hometown of Phthia.[4] And at this stage, he has made his choice: 'Xanthus, why do you prophesy my death? You need not at all. Well I know even of myself that it is my fate to perish here, far from my dear father and my mother; but even so I will not cease until I have driven the Trojans to their fill of war.'[5] Achilles is set on bringing force to bear on the Trojans before he himself goes down. The horse's prophecy merely serves as a reminder of what Achilles – and the *Iliad*'s audience – have known for some time.

And, indeed, the prediction comes true: later in the war, Achilles dies from an arrow wound, inflicted by the god Apollo and fired by the Trojan prince Paris.[6]

SADDLING THE HORSE

Xanthus is not the only ancient animal to go on record as speaking in a human voice. A remarkable line of other, similarly gifted, no less eloquent creatures have done so too.[7] Among them we find many well-known contenders, such as the famous bird and wasp choruses of Attic comedy and various animal protagonists of ancient fables. But the voice of the speaking animal can also be heard in numerous less well-known texts, such as the gnat of Pseudo-Virgil's *Culex*, the speaking eel in Oppian's didactic poem *On Fishing* (*Halieutica*), and a verbose pig and speaking rooster that we will listen to in more detail later in this chapter.[8] In raising his voice on the battlefield of Troy, Xanthus thus stands at the very beginning of a long tradition of speaking animals stretching from the ancient into the modern world where it manifests itself in creatures like the gullible horse Boxer, a fixture of George

Orwell's *Animal Farm* (1945), and Remy, the unlikely and outspoken rodent hero of the Hollywood Blockbuster *Ratatouille* (2007) to name just two.

It may be tempting to dismiss the words of these and other speaking animals as the stuff of storytelling and literary fiction-making. Of course, we all know that animals cannot speak and converse with us in human language (certain exceptions notwithstanding). And yet, to turn a deaf ear to what they have to say would be to miss out on a significant part of a conversation of which the more explicitly philosophical side has gained considerable traction over time.

The ancient world witnessed the rise of a prominent philosophical debate revolving around the questions of whether there is a distinct (essential) difference between humans and animals, what this difference amounts to, and what consequences (if any) should follow from it.[9] Once the conversation was in full swing, the animal's lack of *logos* became the most widespread and consequential argument in favour of human exceptionalism.[10] First invoked as a hard border between man and beast by the ancient Greek philosopher Aristotle (ca 384–322 BCE), *logos* continued to play a key role in ancient conceptions of the animal throughout classical antiquity.[11]

Ancient stories featuring speaking animals relate to the philosophical conversation by what the literary anthropologist Chris Danta has referred to as 'uplifting'.[12] By attributing non-human animals with language, some animal stories momentarily bridge the gap that is thought to separate the human from the non-human animal and thus 'lift' the animal up to the human level. This 'uplifting' temporarily turns what is normally conceived of as a vertical relationship into a horizontal one, with the result that animals can now stand in for humans. The uplifted animal thus features in storylines that help to negotiate human rather than animal concerns. The classic example is the traditional ancient animal fable which uses speaking and otherwise anthropomorphized animals as placeholders for humans, with the ultimate intent of eliciting some moral lesson that can be transferred from the animal into the human realm.[13]

And yet, this evidence is not telling the whole story. For, right from the start of the conversation in antiquity, there was also an alternate tradition. This alternate tradition draws on storytelling and the liberties it affords to imagine a point of view different from those of some Greco-Roman philosophers. And, occasionally at least, this part of the tradition draws on the figure of the speaking animal to offer a surprisingly frank assessment of the human condition and the anthropocentric assumptions on which it is based. It is this evidence which is at the core of this chapter.

Before we listen to what these speaking animals have to say, we will stay with Xanthus a bit longer. What is interesting about his intervention – the first one in Western thought and literature? How does he set the tone for other speaking animals up to this day?

HALTERING THE PROPHESYING HORSE

Xanthus himself raised his human voice early in the history of the ancient world. The *Iliad* was written down at a time conventionally called 'Archaic Greece' or the 'Archaic period' (ca 800–500 BCE) and draws on material that circulated in oral form long before. It thus illustrates that the association between language and the human did not originate with the Greco-Roman philosophers. It was present well before the philosophical conversation turned openly from cosmological considerations about the nature of the universe to the study of the human cosmos.

As early as Homer's *Iliad* and *Odyssey*, there seems to be a close association between language and conceptions of the human.[14] In the world of Homer, this distinction helped to articulate the proximity (or distance) among different groups of people. It was not (yet) used to evaluate it in moral terms, a form of 'othering' that will become a feature of ancient ethnographic writing from the fifth century BCE onwards.[15] Although the Greeks are depicted as busy talkers – about half of both epics consist of speech – non-Greeks appear less proficient in the art of speechmaking, with the inarticulate and uncivilized Cyclops at the other end of the spectrum (see Chapter 4).[16]

It is against this background of the link between humanity and *logos* that Xanthus' speech on the battlefield takes on significance.[17] This is the only time in Homeric epic that we hear an animal speak in a human voice. Even in the more fantastic world of the *Odyssey*, we never hear animals address the human characters within the story. While many weird and wonderful things are possible in the world of ancient epic, a talking animal is a unique event. It stands out.

The singularity of the speaking horse shows that the conventions of epic poetry differ from those of the fable. In the latter, non-human creatures seamlessly converse with each other and with the human characters in the story. In the *Iliad*, by contrast, the blatant violation of what is equinely possible is in conflict with the prevailing naturalistic portrait of animals elsewhere in the poem. It constitutes what one modern commentator has described in regard to speaking animals more broadly as 'a category crisis that demands an explanation'.[18] And this explanation is readily provided before Xanthus can even raise his human voice. None other than the goddess Hera is behind the plot, having endowed the horse with the capacity to speak in human tongue.[19]

At first glance the story of Xanthus' verbose intervention seems to be a classic case of animal 'uplifting' for the sake of human self-recognition. After all, this animal speaks up to address what are ultimately human concerns. But a closer look at the circumstances of Xanthus' speech shows that there is more at stake in his intervention. Rather than supporting notions of human exceptionalism and superiority, the figure of Homer's Xanthus aligns the human with the non-human and redirects our attention to the limits of the human condition.

And yet Xanthus does not speak up merely for himself: he serves as a mouthpiece of the gods. In Greco-Roman culture, the fact that the horse reveals the future is not as unusual as it may seem at first glance.[20] In the ancient world, animals were used widely in divination – the art of predicting the future with the help of the supernatural. The entrails of slaughtered oxen were consulted on the battlefield to gauge the likelihood of military success; the flight of birds provided invaluable insight into auspicious and inauspicious days; and while no example of divination by horse is known from the Greek and Roman worlds, the ancient ethnographic literature reports several instances of prediction by horse among neighbouring peoples.[21] What makes the case of Xanthus stand out, then, is less that he is involved in the revelation of the future but that he does so unprompted, in his own voice, and without human mediation. It is this aspect of the horse's speech that divine intervention explains. In other words: The act of 'uplifting' itself – the horse's momentary endowment with speech – is framed in reference to the supernatural.

And yet, Xanthus does not retain his capacity for long.

What the supernatural gives, the supernatural also takes away. This is the only time we get to hear Xanthus' human voice. As soon as the horse has delivered its lines, its new faculty is promptly revoked by another kind of supernatural creature: the Erinyes (Furies).[22] These primordial deities of vengeance – best known to us from the first part of Aeschylus' drama *Oresteia*, staged at Athens in 458 BCE – make an appearance to rescind Xanthus' verbal powers.[23]

But it is not just the situation in which Xanthus speaks that transcends the natural and points to the supernatural. What he says also alludes to forces beyond the human. Xanthus uses his privileged, speech-endowed position to remind us that humans are subject to fate, which cannot be controlled by human intervention. And not just that: the speaking horse also puts the focus squarely on the physical aspects of human existence and, in particular, the fact that humans, even the best among them, are mortal.

The parallels between human and horse lead ever deeper into the intricacies of the human condition. It is not the humanity of the animal that is at centre stage here, as it is in the traditional animal fable, but the animality of the human. Just as Xanthus transcends the baseline equine condition, so Achilles, too, increasingly transcends the rules and conventions that define human society, and ventures towards both the bestial and the divine. After the death of Patroclus, he is all rage and vengeance. As far as Xanthus and Achilles are concerned, horse and rider come together in standing between the human, the animal, and the divine as different categories of being.[24] The figure of Xanthus reflects and illuminates the character of Achilles.[25] But rather than acting in service to traditional 'uplifting', the orientation here is *downward* to the physical aspects of the human existence (death) and the animality of the fighting human himself.

GOLDEN AGE REMINISCENCES?

And yet, one may wonder whether there is not yet another aspect in play in Xanthus' capacity to speak. In levelling the boundaries between human and animal and those between divine speech and human speech, the figure of

Xanthus points back to a past Golden Age in which gods, humans, and animals lived in much closer proximity.[26] Accounts of this age in Greek thought and literature revolve around a number of set features: the closeness of gods and humans, its simplicity and peacefulness, the absence of disease and hardship of any kind, and the presence of abundant food.[27]

The Greek poet Callimachus (ca 300–240 BCE), for example, explains what happened between the here and now and the legendary Golden Age in which humans and animals could seamlessly converse in a common language. According to one of his fables, a swan once asked Zeus to do away with old age and a fox accused him of not ruling justly.[28] In response, Zeus revoked the capacity of animals to speak like humans. At the same time, he bestowed animal voices on certain humans: one Eudemos received a dog's voice; one Philton a donkey's; the orators sounded like parrots, and the tragedians sported the sounds made by fish – whatever that might mean.

Even though the story carries satiric overtones, it is revealing that the animals' loss of human speech (and the simultaneous attribution of animal voices to individual humans/groups of humans) is presented here as a form of punishment for challenging the hierarchical order that places gods above humans and animals. What the swan and the fox are asking for is precisely the abolition of those markers that set humans *and* animals apart from the gods: their mortality (no more old age) and their subjection to (sometimes volatile) acts of divine justice.

The story thus explains why, in subsequent ages, the human condition is no longer defined by proximity to gods and animals but the distance between them. And this distance is mapped out in a number of ways: the lack of a common language among gods, humans, and animals, in human (and animal) suffering, in disease and old age, and, finally, in those sudden reversals of fortune that seem to suggest that the gods do not care about justice.[29]

Xanthus' intervention juxtaposes the legendary Golden Age with the much more rough-and-tumble realm in which the *Iliad* is set.[30] The world of the Homeric heroes is in stark contrast to this legendary age. It is defined by warfare, human suffering, hard labour, and a distinct gulf between gods and humans. And yet, at the same time, the gap that opened up between gods, humans, and animals after the Golden Age also created space for human ingenuity, ambition, and the winning of *kleos* ('renown') – the very qualities on which the Homeric heroes thrive. When the horse reminds him of his fate, Achilles is thus confronted with one of the basic facts of the human existence: glory has a price. It frequently involves suffering.

Xanthus thus speaks to the condition of a particular human, that of Achilles, its proud owner. But he does so in a way that transcends the 'politics' of traditional animal 'uplifting' to exploit fully the 'poetics' of the speaking animal. By pointing to a past Golden Age during which humans and animals could converse freely and in which the human condition was not (yet) defined by toil and suffering, the horse provides a foil against which the momentousness of Achilles' choice emerges in greater clarity. At the same time, the horse's intercession, the apex of its own anthropomorphism, marks a point at which Achilles' own supernatural and animal sides come to the fore. The categories of human, animal, and divine are all in play again.[31]

So, Xanthus' speech points back to a past Golden Age in which humans and animals could converse freely in a common language. He reminds us of fate as a force beyond human intervention and of the mortality of human and animal alike. All this amounts to a form of 'uplifting' in which the animal does not merely stand in for the human but uses its privileged position and its associations with the gods to point to the limitations of the human condition. As we will see in due course, Xanthus did not remain the last speaking animal striking such a critical tone. Others followed his example.

WHEN REALITY IS STRANGER THAN FICTION

Before we consider what they have to say, it is worth pointing out that speaking animals are, of course, not merely a matter of the literary imagination. Already in the ancient world, the capacity of some real animals to communicate with humans roused considerable interest. As societies based on farming and agriculture, the ancient Greeks and Romans were well-versed in animal husbandry.[32] They were thus well aware that certain domestic and domesticated animals responded to simple human commands.[33] And some animals seemed not just to follow orders but to appear to 'talk' back.

The Greek philosopher Porphyry (ca 234–305 CE), for example, a fervent advocate of vegetarianism (see Chapter 6), tells us about a partridge he once raised. Apparently, this particular pet partridge developed a way to converse with his human companion: 'I observed it not only making up to me and being attentive and playing, but even speaking in response to my speech and, so far as was possible, replying, differently from the way that partridges call each other.'[34] What fascinates Porphyry is not merely that the partridge seemed to respond to his spoken words. It is the animal's use of particular sounds that differ from the way partridges usually communicate with each other that excite the ancient philosopher.

At the same time, the ancient Greeks and Romans also occasionally encountered parrots and other birds able to imitate human sounds and words.[35] But such 'speaking' animals always also retained the air of the uncanny: Aelian (ca 165–235 CE) tells us about a lamb that was once allegedly born to the Egyptians. Apparently, this lamb had no less than eight feet, two heads, and four horns. It was also said to be able to speak.[36] Yet even Aelian found it hard to believe in the existence of this monstrous creature. He includes it as a curiosity but quickly dismisses it as fiction: 'It is right to forgive Homer who bestows speech upon Xanthus the horse, for Homer is a poet . . . But how can one pay any regard to Egyptians who exaggerate like this?'[37] The reference to the Homeric Xanthus as the prototypical speaking animal allows Aelian to delegate the monstrous lamb to the realm of the literary. The purpose of this move: to assure his reader that he and his work remain committed to the authentic and real.

Speaking animals, the example shows, were intriguing and scandalous and worth mentioning for the mere novelty of them. And yet, at the same time, the apologetic tone of Aelian's account of the fantastical Egyptian lamb confirms that the speaking animal belonged more comfortably in the realm of the imaginary. In myth, fables, and other works of literature drawing on storytelling, speaking animals could thrive unshackled by bounds of veracity. And some of the authors writing natural history or philosophy also embraced the animal voice unapologetically and wholeheartedly. They used the freedom of storytelling to take a critical look at the human condition from the animal point of view. It is to this evidence that we now turn.

THE PERSPECTIVE OF THE PIG AND THE ROOSTER-PHILOSOPHER

We are no longer in the Archaic period and the world of epic poetry but in the first/second century CE and that of philosophical conversation. The social and cultural setting has changed dramatically in terms of genre and outlook: By the time Plutarch wrote his treatise *Beasts Are Rational* and Lucian his satirical dialogue *The Dream, or the Cock*, the stakes for stories featuring speaking animals had risen considerably. The capacity to speak had taken a central place in a philosophical conversation about what distinguishes humans from other animals.

As Aristotle put it in *Politics*:

> (m)an alone of the animals possesses speech (*logos*). The mere voice (*phōnē*), it is true, can indicate pain and pleasure, and therefore is possessed by the other animals as well (for their nature has been developed so far as to have sensations of what is painful and pleasant and to signify those sensations to one another), but speech (*logos*) is designed to signify the advantageous and the harmful, and therefore also the right and the wrong; for it is the special property of man in distinction from the other animals that he alone has perception of good and bad and right and wrong and the other moral qualities, and it is partnership in these things that makes a household and a city-state.[38]

Aristotle here acknowledges the fact that animals have their own voice (*phōnē*) in which they can articulate feelings such as pain or pleasure to each other. Human speech (*logos*), he goes on to argue, is different in that it allows humans to make ethical and moral claims. Animal voices are not capable of engaging in such conversation.[39]

This association between animals and the absence of *logos* became so deeply engrained in Greek thought and literature that *ta aloga* ('those without *logos*') became a shorthand for animals.[40] Starting from Aristotle's distinction, various ancient philosophers explored the question of how human speech differs from the way in which animals communicate with each other. Most notably the Stoics – Chrysippus of Soli (ca 280–207 BCE), Diogenes of Babylon (ca 240–152 BCE), Seneca (ca 4 BCE–65 CE) – further investigated the differences between human speech and animal communication.[41] This philosophical school was founded by Zeno of Citium at Athens during the third century BCE. It focused on virtue as the means of a good life and elevated *logos* to a fundamental principle of the cosmos. The Stoics elaborated on Aristotle's view that certain animals can convey information to each other through means other than speech. They agreed with Aristotle that animals lacked *logos/ratio* and that this sets the non-human animal apart from the human animal.

Such views found fierce opposition in the works of Plutarch (ca 46–120 CE), Porphyry (ca 234–305 CE), and a few other ancient thinkers. They took issue with the suggestion that animals did not have *logos,* could not reason, and had no share in justice. These trailblazers in the proclamation of animal rights and capacities argued vigorously against the Stoic position. They were joined by a handful of ancient authors who sought to illustrate animal intelligence in brief anecdotes. Oppian's *On Fishing* (second century CE) evokes examples of cunning and intelligence in sea creatures. Crabs, for example, stealthily insert a pebble into the opening of an oyster in order to prevent them from closing, thus allowing for their consumption.[42] The works of Aelian (ca 165–235 CE) are likewise full of examples illustrating the cognitive capacities and practical skills of individual animal species. Even though he acknowledges the existence of an intellectual gulf between humans and other animals his work, *On Animals* includes numerous examples of animal intelligence: we learn that storks re-occupy their old nesting sites when they return the next season, that wolves form long lines hanging onto each other's tails when crossing a turbulent river, and that honeybees carry a little pebble with their legs in order not to lose their way in strong winds.[43] And when the Greek philiosopher Sextus Empiricus, towards the end of the second century CE, refutes the Stoics, he singles out a creature as particularly intelligent already familiar to us from the beginning of this book: Odysseus' dog Argos.[44]

Why there was suddenly such an uptick of interest in the relation of humans and animals during the second and third centuries CE may be mere coincidence. Or it may be due to the fact that Greece by then had become part of the Roman Empire. The so-called Second Sophistic (ca 60–230 CE) is a time of relative political and economic stability which involved a reorientation towards traditional values, education, and views of the old Greece. It is defined in reference to the figure of the sophist, the critical teacher of rhetoric and persuasion. The themes and outlook of this period, as we will see, are certainly evident in Plutarch's and Lucian's writings, not least in the many references to Homer and the old Greece. We will see below that both the speaking pig and the rooster at some point are referred to as a *sophistēs* ('a sophist').[45] It is against the background of this broader interest in animal intelligence and animal capacities that Plutarch and Lucian refer to the figure of the speaking animal to address the question of the human and the animal not merely indirectly, by example, but head on.

Plutarch's speaking pig takes the floor first. The setting for this remarkable sample of animal rhetoric is quickly explained. We are back in the world of Homer, only this time the setting is not the *Iliad* and the battlefield of Troy but a scene from the *Odyssey*.[46] The opening dialogue features the conversation between the Greek hero Odysseus and the sorceress Circe. According to a famous episode in Homer's *Odyssey*, she had transformed a number of Odysseus' comrades into pigs with the help of magic. In the *Odyssey*, Odysseus convinces Circe to transform his comrades back into humans.[47] Plutarch's dialogue starts with Odysseus wondering whether there are more Greeks among the animals living on Circe's island.[48] When Circe confirms that this is indeed the case, Odysseus asks whether they, too, could be turned back into human form.[49] Not only would this bring him distinction (*philotimia*) upon his return home; it would also liberate these poor creatures from their 'piteous and shameful' (*oiktran kai atimon*) and unnatural (*para physin*) condition.[50]

Odysseus is articulating here the traditional logocentric position according to which humans are superior to animals. And yet Circe is having none of it. She does not share Odysseus' views at all but thinks that the transformation back into humans would leave these creatures worse off. As a witness, she calls on a pig named 'Grunter' (*Gryllus*) and prompts Odysseus to ask whether it actually *wants* to be turned back into a human being.[51] What follows is a heated, surprisingly personal, and frequently hilarious exchange between Odysseus and the pig, in which Grunter lays out his reasons for why it is preferable to remain animal.

The ensuing conversation revolves around a question which plays a central role in philosophical arguments of human exceptionalism and moral superiority: whether only humans have virtue (*aretē*).[52] Odysseus takes the position that animals do not have it. Grunter, however, does not allow himself to be backed into a rhetorical corner. He quickly shifts the argument from philosophical abstraction to actual example, and from the defensive to the offensive.

ODYSSEUS: And what sort of virtue, Grunter, is ever found in beasts?
GRUNTER: Ask rather what sort of virtue is not found in them than in the wisest of men. Take first, if you please, courage, in which you take great pride, not even pretending to blush when you are called 'valiant' and 'sacker of cities'. Yet you, you villain, are the man who by tricks and frauds, have led astray men who knew only a straightforward, noble style of war and were unversed in deceit and lies; while on your freedom from scruple you confer such nefariousness. Wild beasts, however, you will observe, are guileless and artless in their struggles, whether against one another or against you, and conduct their battles with unmistakably naked courage under the impulse of genuine valour.[53]

By launching a straight personal attack on Odysseus, Grunter sets two kinds of conduct against each other: the natural behaviour of (certain) animals on the one hand and the behaviour of (certain) humans on the other. Which, he asks, is more virtuous: the raw and authentic way in which wild beasts assert themselves, or the plotting and trickery of Odysseus himself?

Over the course of their conversation, Grunter and Odysseus go through individual virtues one by one.[54] In addition to courage (*andreia*), the pig sets out to demonstrate that animals also have temperance (*sōphrosynē*), and 'practical wisdom' (*phronēsis*).[55] In making these points, the pig seeks to refute arguments about the purported deficits of animals made elsewhere in Greco-Roman thought and literature.

Here, too, practical examples and personal attacks prevail. Grunter argues that in panthers and lions the female is ready to defend herself just as much as the male. They thus have a better claim to courage than humans. The evidence to prove the point? Odysseus' wife Penelope who, back at home, allows the suitors to wine and dine at Odysseus' expense.[56] In the same vein, Grunter asserts that crows have a better record of fidelity to their partners than humans. His example? Penelope and her dealings with the suitors.[57]

Grunter turns the table on Odysseus by drawing up a list of human deficits. In a direct inversion of the arguments for human exceptionalism, which seek to single out attributes specific to the human only, Grunter highlights those aspects in which animals stand out: animals alone have true courage while humans merely follow social conventions; animals alone restrict themselves to certain kinds of food, while humans are omnivorous and gluttonous; animals alone practise moderation, while humans have a temperance problem, indulging in luxury and excesses of all kinds.[58] The 'animal-only *topos*' of the philosophically inclined pig proves just as pointed and exclusive as the 'man-only *topos*' of the Greek and Roman philosophers.[59] Given these advantages of the animal over the human condition, why would anyone in their right mind want to be turned back into a human being?

The pig uses its 'uplifted', speech-endowed position to launch a blistering attack on notions of human exceptionalism and superiority. Among the arguments that an increasingly baffled Odysseus gets to hear is this: 'Since I have entered into this new body of mine, I marvel at those arguments by which the sophists brought me to consider all creatures except man irrational and senseless (*aloga kai anoēta*).'[60] Grunter cuts right to the core of the ancient philosophical debate on what sets humans and animals apart. He uses his capacity to speak in human language to undermine the Aristotelian position that animals lack reason.[61]

ODYSSEUS: Do you attribute reason even to the sheep and the ass?

GRUNTER: From even these, dearest Odysseus, it is perfectly possible to gather that animals have a natural endowment of reason and intellect. For just as one tree is not more nor less inanimate than another, but they are all in the same state of insensibility, since none is endowed with soul, in the same way one animal would not be thought to be more sluggish or indocile mentally than another if they did not all possess reason and intellect to some degree – though some have a greater or less proportion than others. Please note that cases of dullness and

> stupidity in some animals are demonstrated by the cleverness and sharpness of others – as when you compare an ass and a sheep with a fox or a wolf or a bee.[62]

What Grunter is advocating for here is a more nuanced understanding of how individual characteristics are distributed in the animal kingdom. The pig identifies the category of 'the animal' as too crude to do justice to how different forms of reason and intelligence manifest across the spectrum of all beings. So rather than the Aristotelian conception of non-human animals as *ta aloga*, Grunter points to another conception that, in its rudimentary form, goes back to Aristotle's writings on nature: that of the *scala naturae* – 'literally, the ladder of nature' – the idea that all organisms are related to each other and can be organized in a grand hierarchical scheme according to which differences between them are only gradual in nature.[63]

Once again, Grunter grounds his argument in tangible examples. He names a few remarkably dim-witted individuals, among them the Cyclops Polyphemus as another creature from the world of Odysseus, and adds: 'I scarcely believe that there is such a spread between one animal and another as there is between man and man in the matter of judgment and reasoning and memory.[64] The point here is that there is more variation in the way different characteristics and capabilities manifest themselves among humans than the arguments for human essentialism, exceptionalism, and superiority allow for.

THE ROOSTER'S PERSPECTIVE

The question of virtue is also central to the perspective of another speaking animal whose views resonate with that of the speaking pig: that of the rooster-protagonist of Lucian's *The Dream and the Cock.*[65] This dialogue revolves around the unlikely conversation between Micyllus, a cobbler, and his rooster. It kicks off when the rooster interrupts Micyllus' sleep at an ungodly hour with a hearty cock-crow.[66] And yet, even though Micyllus addresses his grievances directly to the rooster, he apparently does not expect a response.

MICYLLUS: Zeus, god of miracles, and Heracles, averter of harm! What the devil does this mean? The cock talked like a human being!

COCK: Then do you think it a miracle if I talk the same language as you men?

MICYLLUS: Why isn't it a miracle? Gods, avert the evil omen from us![67]

Once again, an animal speaking in human language features as an unnatural occurrence that calls for an explanation. And once again, this demand is met by a reference to the supernatural. Micyllus assumes that the speaking rooster must be a divine sign. In response, the cock points out that, in the ancient world, an animal speaking in human voice is *not* entirely unheard-of and certainly should not be seen as an evil omen.

COCK: It appears to me, Micyllus, that you are utterly uneducated and haven't even read Homer's poems, for in them Xanthus, the horse of Achilles, saying good-bye to neighing forever, stood still and talked in the thick of the fray, reciting whole verses, not prose as I did; indeed he even made prophecies and foretold the future; yet he was not considered to be doing anything out of the way, and the one who heard him did not invoke the averter of harm as you did just now, thinking the thing to be ominous.[68]

This is a remarkably self-conscious statement. The educated rooster seems to be well aware of the larger tradition in which he stands.[69] And yet, despite the reference to Xanthus, the solution to the apparent violation of the 'roosterly possible' consists not in divine intervention. It is not the gods who do the 'uplifting' here but the idea that the soul could be reincarnated in another being after death (*metempsychosis*).[70] Certain (philosophically inclined) circles in the ancient world promulgated the idea that after death the soul could be reborn in another human or animal body. To the surprise of Micyllus – and the amusement of the reader – the cock claims that he is only the latest in a long line of incarnations that include (brace yourself): the Greek philosopher Pythagoras, the Trojan hero Euphorbus, the Greek courtesan Aspasia (partner of the famous Athenian statesman Pericles), the Cynic philosopher Crates, and several animals.[71]

Who will not smirk about this outrageous, puffed-up claim?

And yet, Lucian's satirical dialogue is more complex than its humorous tone might suggest. Central to the conversation between the human and non-human animal here is the question of what makes for a happy human life. Micyllus himself, quite literally, dreams of worldly riches; the rooster, by contrast, in line with his (cynic) philosophical pedigree, advocates for a simpler lifestyle.[72]

Inevitably, perhaps, the conversation eventually reaches the point at which Micyllus asks how the human and animal conditions compare. Drawing on the rooster's prior animal incarnations he wonders:

MICYLLUS: But when you became a horse or a dog or a fish or a frog, how did you find that existence?

COCK: That is a long story you are starting and we have no time for it just now. But to give you the upshot of it, there is no existence that did not seem to me more care-free than that of man, since the others are conformed to natural desires and needs alone; you will not see among them a horse tax-collector or a frog informer or a jackdaw sophist or a mosquito chef or a libertine cock or any other modes of life that you men follow.[73]

For the rooster, as for Grunter, being an animal is preferable to the human condition. Invoking the natural world in ways similar to Plutarch's speaking pig, the cock points out that animals confine themselves to the basics. Humans, by contrast, tend to over-complicate things by striving for ever more. Is this still 'uplifting' for the negotiation of human values? Or is this already the downward gaze that grounds the human by reminding him of just how much human self-fashioning stands in the way of mere life?

And yet one may wonder: do the pig and the rooster perhaps impersonate the sophist who makes a convincing case for what are ultimately absurd arguments? Are Plutarch's and Lucian's texts deeply ironic treatises – illustrating the outlandish positions of the sophists and (in the case of the speaking rooster) mocking core tenets of Cynicism?

It is certainly possible to read both dialogues in this way.[74] The arguing pig and boasting rooster do certainly cut humorous figures – as do their human counterparts. Yet it would be wrong to write off what these animals have to say as mere satire. Plutarch's treatise shows that human claims to superiority are just as extreme as the pig's claims to animal superiority. What he advocates for is a more graded understanding of how individual characteristics, in this case virtues, are mapped across the full range of living beings. Likewise, Lucian is also not going for a quick dressing-down of the cock's views. Here, too, the animal's human voice offers an alternate perspective on the human condition. Both Grunter, the pig, and the rooster-philosopher use their human voices to show us how limited and anthropocentric ideas of human superiority really are. This is not 'uplifting' for the mere negotiation of human values; this is 'uplifting' for the purpose of undermining the very position of the human as a being to which the animal must look up. That both texts carry strong satirical undertones does not take away from this message. Rather, it confirms it. In both instances, the joke is clearly on us.

BEYOND THE ANCIENT: THE HUMANITY OF THE ANIMAL REVISITED

Classical antiquity witnessed the emergence of a conversation around the question of whether human language differs from the way in which non-human animals communicate and, if so, what consequences follow for the status of animals. It did not end there. In the modern world, the debate about animal language, animal reason, and the cognitive capacities of individual animal species has grown considerably in range, scope, and complexity. These days it is not just philosophy that considers this matter; a variety of other disciplines have joined the conversation, including linguistics, moral philosophy, philosophy of mind, cognitive ethology, and behavioural biology.[75]

Some of the positions on animal language and animal reason put forward in the modern discussion resemble those of the ancient conversation.[76] The idea that humans only have *logos* and the capacity to reason is still widely held – as is the idea that it is this difference that places humans on higher moral ground.[77] Despite sustained efforts to discredit it in various ways, the position still holds strong, especially beyond the rather exclusive circles of academia. Owing to the direct line that runs from Aristotle via the Stoics and their reception through Christianity, to modern conceptions of humans and animals, ideas of human exceptionalism and superiority – and the arguments about *logos* on which they are based – are deeply ingrained in Western humanism.

This is not the space to offer a detailed overview of the modern conversation in itself or in its relationship to the ancient debate, nor to discuss individual positions. Rather, in line with the other chapters of this book, we focus again on one particular strand in which the ancient and modern worlds converse. Storytelling as a tool to engage with the question of the human and the animal remain centre stage.

In the modern world, the stakes of the speaking, thinking, and reasoning animal have changed dramatically.[78] The arrival of Darwin's theory of evolution fundamentally altered the way we think of the relationship between humans and animals. The stories we tell reflect these changes. Traditionally the animal fable stood in the service of 'uplifting'. After Darwin it seems that the modern animal fable is increasingly used to explore the animality of the human rather than the humanity of the animal.

Moreover, post-Darwin questions of identity and belonging centre not so much on horses, nor on pigs, nor on roosters, but on the great apes. Owing to their biological and evolutionary closeness to humans, as evident in their physique and their behaviour, it is these apes that, above all, confront us with the question of who we really are.

In Joseph Kafka's brief short story *A Report to an Academy* (published in 1917), an ape by the name of Red Peter (*Rotpeter*) presents a formal report to a learned society. The report eloquently describes the circumstances of his capture in the wild five years earlier, his subsequent transport to human civilization in a small cage aboard a ship, and his ultimate acculturation into the human world. Much of what he has to say sounds familiar as it concerns the key points around which the philosophical conversation evolved. Red Peter's position clearly resonates with that of Xanthus, Grunter, and the rooster-philosopher. And yet, at the same time, the ape takes us from the ancient into the modern world and to the conceptions of the human specific to it.[79]

The story presents the core themes of the debate about the status of the animal but in new clothing: animal speech, intelligence, and virtue – all capacities that were variously evoked as criteria that define the human in the ancient world – again feature prominently. Yet they do so in a way that reveals differences in ancient and modern conceptions of the human.

Crucially, the ape himself is in control of his story. Red Peter is both narrator and protagonist. And the story he sets out to tell is a familiar one: the history of man's evolution from animal origins is compressed into the experience of an individual creature. Indeed, Red Peter's journey away from his own animal nature reflects our own evolutionary journey from animal origins and the philosophically constructed amnesia regarding these origins. Originally prompted by the academy to report on his prior existence as an ape, Red Peter finds himself unable to meet this request. The more that Red Peter adjusts behaviourally to his new environment, the more he forgets what it was like to be an ape. As a result, the only story he feels qualified to tell is that of his transformation and entry into the human world.

The ape's report thus speaks directly to the question of what it takes for a non-human creature to cross the line and become human. And the answer he comes up with is hardly flattering for the human species: not very much, it seems. Or at least not much of consequence.

In order to pass as human, the ape merely imitates a number of human habits.[80] Again, language features prominently. Clearly, this animal too can speak and reason. Yet the capacity to speak is not presented here as a distinct step towards a more human form of existence. Rather, it throws an invariably dim light on the ape's progress. The articulate and reflected voice that speaks to us through the report is in strong contrast to how that very same report describes the undignified circumstances of his first human words:

> What a triumph it was then ... when one evening before a large circle of spectators ... I took hold of a schnapps bottle that had been carelessly left standing before my cage, uncorked it in the best style, while the company began to watch me with mounting attention, set it to my lips without hesitation, with no grimace, like a professional drinker, with rolling eyes and full throat, actually and truly drank it empty; then threw the bottle away, not this time in despair but as an artistic performer; forgot, indeed, to rub my belly; but instead of that, because I could not help it, because my

> senses were reeling, called a brief and unmistakable 'Hallo!' breaking into human speech, and with this outburst broke into the human community, and felt its echo: 'Listen, he's talking! like a caress over the whole of my sweat-drenched body.'[81]

The paltry 'hello' of the intoxicated ape hardly merits the ecstatic response from his human audience. It is the product of imitation – a mere circus trick. And, as with Xanthus the Homeric wonder-horse, the newfound ability to speak is quickly lost again: 'There was no attraction for me in imitating human beings. I imitated them because I needed a way out, and for no other reason. And even that triumph of mine did not achieve much. I lost my human voice again at once; it did not come back for months.'[82] That the audience of this performance consists of a bunch of rowdy sailors who smoke, drink, abuse the ape at whim, and display other kinds of behaviour that hardly do the human species proud, does not help. Even more disturbingly, they coo like pigeons, pointing up their own animal nature.[83] The 'downward' gaze in practice.

Red Peter's emerging humanity thus remains a mere mannerism, a show he puts on in order to find an escape from his plight as a captured animal. Indeed, the ape repeatedly emphasizes that the path he chose and his current position should not be confused with freedom. Freedom is not available to humans (even though they like to hoodwink themselves into thinking it is); it is confined to animals in the wild.

The ape's account of the outcome of his learning also comes with a twist:

> That progress of mine! How the rays of knowledge penetrated from all sides into my awakening brain! I do not deny it: I found it exhilarating. But I must also confess: I did not overestimate it, not even then, much less now. With an effort which up till now has never been repeated I managed to reach the cultural level of an average European.[84]

The average educational status! Of a European!

We might be tempted to be impressed, were it not painfully clear that the education in question does not amount to anything of substance and comes with serious strings attached. In referring to the 'average educational status of a European', Kafka's Red Peter points to the fact that the core of the criticism aired here is directed against the way education is tangled up with both anthropocentrism and Western elitism.

The ape learns everything it takes to pass for a civilized human. The glass of red wine he consumes occasionally acts as a symbol of cultivation and socialization. Ironically, perhaps, we will encounter it again later in this book in the hand of Picasso's Minotaur (see Chapter 9). Yet we cannot shake off entirely the uneasy feeling that the ape's real virtues – his humanity if you will – shine through in spite (and not because) of this instruction in all things human. They become tangible, for example, in his perseverance, ingenuity, and ability to compromise in the face of the limited choices available to him as a result of his capture.

Kafka's ape, like his ancient cousins, speaks to the question of what separates the human from the non-human animal. In his reference of the educational status of the average European, the ape rips off the veneer of Western human self-fashioning. There is only little of substance that distinguishes Red Peter the humanized ape from his ape-ish origins and how little humanity there is in purportedly 'human' traits.

Yet, intriguingly, this congenial move only works because biology itself is largely left out of the picture: that the ape retains his animal form throughout is never thematized as a problem for his humanization. A prominent scar, which gave him the name Red Peter, and a limp are the only things that reveal that this particular specimen has become entangled in the webs of human self-definition.[85] In contrast to the more famous transformation story Kafka tells in *Metamorphosis* (see Chapter 10), there is no transformation here, no physical metamorphosis from animal to human. The focus is squarely on the exterior and behavioural attributes of humanity.

In this modern animal fable, the boundary that separates the human from the non-human animal is more fragile than ever. This is why the ape's animal nature represents a direct danger for those humans surrounding him. In particular, the teachers who assist him in the journey seem to be at risk: 'The ape-nature sped out of me, rolling over and away, so that my first teacher himself almost became ape-ish because of it. Soon he had to give up the instructions and be transferred to a medical institution (*Heilanstalt*). Luckily, he soon emerged from it again.'[86] The ape's fading animality seems to be highly contagious – an existential risk to those humans who come into close contact with it. It is a sickness that can affect and endanger the human condition, curable only through instant transfer into the confined space of the sanatorium as a quintessentially human institution.

Crucially, however, it is not only those who come in close contact with Red Peter who are at risk of infection. We all are. We humans all suffer from this fragility or vulnerability. As Red Peter astutely observes:

> The storm that blew after me out of my past began to slacken; today it is only a gentle puff of air that plays around my heels; and the opening in the distance, through which it comes and through which I once came myself, has grown so small that, even if my strength and my will power sufficed to get me back to it, I should have to scrape the very skin from my body to crawl through. To put it plainly, much as I like expressing myself in images, to put it plainly: your life as apes, gentlemen, insofar as something of that kind lies behind you, cannot be farther removed from you than mine is from me. Yet everyone on earth feels a tickling at the heels; the small chimpanzee and the great Achilles alike.[87]

This is to remind us that every human being shares Red Peter's journey from ape to human. Again, Darwin nods his head here. In putting the focus squarely on such issues, Kafka's story illustrates the fragility, openness, and artificially constructed nature of the divide between man and beast that emerged in the wake of the theory of evolution. It is this particular fragility and openness that sets the modern concept of the human apart from its ancient counterparts. But the storyline in which such considerations are embedded still revolves around the same turning points that shape the ancient conversation.

It matters that the ape invokes the presence of an ancient figure: Achilles. His ominous and vulnerable heel that brought about the hero's death is an image well chosen. Not only does it point to the ancient origins of the concept of the human under investigation. It also reminds us that although humans evolved from animals long ago, our animal origins remain deeply inscribed in our bodies. We all have (an) Achilles' heel if we turn and try to run from those origins. We are all vulnerable in the same spot. And if we do not come to terms with our own animal nature, our humanity may falter more quickly than we are prepared to admit.

BEYOND KAFKA: LUCY AND DR DOLITTLE

Unfortunately, perhaps, the circumstances of Kafka's Red Peter did nor remain confined to the realm of the literary. In the friction they depict between the almost human and the not quite human, the experiences of Red Peter anticipate a trend that reached its peak more than a decade later. During the second part of the twentieth century, it became popular in certain circles in the US, UK, and parts of continental Europe to engage in a particular kind of self-experiment: to raise a baby chimp 'as human'. Inevitably, perhaps, all these cases ended more or less tragically when the cute youngster turned into a grown animal with needs that were impossible to meet in the confines of a family home. But before that there was plenty of time to engage in extensive musings on the human-like qualities of the animals in question. Many years later, the reports of their upbringing have lost little of their captivating allure.

One of them is luridly entitled *No He's Not a Monkey: He's an Ape and He's My Son.* It sets out how one such chimp, who goes by the name of Boris, grew up in a New York two-bedroom apartment during the 1960s. As with a human child, Boris' human parents take delight in every new skill and capacity that their foster 'son' acquires over time. And yet, Boris is never quite able to live up to their human aspirations. When he tries to feed himself with a spoon, he eventually imitates the required movements, but with a crucial difference: the spoon does not carry any food.[88] Boris' behaviour recalls the – ultimately futile – efforts of Kafka's Red Peter, whose 'humanity' also took on the form of mannerisms.

And, yet, at the same time, one cannot shake off the uneasy feeling that Boris, through his mere existence, *does* challenge our thinking of what it means to be human – a feeling apparently shared by those around him:

> Boris seemed to delight as many visitors as he unnerved. Very few could simply relax and enjoy his antics. They felt compelled to respond to him but weren't sure how. They'd joke with him as if he were human and then look embarrassed about it because they knew he wasn't, or they'd sort of pet him like a dog and then look embarrassed about it because he acted too human.[89]

Boris' mere presence seems to raise a question that is as fundamental as it is ultimately unanswerable: where does the human animal end and where does the non-human begin?

The frictions and points of contact between the human and the non-human animal continue to trouble us. They are ultimately irresolvable. They often manifest themselves in a realm that has been invoked since classical antiquity to distinguish man from beast – that of language.

Drawing that line seems less easy than one may think. Lucy, for example, a chimpanzee girl who grew up during the mid-1960s with an American psychotherapist and his family, was taught American Sign Language. Over time, she was able to learn about ninety-four words as well as a number of different names. And Lucy was not unique. Apparently, some other greater apes succeeded in learning even more.

What did Lucy articulate through the new channel of communication available to her? Here is an example of a brief conversation between her and one of the humans she co-habited with about some faeces found on the floor of the family home:

ROGER: What's That?
LUCY: Lucy not know.
ROGER: You do know. What's that?
LUCY: Dirty, dirty.
ROGER: Whose dirty?
LUCY: Sue's.
ROGER: It's not Sue's. Whose is it?
LUCY: Roger's.
ROGER: No! It's not Roger's. Whose is it?
LUCY: Lucy dirty, dirty. Sorry Lucy.[90]

Lucy here tries to deflect the responsibility for the mishap from her to others and apologizes when this is not successful. Is this an example of an animal using human language? If so, what follows from it for how we look at the relationship between humans and other animals?

We leave this question for the reader to answer and move on to another one. Most animals are not able to learn sign language, yet what about their own, species-specific forms of communication? Does human language really differ fundamentally from how other animals articulate themselves?

In his book *Dr Dolittle's Delusion*, the American linguist Stephen Anderson claims that the famous Dr Dolittle – the loveable, eccentric hero of Hugh Lofting's highly successful children's books, a doctor turned vet with the uncanny ability to communicate with animals in their languages – was wrong when he called animal communication a form of language.[91] Anderson argues that human language differs from animal communication in a number of significant ways, including (but not limited to) in the capacity to construct complex sentences and to articulate new ideas and concepts.[92]

> Finally, the very enterprise of asking how human language and animal communication differ does not tell us only about the ways in which the animals fall short of us. Focusing on what it is about humans that fits them to acquire and use languages tells us much about ourselves as well, because languages in the human sense are systems not known to exist in any other organisms.[93]

We do not wish to challenge the scientific insights derived by Anderson here. We merely note that this classical reader at least cannot shake off the uneasy feeling that by emphasizing the uniqueness of human language Anderson presents a modern variant of the so-called 'man-only *topos*'. Of course, Anderson acknowledges the myriad ways in which animal communication resembles human language. And yet in the end he draws a rather sharp line between the human and non-human. Here, too, human language is presented as the stick to which the linguistic capacities of all non-human animals (fail to) measure up. And, here, too, animal speech and animal language are relegated into the realm of storytelling – hence the references to the legendary Dr Dolittle.

More than 2,000 years earlier, Porphyry already developed the perfect refutation of Anderson's position. Right after telling us about his partridge, Porphyry wonders about the following question.

> How then can it not be ignorant to call only human language *logos*, because we understand it, and dismiss the language of other animals? It is as if ravens claimed that theirs was the only language, and we lack logos, because we say things which are not meaningful to them, or the people of Attica said that Attic is the only language, and thought that others who do not share the Attic way of speaking lack *logos*?[94]

What Porphyry is saying here is that there is a certain circularity in play whenever we focus on the way we do things as humans and implicitly or explicitly present it as the only (right) way. Human language might indeed differ from the way in which animals communicate with members of their own species. And yet we are only beginning to understand the principles on which different animal 'languages' are based.

AND SO?

A popular story type included in Stith Thompson's famous index of world narratives reads like this: 'Man riding horse and followed by dog tells horse to jump over a hole. Horse says, "I will not." Man turns to dog and says, "Isn't that strange – a horse talking!" The dog says, "Yes, isn't it."'[95] What sounds like a joke carries serious undertones. This brief fictional conversation exposes a fundamental paradox that is on show whenever animals speak: on the one hand we like to think that the human is different from all other creatures. On the other, in our ultimately futile attempts to define what makes us human, we are invariably directed back to our own animal nature. Storytelling and speaking animals of all kinds thrive on this paradox. In the ancient world as in the modern, the poetics of the speaking animal (r-)evolves against the background of the politics of the speaking (human) animal. But once again, the joke is on us and our preconceptions of who speaks and who is merely spoken to – or should we rather say spoken *about*?[96]

This chapter has shown that ancient stories featuring speaking animals do not always and necessarily privilege the human over the non-human animal. Right from the start of the conversation in antiquity, there was also an alternate tradition of animals speaking to humans from the other side of the divide. This alternate tradition draws on storytelling and the liberties it affords to imagine the ways in which the lives of humans and non-human animals align. And occasionally at least, this tradition also offers a surprisingly frank assessment of the human condition and the anthropocentric assumptions on which it is based. This view, in turn, resonates with how speaking animals feature in the modern world after Darwin put our relationship to non-human animals on a new footing.

To return once more to the question raised at the beginning of this chapter: if animals could speak, what would they say? Listening to Xanthus and his ancient and modern followers, Grunter, the pig, the rooster-fied Pythagoras, and Red Peter the ape, the answer seems clear. There seems to be no innocent way for animals to speak in human voice. If they do, they always and inevitably comment on our humanity. Whether at Troy, on Circe's island, or indeed in Hamburg, Germany, where Kafka's ape was socialized, whether the story in question is ancient or modern, no matter how seemingly removed we are from the highs and lows of the philosophical debate on the question of the animal: the question who is man and what is beast always stirs in the background wherever and whenever an animal uses language to reach out to us. Like an undercurrent or static interference, it is present in whatever else they may have to say.

And occasionally it comes directly to the fore.

Perhaps, then, this is the most anthropocentric of all human appropriations of non-human creatures featured in this book: the idea that *if* animals could speak to us in human voice – and the *if* here remains as conditional as ever – they would have nothing else, nothing better, nothing more interesting or significant to discuss than humans.

CHAPTER 3

The creature at the core of Chapter 3 raises a question that has traditionally been linked to the presence of language, speech, and reasoning: whether animals have a share in justice. Some of the Greek and Roman philosophers argued that animals should not be included in considerations of justice because they cannot conceive of and articulate a moral framework.

In focusing on this problem, Chapter 3 extends a line of argument from the previous chapter – that right from its beginnings in classical antiquity, the animal story served as a medium to challenge such anthropocentric positions. The story of the unlikely encounter between a man and a lion shows that anthropomorphizing is not merely a tool of human appropriation of the non-human animal; it can also bring out real sympathies and correspondences between them. With its particular focus on the capacity to experience pain as a shared feature of humans and animals, the story driving this chapter anticipates modern attempts to bring questions of sentience and suffering into the picture and to reimagine justice as extending beyond the human.

3.1. Georg Stubbs, *A Lion Resting on a Rock* (1788). Metropolitan Museum of Art. © The Elisha Whittelsey Collection, The Elisha Whittelsey Fund, 1949/CC BY-SA (Creative Commons).

The Lion of Androclus (*Panthera leo philanthropus*)

IN CONTRAST TO XANTHUS AND OTHER ANIMALS THAT RAISED their human voices in the previous chapter, the animal at the core of this one remains silent and has no name. Even though its story tells us about an unlikely encounter between human and animal, it does not cross into the realm of the impossible by endowing its animal protagonist with speech. Yet Androclus' lion 'speaks' to us in other ways. By serving as the protagonist of a tale of human/animal friendship, it raises fundamental questions about our engagement with each other and with non-human creatures and, in doing so, reveals something at once specifically Roman *and* universally human.

The story describes an unlikely friendship between a man and a lion that plays out against the backdrop of the social realities of the Roman Empire. The fullest account is offered by the Roman author Aulus Gellius dating from about 180 CE. He included it in his book *Attic Nights* – a compilation of unusual events he jotted down on long winter evenings during his extended stay in the Greek region of Attica.[1] Yet Gellius is not the only author – nor even the earliest – to report this tale. The Roman philosopher Seneca (ca 4 BCE–65 CE) refers to the same story in passing, which suggests it was already in circulation about two hundred years earlier.[2] Gellius apparently came across it in the works of an Egyptian/Greek author – the notorious Alexandrian teacher of rhetoric Apion Plistonices (first century CE) – who claimed to have witnessed the events himself.[3]

The story goes like this.

One day Apion attends one of the bloodthirsty and macabre spectacles routinely held at the Circus Maximus in Rome. The so-called *damnatio ad bestias* ('punishment by beasts') pitted various wild and exotic animals against unarmed humans – prisoners of war, convicts, others who had broken the law, including, in later times, Christian martyrs.[4] On that day, the beast selected for this form of capital punishment is an imposing lion, particularly agile and physically impressive.[5] Yet when this lion lays eyes on one of the humans he is meant to rip apart, a certain Androclus, the unexpected happens:

> When that lion saw him from a distance ... he stopped short as if in amazement, and then approached the man slowly and quietly, as if he recognized him. Then, wagging his tail in a mild and caressing way, after the manner and fashion of fawning dogs, he came close to the man, who was now half dead from fright, and gently licked his feet and hands.[6]

It seems the lion's friendly demeanour is not lost on its human recipient: 'The man Androclus, while submitting to the caresses of so fierce a beast, regained his lost courage and gradually turned his eyes to look at the lion. Then ... you might have seen man and lion exchange joyful greetings, as if they had recognized each other.'[7] Certainly a surprising turn of events.

And one that does not go unnoticed. At the unlikely sight of a lion and a man conversing rather than engaging in mortal combat, the audience erupts in wild cheers and the emperor presiding over the spectacle summons Androclus over. His explanation as to why the lion spared him takes us back in time and from the centre of the Roman Empire to its periphery. It also confirms that in this case appearances were not deceiving: the lion and the man had indeed met before. Their paths had crossed several years earlier under very different circumstances.

Back then, Androclus was a slave in the household of the proconsul of the province of Africa. He was treated so badly by his master that one day he ran off. Seeking shelter from persecution and the fierce climate, he made for a remote cave. A little later a lion entered the same cave, his den. Androclus feared the worst, but there was no growling, snarling, or baring of teeth, nothing – not the slightest trace of aggression.

The reason was that the lion had a splinter (*stirps*) in his paw and was in severe pain. What happened next reads like this in the words attributed to Androclus himself: 'When the lion ... saw me cowering at a distance, he approached me mildly and gently, and lifting up his foot, was evidently showing it to me and holding it out as if to ask for help.'[8] Luckily for the lion, his request did not fall on deaf ears. Androclus removed the splinter and cleaned the wound. By then, he was 'free from any great feeling of fear' – which was just as well.[9] Man and lion cohabited in the cave for three years, sharing not only a common roof but also the food the lion provided for them both.

Human and animal might have lived together happily ever after. Yet this is not what happened. One day Androclus decides to return to civilization. Only three days after leaving the cave, he is arrested, sent to Rome, and condemned to meet his end in combat with wild animals. Although Androclus does not know it, the lion is also captured and sent to Rome – to administer the *damnatio ad bestias.*[10]

And yet the story does not end here. Androclus' account of why the lion spared him is written down on a tablet and passed around among the spectators present at the Circus Maximus on that day. Nothing delighted the masses at these events more than a departure from the usual bloodthirsty script.[11] The tale of an unlikely friendship between human and animal moves the audience. When given the chance to decide Androclus' fate, they vote to set him and the lion free.

Soon there is a new spectacle on the streets of Rome. As Gellius recounts, quoting Apion, 'we used to see Androclus with the lion, attached to a slender leash (*tenui loro*), making the rounds of the shops throughout the city'. Their new fame benefits human and non-human animal alike: 'Androclus was given money, the lion sprinkled with flowers, and everyone who met them anywhere exclaimed: "This is the lion that was a man's friend, this is the man who was physician to a lion."'[12] An auspicious end for at least two of those fighting in the Circus Maximus that day.

***

So, what are we to make of this story? Is this merely an ancient confirmation of the truism that one always meets twice in life? Perhaps. Yet chances are that the events recounted to us here, albeit improbable, are more profound. They point to a further twist in the philosophical conversation on the question of the human.

As we have seen in the previous chapter, it was the ancient Greek philosopher Aristotle who first argued for a firm line separating human and animal. In his view, it was above all the absence of *logos* ('language', 'speech', 'reason') that set them apart.[13] Yet the ancient philosophical debate on the nature and status of humans and animals neither began nor ended with his intervention. Throughout classical antiquity, the absence of *logos* became the basis for a number of other deficits that allegedly set non-human creatures apart – deficits apparently resulting from their lack of *logos*. The claim that animals cannot distinguish right from wrong, that they cannot articulate moral considerations and thus have no share in justice counts among the most consequential arguments made in the course of the ancient philosophical debate.[14] It involves two ideas separate in principle: first, that animals are themselves incapable of acting morally and, second, that they need not be included in human considerations of morality and justice. The second point in particular, that animals can be excluded from human considerations of morality and justice, had devastating consequences for the lives of non-human creatures in classical antiquity. It justified the brutal treatment of animals as evident not least in the mass killings of wild and exotic animals in public spectacles such as the *venationes* ('hunts' revolving around the fatal confrontation between exotic animals and (sometimes) certain humans, such as criminals).

At first glance, the story of Androclus and the lion seems far removed from the intricacies of the philosophical debate. After all, this is the realm of storytelling and not that of abstract reasoning. And yet it is obvious that the story reverberates with several points made by the ancient philosophers.[15] Most notably, perhaps, this particular lion parades a whole set of features typically denied to animals: even if it is not capable of human speech and explicit reasoning, it is able to articulate itself in other ways. By approaching Androclus as someone who can relieve him of his pain, this lion acts towards a preconceived goal.[16] Moreover, later in the Circus Maximus at Rome, the lion recognizes Androclus, thus demonstrating the capacity for memory – another feature that some philosophers attributed exclusively to humans.[17] Most notably, however, Gellius' lion engages with a member of the species *homo sapiens* in a reciprocal relationship of assistance and care. This is all the more remarkable because the lion is not only a wild animal but perhaps *the* apex predator, hence his status as one of the most popular killers in the Circus Maximus and other arenas.

In this story, then, there is a level of mutual recognition and awareness bringing human and non-human animal together and ultimately presenting them as equals: equal in their capacity to feel pain and to suffer; equal in their capacity to experience fear – and joy when they recognize each other; equal in their capacity to understand what is at stake in a certain situation; and, finally, equal in their capacity for compassion – the result of mutual benevolence that outlasts the moment and spans time and space. And with obvious consequences for the way we see the lion: who would want to deny that, in the moral universe of this particular story at least, an animal participates in justice by sparing its human companion's life?

ANIMALS AND JUSTICE IN THE ANCIENT WORLD

The idea that animals had no claim to justice was first raised by the ancient Greek poet Hesiod (ca 700 BCE). In his *Works and Days,* he states that Zeus bestowed a sense of justice (*dikē*) only to humans.[18] With the fourth century BCE and Aristotle's intervention, the argument gained further traction. Aristotle himself variously maintained that humans and animals could not engage in relations of justice because animals had no share in *logos* and so could not communicate notions of right and wrong.[19] He also suggested that animals were for humans to exploit and that humans were entitled to wage a just war against animals. Yet he stopped short of arguing directly that humans were morally superior to animals on the basis of *logos.*[20]

The argument gained greater currency through the reception and continuation of Aristotle's views by the Stoics. In the work of philosophers such as Zeno (ca 335–263 BCE) and Chrysippus (ca 280–207 BCE), the idea of *oikeiōsis* ('kinship', 'affinity') became central to the claim that non-human animals did not participate in justice.[21] As the word itself suggests, *oikeiōsis* started with the *oikos* (ancient Greek: 'household') and the relationships that characterize it; but it soon extended further, sometimes to include all of humanity. For many ancient philosophers – specifically those of the Epicurean and Stoic schools – the presence of *oikeiōsis* constituted the basis for justice. It came into being through relationships of likeness, most notably the joint capacity to reason. Animals were typically excluded from the concept of *oikeiōsis*. They were seen as not enough like humans to warrant inclusion in moral considerations. The Stoics in particular denied animals any share in justice. Referring to animals' lack of reason, they held that *oikeiōsis*, justice, and therefore moral standing were available only to other rational beings – that is, humans.

At the same time, a number of other philosophically inclined authors set out to push back against the notion that animals were different from and inferior to humans. To this end they sought to highlight the commonality of man and animal. An early instance of this part of the tradition comes from Aristotle's successor as the leader of the Peripatetic school, Theophrastus (ca 372–287 BCE). He maintained that humans and animals share 'desires, urges, and even reasonings (*logismois*)'.[22] Further examples include several thinkers roughly contemporary with Gellius. The Platonists Plutarch (the author of the *Beasts Are Rational* from the previous chapter) and Porphyry, for example, promoted a nuanced view of how individual features (such as *logos*) are present among all living beings.[23] Plutarch dismissed the Stoic idea that animals are not included in *oikeiōsis* by illustrating various ways in which they are similar to humans. And Porphyry (ca 234–305 CE) promulgated a broad view of justice that included human and non-human animals alike based on the notion of their kinship:

> Thus also we posit that all human beings are kin to one another, and moreover to all the animals, for the principles of their bodies are naturally the same ... We posit this the more strongly because the souls of animals are no different, I mean in appetite and anger, and also in reasoning and above all in perception. Just as with bodies, so with souls: some animals have brought to perfection, others less so, but the principles are naturally the same in all.[24]

So, did Porphyry and other ancient thinkers fundamentally rethink ancient views of human and non-human animals? At first glance it may seem so and to some extent they certainly did. Yet their contribution to the debate is actually less radical than it might seem at first sight. For none of them appears to have questioned the initial premise of their philosophical predecessors: that reason-possession in itself confers moral value. They merely argue that non-human animals do, in fact, meet the intellectual requirements for inclusion into the company of morally significant beings.[25] In other words, even though they make a strong case for including animals in considerations of morality and justice, ancient thinkers such as Plutarch and Porphyry do not actually pursue fundamentally new lines of reasoning. They merely seek to refute the premises on which the dominant position was based.

Against this background, Gellius' story of Androclus and the lion stands out. It speaks to and inverts typical ways of thinking in the philosophical debate revolving around the presence or absence of reason, language, and memory in non-human creatures. It encourages us to consider new aspects, such as the roles of empathy and loyalty, as additional dimensions in the ways humans and animals meet.[26] Most notably, perhaps, it directs the focus on a dimension of justice that will come to play a key role only millennia later in modern considerations of the moral standing of animals: the shared capacity of human and non-human animal to suffer and feel pain.

PARALLEL STORIES

Before we get into the specifics of this story and the way in which it relates to its Roman context, it is important to address one concern upfront. The critically inclined reader might point out that we are making too much of a single story. In particular, one that appears to be a charming, somewhat mawkish, and ultimately inconsequential tale, the stuff of children's literature, perhaps, but not a worthy subject of serious reflection. This would certainly be true were it not the case that, in the ancient world, the story of Androclus and the lion is less unique than one might think.

Reports of animals showing not just loyalty, but all sorts of complex feelings, are by no means rare. Even though some of the Greek and Roman philosophers denied animals emotions altogether, other ancient authors went on to attribute them with just that.[27] Oppian's didactic poem *On Fishing*, for example, finds complex feelings of jealousy in the Merle-wrasse.[28] And Aelian's *On Animals* features deer acting out of jealousy, fearful leopards, and compassionate mares.[29]

Moreover, there are numerous instances in which animal emotions are directed towards members of the human species. Unsurprisingly, perhaps, companion animals feature particularly frequently in ancient tales illustrating the close emotional ties between humans and other animals. The ancient author Arrian (ca 86–160 CE), for example, describes a level of closeness and intimacy between himself and his dog that leaves no doubt as to the extraordinary loyalty between them.[30] In the ancient world, just as in the modern, companion animals served as a prime way in which human and non-human animals bonded with each other.

And yet we also do hear of instances in which wild animals engaged with humans in relationships of affection and loyalty. Aelian tells us of a seal in love with a woman and a pod of dolphins mourning the death of a man they knew.[31] Such examples show more than mere anthropomorphizing. They illustrate that the divide between animals that were considered capable of emotional bonds with humans and those excluded from them did not always coincide with the divide between domesticated and wild.

At this stage we might infer that the story of Androclus and the lion is not merely a story of human/animal loyalty. It is a story specifically about questions of cooperation and justice. And here, too, parallel stories abound.[32] Indeed, lions seem to feature particularly frequently in ancient tales revolving around questions of justice. Their status as wild and ferocious animals, as apex predators perfectly capable of killing humans, adds further weight to tales of their apparent cooperative behaviour. Aelian tells the tale of two lions whose helpless cubs were killed by a she-bear in an unguarded moment.[33] When the parents return, the bear quickly evades their grief and anger by climbing up a nearby tree. But the lions do not give in easily and come up with the following plan: one of them seeks out a nearby woodcutter. The animal entices the woodcutter to return to the lair with it by wrapping its tail around him and even carries his axe in its mouth. Justice is finally served (or should we perhaps better say, retribution is achieved) when the woodcutter understands what he is supposed to do and chops off the tree so that the offending she-bear can be brought to justice.

The Roman author Pliny the Elder (23–79 CE) knows further instances of lions successfully soliciting help from humans.[34] He tells us about a certain Mentor of Syracuse who seeks to escape a lion but cannot because whenever he tries to get away the lion blocks his way. Mentor eventually notices that the lion's foot is swollen and removes a thorn from its paw.[35] The parallels between this story and the one of Androclus are obvious enough for Aelian himself to point them out.[36] As in the case of Androclus, the lion here suffers and seeks human help.

A third story, also from Pliny, further explores the relationship of man and lion as mutually beneficial. It revolves around one Elpis of Samos who, during a trip to Africa, flees a lion gnashing its teeth by climbing a tree.[37] Devoid of any real way out, Elpis resorts to prayer and finally recalls that the lion had behaved unusually. Why had it not blocked his path even though it could have? And why was it lying down underneath the tree? Was it perhaps not so much gnashing its teeth as begging for mercy? Eventually, Elpis gathers his courage and climbs down the tree, only to find a bone stuck in the lion's jaws which he promptly removes. The lion assists him by holding out and adjusting its foot. Like in Gellius' story, the human helper is later 'paid back' by the lion with food.[38]

None of these examples tells quite the same story as the one of Androclus and the lion. Gellius' tale stands out for its level of detail in how human and non-human animal interact. But the thematic resonances among all these examples are sufficiently strong to point to a larger picture. The story of Androclus and the lion is part of a whole body of similar tales and anecdotes that circulated in the works of certain authors writing during the first two centuries CE. Despite their different outlooks, these stories come together in presenting memorable content in ways that inspire thinking. There was obviously a sustained interest among the ancient authors in concrete examples of how humans and animals act individually and in interaction with each other. And this interest generated a body of knowledge that stood in sharp contrast to the notion that animals differ from humans in insurmountable ways – not least their lack of *logos* – and that they have no moral standing.

ANTHROPOMORPHISM AND ITS DISCONTENTS

At this stage we resist the urge to include ever more tales from the ancient world with a similar storyline.[39] Instead, we return to the tale of Androclus and the lion as told by Gellius with which we started this chapter. How does the human/animal relationship come into focus here?

Gellius' rendering of the tale takes the reader on a wild ride – from Rome and the Circus Maximus, to the lion's den in the African desert, and then back again to the centre of the city where the Romans pass judgement on the events they have come to witness.[40] By starting off in Rome and then moving on to the African back story, Gellius has the reader share in the experience of the audience at the Circus Maximus: the reader, too, is puzzled by the lion's behaviour and keen to find the reason for this unexpected turn of events.

Gellius further shapes the story's focus by highlighting the fact that Androclus is a slave mistreated by his master (a proconsul).[41] The effect of this information: in featuring a slave suffering an injustice, Gellius' story enhances the moral dimension of the tale. Questions of morality and justice appear as central themes.

The story then goes on to juxtapose two main settings for the events that are laid out to us: first, there is the cave as a remote and concealed space beyond human civilization where the values, rules, and hierarchies of Roman society do not apply. And, second, there is the open-air forum of the Circus Maximus at the heart of the city where these same values are very much on display. The story draws on these two very different locations to enact a number of reversals: over the course of the story, the lion turns from a potential threat to a life-sustaining force, from predator to companion. Androclus himself turns from potential prey – unusual for humans who tend to see themselves at the top of the food chain – to a healer, and from someone who receives help to someone who bestows generosity and benevolence on a beneficiary.

There is, indeed, a deep resonance in the way human and non-human animal are represented here both as actors and as beneficiaries of each other's actions: the lion spares Androclus, just as both lion and human will be spared later on in the Circus Maximus. The animal's vulnerability back in the cave foreshadows that of Androclus himself years later in the Circus Maximus. And the assistance Androclus gives to the lion in the African cave finds its parallel in the lion assisting Androclus later at Rome.

By featuring such doubles, the story invites the reader to see the analogies between human and non-human animal: both are at some point in grave danger; both are capable of suffering; both are able to act contrary to their instincts; and both come to rely on each other for their survival. In short: the conditions of human and non-human animal align. By living with the lion in the cave, Androclus himself becomes more animal-like and the lion more like a human. In sparing Androclus, the lion suppresses his natural instinct. As a result, both Androclus and the lion retain not merely their lives but also their freedom.

And yet – and this is crucial – the events recounted to us here never fully eliminate the difference between human and non-human animal.[42] The lion remains a predator, providing them both with fresh meat; Androclus, however, tries to make up for the fact that he does not have access to fire to cook it, having him leave his share out to dry in the sun before consumption.[43] So it only makes sense that eventually Androclus has his fill of the wild and is ready to return to civilization.[44]

What do all these parallels add up to? What is interesting about this story with regard to how it explores the relationship between human and animal?

In her reading of another variant of the same tale (by Aelian), Catherine Osborne has identified anthropomorphism and sentimentalism as two strong yet problematic responses that are frequently ascribed to those humans who promote a kinder, more emphatic stance towards animals.[45] Anthropomorphism, the attribution of human features and feelings to non-human animals, she argues, often feeds into sentimentalism – an overly sympathetic response towards animals in situations in which such a response is not warranted (for example because an animal that allegedly shows human behaviours merely acts out of instinct).

Anthropomorphism and sentimentality play a role in Gellius' version of the tale, too. Gellius seems to be mindful of the risks posed by an overly apparent anthropomorphism. He treads a fine line between reading the lion's behaviour in human terms and avoiding accusations of a misleading sentimentalist anthropomorphism. Rather than speaking the language of fact, he quotes Apion to employ the language of semblance and comparison to interpret the lion's behaviour in human terms: he states that in the cave the wounded lion approaches Androclus 'as if' (*quasi*) looking for help.[46] Upon meeting his old companion in the Circus Maximus, the lion startles 'as if' (*quasi*) recognizing his old friend and helper.[47] Subsequently, they are seen greeting each other 'as if' (*quasi*) they knew each other.[48] In resorting to this turn of phrase, Gellius alerts the reader that what is at stake here is merely a *human interpretation* of the lion's behaviour. The result is a storyline that highlights the role of anthropomorphism in human attempts to make sense of the lion's behaviour without, however, fully succumbing to it.

The story thus confirms that anthropocentrism and anthropomorphism are, at least in principle, different ideas and should be distinguished from each other.[49] While anthropocentrism entails the belief that humans are the pinnacle of evolution and the measure of all things, anthropomorphism involves the ascribing of human features, characteristics, and skills to non-human creatures and things. And while anthropocentrism ultimately serves to elevate the human over the non-human animal, anthropomorphism can actually help us relate to non-human creatures in sympathetic ways. The story is a case in point: Anthropomorphism is mobilized here as a strategy to highlight real similarities between human and non-human animal.

The tale thus allows for and encourages a deeper engagement with the moral and ethical questions raised by its storyline. And among these, questions of sympathy and justice loom large. When both Androclus and the lion finally walk free, our sympathies remain firmly aligned with that of the internal audience witnessing the spectacle within the story. Together with those present at the Circus Maximus, we cheer at the unlikely turn of events and take delight in the lucky escape of human and animal from a cruel death.

The story thus urges us to reconsider the way in which we think about the human/animal relationship.[50] The similarities and correspondences between human and non-human animal come to the fore. In juxtaposing before and after, human and animal, and events occurring at the centre of the Roman world and those at its periphery, the story parades what is perhaps the most powerful feature of stories and storytelling: their 'openness to inspection'.[51] In a nutshell: rather than providing ready-made answers, stories like this one raise questions. They ask us to examine the principles and practices at work in the moral universe they depict. And, in doing so, they allow us to imagine alternative ways in which humans and animals come together beyond those dictated by tradition, convention, and, indeed, philosophical reasoning.

Such a reading of the story is not out of line with the overall character of Gellius' oeuvre. In terms of genre, *Attic Nights*, the larger work from which the story is derived, is best described as a miscellany – that is, a collection of seemingly unconnected material with no apparent purpose.[52] Even though Gellius nowhere sets out an explicit agenda, *Attic Nights* has a strong educational and ethical dimension.[53] This dimension comes out in the numerous short stories that make up this work. Even though, as one modern commentator put it, these stories concern 'virtually every subject under the sun', they raise ethical and educational questions or instigate thinking about a wide array of issues.[54] *Attic Nights* is a compendium of material that Gellius derived from other authors and presented in a way that made the Roman reader think about matters of common concern – among these, the capacities of lions and the intricacies of the human/animal relationship.

THE SLAVE AND THE LION: UNMASKING ROMAN SOCIETY?

Before we move on from the ancient to the modern world to offer some remarks on how the tale of Androclus and the lion resonates in the present, one last look at the story in its specifically Roman setting reveals a dimension that has not yet received the attention it deserves. What is at stake in this story is not just the moral standing of a non-human animal. The moral standing of Androclus, who finds himself condemned to a cruel death in the Circus Maximus, is equally in question. The story of Androclus and the lion, as told by Gellius, raises questions about the human treatment of animals *and* about the Roman treatment of a particular group of humans that were animalized in Roman culture and society: slaves.

To start with, the bloodthirsty setting of the Circus Maximus, which made a sport of human/animal suffering, is an unlikely backdrop for an encounter that foregrounds the bonds and not the differences between humans and animals. It stands for brutality and bloodshed rather than mutual understanding – in distinct contrast to the events occurring within the story. The story of Androclus and the lion is thus ultimately also a story of mercy and compassion, set against the background of the merciless and brutal world of the Roman spectacle.

The Romans knew different kinds of such spectacles. Some of them featured the re-enactment of famous scenes from Greco-Roman mythology with the 'actors' (prisoners) condemned to die at the claws and jaws of wild beasts (or, if this did not finish them off, killed later by human intervention). Others involved elaborate technical devices used as stage props. Others again entailed the brutal slaying of human and animal life without additional embellishments.

From today's perspective, such forms of punishment seem repulsive and inhumane – and they certainly are. Yet in a sense that was exactly the point. The *damnatio ad bestias* involved the dehumanizing of those singled out for this form of punishment. Indeed, those humans subjected to it were seen as little more than beasts themselves. They and the professional *venatores* were called the *bestiarii* (Latin: 'beast fighters'). They were no longer seen as fully human.[55] Through their lawless actions, they were thought to have opted out of the human community. By dehumanizing the prisoners (by linking them to animals), an artificial distance was set between those watching the killing and those being killed.[56] In the eyes of the Roman audience, the fact that wild animals mauled the convicts to death reflected the animalistic nature of the convicts themselves. To eliminate them thus seemed (with very few exceptions) acceptable.

From the Roman point of view, slaves were particularly suited to this form of punishment. In the Greco-Roman world, they were widely associated with animals.[57] Aristotle (384–322 BCE) justifies natural slavery by explaining that those affected have no share in reason.[58] This alleged absence of *logos* ultimately led Aristotle to describe slaves as living 'tools' (*organa*) that could in principle at least be replaced by automation.[59] It also put the slave on par with animals. It is in this sense that Aristotle later asserts that it is acceptable to hunt like wild beasts those humans who refuse to be ruled even though they are 'designed by nature for subjugation'.[60]

Similar connections feature elsewhere in Greek and Roman thought and literature: Xenophon (ca 430–355 BCE) suggests that the strategy to make slaves coincides with that directed at wild animals – to feed them.[61]

Cato the Elder (234–149 BCE) lists elderly and sickly slaves together with worn-out livestock as items to be discarded by the famer as soon as they are no longer productive.[62] Slaves, these examples show, were grouped together with animals and treated as commodities.[63] So it was not just the *damnatio ad bestias* as a particularly cruel form of punishment that dehumanized slaves by associating them with non-human animals but the institution of slavery more broadly.

If the association of prisoners with animals enabled the cruel treatment of other humans, the sudden collapse of this artificial distinction renders it impossible. We know of at least one example in which this applied not just to human but also to the non-human animals in the Circus Maximus. The Roman statesman and philosopher Cicero (106–43 BCE) recalls an incident in which an animal's apparent humanity changed the audience's perception of the spectacle:

> The last day was for the elephants. The groundlings showed much astonishment thereat, but no enjoyment. There was even an impulse of compassion, a feeling that the monsters had something human about them (esse quandam illi beluae cum genere humano societatem).[64]

The mood of the masses turned because the elephants meant to trample the convicts to death seemed all too human. If the dehumanization of humans turned them into creatures suitable for cruel treatment in a public spectacle, the opposite process – the humanization of the animals singled out to participate in bloodthirsty spectacle – made them *un*-suitable. As soon as those fighting for their lives lost their wild, animal-like identity and took on human features, the illusion that allowed the audience to shut off compassion no longer prevailed. The spectacle lost its capacity to entertain.

The dehumanization of certain humans as a form of oppression did not stop with slaves and prisoners. It extended to other suppressed groups and into other areas of life. We find it at play, for example, in Simonides' infamous misogynistic poem which likens women with a variety of beasts in not very flattering ways (see Chapter 10) and in the frequent derogatory association of women with dogs.[65]

Unfortunately, the horrific practice of dehumanizing certain humans by referring to them as animals also did not stop with the ancient Greeks and Romans. In the modern world, the basic treatment of certain humans as animals remains central to the ideologies of racism and genocide. But with such observations we are getting ahead of ourselves. Before we fully leave the ancient world behind, we return once gain to the ancient story to explore how it counters the tendency to dehumanize by (re-) humanizing human and animal alike.

REHUMANIZING HUMAN AND ANIMAL ALIKE

By now it has become clear that the lion and Androclus reference each other on multiple levels. And they do so not just in how they relate to each other but also in the kind of debasement they suffer. Both are marginalized, degraded beings; both are literally and metaphorically voiceless. Within the story, man and lion alike suffer abuse and maltreatment. Both are subject to the caprices of power. Both are captured, deported, and destined to die for the entertainment of others. Human and non-human animal here recognize each other in their shared suffering and marginal status. As objects of vilification and hatred, they perceive each other as beings worthy of care and respect.

Overall, then, the story rehumanizes human and animal protagonist alike. Man and lion actively shape their fate rather than being mere passive sufferers of cruel punishment. Both feature as individuals with a history. By illustrating their capacity to forge a mutual bond of recognition and care, the story challenges the cultural assumptions and prejudices underlying the institution of slavery. It gives the animalized slave and the enslaved animal a face and a story. This makes it impossible not to see them as individuals with hopes and fears of their own. In this light, the very feature sometimes seen as a weakness of the story – the apparent anthropomorphism of the lion – is actually its main point: by breaching the artificial distance created between man and animal, and between one human and another, the story challenges the very assumptions that sustain the abuse of humans and animals alike.

The emphatic recognition of lion and slave in the Circus Maximus thus provides an alternative perspective, another way of looking at those creatures singled out to die there. It puts the focus squarely on the capacity of humans *and* animals to suffer, and thus implicitly challenges the assumptions and ideologies on which the *damnatio ad bestias* and the *venationes* were based. Moreover, in Androclus' compassionate response to the lion's suffering, and in the lion's later decisive response to the helpless Androclus, the story foregrounds compassion rather than bloodshed as a form of engaging with humans and animals alike. And at least the internal audience of the story, the faceless masses at the spectacle on the day, seem convinced: they decide that Androclus and the lion should go free.

Perhaps the external audience should as well . . .?

This reading of the story may seem too great a leap for some of my readers. Yet such a reading is less singular than one might think. Greek and Roman literature holds plenty of examples in which animals are used in similar ways: to act as a mouthpiece and channels of communication for the oppressed.[66] The 'father' of the fable, Aesop, was himself a slave and some of the tales attributed to him (and other ancient authors) used this genre as a form of social critique.[67] In other words, the oppression of certain animals serves as a means to address the oppression of certain humans. In this way, the story anticipates a more recent acknowledgement: that the oppression of women, people of colour, and animals shares the same roots by being grounded in the same conception of the human.

REIMAGINING THE SUBJECTS OF JUSTICE

The lion of Androclus lives on beyond the confines of classical antiquity in more ways than one. The old story of the double encounter with his human companion was variously told and retold over time with Androclus (or 'Androcles', in the Greek rendering of his name) taking on ever new identities, including those of a knight, a shepherd, and – in George Bernard Shaw's 1912 drama – a tailor.[68] In time, the story became sufficiently popular to warrant an entry in Aarne-Thompson-Uther's foundational index of folktales, thus cementing its status as a touching but fictional tale.[69]

Yet rather than indulging in such undeniably fascinating aspects of classical reception, we ask instead: should animals, after all, be included in questions of justice? Where does the debate on this matter stand these days?

In the modern era, the philosophical conversation on animals and their moral standing took a different turn (actually a series of turns).[70] Yet until relatively recently, all these turns addressed the same set of questions first asked in classical philosophy: do humans and animals differ? If so, in what way? And is this difference relevant to their moral standing? Individual contributions diverged merely in the way in which these questions were answered.

For a long time, the conversation revolved around the presence or absence of *logos* as one of the fundamental criteria that set the human apart from the non-human animal. But at least ever since the intervention of the English philosopher Jeremy Bentham (1748–1832) and his provocative and in many ways game-changing line – 'The question is not, Can they *reason*?, nor Can they *talk?* but, Can they *suffer*?' – sentience rather than reason moved to centre stage in considerations of the moral status of animals.[71] By reframing the problem in this way, Bentham's intervention changed the question and with it the course of the debate.

Today, the capacity of animals to feel pain and to suffer provides the basis of a number of arguments for granting them at least some moral status. To name just two: sentience features prominently in the works of the utilitarian philosopher Peter Singer, who has argued that the interest of animals not to suffer in many cases outweighs the interest of humans to exploit them.[72] In different ways, it also plays a role in the capability theory of justice as promoted by the Classicist and philosopher Martha Nussbaum.[73] For her, an animal's capacity to suffer helps to define those aspects of their existence ('capabilities') considered essential for their thriving. In both instances, sentience matters because it points to morally relevant ways in which human and non-human animals resemble each other.

With its emphasis on the shared capacity to suffer pain, the story of Androclus and the lion seems to anticipate such considerations. By depicting the capacity to feel pain as a feature common to humans and other animals alike, the story highlights sentience as a dimension of justice that was not prominent in the ancient philosophical debate. It seems that right from the start of the conversation in classical antiquity, there was an awareness that this physiological commonality mattered in addition to – and perhaps even more than – the presence or absence of *logos* in non-human creatures.

And yet, we may wonder whether what qualified the lion for ethical consideration here is not only or primarily the capacity to feel pain, but the relationship between human and animal that was made manifest. If so, the story resonates with recent efforts (by feminist scholars and others) to move away from rights-based ('deontological') and utilitarian approaches and towards an understanding that it is our capacity to feel empathy with each other which matters.[74]

This makes the tale of Androclus and the lion a story about recognition. The recognition of man and lion within the story points to the much more fundamental recognition of human and non-human animal as fellow living creatures. The story emphasizes our commonality with other animals. It also encouraged its specifically Roman audience to look critically at their own society, the institution of slavery, and the values and cultural practices on which they were based. In this reading of the tale, the human/animal relationship represents the more specific relationship between the Romans and those they considered subhuman.

At the same time, Gellius' tale illustrates the power of storytelling to imagine the human/animal relationship in different ways by instigating the reader to sympathize with the human and the non-human protagonist alike. As such, it is representative of a larger number of short tales depicting the interaction between humans and animals as they became popular in a number of Greek and Roman authors writing in the first three centuries CE. Authors such as Pliny, Plutarch, Oppian, Aelian, Porphyry, and Athenaeus combine an interest in animals and narrative with larger questions of ethical and moral concern.

As far as tales of human/animal encounters are concerned, such stories remain popular and continue to circulate in the present. In the age of the Internet, they come more often than not in the form of short videos illustrating animal capacities and animal behaviour in action. And, in some instances, they recall elements of the old story: Christian the lion – born in captivity, reared by humans, sold at the iconic London department store Harrods and ultimately sent into the wild where he subsequently recognized his former human companions – or any of the numerous other videos illustrating the often astonishing ways humans and other animals interact.[75] All this evidence is part of a body of knowledge that urges us to include non-human animals in our considerations of justice. It parades the bond between humans and non-human creatures that is forged by our joint biological heritage and our shared experience as living beings. That it is mostly culturally prominent quadruped mammals (cats, dogs, horses, lions, etc.) which serve as the heroes of such stories is no coincidence: they lend themselves particularly to projections of sympathy due to their biological (and hence behavioural) closeness to humans.

In the case of Androclus and the lion, at least, this bond between human and animal becomes the focal point towards the end of the story, when both man and lion walk free. The connection between man and animal, established first in a remote cave in a faraway province and proven years later at the centre of the ancient world, is reified in the leash connecting Androclus and the lion when strolling the streets of Rome. I suggest that Androclus holds not a constraining leash here but a lead symbolizing the relationship. As a physical representation of the bond between Androclus and the lion, it illustrates that the stories of human and other animals remain inextricably bound up with each other.

CHAPTER 4

So far, we have investigated the way in which ancient Greek and Roman thinkers draw on animals to explore what it means to be human in fairly general terms. The next four chapters focus on the role of the animal in thinking particular human identities. This chapter kicks off this line of investigation by focusing on the figure of the Cyclops. While in the previous chapter the focus was on inclusion and correspondences between human and animal, here the animal serves to distinguish and differentiate between different levels of humanity. In the encounter between Odysseus and the Cyclops Polyphemus, the traditional vertical relation between humans and animals is mapped out onto a horizontal plane where it translates into one of centre and periphery.

The world of Odysseus and the Cyclops is one in which animality helps to bring out the quintessential 'other' and one in which the margins of the known world coincide with the margins of the human. This spatial concept of the human, however, did not remain restricted to the ancient world but carries on into the modern: the figure of the Cyclops, whose problematic humanity is in sharp contrast to the enlightened, educated, and cunning Odysseus, in many ways anticipates that of 'the savage' as the quintessential 'other' in the modern Western ethnographic imagination. And yet here, too, the question arises as to whether the ancient story does not also expose the kind of hubris at play when we normalize certain ways of being human while dismissing others.

4.1. Johann Willhelm Tischbein, *Polyphemus* (1802). Landesmuseum für Kunst und Kulturgeschichte Oldenburg. Photo © Sven Adelaide.

The Cyclops (*Cyclops inhospitalis*)

THE CYCLOPES OF HOMER'S ODYSSEY ARE HARDLY A BENIGN bunch. They lack everything that the ancient Greeks cherished back at home: they respect neither the law nor each other.[1] They have no political institutions. They do not practise agriculture but live in small families and in mountaintop caves rather than houses or proper cities. Moreover, even though they inhabit an archipelago or coastal landscape somewhere in the Mediterranean Sea, they have no ships and no seafaring skills.[2] As a result, they are stuck on their lands. And for the better. Unlike the Greeks, who maintain elaborate reciprocal relations of *xenia* ('guest-friendship') with those from other lands, the Cyclopes know only one thing to do with hapless strangers who happen upon their island: eat them.

Odysseus himself can attest to this. On disembarking from his ship with his comrades, he notices a mountain cave.

> There a monstrous man spent his nights, who shepherded his flocks alone and afar, and did not mingle with others, but lived apart, obedient to no law. For he was created a monstrous marvel, and was not like a man that lives by bread, but like a wooded peak of lofty mountains, which stands out to view alone, apart from the rest.[3]

Hardly the most welcoming of creatures.

It remains anyone's guess, then, why Odysseus nevertheless thinks it a good idea to pay a visit. Natural curiosity will have played a role; as will the expectation of guest-gifts.[4] And even though the Cyclopes' thunderous voices are clearly audible from a neighbouring island, signs of a common humanity are not entirely absent either: smoke is visible from afar indicating that the Cyclopes know how to light a fire – a cultural technique that, according to Greek mythology, Prometheus once stole from the gods in a hollow fennel stalk and passed on to humans at great personal expense.[5] So perhaps something is, after all, to be gained from making contact?

Upon reaching the cave of this particular Cyclops, who goes by the name of Polyphemus, Odysseus and his men find it deserted. Apparently, the resident Cyclops is out, tending his sheep and goats. So, Odysseus and his comrades look around and make themselves comfortable. They start a fire, offer sacrifice, and sample some of the cheeses the Cyclops stores in his cave.[6]

Soon, Polyphemus returns.

The encounter is ill-fated from the start. The Cyclops' voice is indeed frighteningly loud and deep. At first there are at least no open hostilities.[7] But things quickly turn sour when Odysseus invokes the ancient Greek gods to urge Polyphemus to show kindness:

> We on our part, thus visiting you, have come as suppliants to your knees, in the hope that you will give us entertainment, or in some other manner be generous to us, as is the due of strangers. Do not deny us, good sir, but reverence the gods; we are your suppliants; and Zeus is the avenger of suppliants and strangers – Zeus, the stranger's god – who walks in the footsteps of reverend strangers.[8]

Yet despite the emphatic note Odysseus is striking here, Polyphemus is not happy to submit to Zeus Xenios (the Zeus of guest-friendship) – nor, indeed, to any other Zeus – and he is not afraid to say so: 'You are a fool, stranger, or have come from afar, seeing that you bid me either to fear or to avoid the gods. For the Cyclopes pay no heed to Zeus, who bears the aegis, nor to the blessed gods, since truly we are better far than they.'[9] So, the Cyclopes have not only no law, no political institutions, and no proper houses, but also no respect towards the Greek gods. This is hardly good news.

Next, we hear that the Cyclops eats two of Odysseus' comrades.[10]

***

With the Homeric account of Odysseus' run-in with the Cyclopes, we return once more to ancient Greece and the Archaic period – a time prior to the beginning of the philosophical conversation on the question of the human featured in the previous chapters. Yet even though the creature at the core of this chapter takes us back in time, we push ahead with the larger story at the core of this book. The figure of the Cyclops prompts us to further explore the place of the animal in thinking human difference.

In the case of the Cyclops, the identity in question is that of the non-Greek, the foreigner, the monstrous stranger who inhabits a faraway country at the edges of the known world. In the various non-Greeks that Odysseus comes across during his arduous trip home after the Trojan War, we encounter a world in which the real morphs almost seamlessly into the imaginary. Yet here, too, we will find that notions of the human as opposed to the non-human help to centre certain ways of being in the world while marginalizing others.

WHO ARE THE HOMERIC CYCLOPES?

In ancient Greek, *kyklos* means 'round'. The English words *circle* and *cycle* are both derived from it. So, the name of the Cyclopes means 'round-eyed' or 'circle-eyed' and thus points to the most important distinguishing feature of the creatures in question: the single round eye located in the middle of their foreheads – the emblem of the Cyclopic brand.

Incidentally, the ancient Greeks and Romans knew three different kinds of Cyclopes.[11] All of them have in common a particularly large physique and the central eye prominent in the middle of their foreheads.[12] And yet, in other ways, they could not be more different. A first type includes the three sons of the primordial deities Uranus and Gaia, as described in Hesiod's *Theogony*, who were said to have produced Zeus' thunderbolts.[13] A second type consists of skilled craftsmen who were credited with amazing feats of engineering such as the walls of the cities of Mycenae and Tiryns.[14] They could be immensely helpful to humans, sharing with them their technical knowledge and skills.

Not so Polyphemus and his ilk. The creatures Odysseus encounters on his arduous trip home from Troy constitute a third type of Cyclops that features in Greco-Roman thought and literature, in addition to the primordial creatures and the craftsmen. They have few skills and even fewer manners. They are of no benefit whatsoever to humans. On the contrary, they pose a direct threat to human life. Polyphemus and his like stand out among the Cyclopes of the ancient world in being simple and uncouth, and by their aggressive, man-devouring habit.

As far as Polyphemus is concerned, *his* name is usually taken to mean 'much renowned' or 'much spoken about' (from ancient Greek *polyphēmos*, literally: 'much-talked-about').[15] And much spoken about he certainly is: as the hero of Homer's story, he reached a level of notoriety unmatched by any other Cyclops with numerous ancient authors adding, recrafting, or merely alluding to the same story.[16]

THE *ODYSSEY* AND THE 'ETHNOGRAPHIC IMAGINATION'

The *Iliad* and *Odyssey* may seem unlikely places to look for Greek ideas on non-Greek people. After all, they are works of fiction that variously venture into the realm of the extraordinary and fantastic. So how does ethnography – the study of human cultures – come into the picture?

As members of the genre of epic poetry, Homer's *Iliad* and *Odyssey* follow the conventions of oral performance and storytelling which shaped them. Yet both texts include elements of the real. The Trojan War was fought perhaps sometime during the late twelfth century BCE, but the specific events described in the *Iliad* are the product of the imagination. They reflect and articulate the values and modes of life of the eighth century BCE, when the poem that had circulated orally before was first written down. Similarly, with the *Odyssey*: the story of Odysseus' ten-year voyage back home from the Trojan battlefield to the Greek city of Ithaca reflects the experiences of the perils of travel, seafaring, and overseas settlement.[17] Yet once we get to supernatural intervention and creatures like the sorceress Circe, the Sirens, and, indeed, the Cyclops Polyphemus, we are again in the realm of the imaginary.

There are no one-eyed people anywhere in the world.

Or are there?

The ancient Greeks developed an interest in, and knowledge of, non-Greek peoples long before the arrival of ethnography as a distinct line of inquiry.[18] While the latter emerged during the fifth century BCE as a result of the Greco-Persian Wars (499–448 BCE), information on the customs, cultures, looks, and lifestyles of non-Greek people pre-dates the notion of 'the barbarian' as a summary category for all non-Greeks in its wake.[19] It is already present in Archaic Greek poetry, fragments of early prose texts, painted pottery, reliefs, and other pictorial representations of people inhabiting faraway lands.[20] During this early time, there was not yet a clear polarity between Greeks and non-Greeks ('barbarians'). Greek identity was still cumulative and pluralistic, but an emerging understanding of Greekness also cropped up through the encounter of cultural difference.[21]

From the eighth century onwards, the Greeks increasingly came into contact with other cultures. Through trade, travel, and the foundation of new cities throughout the Mediterranean world, they experienced people living in ways that both resembled and differed from their own.[22] Their sense of what it meant to be Greek thus emerged through their contact with other Greeks and non-Greeks – that is to say, through relations of identity and difference – and everything in between.[23]

Both the *Iliad* and the *Odyssey* include representations of non-Greek peoples.[24] The *Odyssey*, in particular, explores the themes of travel, colonialization, and encounters with strangers, both friendly and hostile, as part of its storyline.[25] Over the course of his protracted return home, Odysseus comes across a variety of different peoples. There are, for example, the Phoenicians – essentially tricksters and traders;[26] the Lotus Eaters, and the Laestrygonians who eat humans.[27] Odysseus' encounters with these and other peoples includes information on their culinary habits, customs, and forms of social organization, later staples of ethnographic inquiry. All this amounts to a rich set of information that allowed the Greeks to compare and contrast their own way of life with that of others.

It may be tempting to put the Cyclopes into a category other than the peoples just mentioned. After all, with their prominent single eye, the Homeric Cyclopes seem more like the Sirens, Scylla, Charybdis, and other marvellous creatures populating the world of Odysseus. Yet there is ample evidence to suggest that Polyphemus qualified for consideration as human even though, as we will see, he may not fully pass the test.

Moreover, in the ancient world, knowledge of human diversity, both physical and cultural, seamlessly morphed into the imaginary the further away one got from home. At least at the outward edges of the known world, blank spaces in the canvas of the known were readily filled with tall tales, hearsay, exaggerations, or mere speculation.[28] The later Greek and Roman ethnographic literature is full of examples of peoples who differed from the human physical norm. In the *Histories,* for example, Herodotus (ca 485–425 BCE) includes an account of northern Scythia which features a tribe of one-eyed people called the Arimaspi, who engage in perpetual warfare with a bunch of gold-guarding griffins.[29] Ctesias, from Cnidus' ethnographic account of ancient India (*Indika,* late fifth century BCE), includes dog-headed men (*kynokephaloi*) and people with gigantic ears covering a good part of their upper torsos.[30] Several centuries later, the Roman author Pliny the Elder (23–79 CE) still mentions Cyclopes, people with eyes in their chests, people with feet pointing backwards, and people sporting a big single foot that, when held upwards, doubles as protection from the sun.[31] So the single eye should not automatically entice us to exclude Polyphemus as a subject worthy of the ethnographic imagination. He merely differs from more mainstream objects of ethnographic enquiry by being part of an extended storyline that illustrates his individual character and brings him face to face with Odysseus – the hero of the *Odyssey.*

The figure of Odysseus is central to the way in which the ethnographic perspective is set up.[32] Odysseus is the quintessential 'traveller-observer' and, as such, resembles the classic nineteenth-century ethnographer: both travel the world; both come in contact with foreign lands and their inhabitants; both show a certain amount of curiosity for the customs and lifestyles of those they encounter; and, most importantly: both present their experiences of foreign lands and their inhabitants in storied form.[33] Odysseus is thus the quintessential outsider who arrives on foreign shores and later returns home to recount his experience. It is through his figure that the ways of non-Greek people are experienced, reflected upon, and laid out to us.

That Odysseus' encounters with the inhabitants of distant lands occurs on the homeward journey back from the Trojan War is therefore no coincidence.[34] This is because in the world of Odysseus (as elsewhere) the ethnographic imagination does not remain a pastime in itself but is closely linked to larger, more pressing considerations concerning things closer to home. In other words: during Odysseus' journey back to Ithaca, the exploration of distant lands and the customs of the people inhabiting them unfolds in reference to what it means to be Greek.

The Cyclopes are a case in point. The account of Odysseus' encounter with Polyphemus features as part of an extended story within a story. It is included in a tale which the Greek hero relates to the Phaeacians, a people who, in many ways, stand in sharp contrast to the Cyclopes.[35] Like Polyphemus, the Phaeacians claim descent from Poseidon, but they could not be more different otherwise. They live a pious, peaceful, and carefree life in a cultured society that, in its natural abundance, is reminiscent of a concept we already encountered in Chapter 2: that of the Golden Age.[36] They know how to sail the seas and till the soil. Their lifestyle thus diverges fundamentally from the primitive, godless, and asocial Cyclopes who lack the resources and cultural techniques to make use of the natural abundance around them. Given these differences, it comes as no surprise that the Phaeacians also differ from the Cyclopes. This manifests itself above all in their reception of Odysseus: The inhospitality of the Cyclopes is in direct contrast to the hospitality of the Phaeacians who wine and dine Odysseus and even offer the king's daughter Nausicaa as wife – a proposition that Odysseus, ever mindful of Penelope back at Ithaca, politely declines.[37] So Odysseus' account of the hostile reception he received by the Cyclopes serves as a contrasting foil to the hospitality of the Phaeacians. Taken together, they sketch opposite ends of a spectrum between extreme civilization and extreme primitivism.[38] Albeit culturally much closer to and more compatible with the civilized lifestyle of the Phaeacians, Greek civilization ultimately differs from both.[39]

So, the Homeric Cyclopes are part of a larger group of creatures inhabiting the world of the *Odyssey* which confronted Odysseus as the story's hero – and with him the Greek audience – with a variety of lifestyles, looks, and likenesses. Even though they ultimately inhabit the realm of the imaginary and fantastic, they represent very real Greek ideas on those inhabiting distant lands. Their geographical remoteness extends into a cultural remoteness that helps to define things closer to home. This makes them an integral part of the way in which Odysseus, by navigating distant worlds, navigates 'the contours of Greek identity'.[40]

THE ETHNOGRAPHIC IMAGINATION AND THE QUESTION OF THE HUMAN

So far, we have examined the kind of ethnographic perspective present in the *Odyssey*. How, then, does the animal come into the picture? The answer to this question emerges from the way in which, in the *Odyssey*, the ethnographic imagination intersects with a more general 'anthropological' perspective. In the tale of Odysseus' travels back home, the question of what it means to be Greek does not stand by itself.[41] Rather, it becomes linked to another, even more fundamental question: what it means to be human.[42] By drawing on the concepts of the human and non-human, the distinction between Greeks and non-Greeks takes on further contours.

To illustrate how this is the case warrants some comments on Polyphemus' identity. In the *Odyssey*, He is referred to as an *anēr*, which means, 'a man'.[43] This word nominates his gender but also sets him apart from gods and animals and seems to suggest that he is human (even though the more straightforward word for human, *anthrōpos*, is conspicuously absent). Overall, he certainly looks the part, single eye notwithstanding. He speaks in a thunderous human voice – and, apparently, even in perfect Greek – and shows a number of other typically 'human' behaviours and skills: he leads the life of a shepherd, even knows how to make fire and produce cheese from milk and wine from grapes.[44] All this aligns the Homeric Cyclopes firmly with human visitors to their island.

Yet at the same time, several features challenge, question, or undermine Polyphemus' human credentials. He is significantly bigger and stronger than a normal man – hence the dehumanizing comparison to a mountaintop. His voice is louder and more thunderous. And then there is that single eye, the most obvious physical marker of deviation from the human norm. But looks are not the only, perhaps not even the most serious problem. Behavioural features support the physical ones in challenging the humanity of the Cyclopes: they drink milk and have some form of wine but do not count among the *andres sitophagoi*, 'the bread-eaters' due to their lack of farming skills.[45]

So, Polyphemus' humanity is, at best, ambiguous.

Ambiguity also defines his affiliation with the divine. Polyphemus traces his lineage from the god Poseidon and from Thoosa, the daughter of Phorcys, a sea nymph.[46] Yet that does not mean all that much. In the ancient world, divine descent does not necessarily bestow divine identity on the offspring. With regard to Polyphemus, there is little to suggest that he is himself divine. Several unmistakable markers of divine status are not present: he is neither particularly knowledgeable (quite the opposite, as we will see) nor immortal. Whether he has any superhuman powers is debatable. Quantitatively, he certainly exceeds human strength. Qualitatively, however, he has nothing more to offer than the average human.

So, Polyphemus is neither divine, nor fully human. At the same time, he also shows several character traits and habits that associate him distinctly with the animalistic and wild – an association that prompted at least one modern commentator, the once-influential German scholar Ulrich von Wilamowitz-Moellendorff (1848–1931), to suggest that the Cyclopes were actually animals.[47] And, indeed, there are several features that support such a view. Consider, for example, his dietary choices. It is, in particular, his man-devouring habit which brings out his animal side. The *locus classicus* for this association of homophagy and animality is a passage from Hesiod's *Works and Days* (about 700 BCE) we have already come across in the previous chapter. In this passage, Hesiod presents the habit of devouring members of their own species as typical only of animals: 'This is the law that Cronus' son has established for human beings: that fish and beasts and winged birds eat one another, since Justice is not among them; but to human beings he has given Justice, which is the best by far.'[48] So Zeus ('the son of Kronos') presides over a world in which animals eat each other and thus do not partake in justice, while man alone has justice – by extension because he does not devour his own kind. This is a variant of the 'man-only *topos*' we touched upon earlier in this book, but one with a particular twist due to the way in which humanity, justice, and the absence of homophagy are linked here.[49]

Incidentally it is not just the fact *that* Polyphemus eats humans that makes him stand out and associates him with a small group of peoples that the ethnographic literature of the ancient world associated with man-eating (homophagy, anthropophagy, or androphagy).[50] *How* he goes about it also attests to his association with the animalistic and wild. Homer describes Polyphemus' meal consisting of two of Odysseus' comrades as follows: 'Then he cut them limb from limb and made ready his supper, and ate them like a mountain-nurtured lion, leaving nothing – ate the entrails, and the flesh, and the bones and marrow.'[51] Like a wild animal, Polyphemus does not restrict his meal to the easily digestible bits but ingests his prey entire, from head to toe.[52] And, like an animal, he devours his food raw, not cooked. What follows the abhorrent meal, then, further highlights his animalistic tendencies: 'But when the Cyclops had filled his huge belly by eating human flesh and thereafter drinking pure milk, he lay down within the cave, stretched out among the sheep.'[53] The image of the Cyclops resting among his livestock again depicts a creature living a life largely free of civilization, a life that is close, physically and conceptually, to the animals he devours.

And yet, despite this association with the animal realm, the anthropophagy of Polyphemus also points back to his humanity. Polyphemus' man-eating habit becomes a problem precisely *because* of his close association with humans.[54] It is this closeness that makes the fact that Polyphemus consumes human flesh a story; otherwise, he would be just another predatory animal – still an unfortunate outcome for those affected (read: eaten) but hardly a scandal. So, the fact that Polyphemus eats humans both reinforces and challenges his humanity, once again revealing a deeply ambiguous figure.

Moreover, it is in relation to their culinary habits, that the refusal of the Cyclopes to acknowledge the Greek gods takes on a particular dimension. That Polyphemus and his ilk have no religion means, above all, that they do not practise blood sacrifice. Against the background of their other deficits this might seem trivial. Yet its significance cannot be overstated. This is because as the central ritual of ancient Greek religion, blood sacrifice symbolically distinguishes between the categories of gods, humans, and animals. The gods are set out as the recipients of the sacrifice, humans as those making the offering, and animals as those being sacrificed. So, blood sacrifice as the central ritual of ancient Greek religion generates and clarifies the hierarchical relationship between gods, humans, and animals. Ancient Greek religion thus conveys the same tri-partite symbolic system that is also at play in the philosophical conversation about the question of the human.[55]

Polyphemus' consumption of flesh, by contrast, not only occurs outside of this ritual practice and the meanings conveyed through it but is represented as precisely the reversal of sacrifice. There is no separation of parts for gods and humans, no cooking, no other rites. The way the Cyclopes kill and devour other living creatures is not regulated by ritual norms. Not only does that brutal affair stand in the random, open, and un-structured eruption of deadly violence that is in distinct contrast to the elaborate and well-timed collective practices that constitute the ritual killing of animals. It also blurs the traditional boundaries that separate those sacrificing from those sacrificed because humans are the victims of this violence. And the subsequent consumption of the flesh derived in this way does little to change the picture. It also falls outside of ritual norms, here those of communal feasting. As a solitary affair, devoid of any decorum, it conveys, above all, one meaning: that the Homeric Cyclopes are indeed lawless creatures that operate in a moral space of their own. Their barbarism is cast in the normative and predetermined language of civilization.

Overall, then, it appears that the Cyclops Polyphemus defies all categories of being. He is neither divine, nor fully human, and his lifestyle associates him with the animalistic and wild.[56] The categories of gods, humans, and animals all come together in his personality. He draws on attributes from all of them, without, however, fully committing to one.

We have already briefly encountered the concept that the ancient Greeks and Romans reserved for such creatures in the figure of the sphinx: that of the monstrous.[57] The ancient Greek *pelōr* or *teras* (Latin: *monstrum*) applies to a wide variety of creatures that stand out in defying the usual categories of being and terrifying the humans that come across them.[58] The Homeric Cyclopes belong firmly in this category. In the *Odyssey*, Polyphemus is variously referred to as 'monstrous' (*pelorios*) or a 'wild man' (*anēr agrios*).[59] In deviating from the usual human norm in his looks and in his behaviour, Polyphemus combines, in one physical body, different kinds of likeness and difference. This makes the land of the Cyclopes a place where insights into the nature of man (anthropology) and insights into human cultural difference (ethnology) converge. In the *Odyssey*, geographical liminality coincides with the limits of humanity. A normative and normalizing dimension emerges that aligns the Greeks with the human and the non-Greeks with the sub- or superhuman.

POLYPHEMUS AND THE PERILS OF *LOGOS*

As far as stories go, that of the encounter between Odysseus and Polyphemus has been invariably successful. Similar stories, or story types, have been found in different parts of the world.[60] Some of these versions and variants seem to have been directly inspired by the Homeric version; others seem to have developed similar figures and story patterns independently. Yet at least in its Homeric rendering, this is a story that presents Polyphemus within a tale of travel to faraway countries, and his encounter with Odysseus as a clash between two individuals, one Greek and one not, one fully human and one whose humanity is, at best, ambiguous and contested. This raises the stakes of the encounter between Odysseus and Polyphemus. It prompts the question of how far the Homeric Cyclopes point to ancient Greek views about other peoples prior to the arrival of ethnography as a distinct mode of critical inquiry.

To put it more bluntly: is the Homeric depiction of Polyphemus an early instance of racism?

To say so would be misreading this story in the light of modern sentiments. The Homeric figure of the Cyclops does not make a point about race.[61] Polyphemus serves to articulate ideas about culture. His function is to shed light on the idea of civilization by personifying a corrupt civilization. His presence helps to raise the question of what it means to be human. How many markers of civilization can be taken away for someone still to count as an *anēr?* It is in this sense that his figure anticipates the stereotypes that parts of the later Western ethnographic tradition projected onto other peoples.

Tales of man-eating, for example, have lost none of their ancient appeal.[62] As the anthropologist William Arens has argued in *The Man-Eating Myth: Anthropology and Androphagy*, such tales are more often than not mere fiction – propelled by our ongoing fascination with and revulsion at what seems to be the ultimate taboo.[63] Moreover, the idea that 'the natives' are for some reason unable to consume alcohol responsibly has long been a staple of the modern ethnographic imagination.[64] In Polyphemus' case, his intoxication serves as an additional marker of his lack of civilization (a weakness that Odysseys exploits by seizing the opportunity to stab the Cyclops right in the eye). We already saw Kafka's ape, Red Peter, draw on a similar image when he reported the successful consumption of wine as a marker of his humanity (see Chapter 2). We will find a similar image at work again in Chapter 9 in the form of the glass of drink in the hand of Picasso's Minotaur. The Homeric account of the Cyclopes and, in particular, the obvious fictionality of the encounter between Odysseus and Polyphemus, opens our eyes to the way in which these sorts of commonplaces and stereotypes are just that: a form of fiction-making that we use to talk up our own 'civilized' humanity by talking down that of others.

Arguably the most consequential way the story of Odysseus and Polyphemus anticipates later views about human difference is through the idea that those who look different, or sound different, or merely do things differently may somehow also *think* differently. More specifically, the way in which the Homeric story ends anticipates the view that the alleged simplicity of other people extends beyond their looks and lifestyles, and manifests itself above all in their minds.

Homer's account juxtaposes Odysseus' superior wits with the apparent failure of Polyphemus to recognize the world in all its complexity. The story of Odysseus' escape from the cave of Polyphemus and his subsequent departure from the land of the Cyclopes is well known and much better told by Homer himself. Instead, we draw out merely three aspects of the story: first, the reversal in the roles of human and animal emerging from the fact that here it is humans who are locked away like puppies in Polyphemus' cave. Second, the particular way in which the Greeks finally manage to escape Polyphemus' cave unharmed and, third, the role that language, words, and naming play in Odysseus' ultimate exit from the land of the Cyclopes.

To touch upon the locked-up Greeks first: by locking them up in his cave, Polyphemus handles Odysseus and his comrades in ways that make it painfully clear what it means to be treated like an animal.

Second: Odysseus and his remaining comrades famously escape from the cave unnoticed by hanging onto the underside of Polyphemus' sheep. This mode of transport not only confirms again the cunning wit of Odysseus.[65] It also beats Polyphemus at his own game, by blurring the categories of human and animal. The very creature who treats the Greeks like a bunch of puppies, which can easily be locked away in the cave while the master is out, is tricked by the temporal amalgamation of human and animal bodies. The particulars of the Greek escape from the cave highlights the incapacity of the Cyclops to perceive what sets the human apart from non-human animals (most notably his sheep).

The third point, the role of wordplay in the escape of the Greeks from the island, then, recalls the role of language as a defining human characteristic, as discussed in Chapter 2. Up to the moment Polyphemus becomes drunk on the undiluted wine that Odysseus serves him, the Greek hero has carefully avoided disclosing his identity. Now, however, he answers the question of who he is: 'Cyclops, you ask me of my glorious name, and I will tell you it; and do you give me a strangers' gift, even as you promised. Nobody (*Outis*) is my name, Nobody they call me – my mother and my father, and all my comrades as well.'[66] Polyphemus' inability to extend anything but the most literal reading of the situation become directly tangible in the way in which he responds to Odysseus' words: 'Nobody (*outis*) will I eat last among his comrades, and the others before him; this shall be your gift.'[67]

A generous offer, indeed! And one based on the understanding of 'nobody' as someone's name.

That Polyphemus has indeed fallen into the trap set for him by Odysseus becomes clear a little later when he howls in pain because Odysseus has just taken out his eye. When the other Cyclopes rush to his help and ask who is responsible, he answers: 'My friends, it is Nobody (*outis*) that is slaying me by guile and not by force.' Given the reassuring tone this seems to strike, the other Cyclopes are satisfied that nobody threatens their comrade: 'If, then, nobody (*mē tis*) does violence to you all alone as you are, sickness which comes from Zeus there is no way you can escape; you must pray to our father the lord Poseidon.'[68] If nobody is threatening Polyphemus, no intervention on his behalf is needed. The Cyclopes quickly disperse.

The joke here is, of course, on Polyphemus. By being incapable of calling Odysseus by his real name, he is unable to identify his assailant to his fellow Cyclopes. And in their response to his call the Cyclopes inadvertently name precisely the power that brings him down: *mētis* – cunning intelligence. Words and their meaning are at centre stage here in more ways than one. Depending on how the Greek word for 'nobody' is used in a sentence, it is pronounced either *outis*, or *mē tis*. In spoken (rather than written) Greek, however, *mē tis* sounds just like *mētis*, which means 'cunning intelligence'. Odysseus' trick draws on both meanings of the word. He is at once 'nobody' and the one who makes use of his astute cleverness. He is the cunning trickster who bests the Cyclops' physical strength through sheer intelligence. By contrast, the Cyclopes have – excuse the pun – no eye for the possible gaps and traps between words and their meaning. They lack a point of reference or perspective to expose the human double-speak.

Even though Homeric epic downplays language as a marker of cultural and ethnic difference, both poems associate the capacity to speak and to speak eloquently with humanity and Greekness.[69] The way in which words and their meaning feature in the encounter between Odysseus and Polyphemus is part of this bigger picture.[70] The whole story illustrates that Polyphemus is not the sharpest cookie in the jar. Even though it would be wrong to say that he lacked *logos* altogether – he can clearly think and speak – he is no match for the crafty Odysseus who manages to escape from the gruesome island and the Cyclops' cave by using his intelligence. In directly juxtaposing Odysseus' success in crafting words and Polyphemus' failure to understand, the situation conveys the sense that the subtleties of the world – reflected in the subtleties of language – are lost on the Cyclopes. And yet, in the end, Polyphemus does resort to powerful language (and acknowledges the gods) when he urges Poseidon to prevent Odysseus from ever reaching his home again.[71] So, the ambiguities surrounding the status of Polyphemus extend to the way in which he is situated between 'mute' animals and the hyper-eloquent Greeks.

This is particularly remarkable in view of the later philosophical debate on the question of the human discussed in previous chapters. Several centuries before the Greco-Roman philosophers argued that humans differed from non-human animals by having *logos*, Homer's *Odyssey* already features language and reasoning in a storyline that sets Odysseus' humanity against the less-than-human qualities of Polyphemus and depicts the triumph of the former over the latter though *logos*.[72] The witty and crafty intelligence of Odysseus, as evident in his use of wordplay, stands out against Polyphemus, whose singularity extends from his single eye to his incapacity to appreciate the complexities of language. Odysseus' humanity also stands in stark contrast to that of another Greek we already encountered before: that of Oedipus (see Chapter 1). While the latter solves the Sphinx's riddling words but fails to understand how they apply to him, Odysseus gets away (from the island and the potentially fatal encounter with the Cyclops) by tricking the ogre through his own use of riddling words. For the moment, at least, *logos* has prevailed.

NO NEWTON: LOGOCENTRISM BEYOND THE ODD SINGLE EYE

The story of the Cyclops does not end with Odysseus' departure from the shores of the Cyclopes. This is because, despite their ancient outlook, the Cyclopes did not become extinct at the end of classical antiquity. Rather, they went on to populate the Western ethnographic imagination far into the modern area. They feature, for example, in the fourteenth-century travel memoir *Travels of Sir John Mandeville.* And even though they are not explicitly mentioned in the so-called 'Nuremberg Chronicle', a world history dating from 1493, they do make an appearance in Hartmann Schedel's famous illustrations of it – and again in Sebastian Münster's *Cosmographia universalis*, an illustrated account of the world published in 1544.[73] The Cyclopes retained such a central place in the ethnographic imagination of distant lands that towards the end of the fifteenth century, Christopher Columbus (1451–1506) still expressed his surprise that he did not come across them during his voyage to those bits of South-East Asia he referred to as 'the Indies'.[74]

With the early modern period, the Cyclopes embarked upon a long and slow retreat back into the realm of fiction where they continue to feature prominently up to this day.[75] Yet at least some of the stereotypes associated with them continue to exist outside of it. Their role as the quintessential 'other' in the stories we tell has been taken over by a number of other figures that continue to represent the ideas of savagery, primitivism, and cultural depravity. Among them are the figure of the 'wild man' (or 'wild woman') who populated the real and imaginary landscapes of medieval and early modern literature and that of 'the savage', a caricature of human difference that had a strong presence in the ethnographic literature and travel writing far into the twentieth century. Both these figures reverberate with the representation of Polyphemus in the *Odyssey* without being identical.[76]

Take the stereotypical 'savage'. A single example of what was not so long ago a standard image of accounts of exploration and travel shall help here to illustrate how this figure recalls many of the very same attributes that also defined the Homeric Polyphemus: Charles Darwin's account of the inhabitants of Tierra del Fuego. In the journal Darwin kept while travelling the world aboard the *HMS Beagle*, he describes their domestic setup, the absence of proper clothes, and accuses them of homophagy. Yet it is above all their alleged lack of intellect that illustrates their civilizational deficits. In his entry of 23 July 1894, Darwin writes:

> How little can the higher powers of the mind come into play: what is there for imagination to paint, for reason to compare, for judgement to decide upon. – to knock a limpet from the rock does not even require cunning, that lowest power of the mind. Their skill, like the instinct of animals, is not improved by experience.[77]

In many ways Darwin's account reads like a blast from the Homeric past, minus the odd single eye. What is on show here again is a strongly logocentric view of humanity that draws on many of the set features that we already found at play in the Homeric depiction of

Polyphemus: physical differences, cultural and civilizational simplicity, and homophagy are all in the mix again. Above all, however, it is their purported lack of brainpower that sets these peoples apart, an absence that prompts Darwin to associate them with animals. More specifically, the native inhabitants of Tierra del Fuego allegedly do not lack just the power of reasoning but also the capacity to learn from experience – a deficiency that associates their practices with the instinctual behaviour of animals.

That this observation is made by the very same thinker who (later in life) developed the theory of evolution is telling. It confirms that, per Darwin, it is not just the physical human body that evolves over time; forms of human social and cultural organization do as well. And unlike the field of biology, where evolution does not necessarily lead to more complexity, it appears that Darwin considered human cultural evolution to lead from simple to more advanced forms of life. His description of the Fuegians shows that, even though Darwin strongly opposed the idea of slavery, he firmly believed in the idea that a deep cultural gap separates Western civilization from the alleged 'primitivism' of 'the savages'.[78]

To flesh this out Darwin draws on a familiar image. He concludes his reflections on the simple-mindedness of the Fuegians by posing the following question:

> Although essentially the same creature, how little must the mind of one of these beings resemble that of an educated man. What scale of improvement is comprehended between the faculties of a Fuegian savage & a Sir Isaac Newton – Whence have these people come? Have the remained in the same state since the creation of the world?[79]

The questions raised here are, of course, entirely rhetorical, their answer clear from the start: the inhabitants of Terra del Fuego ain't no Newton. By setting the figure of the quintessential (but amorphous and nameless) 'savage' against the famous Englishman, Darwin here juxtaposes once again Polyphemus and Odysseus. Once again primitivism comes face to face with *logos* and civilization.

What sets the Homeric example apart from such modern forms of 'othering', then, is the absence of any obvious colonial overtones. Even though there is some suggestion in Homer's *Odyssey* that the nearby goat island lends itself to exploration and cultivation, the focus of the story here is not on the Greeks but on the island of the Cyclopes and its inhabitants who cannot explore and cultivate. Odysseus' encounter with Polyphemus is not driven by any desire to control and exploit.[80] What is already in place in the Homeric account, however, is the violence that in the modern world came to define the encounters between Western civilization and those it dismissed as 'savages'.

And yet, the Homeric account of Odysseus' run-in with the Cyclopes also allows for a reading that casts Polyphemus in a more sympathetic light and Odysseus as an individual prone to hubris. The (more) sympathetic view of Polyphemus appears in his gentle and caring interactions with his livestock, such as when he converses with his old ram.[81]

> Beloved ram, why is it that you go out through the cave like this, the last of the flock? . . . Surely you are sorrowing for the eye of your master, which an evil man blinded along with his miserable fellows, when he had overpowered my wits with wine . . . . If only you could feel as I do, and could get for yourself the power of speech to tell me where he skulks away from my wrath . . .[82]

If Polyphemus here articulates empathy and sentiment towards a non-human creature, Odysseus parades his hubristic side. He not only endangers the life of his comrades by verbally provoking Polyphemus during their exit from the island.[83] He also shows no gratitude to the ram who had carried him to freedom, sacrificing it shortly after the escape from the cave. By allowing for such a reading, the story reclaims at least some of the profound othering on which it is based. Perhaps it challenges us to rethink where exactly our sympathies lie?

TARGETING THE SINGLE EYE

We leave this question to the reader to answer and return – in lieu of a conclusion – to another one, raised earlier: What does the single eye stand for? What does it represent? What is there *for us* to see?

The odd single eye of the Cyclopes serves as what the French critic, philosopher, and literary theorist Roland Barthes in another context has referred to as a *punctum*.[84] In his acclaimed book *Camera Lucida*, Barthes introduces the term in the course of his discussion of photography. He uses it to describe the quality of certain images to bind the observer's gaze and draw them into their story. The *punctum* is an outstanding feature, mark, or detail which suggests that there is more to an image than meets the eye. It is a visual clue, a disturbance, that at first does not make sense because it falls outside the codes of sense-making that inform its surroundings.[85] It invites further investigation.

The concept of the *punctum* is, I believe, well suited to describe the effects of the Cyclopes on those humans, past and present, looking at them. The single eye mesmerizes. Its presence disturbs because it upsets our expectations of what makes a normal human body. It transfixes the onlooker, drawing and holding our own eye as inevitably as the metaphorical bull's eye. Hence, the central role of this physical feature in artistic representations of the Cyclopes of all kinds, past and present (see, for example, Figure 4.2).

4.2. William Baziotes, *Cyclops* (1947). The Art Institute of Chicago 1947.468. © Estate of William Baziotes. Photo © The Art Institute of Chicago/Art Resource, NY

The single eye of Polyphemus as the quintessential *punctum* points us, I think, to three different ways of looking. First and foremost, it represents the outlook of the Cyclops. As I have shown above, Polyphemus' singularity extends from his single eye to his plain reading of the world. He is easily the most one-dimensional, literal, single-focused creature inhabiting the *Odyssey*, incapable of appreciating ambiguity.

At the same time, however – and this is my second point – Polyphemus' single eye also serves a target for our own gaze, for the way in which *our own eyes* are invariably drawn to human difference in general and, in particular, to its *physical* manifestations. We still forget sometimes that, despite its undeniable strengths and benefits, logocentrism comes at a certain price. The idea of the human as part of a radically separate order of being defined by reason draws on the idea of a lower order that comprises physical aspects of our existence (the body), animals, and certain humans (foreigners and slaves) typecast as subhuman. So, the single eye of the Cyclopes also highlights the manifold ways we conceive of certain forms of human differences in terms of the absence of those very qualities we posit as central to the human condition. It stands for the way we normalize certain ways of being human and marginalize others by dehumanizing them.

In this sense, Odysseus' successful efforts to take out Polyphemus by targeting his single eye is no coincidence. The move makes sense within the logic of the story. It is motivated first and foremost by the need to incapacitate Polyphemus without eliminating him entirely. Yet it is difficult not to see this also as some sort of symbolic act. As the physical marker of human difference, the single eye represents all the ways in which the Cyclopes differ from the human norm. By taking aim at the eye, Odysseus takes aim at all the (frightening and dangerous) ways in which Polyphemus stands out.

My third and final point: If we consider the way in which the figure of the Cyclops resonates with subsequent conceptions of human difference, the single eye also serves as an icon for how the world looks at *us*. In recent years, calls to 'decolonize' the Classics have gained momentum.[86] While in some instances this has involved the radical suggestion of dispensing with Classics as a discipline altogether, the story of Odysseus and Polyphemus draws attention to the fact that some of the important work to be done needs to occur within classical studies itself. More specifically, what is needed is a critical reassessment of the normative dimensions inscribed in Western humanism. In order to re-think, de-centre, and de-normalize our notions of 'the human', we need to make visible the hidden symbolic transactions on which these notions are based. And to get such considerations going, the Homeric Cyclops and his mesmerizing single eye are not a bad place to start

CHAPTER 5

Why did the Greeks choose to hide in the shape of a gigantic wooden horse to trick their way into Troy? And what motivated the Trojans to accept the deadly gift? This chapter revolves around the famous story of how the Greeks managed to get into the city of Troy concealed in a gigantic wooden horse – and so win a long and drawn-out war.

In following this story and the odd human/animal hybrid at its core, this chapter continues to probe the place of animals in thinking about particular human identities. More specifically, it explores how notions of animality define the human at war. Moving away from the 'othering' at work in the previous chapter, this one illustrates an area of existence in which analogies between human and animal prevail. Fighting emerges as an area of life in which our animal side comes to the fore.

5.1. Giovanni Domenico Tiepolo, *The Procession of the Trojan Horse into Troy* (detail) (1773). The National Gallery, London, NG3319. © The National Gallery, London.

The Trojan Horse (*Equus troianus*)

IMAGINE YOU ARE IN A LONG, DRAWN-OUT, FOREVER WAR. YOUR enemy has laid siege to your city for years on end. Nerves are frayed, anxieties high, spirits, supplies, and morale low. One morning you find the enemy has suddenly disappeared. The shoreline lies deserted, encampments gone. All that's left is a gigantic wooden horse outside the gates of your city. There has never been anything quite like it. Moments later, you chance on one single man claiming to be a deserter from enemy lines. He identifies himself as Sinon and explains the horse as a gift of devotion ('a votive') to Athena. The horse, he says, was left by your opponents to appease the goddess for past religious offences and to ensure safe passage home.

What would you do?

Would you pull down the barricades, open the city gates, and welcome the unusual trophy in? Or would you act cautiously and examine the object before you made a move?

Chances are most of us would like to think that we would have acted with extreme caution and first checked the horse out. This is because the proverbial Trojan horse has become a commonplace in the symbolic landscape of the West. Following the famous line from the Roman poet Virgil (70–19 BCE), we have learnt not to trust Greeks bearing gifts.[1] Or have we? We return to this question later in this chapter.

Meanwhile, the Trojans under their king Priam are stunned by the fact of the horse. Right away, it commands the attention of the entire city. Initially, several sceptics (the Trojan priest Laocoön and the seer Cassandra among them) express concern about the nature of the gift and warn their fellow Trojans to be vigilant. Could this be some sort of war engine? Or a device crafted to provide the Greeks with intelligence from inside Troy? Even the concern that the horse may be carrying unwanted soldierly cargo deep inside is voiced.[2]

The captured Greek seeks to disperse such concerns. He explains that the horse is of such gigantic proportions because the Greeks hoped it would prove impossible for the Trojans to bring it into their city in one piece. To do so would require them to dismantle it, so incurring the wrath of the gods for violating the offering.

The tall tale has the desired effect. Concerns as to the true nature of the horse are quelled and further critical voices ignored. Virgil has the Trojan hero Aeneas later recall the passage of the horse into the city as follows:

> All gird themselves for the work; under the feet they place gliding wheels, and about the neck stretch hemp bands . . . Around it boys and unwedded girls chant holy songs and delight to touch the cable with their hands. Up it moves, and glides threatening into the city's midst. O my country! O Ilium, home of gods, and you Dardan battlements, famed in war![3]

The Trojans are obviously relieved that the lengthy conflict is finally over. And some of the ensuing enthusiasm is directed towards the unlikely object in front of their gates. Soon, the horse is inside the city.

At first everything seems fine. The mood is festive and joyous, and wine flows freely.[4] But at night, when everyone is fast asleep, Greek fighters – 30, 50, 100, accounts differ – emerge from inside the horse with Sinon's help.[5] They open the city's gates to their returning comrades.

Troy falls.

***

The trick involving the horse is arguably the most well-known part of the story of Troy's fall. Already in the ancient world, the way in which the Greeks duped the Trojans into transferring their fighters into their city with the help of the artificial horse aroused considerable interest. In classical antiquity, the sack of Troy was a popular theme inspiring numerous writers and artists from the Archaic period onwards.

But is the story real? Did the sacking of Troy really happen? Did the Greeks *really* manage to breach the city walls by smuggling the fighters into Troy inside a gigantic wooden horse? To date, lots of effort has gone into finding an answer to these questions.[6] By contrast, there is surprisingly little on other questions that could be brought to bear on the ancient evidence.

This chapter draws on the 'anthropology' of warfare to dismantle the horse and inspect the human cargo within. It explores how the Trojan horse as a peculiar human/animal hybrid brings out conceptions of the human and the non-human animal at war. Doing so allows us to acknowledge the horse for what it really is: the Greek and Roman imagination of a real object that is deeply grounded in the meaning and status of horses on the battlefields of the ancient Greek world.

We start from the role of horses and horsemanship during the Mycenean period (the time when the Trojan War would have taken place) and move on to the specifics of the way in which the horse features within the story of the sack of Troy, ending with the famous Roman telling of the story by Virgil.

HEROES AND HORSES AT WAR IN MYCENEAN GREECE

The trick involving the artificial horse was, of course, not a standard military tactic but a one-off. It only worked as a surprise ambush.[7] Within the myth, the idea is attributed to Odysseus and the skills in carpentry of a certain Epeius, who assembled the horse with the help of the goddess Athena. Yet besides such specific explanations of who brought the Trojan horse into existence, its role in the fall of Troy reflects the wider use of horses in early Greece. From the earliest times onward, real horses had a distinct presence on the battlefields of the ancient Greek world.

From as early as the Mycenean period, there is evidence of horses and horsemanship in the realm of warfare, mostly in the form of small figurines of horsemen that were dedicated as votive offerings in sanctuaries.[8] There are also some depictions of horsemen on Greek painted pottery from this period (see, e.g., Figure 5.2). At least some of this evidence seems to show mounted warriors, as suggested by body armour and

5.2. Mycenaean krater (ca 1400–1300 BCE) showing a Late Bronze Age horse-drawn chariot (detail). National Archaeological Museum, Athens NAM P7387. © Hellenic Ministry of Culture and Sports/Hellenic Organization of Cultural Resources Development

weapons. None of this evidence appears to relate directly to the sack of Troy. And yet, it does throw light on the role and function of horses at the time when the Trojan War would have taken place (the twelfth century BCE). Even though the overall number of examples is not extensive, it is substantial enough to suggest that members of the Mycenean aristocracy were well-versed in the handling and riding of horses and made use of these skills on the battlefield.[9]

More extensive evidence for the presence of horses in Mycenean warfare attests to their role in pulling chariots. Chariots carrying anywhere from one to three riders feature widely on Greek painted pottery and murals dating from this period.[10] Again the military setting is evident in the presence of arms (in particular, shields and spears). However, exactly how these chariots were used is much harder to make out. The static images are difficult to read.[11] They show few examples of horsemen directly engaged in military confrontation and many depict the chariot as merely 'standing by'.[12] Moreover, the obvious military advantage of chariots – to launch attacks in clusters and to throw spears or shoot bows into enemy lines from the elevated position of the moving vehicle – does not seem to be realized at all.[13]

No matter what was the exact role of these chariots, the presence of horses, horsemen, and chariots on the battlefields of the Mycenean period shows that the horse was associated with the fighting of wars. So, it was not just any animal that the Greeks chose for the hidden transfer of soldiers into the city, but one with a strong military presence.

HORSES AND HORSEMANSHIP IN HOMER

By the Archaic period (ca 800–500 BCE), we get the first written accounts of the Trojan War in the form of epic poetry and the now largely lost works of the so-called Epic Cycle (a set of early Greek poems concerned with the Trojan War). Unfortunately, the latter are too fragmentary to allow for a detailed investigation. As far as Homer is concerned, both epics relate (to) the story of Troy. Yet contrary to what one may expect, they do not actually include a comprehensive account of the trick involving the horse. Homer's interests lie both earlier and later – in the war itself as recounted in the *Iliad* and in its later aftermath – Odysseus' extended trip home, the stuff of the *Odyssey*. The *Iliad* thus contains only a few vague references in passing to the horse escapade. And although the *Odyssey* features three accounts of the role of the horse in the sack of Troy, these remain too brief and cursory to allow for a detailed investigation.

The three times the horse does appear in Homer's *Odyssey* it is always within a narrative one character in the story tells another: it features in Menelaus' account to Telemachus during the latter's visit to Sparta, in the story of the sack of Troy recounted by the bard Demodocus at the court of the Phaeacians, and in the events that Odysseus relates to the ghost of Achilles during his visit to the Underworld.[14] Each of these characters is not telling the whole story that stretches from the conception of the horse, to its production, to any debates that the Trojans have about it before or after they move it into the city. Rather, they tend to focus on one brief section of it. As a result, the part where Sinon pretends to desert Greek ranks and gives the horse a false pedigree does not appear in the *Odyssey* at all.

And yet, Homer fleshes out other parts of the story: we hear that Helen tried to entice the Greek fighters hidden in the horse's belly to give themselves away by speaking to them from outside in the voices of their wives. She ultimately failed because Odysseus (as one of the soldiers hidden inside the horse) prevented his comrades from responding.[15] Yet despite such amusing detail, Homer's renderings of the tale remain short and partial. For an extensive account about the Trojan horse, we will need to look to later authors.

But Homer has more to offer than the first short references to the infamous trick. The *Iliad*, in particular, contains detailed information on the role and standing of horses in the larger context of the Trojan War (as recounted during the Archaic period). And the *Odyssey* features at least a few revealing passages which further shed light on the matter. They include invaluable information about the kind of meaning that the Greeks associated with horses and their presence on this particular battlefield. It is here that we first get an inkling as to cultural associations and meanings that may have been 'embedded' in the Trojan horse.

In the *Iliad*, horses are represented as central to the experience of war.[16] Their thundering hooves blend in with the other sounds of fighting, the clashing of armour, the clanging of weapons, and the shouts and cries of those in combat. 'The whole plain was filled with men and horses and aflame with bronze, and the earth resounded beneath their feet as they rushed together.'[17] In Homer's *Iliad*, horses and humans fight alongside each other. Throughout Homer's account of the Trojan War, we find them sharing in the experience. Indeed, the poem goes out of its way to highlight the parallels between human and horse: 'Wet with sweat about the chest of many a man will be the strap of his sheltering shield, and about the spear will his hand grow weary, and wet with sweat will a man's horse be, as it strains at the polished chariot.'[18] In the *Iliad*, the physical effects of warfare are experienced by horses and humans alike.

To the Homeric hero, warfare was an opportunity to excel and ultimately become the subject of song. The winning of glory (*kleos*) was central to the heroic code and the battlefield was one of the prime platforms to show one's bravery and skill in fighting.[19] The Greek concept of *aristeia* ('excellence', 'prowess') is central to how this pans out in epic poetry. The *Iliad* is full of moments in which the spotlight is on the attempts of an individual hero to distinguish himself in warfare and win eternal renown.

Curiously, perhaps, this striving towards excellence seems to have extended from hero to horse. A passage that follows right after the so-called catalogue of ships (a lengthy enumeration of the individual Greek contingents fighting at Troy) starts with a fresh invocation of the Muse that recalls the one from the beginning of the epic, followed by the wish to hear more about the excellence of humans *and* horses:

> These were the leaders of the Danaans (Greeks) and their lords. But who was far the best among them do you tell me, Muse – best of the warriors and of the horses that followed with the sons of Atreus. Of the horses best by far were the mares of the son of Pheres, those that Eumelus drove, swift as birds, like of coat, like of age, their backs as even as a levelling line could make ... And of warriors far best was Telamonian Aias, while Achilles continued his wrath; for Achilles was far the mightiest, he and the horses that bore the incomparable son of Peleus.[20]

The particular excellence of the Homeric hero here finds its extension in the particular excellence of his horses. Of course, it matters that the horses in question here are not just your normal run-of-the-mill ones: they are special, supernatural horses that Achilles received from his father Peleus who, in turn, received them from the gods. One of these was Xanthus, the speaking horse that addressed us in perfect Greek in Chapter 2. Together with another supernatural specimen called Balius, it was thought to have been descended from the West Wind and a Harpy (the personification of storms combining a human head with a bird's body).[21]

Achilles was by no means the only fighter at Troy who owned supernatural horses. On the Trojan side Aeneas, too, sports special horses. And like Achilles, he prizes them highly and brags to Pandarus (a fellow Trojan): 'But come, mount my chariot, so that you may see of what sort are the horses of Tros, well skilled to course swiftly here and there over the plain whether in pursuit or in flight.'[22] The horses Aeneas shows off to Pandarus are bred from the immortal stallions Zeus once gave to Tros, the mythical founder of Troy.[23] Later on in the epic, Aeneas will lose them to the Greek hero Diomedes who will later parade them at Patroclus' funeral games.[24] Owning such special horses also connected those humans with the Homeric gods. Throughout the *Iliad*, Zeus, Hera, and their like move about using splendid chariots and special horses that are themselves supernatural.[25]

Homer's *Iliad* thus depicts a world in which there is a fundamental analogy between horse and hero.[26] Horsemanship was one of the modes of aggrandisement and self-representation of those fighting at Troy; special horses and splendidly equipped chariots directly reflected their elevated position in society. Indeed, the elite aristocratic warriors on both sides of the conflict used their horses to show off and outdo each other.

The way horses help to characterize and define human identities extends from special horses to the use of horse-related epithets. These are short, formulaic descriptions that are applied to individuals or groups of people in the epic. They originate in the oral nature of epic poetry in which they served as mnemonic aids and to sustain the meter. It may be tempting to dismiss them as 'merely formulaic', yet this would be to ignore the complex cultural meaning inscribed in them. Throughout the *Iliad*, horse-derived epithets feature frequently. Atreus (the king of Mycenae), the Trojan heroes Hector and Antenor, and the Greek fighters Diomedes and Thrasymedes are all referred to as 'tamers of horses' (*hippodamoi*).[27] Mentor's son Imbrius is called 'rich in horses' (*polyhippos*), and Pelops, Oileius, and Menestheus are 'drivers of horses' (*plēxippoi*).[28] And it is not just individual identities that are cast in this way: the Greek city of Argos is 'grazed by horses' (*hippobotos*) and the Phrygian warriors feature as 'masters of quick moving steeds' (*aiolopōloi*).[29] Collective identities were also shaped relative to horses.

Incidentally, one people in particular were associated with horses: the Trojans. Throughout the *Iliad,* they are referred to as 'tamers of horses' (*hippodamoi*).[30] Moreover, several of the Trojan fighters carried horse-derived names (as evident in that they feature a derivative of the ancient Greek word for horse – *hippos*: Hippasos, Hippodamas, Hippodamos, Hippothoos, Hippolochos, Hippomachos, and Melanippos all feature within the text.[31] Horse breeding was a central feature of the Trojan economy.[32] The Trojans probably derived their knowledge of horsemanship from the nearby Hittites, a kingdom to the east in which horses and horse-breeding was sufficiently important to warrant the existence of an equine deity.[33]

So, the object the Greeks left at the gates of Troy will have appealed to the Trojans as 'tamers of horses'. The idea that the presence of the statue inside Troy would protect the city against a hostile takeover further enhances the horse's association with the Trojans themselves. Indeed, it seems a particular irony of the story that the 'tamers of horses' are themselves 'tamed' by (those hidden inside) the horse.[34]

So, what are all the horses and horse-drawn chariots really about?

To state the obvious: horses served as status symbols for members of the aristocracy.[35] They were costly and expensive to maintain and so allowed ample opportunity to show off wealth and demonstrate social standing. Their possession and handling are fundamental to how the Homeric heroes define themselves.

On the battlefields the stories of the humans fighting at Troy and their horses are entwined in moments of success and bravery and in death and annihilation. This is why the death of Trojans fighting outside of their city is described with a reference to horses which pulled empty chariots in search of their riders: 'so beneath Agamemnon, son of Atreus, fell the heads of the Trojans as they fled, and many horses with high-arched necks rattled empty chariots along the lines of battle, longing for their incomparable charioteers; but they lay on the ground dearer far to vultures than to their wives.'[36] The fate of the Trojan fighters is experienced through their horses.

Humans and horses also serve as proxies for each other in other ways. In his fight with Patroclus, the Trojan ally Sarpedon misses the Greek hero, but he makes a lethal strike on one of Achilles' special horses instead: 'But Sarpedon missed him with his bright spear, as in turn he set on him, but struck with his spear the horse Pedasus on the right shoulder; and the horse shrieked aloud as it gasped out its life, and down it fell in the dust with a moan, and its spirit flew from it.'[37] The death of the horse at the hand of Sarpedon anticipates Sarpedon's own death. Moments later he, too, will lie on the ground in front of his horses, 'moaning aloud and clutching at the bloody dust'.[38] Here and elsewhere the shared mortality of horse and human draws attention to the physical aspects of the human existence.[39]

This fundamental analogy and parallelism between horse and human also explains a feature of Homeric epic that may strike the modern reader as puzzling: some of the special horses cry, mourn their human handlers, and show other distinctly human characteristics such as speech (as in the case of Xanthus, Chapter 2).[40] Of course, such spates of anthropomorphism are possible only because these are special, supernatural horses. But they also sit well in the way human and equine identities overlap in Homer's *Iliad.* That the heroes in the story, despite their masculine self-fashioning as tough fighters, are unafraid to show emotions and burst into tears in public is of course well known.[41] The horses resemble their owners in this way too.

In the world of the Homeric hero, real horses thus served as pricy and desirable possessions central to the experience of war, as status symbols of the aristocratic elite warrior, and, occasionally at least, as his physical extensions, placeholders, and substitutes. All these associations make the horse an obvious choice for the transfer of fighters into the city. The idea of hiding the humans inside the horse resonates with the status of horses and the close association between human and equine identities on the battlefield of Troy.

ENTER ATHENA

So far, we have considered the role of horses and horsemanship during the Mycenean period and their presentation in later accounts of the war. It is about high time to return to the particular horse at the core of this chapter. This horse is associated not just with the humans in the story. As with most of the creatures discussed in this book, the divine element has a part to play too.[42] More specifically, several kinds of evidence link the horse to one particular deity with a distinct affinity to horses: the goddess Athena.

Some ancient authors name Athena as the recipient of the gifted horse, presenting it as an offering made by the Greeks to ensure their safe return home.[43] Several also credit her with a role in the horse's production.[44] The horse is said to have emerged from a collaboration between Odysseus, another Greek fighting at Troy by the name of Epeius, and the goddess Athena herself.[45] But what exactly her involvement amounted to remains unclear: did she inspire Odysseus' plan? Did she endow Epeius with the woodworking skills? Or, did she merely endorse the whole operation? Did she perhaps even ordain it?[46]

The most detailed account of the horse's construction that has come down to us seems to suggest so. It comes from the Greek author Quintus of Smyrna. In his epic *The Fall of Troy*, now thought to date to the third century CE, he describes the process of the horse's construction as follows:[47]

> Epeius first
> fashioned the feet of that great Horse of Wood:
> The belly next he shaped, and over this
> Moulded the back and the great loins behind,
> The throat in front, and ridged the towering neck
> With waving mane: the crested head he wrought,
> The streaming tail, the ears, the lucent eyes –
> All that of lifelike horses have. So grew
> Like a live thing that more than human work,
> For a God gave to a man that wonderous craft.
> And in three days, on Pallas' suggestion (*Pallados ennesiēsi*),
> Finished was all.[48]

For Quintus, at least, Athena endowed Epeius with the technical skills to craft the horse. She apparently also suggested its construction. Earlier in the same book, Quintus had Athena appear to Epeius in a prophetic dream instructing him to build the horse and promising her help.[49]

That the link between Athena and the Trojan horse is more than the product of a 'late' author's imagination becomes clear when we consider some earlier pictorial representations of Athena on Greek painted pottery. One of them, a *kylix* (a drinking cup used for wine) dating from the fifth century BCE, shows Athena wearing an *aegis* (a protective animal skin) and standing beside a sculptor crafting a model of a horse (see Figure 5.3). Could this be Epeius and the horse a model of the Trojan horse?[50]

A red-figure *oinochoe* (wine jug) depicts the goddess herself crafting a statue of a horse out of clay (Figure 5.4). A saw, drill, and bow can be seen to the left of the goddess. The size seems not quite right for the horse to be the Trojan horse. As in the previous image, it is significantly smaller than the goddess herself. If we assume the goddess to be of

5.3. Athenian red-figure kylix from Vulci (ca 480 BCE) showing Athena visiting a workshop crafting a marble horse (detail). Munich, Antikensammlung 2650. © Antikensammlung, Munich

5.4. Attic red-figure oinochoe from Capua (ca 470–460 BCE) showing Athena producing a clay model of a horse (detail). Berlin, Antikensammlung F2415. © Antikensammlung Berlin. Photo © Johannes Laurentius

5.5. Attic red-figure kylix attributed to the Sabouroff Painter (ca 470–460 BCE) showing Athena making a horse. Museo Archeologico Etrusco, Florence V57. © Museo Archaeologico Etrusco. Photo © Scala, Florence.

human size, this would rule out the actual Trojan horse. Again, it has been suggested that Athena here is producing a clay model.[51]

A third example features Athena crafting a horse so big that we see only its head, neck, and upper torso (Figure 5.5). It is not clear whether the horse in question is the Trojan horse. This time its size would be more appropriate for the actual horse; its decorations also support the interpretation that this is a votive of some kind. If these images indeed depict the making of (a model of) the Trojan horse, they bring out Athena's technical and conceptual 'hand' in its production. But even if the horses in question were merely generic, such representations confirm that the ancient Greek cultural imagination extended Athena's particular expertise with horses to include the production of artificial ones.

It matters here that Athena's association with the horse differs from that of Poseidon, the other Greek deity associated with this animal. Like Poseidon, she was worshipped as *Hippia* ('of the horse') in several Greek cities as early as the sixth century BCE (if not earlier), most notably in Corinth and Attica.[52] But in contrast to Poseidon, she represents the human technical mastery of the horse (through bridle, yoke, bit, and chariot, for example).[53] Poseidon, by contrast, relates to the unbridled, thundering, and ferocious aspects of the horse, its uncontrolled and terrifying attributes. So, the idea of the horse as a technical device to enter a city very much fits Athena's area of expertise. It is the harnessed and instrumentalized horse that takes shape in the wooden construction at Troy, the horse as a product of ingenuity and as part of a larger, cunning plan, and not the wild and untamed animal.

At this stage, some comments on the status of the resulting artefact are warranted: what kind of thing is the Trojan horse? We might be inclined to call it a 'machine' insofar as it is designed to reduce the human effort needed to perform a certain task: in this case, the incursion of Greek soldiers into the city. And yet, given that it does not include any automated bits and is single-use only, 'device' seems more appropriate. Its trick rests on the fact that during the crucial moments of its operations, it is powered by the Trojans themselves thus giving them a (false) sense of security that they are in control of what is happening. As an artefact, it thus conceals the Greek war effort and foregrounds the Trojan input in its operations. In other words, the horse makes it possible for the Trojans to play an active role in the fall of their own city.

And yet we may wonder: how does all this relate to the way the Trojan horse points to conceptions of the human at war?

Athena's involvement in the horse's creation encourages us to think about the forces that have shaped the horse in more abstract terms. And these point, above all, not only to the divine but also to the human realm: Odysseus' cunning and Epeius' technical skills are represented in and endorsed by the goddess who decreed and helped craft the horse. Athena personifies and deifies the *human* traits that have shaped the horse. As such, it serves as a reminder that warfare is about more than the physical aspects of fighting; it is just as much about scheming, forethought, and the technical skills to turn plans into action.

But that is not all Athena brings to the story. The presence of the Trojan horse also intersects with her expertise in horsemanship and warfare more broadly, thus tying together the meanings and cultural associations of horses discussed above. Taken together, *all* these different dimensions add up, giving the horse a presence that represents the status of those fighting at Troy, the particular Greek traits that ultimately lead to the city's fall, and, finally, the role played by the supernatural in the events. *If* the Trojan horse does, after all, serve as a symbol, it does not denote a war engine, or an earthquake, or another external force that brings down the walls of the city *but the war itself.*

VIRGIL'S HORSE: BRINGING THE WAR INTO THE CITY

We finally return to Virgil and what is arguably the most detailed and influential account of the sack of Troy. By the time he composed the *Aeneid* (in the first century BCE), the ancient world had changed fundamentally. Greece had become part of the Roman Empire and the Roman authors reimagined the old tales in new, Roman ways. Moreover, there was now already a long tradition of ancient accounts of the sack of Troy to look back on which influenced later tellers.[54] In particular, Homer and the now largely lost works of the Epic Cycle provided a story with which later authors had to grapple. It is against this background that Virgil carved out his rendering of the story. How did he handle the trick with the horse in an account that turns a story of Greek cunning and Trojan defeat into a foundational narrative for Rome?

One dimension of the Trojan horse that has perhaps not received the attention it deserves is the extent to which it is entangled in the practice of storytelling.[55] It is not only that the ancient authors themselves tell the story of Troy in their own voices; several of them also present the horse-bit as a story within a story. Homer's brief references to the story (as mentioned above) are a case in point. Storytelling is also prominent in Virgil's *Aeneid*, which has Aeneas relate the events resulting in the demise of Troy and his escape from the burning city to Dido, the queen of Carthage. And what he has to say also highlights the power of storytelling.

It is easy to overlook that there is more to the trick than just the horse.[56] This is because the unusual object itself has a similar effect on us today as it had on the Trojans: its surprising and monumental presence stuns and evokes a sense of awe. 'Some are amazed at maiden Minerva's (Athena's) gift of death, and marvel at the massive horse.'[57] This horse is certainly an eye-catcher. Yet the trick works only because it comes with a false but ultimately convincing tale. I refer here, of course, to the way in which Sinon (the Greek left behind at Troy from the beginning of the chapter) explains the presence and purpose of the horse to the Trojans when he claims that it is a votive offering to Athena. Even though this dimension of the story is alluded to in several ancient authors, it is particularly prominent in Virgil's rendering of the tale.[58]

In order to persuade the Trojans to spare him and to move the horse into the city, Sinon embarks on an extended account that serves several purposes at once. First, he explains his own presence at Troy, and it is here that he first invokes religion in a false narrative to achieve his goal. He claims that he deserted from the Greek ranks because he feared for his life. Apparently, the Greeks had decided to sacrifice him after an oracle from Delphi advised them to do so. The oracle allegedly said that in order to return home they needed to sacrifice one of their own, just as they had to sacrifice a human life (Iphigeneia) to appease the winds when they first came to Troy.[59] Second, Sinon goes on to explain the presence of the horse itself and here, too, religion matters. He tells them that the Greeks put together the Trojan horse on the advice of their seer Calchas who spoke of the need to return to Troy the Palladium (a statue of Athena, see below), which the Greeks had once taken, and to compensate for that offence by offering Athena another object associated with her: the horse.[60]

Sinon's account of the situation is, of course, a clever trick that uses religion and storytelling to prey on human psychology. It appeals to anti-Greek sentiments among the Trojans as well as to feelings of relief after years of warfare and siege. At the same time, it presents the desired outcome – sparing Sinon's life and moving the horse into the city rather than destroying it – as desirable for the Trojans. In reality, things are quite the opposite: the Greeks *want* the Trojans to let Sinon live; they *want* the horse and its human contents to be transferred into the city. And sure enough Sinon's performance, the invocation of religious authorities (Delphi, the seer Calchas) and fake religious arguments (the threat of divine vengeance if the votive horse is disassembled) laced with much lamentation, pleading, and (false) appeals to the truth, ultimately have the desired effect: the Trojans are lulled into thinking that Sinon, his story, and the horse pose no threat to them whatsoever.

Never mind that there is a plethora of prophets, predictions, and omens lining up to forecast in no uncertain terms that bringing the horse into the city would be its downfall. Among them are the famous seer Cassandra and Laocoön, the priest of Poseidon/Neptune. But to no avail. As so often in human history, the wise advisors' words are ignored. Too stunning is the sudden turn of fortune; too alluring the gigantic object in plain sight. Together with the horse, the Trojans accept the story that comes with it. For an evening, they live the happy life of those whose daring and stubborn persistence seems to have finally paid off. That is, until they learn that with the horse, they welcomed the war into the heart of their city. Thus, where neither persistence nor brute military force had made the difference, the clever trick with horse and humans did.

With the benefit of hindsight and the distance of time, it is easy to make out the kind of trickery at work. The horse itself reflects the larger strategy of which it is part. It is not just Sinon's story which presents things as opposite from what they actually are. The horse, too, is the opposite of what it appears to be: it is a human product (conceived of and created by humans) *and* divinely inspired (by Athena). Despite its animal form, it is filled to the brim with humans. The votive offering ostensibly acknowledging Greek defeat turns out to be an offensive human weapon; the *de*-struction of the city is achieved with the help of the *con*-struction of the horse. The trophy of victory turns out to be the facilitator of defeat. At Troy, things are never quite what they seem. The Trojan horse is the most deceptive packaging in the history of human sales.

Ultimately, then, the Trojans fall victim to that quintessential Greek trait that already featured prominently throughout this book: cunning. In ancient Greek warfare of the Archaic and Classical periods, the use of deception and trickery was widely used and well regarded.[61] Yet Virgil does not tell a Greek story celebrating this most powerful of all Greek weapons, but a Roman one. And in this Roman story Greek cunning becomes mere deceit. His rendering of the tale highlights the horse's standing as the product of plotting and trickery. This is why Virgil's Aeneas speaks of 'Greek treachery' (*Danaum insidias*) and 'wickedness' (*scelus*) in reference to the horse.[62] Rather than the product of ingenuity, this horse is the product of deceit.

One dimension of the horse in particular comes to the fore: its role as a manifestation (a symbol for) the war itself. The *Aeneid* describes the horse's extraordinary size: it is 'of mountainous bulk' (*instar montis equum*).[63] In its extraordinary dimensions, the horse mirrors the extraordinary length of the war (ten years). From the Trojan point of view, its presence at Troy is as unusual and surprising as the sudden Greek retreat. All this makes the horse a perfect display trophy to commemorate the war and its sudden end.[64]

Virgil's account of the city's fall is driven by complex charade between inside and outside: inside the horse – outside the city. Inside the horse – inside the city. And finally: outside the horse – inside the city! The sack of Troy is already anticipated in the human takeover of the horse's wooden body. This mare is 'pregnant' with humans, as indicated in Virgil's reference to the men inside its 'womb' (*uterus*).[65] In the end, when the horse 'gives birth' – when the Greek fighters emerge and descend on the city – we have come full circle and the charade is complete. Such meanings are already inherent in the myth itself. But they really come to the fore in Virgil's telling of it. Homer had the Trojans debating the horse once it is inside the walls. Virgil, by contrast, delays the moment of the horse's transfer into the city, thus making space for the Trojan debate when it is still outside.[66]

In this context, it matters that Aeneas, who tells the story of Troy's fall to Dido, is not just talking to the queen of Carthage but seducing her. So what exactly is it that Dido is offered here in storied form? It seems that together with the story of the Trojan horse, Dido is taking destruction into her heart and into her city. After Aeneas' departure she will die from her own hand, leaving her people without a leader.

The ambiguity of horses and their capacity to represent both war and peace, destruction and stability is also articulated later in the *Aeneid*, when Aeneas recounts several omens that appeared the very morning of their landing in Italy:

> Here, as a first omen, four steeds I saw on the turf, grazing at large over the plain, as white as snow. Then father Anchises: ''Tis war you bring, land of our reception; for war are horses armed, war these herds portend. But yet,' he cries, 'those same steeds at times are wont to come under the chariot and beneath the yoke to bear the bit in concord; there is hope also of peace!'[67]

So, horses serve as symbols for war and peace, victory and defeat, depending on which side one mounts them. Again, it is the double nature of the horse that matters here.

And yet in Virgil's *Aeneid*, warfare has a meaning different from that in Homeric epic.[68] For Virgil, the battlefield is no longer an arena in which humans can distinguish themselves and win eternal glory. Rather, warfare is an unsettling business that upsets the order of things and blurs distinctions otherwise firmly in place. Virgil wrote his account of the fallout of the sack of Troy during the Augustan Age (43 BCE–18 CE) – a time of relative peace and stability under the newly founded *Pax Romana* that followed the turbulent civil war and a plethora of assassinations and deadly conspiracies in the preceding years. The memory of the unsettling effects of internal and external strife and armed confrontation colours his description of warfare. It feeds into the way in which Virgil, in the *Aeneid*, draws on antithetical terms and concepts (dark and bright, male and female, Jupiter and Juno, etc.) to sketch a world driven by fate and the tension between opposites, a world in which the fall of one city (Troy) ultimately leads to the founding of another (Rome).[69]

The Trojan horse fits into this larger scheme. Combining human, animal, and divine dimensions, a monumental physical presence and a scheming core, the horse is a destabilizing and ambiguous force. It helps bring about the fall of one city but also stands at the beginning of a chain of events that will lead to the rise of a new one. In the *Aeneid*, Virgil pairs it with the Palladium as another object connected to the fate of Troy mentioned before. The Palladium was a small wooden statue of Athena bearing arms. It was thought to have dropped from the sky and subsequently served the Trojans as a talismanic guardian statue. As long as it was within the city, Troy was safe from attack and onslaught.[70] According to some authors, the Palladium was removed from the city by Odysseus and Diomedes thus bringing about its sacking. In some accounts, the Palladium later made it back to Aeneas and found a new home in the city of Rome.[71] In the *Aeneid*, Sinon presents the horse as appeasing Athena for the removal of the Palladium from the city; but the story Sinon tells linking the horse to the removal of the Palladium is as false as the horse's status as a gift.

In many ways, then, the *Aeneid* tells a tale of change and transformation, propelled by the inscrutable forces of fate towards a preordained *telos* (end) – the foundation of Rome. This is a world in which opposing forces ultimately cancel each other out or supplement each other to constitute a newly unified whole. The Trojan horse is central to this endeavour. It represents both Greek ingenuity and Greek deceit, the end of the story of one city and the beginning of another, and human, divine, and animal identities. Above all, however, Virgil includes it as part of a narrative in which Sinon's false story matches the concealed human contents of the horse to form a compelling strategy by which the Greeks trick their way into the city. And yet, unlike his Greek counterparts, Aeneas, the hero of Virgil's *Aeneid*, cannot boast about having been one of the fighters hidden in the horse. His humanity emerges when he flees the horse's deadly human cargo – and turns a story of destruction into a story of a new beginning.[72]

WARFARE AND ANIMALITY

In the last section of this chapter, we finally dismount the horse to consider in more general terms how the identities of the human and non-human animal merge on the battlefield. To this end, we deploy the Trojan horse like its proverbial modern cousin: to introduce – stealthily – further dimensions of the larger theme of this chapter that transcend the core story. Ultimately, this will allow us to leap from the ancient into the modern world. And with this 'leap into the modern', I do not refer to the – by now somewhat tired – metaphorical use of the Trojan horse as a form of computer-based warfare of the present era. The horse and its human contents point to the larger nexus between humanity and animality in the realm of war both ancient and modern.

Warfare is an area of life that defies many of the principles and practices that apply elsewhere. In particular, the close-combat warfare of the ancient world was an intensely physical affair. The Mycenean period, when the Trojan War would have taken place, pre-dated the arrival of the phalanx – a military formation consisting of several rows of infantry that came to define the way in which wars were fought in the world of the Greek *poleis.* The Greek and Trojan fighters engaged each other individually or in small groups and with spears and swords at close range.[73] This means that those fighting (at Troy and elsewhere) will have experienced the gruesome and deadly effects of their actions close up. The *Iliad* is full of grisly descriptions of soldiers groaning in pain, body parts spilling onto the ground, lives expiring. Even though strategizing played an important role in this kind of combat, too, fighting involved a complex set of emotions: we hear of fear, anger, rage, fury, panic, grief, and despair. And warfare was an area that involved the wounding and killing of other humans. All these aspects make warfare a dimension of life that was associated with the animalistic side of the human.

Various ancient sources bring this side of warfare to light. The animalistic and wild informed the choice of motif for Greek shield devices. Among the images represented on Greek shields of the Classical period, we often find wild and ferocious animals.[74] Boars, eagles, serpents, and scorpions (to name just a few examples) were all common. Sometimes we also encounter depictions of ferocious animals ripping weaker ones apart: an eagle carrying a snake in its fangs; a lion ripping into a stag; a boar devouring a fish.[75] Not all animal representations on Greek shields can be explained in this way. There are also others selected for other reasons – owls for Athena, for example, or horses due to their real and symbolic role in ancient warfare as described above – but these animals, at least, were chosen because they articulate a dimension of warfare that associates the fighting human with the behaviour of predatory animals.[76] They were meant to terrify those on the receiving end of the Greek weaponry.

The link between the fighting and killing humans with wild and deadly animals also comes to the fore in some of the Homeric animal similes. These are short or extended analogies that compare situations within the story with a parallel reality derived mostly from the natural world. Like the epithets, they were once dismissed as formulaic but are now seen as conveying complex thoughts that supplement, and in some cases extend, the main storyline.[77] And many of these similes are derived from the natural world and the realm of animals in particular. The two Ajaxes holding up Imbrius to strip him of his armour, for example, are compared to two lions snatching a goat away from some dogs holding it high in their jaws.[78] Lions served as a frequent point of reference for the humans fighting at Troy.[79] By bringing out the animal (lion) within the human, such similes invert the idea of the human within the animal (as in the Trojan horse).

Other ferocious animals are also drawn upon to describe the human at war. The cry uttered by the dying Hippodamus is likened to the bellowing of a bull being dragged to sacrifice.[80] Menelaus' joy in spotting Alexander among the fighters is compared to a hungry lion who feels glad when he detects the body of a deceased animal.[81] We could extend the list to include further examples of similes that animalize Greek and Trojan fighters here. Yet the general principle has already become clear: animal similes frequently feature in the *Iliad* to convey particularly animalistic human traits. These traits range from physical similarities between the fighting heroes and wild beasts to more complex emotional and behavioural ones.[82]

But it is not only through similes and analogies that such ideas are articulated. The human body itself can be the locus in which such transformations occur.[83] Again Homeric epic provides examples. The Greek and Trojan soldiers leap out (*throskein*) and spring like dogs (*eporouein*).[84] They fly with swift feet when in fear.[85] At the same time, the sharp, piercing cries of those fighting echo across the battlefield of Troy.[86] More than words, these kinds of animal-like shrieks provide a suitable backdrop to, and commentary on, the action.

In particular, the figure of the Greek fighter Achilles assumes distinct animal traits in the latter part of the *Iliad*. When he joins the fight again to avenge the death of his friend and protégé Patroclus, he shows himself at his most beast-like. As John Heath succinctly put it: 'His (Achilles') viciousness in battle, his rejection of social norms such as oaths and suppliants, his scavenging, and his similes reveal a man on the edge of humanity.'[87] And that edge is defined by the way Achilles crosses over into the territory of the bestial and wild.

One of the social norms questioned in this part of the story is the right to a proper burial. Achilles himself and several other characters in the story would prefer their dead enemies to be left unburied so that animals can rip them apart.[88] But when Achilles goes even further and considers to do the ripping apart himself, the possibility of androphagy rears its ugly head again: 'I wish that somehow wrath and fury might drive me to carve your flesh and myself eat it raw because of what you have done.'[89] That the raging Achilles craves the raw flesh of his opponents is a strong indicator of a lack of humanity that we also find at play in the case of the Cyclops in the previous chapter and elsewhere in this book.

Such considerations are a long way from the Trojan horse and the kind of humanity contained in it. Yet the horse's presence and the way in which it contains those fighting at Troy, both physically and symbolically, points to the larger way in which human and animal identities merge in the realm of war. Indeed, in Aeschylus' tragedy *Agamemnon*, the Greek fighters emerging from the horse jumping to the ground from inside the horse's wooden belly themselves transform into an acrimonious beast (*Argeion dakos* – 'Argive beast'). Their long leap down from the huge horse to the ground – referred to elsewhere as 'the Trojan leap' (*Trōikon pēdēma*) – is compared to a lion: 'a lion, eater of raw flesh, leaped over the walls and licked its fill of royal blood'.[90] So in some sense, the Trojan horse incubates the Greek fighters to turn into leaping, deadly beasts.

Clearly, the stories we tell ourselves about the human at war reference the realm of animals, the animalistic, and the wild in more ways than one.

And some of these stories live on from the ancient world into the modern. Nowadays, we no longer carry shields featuring lions, scorpions, and snakes. But we still tap into the same link between warfare and animality when we name a war machine such as a tank or fighter aircraft after a predatory animal ('leopard', 'lion', 'panther'). The animal attributes of stealth, camouflage, and, of course, deadly force, are all in play here. This is because the experience of war continues to appeal to our animal side. Warfare, then, is an area of life in which humans, at least on occasion, take on animal traits, and in which some animals turn out to be surprisingly human inside.

AND FINALLY . . .

In lieu of a conclusion, we return once again to a question raised at the beginning: what would we do if we found ourselves facing the Trojan horse? Would we welcome it into the city? Or would we tread more carefully? These days we may deride the trusting nature of the Trojans and convince ourselves that surely we would not fall for the same old trick. We have come to believe we are clever enough to see through the horse's deceptive animal form to reveal the human within. But arguably this is only because we know the ancient story far too well to see this particular horse for anything other than what it really is.

Nowadays, Trojan horses come in many different forms, shapes, and sizes. These days, the Trojan horse has become an item and a symbol for all things introduced by stealth. What qualifies these modern horses as members of the Trojan breed is that they combine an item or presence that appears attractive (but is actually potentially harmful) with a story that presents this item or presence as something not only harmless but even desirable. And with great success. In the age of the Internet, ruses and scams drawing on the same kind of mechanism we found in the original horse are still rife.

So, it seems that, after all, we do still fall for the same old trick if it is presented to us in new clothing. In other words: even though modern wars are fought on different battlefields, they still tap into the same psychology that drove the ancient ruse. That we dress this trick in animal skin says something about the kind of humans we are; that we call it 'Trojan' says something about the role of classical antiquity in the shaping of this conception of the human.

CHAPTER 6

This chapter revolves around meat-eating as an important way by which humans define themselves and explores it as part of a broader 'anthropology' of food and eating. It tells the story of a boastful consumption of a wild boar at a (fictional) Roman dinner party to show that in the ancient world (as in the modern), what you eat is who you are.

In the Greco-Roman world, there is a distinct connection between meat-eating and the forging of male social and political identities. This connection plays out against the background of sacrifice and hunting as two ancient cultural practices resulting in the generation of red meat for collective and individual consumption. At the same time, the link between meat-eating, masculinity, physical vitality, and power points back to some of the arguments made in the philosophical debate discussed in the beginning of this book.

And yet, not everybody participated in the feast. Already in classical antiquity there were people who forged their identities along different lines by consciously opting out of this defining association. Intriguingly, perhaps, some of the arguments made over 2,000 years ago promoting vegetarianism resonate with modern advocacy of a meat-free diet.

6.1. James Ward, *A Wild Boar* (1814). Yale Center for British Art, Paul Mellon Collection B2002.2.1326. © Public Domain.

The 'Trojan' Boar (*Aper troianus ostentator*)

SOMETIME DURING THE REIGN OF THE EMPEROR NERO (54–68 CE), somewhere in the Bay of Naples in southern Italy, an illustrious group of friends and acquaintances descends on the residence of a certain Trimalchio for a lavish feast.[1] Like his friends, Trimalchio is a former slave (a 'freedman'). He amassed considerable riches after his release and, like many who come to wealth later in life, he feels the urge to parade a lifestyle that confirms he has indeed made it and attained considerable social standing.[2] Trimalchio uses the presence of his peers as an opportunity to show off his wealth and generosity.[3]

And show off he does! The dinner features idle conversation, harmless banter, pompous grandstanding, a bit of mansplaining, and plenty of misquoting of classical literature – highlighting first and foremost an embarrassing lack of education.[4] All this is topped off by a somewhat eccentric, narcissistic, and incontinent compère who is obliged to leave the dining room for an extended period of time to attend to his business.[5] Needless to say, there is also plenty of drink and a succession of courses to make the most ostentatious banquet pale in comparison. By one count, a whopping sixty-two separate foods were served up at Trimalchio's house that night.[6]

Well into the feast, the doors to the *triclinium* ('dining room') open and servants bring in coverlets for the dining couches decorated with hunting paraphernalia. When a pack of hunting dogs enters and begins to forage around the guests, the scene is set for what promises to be the culinary highlight of the evening.

The doors open again and what follows reads like this in the words of one present:[7]

> A tray was brought in . . . with a wild boar (aper) of the largest size upon it, wearing a cap of freedom, with two little baskets woven of palm-twigs hanging from the tusks, one full of dry dates and the other of fresh. Round it lay sucking-pigs made of simnel cake with their mouths to the teats, thereby showing that we had a sow before us. These sucking-pigs were for the guests to take away.[8]

Surely, this dish would have been a serious contender for the prize in best food presentation prior to the invention of Bavarian-style pork knuckles and the hot wiener?!

But this is not the end of it. Next, a person enters the room, 'a big bearded man with bands wound round his legs, and a spangled hunting coat of damasked silk, who drew a hunting-knife and plunged it hard into the boar's side. A number of fieldfares flew out at the blow.'[9] Although the sudden emergence of living birds from inside the boar astonishes those present, their appearance is not accidental but part of a tightly choreographed script: 'As they fluttered round the dining room there were fowlers ready with limed reeds who caught them in a moment.'[10] The host, never lost for words, rounds off the presentation with witty commentary: 'Now you see what fine acorns the woodland boar has been eating.'[11] Subsequently, the baskets carrying the dates are removed from the boar's tusks and their contents distributed among the guests.

SETTING THE TABLE

The vivid description of Trimalchio's dinner party is part of a work called *Satyrica* by the first-century CE Roman author Petronius.[12] It is fiction, but like all good satire, it hits hardest where it hurts most: accentuating and exaggerating the habits of real people.[13] The *Satyrica*, and, in particular, the section describing the events at Trimalchio's house that night (usually referred to as the *Cena Trimalchionis*, or 'the dinner of Trimalchio'), casts a critical eye on the milieu of those who made it in Roman society from relatively unpromising beginnings.[14] It depicts these *nouveaux riches* as perverted by the temptations of excessive wealth and conspicuous consumption. In their indulgent exuberance, they are presented as lacking both education and true class.[15]

Like many of the foods served up at Trimalchio's house that night, the stuffed boar points to what is arguably the most physical and certainly the most destructive human way to relate to non-human creatures: their consumption. Its ultimate fate in the digestive tracts of the freedman's guests exemplifies the most ubiquitous way in which human and animal bodies, human and animal identities merge: not through metamorphosis or hybridity – the subject of later chapters of this book – but through the very real human habit of eating the meat of certain animals.

Questions of human identity are never far away whenever humans sit down together to share a meal. And those interested in the so-called 'ethnography' of food and drink (the link between food, drink, and culture) have taken notice. They have shown that gatherings at formal dinners, cocktail parties, or indeed the humble kitchen table are about much more than the mere intake of calories. They reveal who we really are or indeed, who we aspire to be. *Everything* to do with how humans prepare, present, and consume their meals matters: the origin, choice, and succession of dishes, the mode of their preparation, their combination, the occasion and setting, and, finally, the question of who is included in the party (and who is left out). Food thus is – and has always been – a social 'code' that allows us to articulate complex messages of identity and belonging.[16]

Unfortunately, we cannot time-travel back to the ancient world and engage in the main method of ethnographic study: 'participant observation' – the full immersion into the culture under investigation with the ultimate intention of exploring its inner workings. But we can apply some of the questions and approaches that ethnographers use to decipher meals in all their complexity to sources like Petronius' account of Trimalchio. That the text in question is not only fictional but satire is by no means a disadvantage. As we will see, the comic treatment of matters of identity and belonging only adds further spice to the story.

FOOD AND HUMAN IDENTITIES: ANCIENT AND MODERN

In her study of human feasting habits, the notable British social anthropologist Mary Douglas has drawn attention to the fact that food, drink, and their consumption include an array of social messages.[17] She has shown what all, or at least those of us who entertain friends and acquaintances at our dinner tables, have always intuitively known: that common meals can be tightly choreographed affairs in which the choice and succession of dishes convey a rich array of meanings. They allow us to make claims about ourselves, our place in society, and the way we relate to our guests. It matters whether we serve vegetarian quiche, or fish, or a big fat Porterhouse steak. And whether we serve it with some expensive Champagne of a well-known brand (that will go unnamed here) or merely cheap booze grabbed last-minute from the supermarket shelves. On an individual level, such choices are invariably revealing in terms of how we position ourselves in a particular social milieu. Taken together they point to the way in which cultural meanings are inscribed in everyday activities such as the consumption of food and drink.

In this point, Douglas' work intersects with that of another famous anthropologist: Claude Lévi-Strauss. Lévi-Strauss is well known for having founded a mode of interpretation called 'structural anthropology' – the study of cultural meanings encoded in webs of dual opposites and differences such as day and night, male and female, summer and winter. In his acclaimed study with the same name, Lévi-Strauss distinguished between the 'the raw' and 'the cooked' (French: *le cru et le cuit*, literally perhaps better 'the raw' and the 'prepared' or 'processed') to illustrate how empirical categories can point to deeper modes of thought specific to a given culture.[18] Lévi-Strauss exemplifies his claim by studying the mythological tales of the tropical America of his own present and his focus exceeds communal consumption. And yet food-related pairs such as 'the raw' and 'the cooked', 'fresh' and 'rotten', 'moist' and 'burnt' are central to his work. They have variously been used to explore the ways in which individual cultures and subcultures prepare their foods.

Where does this leave us with regard to Trimalchio's dinner party and the overall themes of this book?

Of course, it would be perfectly possible to go through the succession of dishes served up by Trimalchio one by one in order to tease out how they relate to each other, to Trimalchio's social peers, and Roman society at large. Yet that would not only take up too much space. After all, who would want to digest the cultural meanings of sixty-two individual dishes! Doing so would also take us too far away from the human/animal entanglements at the core of this book. So instead, we concentrate on a single dish, that of the stuffed boar – the main course of the meal – and that part of Petronius' story that is concerned with its presentation.

Already, the chapter on the lion of Androclus mobilized the categories of 'the raw' and 'the cooked' to distinguish the human from the non-human animal. In this particular story, the lion ate his prey raw and unrefined, while Androclus cooked or at least dried the meat that he derived from the lion before he consumed it. As the main course of Trimalchio's party, the stuffed boar seems to belong firmly in the category of 'the cooked'. And yet, as we will see, the modes of its preparation prior to its spectacular arrival on Trimalchio's dinner table also point back to the raw and wild: the stuffing of live birds not only evokes the natural world. It also points to hunting and, specifically, boar hunting as a popular activity in the ancient Greek and Roman worlds.

Before we explore the specific cultural seasonings of this particular dish, we shall cast our net a bit more widely and start from some observations about the larger category to which the cooked boar belongs – that of meat.

MEAT-EATING IN THE ROMAN WORLD

In ancient Greece and Rome, the consumption of meat was by no means as widespread as it became after the Industrial Revolution, the arrival of intensive farming, and the mass production of meat. The typical Mediterranean diet consisted of cereals, beans, pulses, olives, and vine fruits, with other foodstuffs serving merely as supplements, depending on local climate, growing conditions, proximity of trade routes, and of course the seasons.[19] Cheeses and milk were widely available. Fruit and vegetables were accessible, again depending on local climate, soil, and season.

The extent to which meat was part of the diets of regular Greeks and Romans is controversial.[20] Classical scholars have pointed out that its consumption by members of the middle and lower classes was limited mainly to special occasions. In ancient Greece and Rome, the communal sacrifices carried out by the city provided one such occasion, as did large banquets organized by well-off hosts, which, from the last quarter of the fourth century BCE onwards (the beginning of the Hellenistic period), allowed for a wider distribution of meat, in particular high-quality meat.

Yet cheaper meats were also available at local markets and – the ancient equivalent of 'pub food' – at restaurants and inns. Meat and meat-based products such as sausages and blood pudding feature regularly in the evidence from Greece and Rome.[21] They were a welcome addition to the fare of regular Greeks and Romans unable to afford prime cuts. Moreover, meat was available to those who served the Roman Empire in uniform. The Roman army provided its members with regular portions of meat – mainly bacon, but beef as well.[22] To others, meat eventually became available through food handouts. The Roman emperor Aurelian, who ruled the Roman world between 270–275 CE, gave free pork (and a number of other foodstuffs) to those segments of Roman society already receiving grain supplies.[23] Overall, then, meat and meat-based products were available at least occasionally to non-elite segments of society.

To complicate things further, there were fundamental regional differences in the kind of meat available. While pigs were bred widely in different parts of the ancient world, other types of animal products were local. Rural areas provided opportunities for supplementing farmed meats through the hunting of game (boar, hare, deer). Fish was more readily available in settlements close to the coast than in landlocked cities. Beef and cattle flourished in communities on or near fertile ground.[24] I say 'more readily available' because, again, there were exceptions: the ancient Greeks and Romans knew several food preservation techniques – the salting and drying of fish and meats, and the pickling of vegetables – that extended their lifespan significantly and allowed their transport into other parts of the ancient world.[25] The Roman author Strabo (ca 64 BCE –after 21 CE), for example, mentions that ham from the region now called France was a prized delicacy in ancient Rome.[26]

Finally, we also hear about the ancient appetite for animals no longer consumed in Western societies: foxes, hedgehogs, songbirds, camels (in Roman Egypt and Mesopotamia), even certain insects (locusts, cicadas) all landed occasionally on the table of the ancient Greeks and Romans.[27] Yet such items remained culinary outliers. In the Greek and Roman ethnographic literature, the consumption of exotic foodstuffs, including animal meats, is a feature that set other people apart.[28] As does the apparent lack of culinary sophistication in terms of both choice of meats and the mode of preparation. It is in this sense that the Roman author Tacitus (ca 56–120 CE) describes the German tribe of the Fenni as indiscriminately eating what is essentially raw animal flesh. And its preparation does not redeem it either: Apparently, the Fenni merely warm the meat by tucking it into the folds of their horses' thighs.[29] It is the absence of proper cooking, the consumption of raw meat, and the indiscriminate choice of animal that communicate the lack of refinement of the people in question here. In the ancient world as in the modern, you are what you eat.

Overall, then, regardless of which meat was consumed, when, and by whom, meat in ancient Greece and Rome was never really a staple. In particular, high-quality red meats remained special and exclusive. Tellingly, it is a *cholikion* ('guts') – that the prototypical 'shameless man' by the Greek author Theophrastus (ca 372–287 BCE) shoplifts from the food stalls in the city.[30] Not to read too much into this example: it is part of a caricature in a work of fiction. But it is no coincidence that meat is the object of desire and unauthorized appropriation here. So meat was a food apart, an object of individual craving and symbolic embellishment.

What, then, did the consumption of meat entail? Which human identities are nourished by it and how?

MEAT-EATING AND MASCULINITY

In the ancient world, there was a distinct link between meat-eating and power, both political and physical. During the Classical period (480–323 BCE), the levelling ideology of ancient Greek democracy articulated itself, for example, in the distribution of equal cuts distributed to all citizens of the *polis* after communal sacrifices.[31] The Hellenistic period

(323–31 BCE) witnessed the arrival of large formal dinners hosted by those of elevated social standing. This kind of banquet (or 'symposium-feast' as one modern commentator put it) alluded to the old Greek tradition of the aristocratic drinking party called the *symposium*, but in effect they were more food-oriented, hierarchical, and driven by altogether different considerations and ideologies.[32] In contrast to the ideology and the opportunities for aristocratic display that underpinned the *symposium*, feasting during the Hellenistic period propagated hierarchical relationships between benefactors and beneficiaries. In the Roman world such occasions and the human relationships fostered by them thrived. Emperors hosted lavish banquets, as did many lesser office-holders and members of the aristocratic elite. At the same time, the private dinner party such as the one hosted by Trimalchio became a welcome occasion for the well-off to flaunt their social status and for the less well off to participate in their hosts' luxury and conspicuous consumption.[33]

In the ancient world, there was a distinct link between meat-eating, physical strength, and masculinity. It is evident early in the history of the ancient world in the excessive meat consumption of Homeric heroes. Later ancient authors variously noted that even though much of the action in the *Iliad* and the *Odyssey* happens on or near the sea, there is a notable absence of fish among the food items consumed.[34] Instead, both epics portray Achilles, Hector, Odysseus, and their likes as enthusiastic meat-eaters. The consumption of red meat is part of the so-called 'heroic code'. Meat-eating makes a Homeric hero.[35]

This is because it reinforces notions of masculinity, physical strength, and daring central to the heroic code. The Greek hero Agamemnon tries to kindle the spirit of battle in his men with the following words: 'Where have our boastings gone, when indeed we used to say that we were bravest, the empty boasts that you uttered when you were in Lemnos eating abundant flesh of straight-horned cattle and drinking bowls brim full of wine, saying that each man would stand to face in battle one or two hundred Trojans!'[36] It is not merely courage that Agamemnon attempts to inspire here, but also a special prowess surpassing that which is normally possible and articulating itself above all in the confidence to be able to take on hundreds of Trojans at once.[37]

The traditions about the Greek mythical hero Heracles tap into such sentiments. This figure, known for his heroic feats – many of which involved the conquest of monstrous animals such as the Nemean lion and the Erymanthian boar – was said to have once eaten two bull-carcasses for dinner.[38] Already in heroic times, it seems, the consumption of meat is linked to the idea of bodily strength, masculinity, and toughness, both physical and mental. At the same time, the figure of Heracles also reveals that the large consumption of meat is not a straightforward praise. Here and elsewhere, it borders on the comical and carries the whiff of excess. It thus fits the picture that another Greek mythical figure (that of Erysichthon) was punished by the gods for committing an impiety by instilling him with an insatiable hunger.[39] The more he consumed, the hungrier he got, ultimately resulting in his financial ruin. Overall, then, it appears that the link between food and identity, and, in particular, between meat-eating and masculinity, resonates in the mythical as well as in the real world and it does so in ways that do not always shed the most favourable light on those munching away on their (real and metaphorical) beef.

Beyond Heracles and his like, it is ancient athletes in particular who are on record as having enhanced their physical capacities through the excessive consumption of red meats. During the first half of the fifth century BCE, the famous Greek boxer Theagenes from the island of Thasos in the northern Aegean racked up numerous victories in athletic competitions and once, allegedly, ate an entire bull on his own.[40] Of a certain Herodotus (not to be confused with the famous ancient Greek historian of the same name) we hear that, in addition to large amounts of bread and wine, he consumed 20 pounds (about 9 kg) of meat.[41] He not only won numerous competitions in trumpet-playing but was able to play two trumpets at the same time and so loudly that it spurred soldiers on to their last reserves of strength when besieging the city of Argos. Milo of Croton, another athlete, was also capable of consuming 20 pounds of meat in one sitting. Even more impressively, he famously carried a heifer on his shoulders around the stadium at Olympia, before slaughtering it and gobbling it up all in one go.[42] According to another tradition, he gained his legendary physical strength as a boy by carrying around a heifer on his shoulders every day until he was a grown man – and the heifer a full-sized bull.[43] No matter what one makes of such accounts, the overall message is clear: the size of a meal, the speed at which it is consumed, and the fact that it is (usually) meat that is consumed all highlight the notion of physical vigour. Extraordinary male bodies, it seems, are built on the extraordinary consumption of red meat.

GOING MEATLESS: ANCIENT VEGETARIANISM

If the consumption of meat supported individual and collective identities in the ancient world, opting out of it provided a potent strategy for those who wished to set themselves apart from mainstream society. Even though ancient vegetarianism was not as widespread as it has become over the past two centuries – ever since the foundation of the first vegetarian society in the UK, in 1847 – it was already a viable option to those Greeks and Romans wishing to make a point by adopting a diet different from those around them.

In the ancient world, a vegetarian diet was followed primarily (and widely) among the adherents of certain philosophical or religious movements and by charismatic individuals seeking to develop a following.[44] Most notably, perhaps, Pythagoras and his disciples ('the Pythagoreans') promulgated abstinence from eating animals, as did those adhering to Orphism, a religious movement centred on the figure of Orpheus (a mythical singer/poet).[45] Empedocles, Plato, Plutarch, Porphyry, and Plotinus (among others) all at some point promote vegetarianism in their works.[46] Some may also have adopted the vegetarian habit temporarily only: the Roman philosopher, statesman, and author Seneca (ca 4 BCE–65 CE), for example, gave up eating animals for a year. Apparently, he enjoyed the experience but was ultimately talked back into meat-eating by his carnivore father.[47]

So, what considerations drove some of the ancient Greeks and Romans to opt out of the consumption of meat and the associated identity politics? Several texts in support of vegetarianism have come down to us from the ancient world. They include a long speech attributed to the philosopher Pythagoras in Ovid's *Metamorphoses*, Plutarch's treatise *On the Eating of Flesh*, and Porphyry's *On Abstinence from Killing Animals*.[48] Some of the considerations featured here and elsewhere sound surprisingly modern in that they resonate with similar arguments still circulating today. Many others, however, are uniquely Greek and Roman and illustrate the cultural and historical gap that separates us from the ancient world.

The belief in the reincarnation of the soul after death (*metempsychosis*) played an important role in ancient justifications of vegetarianism.[49] Ovid's Pythagoras, for example, draws on the principle of *metempsychosis* to argue why it is morally wrong to eat animals. He asserts that 'all things are changing; nothing dies. The spirit wanders, comes now here, now there, and occupies whatever frame it pleases. From beasts it passes into human bodies, and from our bodies into beasts, but never perishes.'[50] The belief that the human soul can be reborn in the body of an animal and vice versa was held by various ancient authors. As Peter Garnsey has pointed out, to those following this doctrine, eating meat was in effect a form of cannibalism.[51] This connection is drawn directly in Plutarch's explanation of why the consumption of animals is wrong. He states that even if the transmigration of the soul after death cannot be proven with ultimate certainty, better to err on the side of caution. Surely nobody would want to run the risk of killing an animal that carries the soul of a friend or relative or another human being? In a direct swipe at the Stoics, a philosophical school that allowed for the consumption of animals based on the idea of a fundamental divide between human and non-human animals, he asks:

> Do but consider which are the philosophers who serve the better to humanise us: those who bid us eat our children and friends and fathers and wives after their death, or Pythagoras and Empedocles who try to accustom us to act justly toward other creatures also? You ridicule a man who abstains from eating mutton. But are we, they will say, to refrain from laughter when we see you slicing off portions from a dead father or mother and sending them to absent friends and inviting those who are at hand, heaping their plates with flesh?[52]

The idea of *metempsychosis* invoked here helps Porphyry to mobilize the taboo of eating human flesh for the purpose of promoting vegetarianism. Who would want to argue against it when presented with such a drastic choice? And yet the belief in the transmigration of the soul was also invoked in support of the consumption of meat. Some argued that killing animals actually liberated souls from their animal bodies and thus contributed to the possibility of a swifter reincarnation in human form.[53]

Beyond the issue of reincarnation, ancient proponents of vegetarianism present the consumption of other living beings as brutish – a practice that puts man on a par with wild animals.[54] For Ovid's Pythagoras it is a form of degeneration, a fall from the Golden Age, that mythical time in the beginning when humans and animals lived in harmony together: 'But that pristine age, which we have named the Golden Age, was blessed with the fruit of the trees and the herbs which the ground sends forth, nor did men defile their lips with blood.'[55] The consumption of animals features here as particularly unfair because humans consume the meat of creatures such as oxen that help by ploughing their fields. Humans owe them. Instead, they eat them. Although he supports the killing of wild animals which pose a threat to human lives, he still considers their consumption wrong.[56]

Meat-eating also features as a form of moral decline in Plutarch's treatise *On the Eating of Flesh*.[57] But rather than ruminating wistfully about a Golden Age, Plutarch puts the focus squarely on those who first killed and consumed animals. In what is perhaps a veiled reference to the mythical stories of Hyperbius or Prometheus (who were said to have first killed an unspecified animal and an ox, respectively), he suggests that the practice originated during a much more primitive age when humans had no other way to sustain themselves, such as through agriculture and farming.[58] This age is juxtaposed with Plutarch's own present – the first/second century CE – in which humans kill animals not out of necessity (such as to avoid starvation or to fend off danger) but as a luxury, for mere gluttonous pleasure: 'But you who live now, what madness, what frenzy drives you to the pollution of shedding blood, you who have such a superfluity of necessities?'[59] Citing examples of humans mistreating animals to fatten them up or to make them tastier, Plutarch suggests that the human killing of animals for pleasure is against nature (*para physin*) and incurs pollution.[60]

And yet, despite such impassioned arguments against meat-eating, even some ancient proponents of vegetarianism believed that a vegetarian diet may be unsuitable for those with particular physical needs. Porphyry, for example, explicitly excludes manual labourers, athletes, soldiers, and sailors as well as, curiously, orators and others engaged in public affairs.[61] Moreover, he concedes that it is good practice for athletes and those recovering from an ailment to eat meat.[62] The reason: Meat-eating bestows physical strength and a taste for fighting.[63]

The Homeric heroes and the Roman soldiers nod their carnivorous heads . . .

Several of the ancient authors sought to make a connection between vegetarianism and the capacity to engage in philosophy as an endeavour of the mind. Plutarch, for example, explains that the eating of animals corrupts because it 'makes us spiritually coarse and gross by reason of satiety and surfeit'.[64] As an explanation, Plutarch maintains that the consumption of animals strengthens the physical human body but weakens the soul. On this point Plutarch finds agreement in the words of the later Neoplatonic philosopher Porphyry (ca 234–305 CE) who argues that it is, above all, temperance (*sōphrosynē*) which allows the philosopher to see more clearly.[65] This observation applies to all kinds of temperance but in particular to meat-eating.[66] Vegetarianism is considered once again part of a lifestyle designed to enhance one's proximity to the divine.

In invoking the supernatural here, Porphyry's argument recalls similar thoughts of earlier authors. Already Ovid's Pythagoras had maintained that to draw the gods into the business of meat-eating by virtue of their roles as recipients of blood sacrifice is based on the erroneous assumption that they enjoy the bloodshed.[67] And Plutarch had pointed out that it is impious to imply that the gods do not provide humans with enough alternative fare to live.[68] All of this amounts to a veritable attempt to rebrand religion – traditionally a major occasion for the consumption of meat – by drawing it into an argument for vegetarianism.

So, what does all this add up to? Ancient justifications of vegetarianism reveal that the link between meat-eating (or its absence) and human identities, both collective and individual, was established long before Trimalchio served up his gigantic boar. And with this point we end our brief foray into the identity politics of ancient meat-eating and vegetarianism and return to the Roman dinner table.

ANCIENT MEAT-EATING BETWEEN HUNTING AND SACRIFICE

To the modern reader, the scene that presented itself to Trimalchio's guests – the dead boar, the pastry suckling piglets, the very real birds emerging from the carved-up body – seems over the top, if not downright revolting. Modern paleo-diets notwithstanding, we are no longer used to having the animal origins of our meals paraded before our eyes and under our noses, let alone stage-managed as Trimalchio did. It is not merely that we buy what has been called 'sanitized meat' in small portions, wrapped in clean plastic packets, available in modern supermarkets that betray nothing of their animal origins, let alone the violent and bloody ways these came about.[69] We habitually dress up our animal-derived foods as something else altogether: We consume 'beef' and not cow, 'pork' and not pig. Even the word 'meat' itself covers up the fact that it is the flesh of other creatures that is served on our dinner plates.

In his book *The Civilizing Process*, the sociologist Norbert Elias has traced changes in Western etiquette from the Middle Ages to the present. In a chapter on shifts in table manners, he includes a special section on meat-eating in which he states:

> Today it would arouse rather uneasy feelings in many people if they or others had to carve half a calf or pig at table or cut meat from a pheasant still adorned with feathers . . . This direction is quite clear. From a standard of feeling by which the sight and carving of dead animal on the table are actually experienced as pleasurable, or at least not at all unpleasant, the development leads to another standard by which reminders that the meat dish has something to do with the killing of an animal are avoided to the utmost. In many of our meat dishes the animal form is so concealed and changed by the art of its preparation and carving that, while eating, one is scarcely reminded of its origin.[70]

At one time, it seems, humans did not mind facing the animal origins of their foodstuffs. Throughout the ages, the etiquettes pertaining to food consumption and preparation underwent fundamental changes with consequences not just for the meat presented but also for those involved in its processing. In other words, the butcher or meat carver is no longer fit for presentation at the dinner table. At Trimalchio's feast, by contrast, the person cutting the boar himself becomes a central ingredient in the way the dish is served up.[71] To recall his performance from the beginning of this chapter: he 'drew a hunting-knife and plunged it hard into the boar's side'.[72] The man's robust appearance together with the vigour with which he carries out his task indicate that the whole scene is meant to point up (rather than subdue or conceal) the provenance of this dish and its violent origins. More specifically, by serving up the stuffed boar, Trimalchio sought to tap into connotations of hunting as evident in the emergence of hunting dogs and the decorations of the dining couches featuring hunting articles.

So, what kind of associations did this cultural practice convey in the ancient world in general and the Roman Empire in particular? And, how did Trimalchio make use of them?

The meanings associated with hunting emerge in particular clarity if set alongside the other way in which meat was derived for consumption in the ancient Greek and Roman worlds: through sacrifice. Hunting differs from sacrifice above all in that it targets wild animals rather than the domesticated species that provided the vast majority of sacrificial victims. It thus did not come with the guilt that is sometimes mentioned in the ancient sources in association with the killing of domesticated animals, in particular useful ones, such as oxen. Instead, it carried the whiff of the dangerous. It belonged in the wild rather than the civilized sphere of the city.

In contrast to the highly choreographed sacrificial rituals that formed the core of Greco-Roman religion, the hunt was a much more uncontrollable and dangerous affair that provided ample opportunities for individuals to prove themselves. In sacrifice, the roles of those involved (as priests or assistants of various kinds) were clearly set out right from the start. The hunt, by contrast, required skill, daring, flexibility, and the willingness to improvise in response to unexpected turns of events.

A final difference between hunting and sacrifice concerns the way in which both draw on and mobilize the categories of gods, humans, and animals. Sacrifice makes a fundamental distinction between those conducting the sacrifice (humans), those sacrificed (animals), and those in whose honour the sacrifice is carried out (the gods). It conveys the very same hierarchical structure with gods at the top, animals at the bottom, and humans sandwiched in between that was also promoted in parts of the philosophical debate.[73] In hunting, by contrast, the role of human and non-human animal, hunter and hunted, are much more aligned. There is a direct connection between the physical vitality of the hunter and that of the hunted. Simply put: the bigger, more difficult to hunt, and more dangerous the hunted animal, the more credit goes to the one who pulls off the feat. In contrast to sacrifice as a religious ritual, the gods play a more remote role in hunting: they are usually invoked before the hunt, to secure a good outcome, or thanked for their support in the case of its success thereafter.

In the ancient world, hunting served as an opportunity for well-off young men to prove themselves. The ancient Greeks praised it as a particularly masculine pastime that required not only special equipment and well-trained dogs, but also bravery and courage.[74] In Greek thought and literature, the hunt features as a rite of passage for young men and an important social activity to pursue, in particular for those of elevated social standing.[75] Moreover, in his treatise *On Hunting*, the Greek author Xenophon (ca 430–350 BCE) praises the hunt as preparation for warfare – that other aspect of life in the ancient world in which courage, physical strength, virility, and skill in handling weapons mattered.[76] Hunters, he explains, are used to strenuous marches carrying weapons, to sleeping on hard grounds, to keeping a watchful eye at all times, to coordinating their own efforts with those around them, and to pursuing their prey relentlessly – all skills that come in handy in warfare as well. And the Greek author Oppian (second century CE) compares the soundscape of humans engaged in extracting a large monster from the depths of the sea with that of the battlefield.[77]

In the Roman world, hunting carried similar connotations. The Romans hunted from the earliest times onwards and they did so for a variety of reasons: to control dangerous animals, as an additional source of food, as an initiation into the military service, and as 'sport'.[78] For the first three reasons, hunting was practised by larger segments of society. Small farmers in rural areas hunted to defend their livelihoods from dangerous predators as well as to supplement their diet. Young men from different social and economic backgrounds – the so-called 'citizens of the middle ranks' – engaged in the hunt in preparation for their military service.[79] And yet, it is in particular the last function, the communal hunt as a pastime of the well-off, that came to define the image of hunting and the hunter in Roman culture.

The communal hunt thus carried associations of entitlement and elevated social standing.[80] As a pastime of the elites, it was seasoned with privilege sustained by notions of masculinity, physical strength, and courage. Roman law provided for wild animals to be hunted by everyone on one's own property as well as that of others. The exception to this rule was the private game parks (*vivaria*) – mentioned by various ancient authors – that some of the well-off maintained for privileged access to huntable game.[81] Those were available to their owners only and their favoured guests and friends.

Among the animals hunted by the Romans, the wild boar stands out. The abundant ancient hunting literature tells us that this animal was widely available in different parts of the Roman Empire. Owing to its ferocity, it required special skills and equipment and carried particular risks. We will consider the cultural meanings of wild boar as a hunted animal and as a food item in more detail below. Here, we merely say that in serving wild boar at his dinner party and in playing up the hunting theme, Trimalchio seeks to align himself with the ideologies and meanings associated with hunting.[82] By highlighting the hunt as the way in which the boar ended up on his dinner table, Trimalchio emphasizes his claim to elevated social standing.

At the same time, the robust means of the boar's presentation that makes no secret of its violent origins also taps into notions of masculinity, courage, and physical strength. Indeed, the dish thematizes life and death in more ways than one: the dead boar is resurrected as a female nourishing its own (artificial) offspring – the suckling pastry piglets. At the same time, the butchered boar gives birth to live birds, thus tabling, quite literally, the subject of life and death administered by human hand. Moreover, in the intervention of fowlers catching the birds emerging from the boar's carved up body, Trimalchio restages the trapping of animals in general, and birds in particular, as central parts of the ancient hunt.

DEGUTTING THE BOAR

Further 'flavours' of Trimalchio's dish then emerge from the boar as the animal at the heart of the drama. Boars were abundant in the forests of central Greece and all over Italy. As omnivores, they were highly flexible in adapting their diet.[83] In particular, shrubs, roots, mushrooms, fruits, berries, and other plant parts provided ubiquitous food sources and ensured that populations flourished, especially in rural areas.

In the ancient world, boar hunting was popular among those of elevated social standing. As far back as Homer, Greek heroes are portrayed pursuing boar as a source of meat, or to fend off danger, and to showcase their skill and daring. The Greek hero Odysseus, for example, proves himself by chasing a wild boar on the slopes of Mount Parnassus.[84] Killing this boar not only brings him fame and foreshadows his execution of the suitors towards the end of the *Odyssey*, but also earns him the distinctive scar on his leg by which his wet nurse recognizes him many years later.[85]

6.2. Black-figure lekythos showing Heracles and the boar. Athens, ca 525–500 BCE, attributed to the Leagros Group, Nicholson Collection, Chau Chak Wing Museum, The University of Sydney NM 46.52. © Chau Chak Wing Museum, Sydney

Other iconic boar hunts in Greco-Roman thought and literature include that of the so-called Calydonian boar – a ferocious beast sent by the goddess Artemis to terrorize the region of Calydon in Aetolia – as well as the Crommyonian sow and the Erymanthian boar, finished off by Theseus and Heracles, respectively (see Figure 6.2). Such high-profile events involving famous heroes of Greco-Roman mythology show that already in heroic times, boar hunting was a rite of passage – an important test for the aspiring hero to pass.[86]

Yet it was not only mythical heroes who indulged in this pastime. In historical times, boar hunting lost nothing of its epic allure. In the ancient world, the boar was one of the most difficult and potentially dangerous animals to hunt. Xenophon's *On Hunting* includes a whole chapter describing the dangers involved. It includes cautious instructions on best practice:

> Let one man, the most experienced, urge on the hounds, while the others follow in regular order, keeping well behind one another, so that the boar may have a free passage between them; for should he beat a retreat and dash into a crowd, there is a risk of being gored, since he spends his rage on anyone he encounters.[87]

Surely those finishing off such a ferocious beast were entitled to boast about their accomplishment. Other animals hunted frequently in ancient Greece and Rome include the hare, deer, wild goat and, of course, numerous birds – none of which pose the same risks to the hunters. Given the well-attested ferocity of the boar in Greek and Roman literature, it thus comes as no surprise that up until the second consulate of Gaius Marius (104 BCE), it served as one of only five creatures to be represented on the standards of Roman legions.[88] The boar features as a symbol at the intersection between hunting and the military service with its presence highlighting values such as physical strength, courage, and daring. At least some of these flavours were presented to Trimalchio's guests in the form of the boar.

THE INFLATIONARY BOAR

When it came to boars at Roman banquets, size mattered, as did number and presentation. To serve boar was one thing. To serve up a specimen that was not merely presentable but awe-inspiring was something else altogether. In a poem by the Roman author Martial (ca 40–102 CE), a guest complains about the size and mediocrity of a boar served up at a dinner party:

> Twice thirty of us were invited to dinner yesterday, Mancinus, and nothing was set before us but boar: no grapes preserved from late-maturing vines nor honey-apples that rival sweet honeycombs nor pears that hang tied with length of broom nor pomegranates looking like roses cut short. Neither did rustic Sassina send her milky cones nor came olives from Picene jars. No, naked boar, and a tiny one at that, such as an unarmed midget might lay low. And nothing of it came our way, we all just watched. The arena is apt to serve us boar in that fashion. After such behaviour I hope that boar will never again be served you, but that you will be served to the same boar as Charidemus.[89]

What is found wanting here is exactly the kind of exuberance and excess that defines Trimalchio's dinner. This boar is too bare to impress. There is no orchestration of meanings through the foodstuffs surrounding it. Moreover, it was only a small specimen. This boar is so pathetic that it could be finished off by anybody, even someone small and unarmed. A connection is drawn between the physique of the hunted and that of the hunter. Trimalchio's boar, by contrast, is explicitly said to be a big specimen (*primae magnitudinis aper*) with enough *gravitas* to impress those present. Surely, on the scale of inflationary boar, Trimalchio's dish ranks highly?

In particular, the boar's frequently impressive tusks – capable of inflicting horrendous wounds – served as objects of admiration and veneration. Like no other body part, those tusks bundle the boar's ferociousness.[90] Its lower tusks also play a role in the presentation of Trimalchio's dish, recalling the past ferocity of the animal now before the guests. In more practical terms, they also provide a hook for the baskets carrying the dates.[91]

Wild boar had a rightful and cherished place on ancient Roman dinner plates, particularly among the well-off. It was considered a delicacy steeped in cultural and social flavour.[92] To the ancient Romans, wild boar was not just a tasty roast but the opportunity to showcase a broad array of ingredients: a pinch of virility, a cup of heroic bravery, a spoonful each of wealth, exclusivity, and social standing – and lashings of luxury. Trimalchio's boar is seasoned with all of these.

Speaking of luxury and excess, there is ample evidence to suggest that when it came to consumption in general and wild boar in particular, Rome's elites overdid it a bit. Here is what the Roman author Pliny (23–79 CE) says about excessive consumption of wild boar:

> (W)ild boar has been a popular luxury. As far back as Cato the Censor we find his speeches denouncing boar's meat bacon. Nevertheless a boar used to be cut up into three parts and the middle part served at table, under the name of boar's loin. Publius Servilius Rullus ... first served a boar whole at his banquets – so recent is the origin of what is now an everyday affair; and this occurrence has been noted by historians, presumably for the improvement of the manners of the present day, when it is the fashion for two or three boars to be devoured at one time not even as a whole dinner but as the first course.[93]

Roman dinners of the type hosted by Trimalchio seem to have expanded in size and indulgence in the centuries leading up to the dinner party described by Petronius. Such suppers typically consisted of a succession of dishes.[94] A first part (*gustatio*) offered an array of lighter foodstuffs, such as salads, fish, vegetables, or egg-based dishes – what we might refer to as 'starters'. The second part (*mensa prima*) consisted of a number of dishes of meat, game, and/or fish, including the *caput cenae*, the main dish. The third part, *mensa secunda*, featured what we would consider typical (sweet) desserts or cheeses but sometimes also included more hearty things like molluscs. To serve up a whole boar, not to mention several, in a single course was evidence of a sort of culinary arms race widespread among the Roman elites. The inflationary use of boar was one way the well-off sought to one-up each other at the dinner table.

Trimalchio tried to outdo them all by serving up a specimen that was not merely big and beautifully decorated; he trumpeted his virility by reanimating the boar as a lactating female by virtue of the pastry piglets. The stunt of having live birds emerging from this boar was meant to surprise and to draw attention to the host's capacity to pull off such a spectacle.

Incidentally, the Roman author Macrobius (fourth century CE) decries a similar dish as an example of especial decadence.[95] The dish in question is aptly and charmingly called '*porcus Troianus*' ('Trojan pig') and consisted of a gutted pig stuffed with the meats of other animals. Macrobius mentions it in his stinging critique of Roman excess and explains its association with the more famous Trojan horse by analogy. The pig, he states, 'is "pregnant" with other animals enclosed within, just as the famous Trojan horse was "pregnant with armed men"'.[96] The decadence infiltrates the dining room by stealth, just as Greek soldiers once invaded the city of Troy (see the previous chapter). Of course, we should not mix up pig with boar. As we have seen above, it matters that Trimalchio is serving up boar here, a wild animal, and not its domesticated counterpart, the pig. And yet at least in the mode of its preparation, Trimalchio's stuffed boar constituted a variation of a dish that became synonymous with the most extravagant forms of gluttony and decadence. By serving up what, following Macrobius, we may want to call 'Trojan boar', Petronius parades a dish rich in symbolic flavour. The boar in question is stuffed with a variety of social connotations that bring out different aspects of human identity: it combines notions of social class and masculinity; in its decadent exuberance it also helps to expose the futile efforts of those at the margins of Roman society to make their way to its core.

Over time, unchecked and conspicuous consumption at private banquets and dinner parties became a veritable problem for the Roman state. During the third, second, and first centuries BCE, it thus tried to curb these excesses through officialdom and governance. A number of sumptuary laws (*sumptuariae leges*) were passed which sought to confine the most egregious.[97] And yet, Hellenistic and Roman literature abounds in examples of privileged overindulgence. Whether meat was involved or not – it often was – excessive consumption of local and exotic foodstuffs became the craze of the day. A whole literature on dining reflected ever more pompous presentation of food, drink, and entertainment at dinner parties. Some authors described the lavish dinner parties of the upper classes both past and present, extending them into the realm of (an equally exuberant) literature.[98] Others struck a more critical tone, highlighting them as perversion and overindulgence and calling for moderation.[99]

Incidentally, in the critical responses to culinary overindulgence, the boar was singled out to represent the worst forms of excess: among the critical voices we find one already familiar to us: that of Cato the Elder (234–149 BCE). As Censor, he decried the consumption of boar bacon as an unacceptable luxury.[100] And it is also not just the over-consumption of boar that became the subject of criticism, but the hunt itself could be portrayed as excessive through satire: in his play *Casina*, the Roman author Plautus (ca 250–184 BCE) represents himself as a hunter who sets out to kill not one but two wild boars all by himself.[101]

Most of these critical voices speak to us from the Republican period (509–27 BCE), while Petronius wrote his *Satyrica* during the Early Empire, when Rome had become a monarchy again. Yet Trimalchio's *Cena* belongs firmly in this context.[102] Overindulgence, competitive consumption, and exuberant luxury continued to spread during the empire, with some of the worst excesses now being committed by the Roman emperors themselves.

In the figure of Trimalchio, the freedman who seeks to parade his wealth and social standing in front of his peers, Petronius represents the practice of competitive consumption by actual and aspiring members of the elite and renders it *ad absurdum*. What Petronius offers as a parody is in effect a scathing criticism of the social realities of Rome during the early years of empire. In particular, he points to the fact that during this period, substantial numbers of ex-slaves turned freedmen could attain considerable wealth through the economic possibilities that presented themselves without ever being able to join the ranks of the prime movers and shakers politically: they were not admitted to senatorial class, could not hold public offices, and were excluded from state priesthoods. Moreover, as the figure of Trimalchio painfully reveals, as far as Petronius is concerned, wealth does not necessarily bring true class. In Petronius' view, it takes tradition, the right outlook that only old money will bring, and, above all, an education.

In the end, the host might have excited his impressionable guests of fellow freedmen, but not the reader of Petronius' story. Trimalchio's dish – like his dinner party more generally – is all smoke and mirrors. Some of the dates served with the boar seem to be substandard.[103] And the boar itself is also not what it seems. The attentive reader may recall that it is decorated with a 'cap of freedom', the symbol and sign of manumission. This is because it had already served as the centrepiece at another, similar occasion the night before. 'Yesterday when this animal appeared as *pièce de resistance* at dinner, the guests let him go; and today he comes back to dinner as a freedman.'[104] The boar, it turns out, is yesterday's leftovers. Because it was spared the day before, Petronius is able to present it a second time – now adorned with the *pilleus*, a kind of felt cap that was typically worn by those who had just been released from slavery.[105] That the boar is presented here as a 'freedman' (*libertus*) is, of course, deeply ironic. After all, those about to devour it are themselves freedmen. Just as this peculiar 'freedman' is not really free, the guests of Trimalchio's party remain hogtied by their very own pretension and aspirations without ever being able to demonstrate true class.

DIGESTIF ANYONE?

It might be tempting to think that the days of Trimalchio and his like are long gone. And yet in the modern world, exuberant dinner parties have lost little of their captivating alure. The traces of Petronius' *Dinner of Trimalchio* are still prominently on show in F. Scott Fitzgerald's famous novel *The Great Gatsby* (1925). Prior to its publication the novel went under the title 'Trimalchio' or 'Trimalchio in West Egg'. Apparently, Fitzgerald was argued out of such an overt classical reference by his editors who – in an ironic twist on the educational deficits of Trimalchio and his guests – considered his name too difficult for modern audiences to digest.[106] And yet, in this scathing – and highly amusing – critique of Long-Island society and its peculiar blend of old and new money during the so-called 'Jazz Age' (roughly the time during the 1920s and 1930s), Fitzgerald evokes a milieu that recalls the excesses of Trimalchio and his admirers in various ways. Even though wild boar is not on offer at the social gatherings taking place in the Gatsby residence, 'spiced baked hams crowded against salads of harlequin designs and pastry pigs' very much are. Obviously pretentious foods and drink and show-offish banter still make the day.[107]

As far as wild boar is concerned: it remains an important food item in Italian cooking, where *cinghiale* is a prized delicacy even though these days it is rarely, if ever, served-up 'Trojan-style'. Beyond this particular dish, it is certainly true that, in the present, meat has lost little of its symbolic value.[108] Many people still find it an essential item on the dinner table, especially when entertaining.

It should therefore come as no surprise that we continue to define and evaluate individuals and even whole peoples by their meat-eating habits. The French refer to the English as 'les rosbifs' ('the roast-beefs') and the English to the French as 'frogs'. The latter references the fact that frog legs have traditionally made an appearance on French menus. But it is not just here that we single out those who consume the 'wrong' kind of meat. Frog leg is one thing. Horse meat another. Fried insects or – particular horror – dog meat is beyond acceptable. Hot dog is ok albeit not exactly a marker of high social standing.

As one of the most succinct expressions of the hierarchical view of human and non-human animals that has dominated Western thinking (at least) since classical antiquity, the consumption of meat (or the conscious abstinence from it) is tied up with notions that define aspects of the human animal. The association between meat-eating, masculinity, physical strength, social standing, and influence is still going strong, even if the particulars of this symbolic link may take on different forms and formulations in the present.

In the ancient world, being a vegetarian meant being excluded from most public festivities and banquets which revolved around the communal consumption of meat. In the modern, practising vegetarians are no longer social outsiders. There is now a growing number of people – both male and female and mostly urban, middle-class, and well-educated – who pursue another kind of vegetarianism that seeks the conscious break with a tradition linking masculinity with the consumption of meat and human with the exploitation of animals. Some men have sought to develop a different masculinity, one that no longer defines itself through the consumption of meat and other traditional markers of maleness. To them, abstinence from animal products is a form of rebellion, a turn away from the traditional expectations of males and male bodies and towards a mode of existence that steps out of the old patriarchal structures. This form of masculinity places more emphasis on ecological and ethical concerns and arguments. Even if – unlike the ancient philosophers practising vegetarianism – they rarely live what the ancients would recognize as 'a life of the mind', they certainly seek a more mindful existence.

And yet, it remains to be seen whether this form of dietary choice and the human identities it supports can ever reach the centre of society. Until this is the case, we continue to chew on our Sunday roasts and dream of being better, healthier, more principled, more ecologically conscious humans than many of us – the author of this book included – really are.

CHAPTER 7

The next two chapters focus on the role of the animal in the shaping of political identities, ancient and modern, collective and individual. Chapter 7 revolves around a peculiar human habit that seems to have been popular in the ancient world but that is still with us today: attributing political qualities to honeybees. By distinguishing a 'queen bee' from 'workers', we continue a tradition that has its roots in classical antiquity and in Aristotle's inclusion of honeybees among the *zōa politika* (the 'political animals').

But why do honeybees 'need' politics? And why does human politics 'need' honeybees? The answer to these questions in the context of the ancient world shows what is at stake in the current attempt to compare humans and other social animals, not merely for the purpose of theorizing about human politics but in the scientific study of the natural world itself.

Unlike other chapters in this book, this one does not start with a story. And yet aspects of narrative and storytelling come into the picture in other ways. Narrative here appears as both a force inscribed in nature itself and as a form of sense-making that allows us to humanize the behaviour of animals by attributing them with human intentions and motivations. At the same time, to naturalize often means to normalize a political system in ways that draws on the idea that because something occurs in nature it is by definition good.

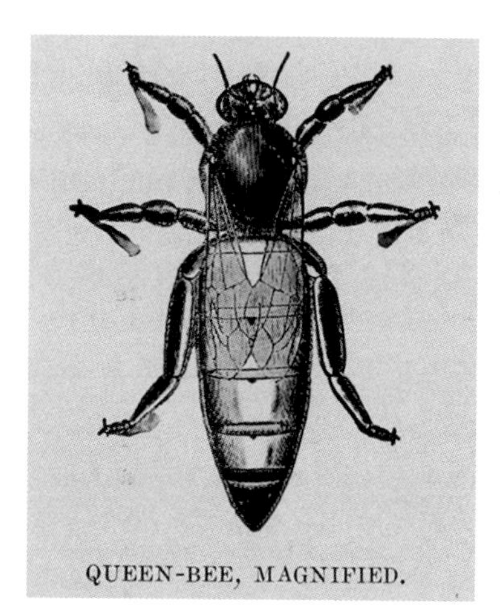

7.1. Queen-bee (magnified), From E. F. Philips. *The Habits of the Honeybee* (1914). © Wikimedia Commons.

The Political Bee (*Apis politica*)

In his book Honeybee Democracy, Thomas Seeley, a biologist at Cornell University, states that we get it all wrong when we think of the honeybee (*Apis mellifera*) as living in gigantic monarchies, gathered around a single, dominant queen. 'There is one common misunderstanding about the inner operations of a honeybee colony that I must dispel at the outset, namely that a colony is governed by a benevolent dictator, Her Majesty the Queen.'[1] Rather, he argues that it would be more accurate to view honeybee populations as a form of democracy in which decision-making rests with the common people. It is the 'workers' and not the 'queen' in charge of the operations of the colony; they carry out this task collectively and in communication with each other. The so-called 'queen' provides little more than reproductive leadership – all the 'workers' and 'drones' descend from her.

Honeybee colonies, Seeley argues further, are governed by complex collective decision-making processes. These processes are in play whenever a bee colony that has swarmed looks for a new place to live: 'When a honeybee swarm chooses its future home, it practises the form of democracy known as direct democracy, in which the individuals within a community who choose to participate in its decision-making do so personally rather than through representatives.'[2] Seeley shows that honeybees use their famous waggle dance like a language not only to inform each other of nearby food sources but also to indicate the location and quality of prospective sites to establish a new colony.[3] Individual scout bees identify and later promote different sites, trying to inspire additional dancers to support their choice. Once the swarm is in agreement, it takes off for the new home. Seeley thus concludes that rather than subjecting themselves to the overarching will of a single, dominant individual, implicit in the notion of a 'queen', honeybees participate in complex processes of decision-making and consensus-finding.

We will return to Seeley and his way of crediting honeybees with political qualities later in this chapter. Meanwhile, it must be said that he was by no means the first person to make such a connection. In re-badging honeybee society as a democracy, Seeley extends and revises a tradition with origins deep in the past: that of politicizing certain kinds of social animals, in particular the bee. The ancient Greek philosophers Plato, Aristotle, and Plutarch, the Greek authors Homer, Aristophanes, and Xenophon, and the Roman writers Varro, Virgil, Seneca, Columella, Pliny, and Aelian (to mention just a handful of examples), all set honeybee society in relation to human politics and society.[4] Indeed, the very idea Seeley seeks to revise – that of honeybee society as a monarchy – has an astonishingly long and influential history that leads right back to the classical past – and beyond.[5] Numerous ancient authors believed honeybees to be guided by a strong monarch and, in line with the gender realities in the ancient Greek and Roman city, they imagined this monarch to be male.[6]

Where did this interest in and knowledge of honeybees come from? In addition to the possibility of encountering them in the wild, domesticated (or perhaps better cultivated) honeybees had a ubiquitous presence in the ancient Greek and Roman countryside (but could be found in urban settings too).[7] In the ancient world, beekeeping became a widespread cultural practice and apicultural knowledge was accordingly well advanced, as evident in numerous surviving texts about beekeeping.[8] Beehives and the honey and wax generated by them provided sweet sustenance and additional sources of income. In addition to this economic significance, honeybees and the honey produced by them took on symbolic meanings. From Pindar (ca. 518–438 BCE) onwards, honey and honeybees were associated with poetry and the figure of the poet whose language was frequently thought to be as 'sweet' as honey.[9] Honey also came to play an important symbolic role in several rituals; local lore connected the bees producing it with the supernatural.[10] It is this economic, literary, and religious meaning of the honeybee in the ancient Greek and Roman worlds that provides the backdrop for the interest of thinkers in the inner workings of the hive.

Before we inquire into the buzzing of the political bee, we add that the humanizing and politicizing of honeybees did not end with classical antiquity. Rather, it was revisited and revived time and again in later periods. The idea that honeybees constitute some sort of polity analogous to human forms of government and social organization is one of the most widely used and persistent images in political philosophy from antiquity to the present.[11] Over time, it came to be invoked in support of different, even opposing, political ideologies: both Feudalism and Mercantilism drew on it, Napoleon Bonaparte made use of it, as did the French Revolutionaries and Nazi Germany.[12] Even the Vatican pointed to the communal life of bees to reference its own hierarchical structure with a single individual at the top.[13] And it is not just different political systems and forms of governance that appropriate the honeybee for their purposes, but the political philosophies supporting them too. Bees feature as an analogy to humans in Thomas Hobbes' *Leviathan* (1651), in Bernard Mandeville's controversial political treatise *Fable of the Bee* (1705/1714), and in Karl Marx' *Capital* (*Das Kapital*, 1867).[14] As the appositely named historian of ideas Bee Wilson put it: 'The hive has been, in turn, monarchical, ... communist, anarchist and even fascist.'[15] The kind of society honeybees were thought to inhabit changed together with the cultural and historical context and the political preferences of the day. Or, in other words: While life in the beehive will have remained the same throughout human history, the volatility of human politics is reflected in the different political qualities attributed to honeybees.

POLITICIZING THE NATURAL – NATURALIZING THE POLITICAL

The persistent buzzing of the political bee throughout the ages raises a question that goes right to the core of our understanding of politics: why does 'the political' need the honeybee? Given the human tendency – as evident in many other chapters of this book – to distinguish human nature as much as possible from that of other animals, the equating of human and animal societies is a curious move. Whereas other forms of human/animal entanglement follow, explore, challenge, and sometimes invert a sharp (essential) difference between man and beast, this way of relating humans to animals is grounded in the assumption of a fundamental analogy between them.

The political bee reveals a dimension of the conception of 'the political' that is not always apparent: its affinity to the natural world and to biology in particular. This affinity can take on many different forms and goes well beyond the politicizing of the honeybee, both past and present. It becomes evident, for example, in what has been termed 'bio-politics' – the inclination of certain political ideologies to administer, regulate, and control life in all its forms, as evident in the current struggles about abortion and reproductive rights in the United States.[16] It is also on prominent display in the way in which culture politics from the 1960s onwards has drawn upon socio-biology as an area of study that seeks to explain the behaviour of social animals (including humans) with reference to evolutionary biology.[17] In the highly contested arguments about whether evolutionary pressures determine our stance on questions of altruism and diversity (to give just two examples of the use and abuse of socio-biology to explain human behaviours) biology and political ideology remain uneasy bedfellows.

We shall return to the link between biology and politics in the modern world towards the end of this chapter. One more point, however, deserves mentioning up-front: with regard to the way in which the honeybee features in the ancient evidence, the affinity between politics and biology more often than not involves arguments from nature. That is to say that certain socio-political institutions and the values underpinning them are located in honeybee society with the ultimate aim of presenting them as natural – and thus universal. This move, in turn, allows these institutions to claim a higher degree of legitimacy than if they were merely human conventions. As Lorraine Daston (a historian of science) and Fernando Vidal (a modern political philosopher) point out in *The Moral Authority of Nature*: 'Naturalization imparts universality, firmness, even necessity – in short, authority – to the social.'[18] Indeed, this use of the natural world implicitly draws on the idea that because something occurs in nature it must be good. In a nutshell, then: numerous ancient and modern authors have politicized the honeybee in order to naturalize human politics.[19] This strategy has the effect that nature and the natural world can serve as seemingly impartial points of reference to evaluate human politics. I say 'seemingly impartial' because, contrary to all appearances, this normative conception of nature is just as much a human (ideological) construct as the idea of 'the political' itself.

ARISTOTLE'S POLITICAL BEES

In the ancient world, the naturalizing of the political found an early and prominent advocate in the works of the Greek philosopher and polymath Aristotle (ca. 384–322 BCE). And yet, he is not the first ancient author who politicized the honeybee. This honour arguably belongs to Homer who compares the constant trickle of Greeks gathering in an assembly with swarming bees emerging steadily from a cleft rock.[20] Yet Aristotle makes a good point of departure to start an inquiry into the link between honeybees and politics for two reasons: first, because of the influence he had on later authors; second, because his work brings together two traditions – political philosophy on the one hand and natural-historical observations on the other. Besides his famous works on political and moral philosophy, Aristotle also wrote extensively on natural history. Several of his works describe how individual physical and behavioural features map across the animal kingdom (humans included), and honeybees are one of the many species he refers to in detail for this purpose.[21]

That Aristotle, in his biological works, politicizes the honeybee and that he does so in ways that recall the political and social structures of the ancient Greek *polis* ('city-state') is not difficult to discern. It is already evident in his description of the members of honeybee society itself. Even though he acknowledges that some people call the 'queen' bee *mētēr* ('mother') – an apparent nod to her reproductive function – he does not himself do so. Like most other ancient authors, Aristotle, too, has honeybees governed by one or several kings (*basileis*) or commanders (*hēgēmones*). In addition, he is aware of the presence of other kinds of bees including 'worker bees' – simply *mellitai* ('honey bees'), *chrēstai mellitai* ('productive bees') or *ergatides*, from ancient Greek *ergazomai* ('to labour', 'to work'), and *kēphēnes* ('drones'). He also distinguishes between worker bees carrying out different functions in the hive.[22]

We should not make too much of this point. After all, Aristotle here is merely following contemporary nomenclature. And yet, the way in which he distinguishes between different inhabitants of honeybee society already has a decisively humanizing slant and betrays a distinct focus on those in power. It arguably also reflects a distinct preference for male over female leadership in ways that reflect the socio-political realities of the ancient Greek city.

The political slant of Aristotle's description of honeybee society and its analogy to the ancient Greek *polis* comes fully to the fore when he extends his empirical observations to questions of governance and leadership. Incidentally, both themes also feature prominently in his political philosophy in the context of human statecraft, where he shows an extended interest in the roles of the statesman, politician, and lawgiver. In *History of Animals*, we find it applied to the communal life of honeybees. He states that 'in each hive there are several "leaders" (*hēgēmones*), not only one; a hive comes to grief unless it has enough "leaders" in it'.[23] The way in which politics and biology come together becomes evident in how he accounts for this observation. He states that 'this is not because of any resulting lack of leadership but (so we are told) because they contribute towards the generation of the bees'.[24] So questions of reproduction directly matter to the internal stability of the hive. The underlying principle at work here is that of 'a balance between productive and reproductive forces'.[25]

Questions of leadership and good governance return again in the observation that follows; this time they are not explained away with a reference to the reproductive dimension. As Aristotle goes on to say: 'A hive will also fail if the "leaders" are too numerous: they produce factions in the hive (*diaspōsi gar*).'[26] No matter whether such observations are grounded in biological reality – occasionally hives do indeed produce more 'queens' which then take part of the hive off to found a new colony – how this information is presented here is telling.[27] Aristotle clearly seeks to formulate a general rule of what constitutes a stable bee society, and he does so by establishing a link between the number of leaders and the stability of the hive. The observation of nature almost seamlessly turns into theorizing about the principles and practices at work. When it comes to leadership in the beehive, there is an optimal number of leaders. Every deviation from this ideal – every more or less – results in a loss of stability of the community as such. Even though such observations about the principles and practices of bee leadership remain just vague enough not to encourage direct comparisons with any particular historical situations and constellations, the politics of the city-state is never far away in this description of life in the hive.

The concept informing such observations is the ancient Greek idea of good measure, according to which both too much and too little of something has adverse effects.[28] More specifically, it recalls Aristotle's principle of the mean (*mesotēs*), or 'golden middle', according to which an ideal state lies between excess on the one hand and a lack or dearth on the other. Aristotle developed this concept as a general principle informing various aspects of his philosophy. Most notably, perhaps, it shapes his virtue ethics and his political philosophy, both of which likewise feature a middling ideal.[29] Here we find it applied to honeybees.

So, how are we to explain the presence of a political dimension in Aristotle's account of the honeybee? What kind of considerations underpin it?

The answer lies in one of Aristotle's most famous and influential political conceptions: that of man as being by nature a *zōon politikon* (a 'social' or 'political animal', a 'creature of the *polis*').[30] That this conception is at the core of his understanding of the political as developed in his *Politics* and elsewhere is, of course, well known. What is perhaps less well known, in particular outside of the circle of those with an interest in classical philosophy, is the fact that humans are not the only species Aristotle includes under this label.[31] In a famous statement in the *History of Animals*, he also includes a number of other creatures. He states that 'the social animals (*politika*) are those which have some one common activity (*koinon ergon*); and this is not true of all the gregarious animals. Examples of social animals are man, bees, wasps, ants, cranes.'[32] So some gregarious animals share with humans the capacity to pursue a common *ergon* (a 'task' or 'matter'), and it is this feature, combined with their gregariousness, that qualifies them as a *zōon politikon*.

But this is just one of two meanings of a *zōon politikon* used by Aristotle.[33] In addition to this broader zoological sense that encompasses social animals of all kinds, Aristotle also applies the term in a narrower, political sense: this narrower sense refers to the ancient Greek *politikos* as simply meaning 'pertaining to the *polis*' and refers to a creature inhabiting a city – only the human.

So at least in the first, zoological sense, humans are not the only political animal; that group also includes others, like honeybees. And yet the human political animal does hold a special place in Aristotle's account of the continuum of living beings.[34] In Aristotle's oeuvre, humans serve as 'model or supreme, paradigmatic animal'.[35] This exemplary character explains why Aristotle's account of the socio-political life of honeybees seems to be modelled on human politics. Yet at the same time, there is also a reverse implication: *because of* their capacity to cooperate with each other in ways that resemble, however vaguely, human forms of social and political interaction, certain animals have the capacity to illustrate what it means to live a political life. This applies to all those belonging to the exclusive club of the *zōa politika.*

Aristotle's account of the principles and practices of honeybee society draws on their capacity to illustrate general principles at work. The normative element in his empirical theorizing about honeybee society emerges not only whenever the focus is on 'leaders' or 'kings'. It also shows in other ways. When he discusses the capacity of bees to collaborate and to contribute to a common task, he distinguishes between different kinds of bees according to their capacity to constitute a stable community: 'Now the good working bees (*chrēstai melittai,* literally: 'the useful bees'/'the productive bees') work to make the combs even, with the outer covering all smooth ... But the long bees (*hai makrai*) make the combs uneven (*anomala*) and the cover bulging ... and moreover the embryos and everything else (are) placed at random.'[36] This is to say that not all bees are created equal when it comes to their capacity or willingness to contribute to the common task. Some seem unable to execute certain well-established patterns and proportions. Aristotle's description of honeybee society is coloured by assumptions of the orderly and the disorderly, balance and imbalance, as evident in the language he uses to describe the working of the hive. The normative element of these observations is hinted at in the alignment of pairings of odd and even combs, regular and random arrangements of things in the hives, productive and unproductive hives, and productive and destructive bees. In short: it is the successful running of the hive's common task that provides the point of reference for the evaluation of its individual members.

Again, we could add further examples here. Aristotle's evaluation of honeybee politics extends into his account of factionalism in the beehive and his comments on a bee he calls 'the robber' (*fōr*) – the quintessential rogue element in honeybee society.[37] Yet one thing has already become clear: Aristotle's naturalism variously includes an evaluative dimension, and it does so in ways that recall the politics of the ancient Greek city-state. Even though the precise nature of this evaluation differs depending on whether the main focus is primarily on the natural world (as in Aristotle's writing on animals) or on human politics, it is always present when Aristotle speaks about sociality.[38]

By illustrating that man is not the only *zōon politikon*, Aristotle is able to make the case that life in a political community is not merely a human invention, the contingent outcome of cultural development, or a mere social convention, but the realization of a *natural inclination* that humans share with certain other animals.[39] The communal life of honeybees, as presented by Aristotle in those parts of his oeuvre that focus on the study of nature, thus reveals some of the underlying principles that also apply in human politics. In his account, principles such as cooperation and good governance appear to be already inscribed in nature (*physis*) itself.[40]

What drives such considerations is ultimately a form of looking at the world that has become deeply inscribed into the Western scientific tradition: that of analogical reasoning. Analogical reasoning is a form of thinking that sets two things in relation to each other in the ultimate intent to explain one through the other through shared features. In ancient Greek and Roman thought and literature, analogical reasoning has a long tradition. It goes all the way back to Homeric epic and the extensive use of similes to draw multiple lines between the human realm and the natural world.

Analogical reasoning is central to Aristotle's biological works.[41] He makes sense of the natural world and the place of the human animal within it by highlighting the apparent and less apparent similarities and congruences between them. By looking for parallels rather than differences between humans and other animals, Aristotle seeks to establish the larger patterns at play in the workings of nature.

This grounding of the political in nature allows Aristotle to refer to the natural world as an independent point of reference.[42] Aristotle's political philosophy takes nature to be a primary point of reference – a potentiality – which allows for an assessment (an evaluation) of how the political has been realized in a particular realm. In his oeuvre, the natural world thus features as a force deeply embedded in the lives of both human and non-human animals.[43]

NATURE'S NORMATIVE FORCE BEYOND ARISTOTLE

In the ancient world, the moralizing through honeybee society that we saw at work in Aristotle, was unfailingly attractive. It manifests itself in numerous Greek and Roman authors, writing in different genres. The conversation revolved around a number of recurrent themes: how do bees propagate?[44] Does the king bee have a stinger? If not, what does this say about his capacity to lead by softer, less intrusive, less piercing means? What does the example of the lazy drones and the way they are treated by the workers reveal about how labour is, could be, or should be distributed in society? These kinds of questions resonated widely.

The establishing of analogies between human and honeybee society is central to this endeavour. Unlike Aristotle, who inscribed political considerations directly into his description of honeybee society itself, many other ancient authors chose to detour by drawing parallels. This had the benefit of allowing for a more pointed comparison of humans and honeybees, and more explicit moralizing.

Two examples: in the writings of the Roman philosopher and statesman Seneca (ca. 4 BCE–65 CE), the king bee parades the qualities a good king should possess.[45] These consist, above all, in his *clementia* ('mercy', 'mildness', 'forbearance') – that is, his capacity to exercise restraint rather than to punish and pursue – a trait that Seneca deduces from the (mistaken) assumption that the honeybee at the top of the hive (his king bee) lacks a stinger. His account of the kind of leadership qualities of the king bee is rounded off in a way that makes sure that the moral of this observation is not lost on his human audience. As Seneca is quick to assert, 'Great kings will find herein a mighty precedent; for it is Nature's way to exercise herself in small matters and to bestow the tiniest proofs of great principles.'[46] The purpose of this analogy is not difficult to discern. If only human leaders – above all the Roman emperor Nero (37–68 CE) at whom these remarks are directed – could be convinced to follow nature's lead.

That not all human leaders do, in fact, follow the example set by the bee, is pointed out by another ancient author we have already variously come across in this book: Aelian (ca. 165–235 CE) – our second example. In *On Animals*, he draws on bees to contrast the benefits of kingship with the dangers of tyranny. As with Seneca, Aelian's honeybee monarch 'is at once gentle and inoffensive and also stingless'.[47] He provides a form of charismatic leadership which becomes evident in the fact that when he swarms and leaves the hive, he is readily tracked down by his subjects, who swiftly return him to the hive and reinstall him in his position 'of their own free will, indeed eagerly, for they admire his disposition'.[48] While the honeybee king thus enjoys great reverence and respect, this is not always the case with human leaders. As Aelian is quick to point out, 'but the Athenians drove out Pisistratus, and the Syracusans Dionysius, and other states their rulers, since they were tyrants and broke the laws and could not exhibit the art of kingship which consists in loving one's fellow-men and protecting one's subjects'.[49] Again, the moralizing message is hard to miss. For Aelian at least, the kind of stingless leadership exerted by the king bee is much more powerful – and hence stable – than the, at times, violent mode of governance exerted by the ancient Greek tyrants.

We could easily expand the list of examples here. In particular in Augustan literature, apian imagery, moralizing by honeybee nature, and political analogies and allegory abound. The political bee buzzes its way right through the writings of different authors and genres, some more literary, others more philosophical or, indeed, political. And sometimes the making of analogies morphs into the equally persuasive, but less obviously moralizing allegory, as in the works of the Roman poet Virgil (70–19 BCE) whose honeybees labour to sustain both king and community.[50] Yet the general thrust of this use of honeybee politics to naturalize human politics has already become clear: By highlighting real or perceived analogies to Greek and/or Roman political institutions in honeybee society, they are presented as natural and thus eternal.

HONEYBEES IN ROMAN WRITING ON NATURE: THE BEEHIVE AS *RES PUBLICA*

As it happens, the ancient conversation on honeybee politics includes a number of authors whose primary interest was not politics but the study of nature and the advancement of knowledge through its observation. This part of the conversation differs from the overt moralizing, politicizing, and allegorizing literature in that the ideological dimension here emerges merely as a by-product of the genuine aim of furthering an understanding of nature. The dissemination of knowledge about the communal life of honeybees through empirical observation remains at centre stage at all times.

A separate set of questions apply here: the point is not so much why does the political need the honeybee, but rather, why does the empirical observation of honeybees 'need' politics? In other words, why and how does the observation of nature end up in the vexed territory of politics? We will find that here, too, humanizing and politicizing readings of honeybees abound, but they occur in the service of an attempt to gain a deeper understanding of nature.

The example of the Roman author Pliny the Elder (23–79 CE) helps to illustrate this point. Pliny wrote an encyclopaedic work on nature from different points of view (cosmological, meteorological, geographical, natural history, mineralogical, and medical), including a book predominantly on insects.[51] It is here that we find his thoughts on honeybees.

If Aristotle's account of the communal life of honeybees recalls the ancient Greek *polis*, Pliny's evokes the Roman *res publica*. And again, as in Aristotle's case, this is evident above all in the kind of members that constitute honeybee society. In analogy to the Roman plebs, Pliny refers to the 'worker' bees as *plebes* ('plebeians', 'commoners'), while the 'drones' are called *fuci* (from Latin *fucus*, 'disguise', 'sham'), which he describes as 'imperfect bees' (*inperfectae apes*) presumably because they have no stingers and do not contribute anything obvious to the common good.[52] At the top of Pliny's honeybee society, however, we again find a strong male figure: a king bee (*rex*), ruler (*imperator*), or leader (*dux*).[53] This bee is of exceptional size and inhabits 'splendid separate palaces' in the bottom part of the hive.[54] Like the imperium-holding magistrates of his own time and the Roman kings of old, Pliny's king bee is surrounded by lictors (*lictores*) who protect his authority (*auctoritas*).[55]

In order to describe what he saw, and to make the life of honeybees intelligible to his readers, Pliny refers to words and concepts familiar to him and his audience. When it comes to honeybees, the realm of politics lends itself to this purpose. It provides Pliny not only with a language with which to describe the members and institutions of honeybee society but also a blueprint of its inner operations. This is to say that Pliny's account of labour and social stratification in honeybee society is modelled after the Roman socio-political order. It is not that Pliny's account ever loses its grounding in the observable and real: the observation of the collective life of honeybees remains his point of departure throughout. And yet, he seems selective in the kind of information he included. More specifically, he put the focus squarely on those aspects of honeybee society that resonate with the socio-political structures of his own time while ignoring others.

It is not just the members of Pliny's honeybee society that look strikingly Roman; the operations of the hive too look familiar. Pliny states that, 'they endure toil, they construct works, they have a government (*rempublicam habent*) and individual enterprises and collective leaders, and, a thing that must occasion most surprise, they have a system of manners (*mores*) that outstrips that of all the other animals, although they belong neither to the domesticated nor to the wild class'.[56] This is, as Pliny himself acknowledges, an astonishing observation. Not only does it articulate a distinct interest in a creature that does not fit into neat human distinctions. It also attributes to honeybees both a fully-fledged polity, Roman-style, and a system of social practices and conventions underpinning it (Latin *mores*: 'customs', 'manners', 'habits').

So, Pliny extends not just the institutions of Roman politics to honeybees but also the values underpinning them; he endows them with not just a *res publica*, but also the *mores* that sustain it. And these *mores* manifest themselves to a significant extent in the way in which honeybees go about their business of making honey, propolis (a kind of glue produced by the bees), and wax. Like Aristotle, Pliny attributes honeybees with a remarkable work ethic. He states that 'they go out to their works and to their labours, and not a single day is lost in idleness when the weather grants permission'.[57] Pliny notes that this capacity towards collective organization extends further into an impressive division of labour by which different worker bees pursue different tasks. 'For they do not feed separately, so that there shall be no inequality (*inaequalitas*) of work or food or time.'[58] At least among the commoners – the *plebes* – the notion of an equal share applies. This sense of equality extends to the policing of those who do not pull their weight: 'They keep a wonderful watch on the work in hand; they mark the idleness of any who are slack and chastise them, and later even punish them with death.'[59] So it seems, being a sluggard and slacking off at the expense of others is not an option in honeybee society.

This applies, above all, to those bees that we call drones (Pliny's *inperfectae apes*, or 'imperfect bees'). In his account, Pliny speculates that they may be stingless and that their sole role seems to be to assist the worker bees 'who consequently order them about, and drive them out first to the works, punishing laggards without mercy'.[60] What this punishment may involve becomes clear a little later when Pliny informs us that the worker bees drive drones out of the hive when there is a shortage of honey and that they also execute them.[61] Both observations are grounded in nature as one would still see it today: worker bees do indeed kill drones each autumn when food gets scarce.[62] It is the interpretation of their motivations by Pliny that includes a normative dimension into the description of their behaviour. By presenting the punishment of the drones as a direct consequence of their lack of effort in working towards a common goal, honeybee society seems to follow considerations of social justice and equality.

The examples show that Pliny draws on elements of narrative and storytelling to combine observation, description, and political interpretation. The Roman polity did not only guide his observations of nature but directly *shaped* the way he made sense of what he saw in honeybee society. The means by which this occurs is through 'emplotment'. Pliny's observations of the natural world feature honeybees as agents with complex motivations, intentions, and desires. Like characters in a story, individual bees, such as the king or the drones, fulfil certain roles. His empirical observations always retain the air of the descriptive and real, and never evolve into outright storytelling mode. And yet, by sketching scenes of life in the hive, Pliny's account of honeybee society draws on aspects of the story in ways that allow him to expose its inner workings. In particular, he uses the capacity of narrative to establish relationships of cause and effect to illustrate the kind of values that bind honeybee society.

The transition from the mere observation to evaluation is also evident in Pliny's account of the standing of the honeybee king. He emphasizes that the king's power is grounded not in brute force but in good leadership. Like Seneca and Aelian, he believes that the ruler or king does not need a stinger. But he does acknowledge the speculation of certain unnamed authorities on the topic who claim that the king either has a stinger and cannot use it or has none and 'is armed only with the grandeur of his office' (*maiestate tantum armatus*).[63] Despite – or perhaps because – of his *maiestas* ('dignity'), Pliny's honeybee king or leader enjoys great popularity among his subjects: 'The commons surround him with a marvellous obedience.'[64] The extent of this reverence is on full display when the hive swarms: 'When they have started, each one wants to be next to him and delights to be seen on duty; when he is tired they support him with their shoulders, and carry him entirely if he is more completely exhausted.'[65] If a king passes away, the resulting collective grief is so intense that the bees cease to leave the hive altogether, not even to collect food. Their response is 'to mass themselves round his body with a sorrowful buzzing'.[66] One cannot shake off the feeling that the king bee here enjoys a final farewell reminiscent of the great funerals of the Roman Empire.

The humanizing here emerges again in Pliny's speculation about the motivations of certain behaviours. To attribute feelings such as loyalty and grief to honeybees is to bestow a quasi-human touch. In Pliny's account, the values, considerations, and emotions driving the individual and collective life of honeybees are decidedly those of human society. And not just human: in several crucial aspects, the *respublica* of the honeybee is indisputably Roman. It is not only that the distribution of roles, powers, and loyalties in the hive resembles that of the Romans of the first century CE, but that the similarities extend to concepts like the king bee's *maiestas* and *auctoritas.* It seems that the words and concepts Pliny uses to describe honeybee society carry considerable cultural baggage which colours his further interpretation of the communal life of the honeybee in decisively Roman terms. He is looking at the natural world through Rome-tinted glasses.

It may be tempting to dismiss this simply as a lapse by an author writing at a point in time when the standards that guide scientific observation today were not yet in place. But to do so would not only disregard the fact that some of the fundamentals of our understanding of the natural world are already 'emplotted' in nature itself.[67] More importantly, perhaps, it would suggest that in the modern world scientific debates are conducted outside of prevailing cultural norms and values. This is not so.[68] In the modern world, too, our questions, insights, and modes of sense-making, scientific and otherwise, are deeply shaped by prevailing interests, cultural assumptions, and historical paradigms. This is not to say that science does not aim at (and, to some extent, achieve) an understanding of the authentic and real. But despite all its claims to neutrality, scientific inquiry always also points back to those (humans) at the other end of the looking glass.[69] It is just that this link is easier to discern in times and places other than our own. Pliny's humanizing and Romanizing account of the social life of the honeybee thus points to the deeply and unavoidably anthropocentric nature of *all* human inquiry, even that which wears the mantle of a seemingly impartial observation of nature.

SEELEY'S DEMOCRATIC BEES REVISITED

Returning from the ancient to the modern world, we may wonder whether it is really fair to include Seeley in this picture. Is there a link between the Cornell professor and the ancient literature on honeybee politics as suggested in the beginning of this chapter? More specifically, is there a difference between Seeley's fascinating study of honeybee consensus-finding and those ancient observations of nature which project political systems onto honeybee society? Or is this the same kind of anthropomorphizing and politicizing of the honeybee we found at play in the ancient world? Is it merely presented to us here in new, modern, democratic clothing – a clothing that we may find less conspicuous than the ancient attempts at naturalizing aspects of the political simply because it is more familiar?

Of course, apicultural knowledge has advanced considerably since ancient times. In its modern, institutionalized, and academic setting, the inquiry into nature – including that into honeybees – has refined its methodology, research design, and overall approach. It has gained further instruments of study through technological advances of all kinds – microscopes for a close-up look at honeybee physiology, more sophisticated observation hives, and, finally, high-resolution cameras that are able to track swarming honeybees in flight – all innovations that feature prominently in Seeley's account. As a result, it is undeniable that Seeley's work is grounded in more sustained and methodologically informed observation than that of his ancient predecessors. And yet there are parallels between his work and that of Aristotle and Pliny which reveal some underlying connections.

Seeley shares with some of the ancient tradition of nature writing not only the inclination to attribute to honeybees a political life similar to that of humans but also a disposition to regard them as exemplary in this respect. He pursues an explicit aim to derive 'lessons' from honeybee democracy for its human counterparts. These 'lessons' consist in a number of insights that he presents as directly transferable from honeybees to humans: 'Swarm smarts' as he calls them – whether bee or human – work best in relatively coherent groups (in terms of interests and reciprocal respect), if the influence of the 'leaders' is limited, if there are a number of different solutions to a problem to choose from, if there is ample space for debate, and if a quorum is sufficient to prompt a departure (literally, in the bees' case). When such a departure is warranted, a compromise is sought between accuracy and speed in decision-making.[70] All of these aspects make 'honeybee democracy' an example of a populace in which the collective intelligence of the swarm is greater than the sum of its parts.

Seeley argues that the closest equivalent to the form of direct democracy practised by honeybees can be found in typical New England town meetings, 'in which the registered voters who are interested in local affairs meet in face-to-face assemblies, usually once a year, to debate issues of home rule and to vote on them, rendering binding decisions for their community'.[71] Seeley finds truths close to home. He sets out to inquire into strategies of consensus-finding and decision-making among honeybees, whereas the ancient authors were interested in questions of good leadership and governance.

Like Pliny and other ancient authors before him, Seeley attributes to honeybees a high level of perfectionism in the procedures fundamental to their community. Indeed, he does not shy away from attributing them with a form of intelligence similar to humans. 'Swarm smarts' is only one way of putting this. Elsewhere he states that 'the reality of honeybee swarms making good decisions shows us that there really are ways to endow a group with a high collective IQ'.[72] So collectively, the inhabitants of the hive illustrate an intellectual capacity that significantly transcends that of its individual members. And, like some of the ancient authors, Seeley sets honeybee intelligence in direct relation to human forms of intelligence.

The main difference between Seeley and the ancient naturalists (including Aristotle), then, is that he draws on a conception of nature that, while related to that of the ancient authors, differs in its capacity to explain. In the twenty-first century, thinking about the relationship between humans and other animals is no longer grounded in vague notions about their kinship and the formative power of nature as was the case in some of the ancient authors. With Darwin's theory of evolution (and the rebuttal of creationism that came with it), the insight into the relatedness of phenomena in the natural world has been put on a firm scientific footing. Darwin's *On the Origin of Species*, first published in 1859, provided an explanation for the gradual presence of physical (and behavioural) features across the plant and animal kingdoms. His study *The Descent of Man*, published in 1871, extended the theory that he originally explained for plants and non-human animals to include humans. Homology in design and/or function across different species and the variation of forms within individual species could now be understood as the result of evolutionary pressures. With the principles of variation and natural selection, it named the kind of forces at play behind the continuum of phenomena in the natural world.

In his explanation of why the collective behaviour of honeybees is relevant for other creatures, most notably humans, Seeley draws on the theory of evolution. He states that 'evolution has repeatedly built higher-level units of biological organization: by assembling unified societies of lower-level units'.[73] That is, nature built more complex designs in form and function out of much simpler structures. This is why it is possible to compare human forms of governance and decision-making with their honeybee equivalent: 'The same sort of selection for extreme cooperation also happened with some societies of animals to produce the thoroughly harmonious, smoothly running insect societies that we can call superorganisms.'[74] Evolutionary pressure selected for optimal processes of decision-making results in similar forms and procedures among different kinds of beings.

To illustrate this point, Seeley takes us to a level of observation which is at once larger than a honeybee and smaller than a human. He sees honeybees as superorganisms which, in their design for information-sharing and decision-making, resemble the more complex design of the human body: 'Just as a human body functions as a single integrated unit even though it is a multitude of cells, the superorganism of a honeybee colony operates as a single coherent whole even though it is a multitude of bees.'[75] This complex design makes the insect swarm similar in acquiring and processing information to the human (or mammalian brain). 'We will see that natural selection has organized honeybee swarms and primate brains in intriguingly similar ways to build a first-rate decision-making group from a collection of rather poorly informed and cognitively limited individuals. These similarities point to general principles for building a sophisticated cognitive unit out of far simpler parts.'[76] So, evolutionary theory provides Seeley with a scientific basis for comparing honeybee and human forms of decision-making.

In 'swarm smarts', Seeley pursues an area of study that has recently gained considerable momentum in the biological sciences: collective forms of decision-making by non-human animals. This area of investigation seeks to draw on the behaviour of flocks, swarms, packs, and schools of animals to model collective human behaviour.[77] It is part of a broader interest of learning from the behaviour of animals, and insects in particular.[78] In the biological sciences, it is one of the most rapidly growing and vibrant areas of current debate.

Inevitably, this line of inquiry involves some degree of humanizing and anthropomorphizing. To make humans and honeybees comparable, scholars pursuing this line of inquiry have to map out the common ground between them. To speak of 'honeybee IQ' and 'honeybee democracy' is one way of doing this. Another way is to speculate about possible equivalences between them, as when Seeley states that 'it may be that finding a desirable tree cavity feels to a homeless scout bee as inherently pleasurable as feasting on a delicious meal does to a hungry human being'.[79] A third way takes a somewhat arresting turn: 'Bees ... serve as flying penises for the plants.'[80] Whatever one makes of this virilizing observation, it brings the wonderful and at times bemusing world of social insects in line with the much more familiar human one.

Again, it may be tempting to dismiss such statements and many biologists certainly shy away from using such language altogether. But to do so is to deprive us *a priori* of acknowledging that we are in many ways closely related to our furry and buzzy friends, that we share with them many features, and that we are able to learn about us by learning from them.

By highlighting those aspects of the collective life of honeybees that have an analogy (however remote) in human society and by describing them in the language of human politics, Seeley prepares the ground for their comparison. At the same time, he also makes the operations of the hive intelligible to a wider readership. And last but not least: the democratic reading of honeybees is also an attempt to make his data relevant to a group of readers who may not otherwise be interested in the operations of the beehive: those with an interest and stake in questions of statecraft and governance.

AND FINALLY ...

To sum up: honeybees constitute neither a democracy nor a monarchy – nor, indeed, any other form of human government. Of course, they are social insects in the definition of the American biologist Edward O. Wilson, in that they constitute 'a group of individuals that belong to the same species and are organized in a cooperative manner'.[81] But to refer to them in the language of constitutions and human politics is merely a way of saying that the collective life of bees in the hive *in some ways* resembles that of humans living in a democracy or monarchy. *In other ways*, however, for example in the exclusion of male drones from such decision-making, they are thoroughly undemocratic.

On the most general level, the buzzing of the political bee in select works of natural history, both ancient and modern, thus reminds us that all knowledge, even that which seems to be the product of impartial observation, is not value-free: it does not exist – or indeed, come into existence – in a vacuum but remains deeply embedded in our human ways of organizing and making sense of the world. What some may dismiss as a weakness of Seeley's account – its apparent and unapologetic anthropomorphizing – may thus be its greatest strength. Rather than hiding the human dimension under the mantle of a seemingly impartial scientific observation, Seeley embraces it and brings it to the fore. In doing so, he allows us to consider its implications.

Seen in the larger historical context of the human tendency (variously pursued throughout the ages) to project human politics on honeybee society, then, Seeley's work exposes a dilemma fundamental to all good scholarship: in order to be relevant to our lives, to have impact beyond the pursuit of knowledge for its own sake, our inquiries (scientific and otherwise) must speak to questions that matter. And what matters emerges in relation to us. But as far as the study of nature is concerned, the focus on relevance and impact does not come without its own challenges. This is because the establishment of analogies between human and animal lives often results in efforts to humanize and anthropomorphize. Again, we are left with the ambiguity of anthropomorphizing as a means of understanding real parallels and sympathies on the one hand and its distorting, anthropocentric qualities that we already noted in Chapter 3.

So, in a nutshell, the buzzing of the political bee in select ancient and modern authors raises a question which is as pressing as it is ultimately unanswerable: where does humanizing and politicizing end and where does genuine learning from nature begin? Or is there ultimately little difference between the two?

CHAPTER 8

This chapter extends the focus of the previous one by remaining in the realm of the political. Yet rather than collective political identities, it is the identity of the individual, critically inclined citizen who might deviate from the collective hum of the hive that is at stake here. To this end, the chapter investigates what Socrates may have meant when, in his infamous appearance before a jury at Athens in 399 BCE, he referred to himself as a *myōps* – typically translated as a gadfly. The chapter illustrates that the natural world (and non-human animals as part of it) does not just serve to naturalize (and thus normalize) collective political systems that are already firmly in place, as in the previous chapter. It also serves as a potent strategy to seek to naturalize (and thus normalize) the individual political stance outside of the collective. By carving out a space for dissent, Socrates defined a form of citizenship that resonates far beyond the ancient world. We will find it elaborated in Hannah Arendt's political philosophy, which touches on the Socratic gadfly in her critique of the perils of modernity.

8.1. Horsefly. © Wikimedia Commons/Person Scott Foresman Donation.

The Socratic Gadfly (*Haematopota oxyglotta socratis*)

ATHENS, 399 BCE. BEFORE A COURT OF 501 CITIZEN JUDGES, the philosopher Socrates – charged with corrupting the city's youth, not acknowledging the city's gods, and introducing new deities – makes the following statement, in which he compares himself to a gadfly and the city of Athens to a horse.[1]

> Now therefore, my fellow Athenians, far from making a defense on my own behalf, as one might suppose, I must make it on your behalf to prevent you from making a mistake regarding the gift the god has given you, by condemning me. For if you put me to death, you won't easily find another like me, literally, even if it's rather comical to say so, attached by the god to the city as if to a horse that, while it's large and of good stock, nevertheless is rather sluggish because of its size and needing waking up by some gadfly (*myōps*).[2]

This evocative statement is part of Plato's account of the trial, written after the death of his famous teacher. And yet, it is far from the most provocative claim Socrates makes on that day. His defence also includes the request that he not be punished but rewarded for his services to the community – preferably with free meals at public expense, like an Olympic victor.[3] All these claims may make us wonder: did Socrates on that fateful day at court (as represented by Plato) even try to defend himself? Or did he merely use the attention to give another example of his legendary methods of examining, questioning, and refutation, known as the *elenchus*, the 'Socratic method'?

In the years preceding the trial, Socrates had roamed the streets and public spaces of Athens, always on the lookout for suitable targets to exercise his skills in questioning and examination. In the present-day academy, Socrates would have been in serious trouble: throughout his life and career, he never published anything. Back then, however, 'publish or perish' was not yet a thing. All his thinking is known to us only because some of his most faithful pupils, in particular Plato, wrote it down. What is rhetoric? What is love? What is virtue? And: What do we know? How do we know? What is knowledge, anyway?[4] These are the kinds of questions Socrates explored in conversation with anyone and everyone available and willing to engage.

Socrates' defence as presented in the *Apology* addresses the specific charges but also speaks more broadly to the prejudices against him on the part of the populace. Some passages read more like a polemic, including his call for reward rather than punishment. Yet whether or not Socrates actually meant what he said during his day in court, his words certainly made an impression. It was just that, far from acknowledging Socrates' service to the community, the jurors seemed put off by the gadfly: the trial ends with Socrates being found guilty, handed the death penalty, and executed by the poison hemlock soon after.

What happened? And Why?

That Classical Athens – a vibrant city renowned for its democracy and the attractive environment it offered artists, intellectuals, and thinkers of all kinds – put to death one of its most illustrious public intellectuals remains difficult to explain. Modern commentators have variously suggested that the persecution for impiety (*asebeia*) – a notoriously vague charge – was merely a pretext and that the trial of Socrates was ultimately political in nature.[5]

A few years before the trial, the Athenian democracy had suffered two serious, if short-lived, blows in the form of an oligarchic coup.[6] The Peloponnesian War between 431–404 BCE, in which Athens and her allied states fought against Sparta and her allies, was the backdrop to this gap in the Athenian democratic tradition. In the wake of the harrowing Athenian defeat at Sicily, the democracy was overthrown in 411 BCE and replaced by a regime of 400 oligarchs. Even though their rule was quickly broken up, the underlying tensions did not resolve, resulting in a second coup in 404 BCE which lasted almost a year. As the teacher of Alcibiades and Critias, the latter of whom was a leading figure among the

Thirty Tyrants, Socrates was implicated in the politics of the day. His trial for impiety probably also reflected adverse sentiments towards a public figure viewed as a troublemaker when the political order of the city seemed more fragile than ever.

By referring to himself as a *myōps*, Socrates sketched an iconic image of his role that has resonated well beyond the ancient world. And yet we may wonder: why? The conceit of philosopher as stinging fly and of Athens as sluggish horse is certainly curious (Socrates himself refers to it as *geloioteros* – 'absurd' or 'fairly ridiculous').[7] After all, the blood-sucking, sleep-depriving, itch-producing gadfly is considered annoying rather than helpful. While horses frequently serve as metaphors and points of reference for political similes of all kinds, the gadfly is nowhere else associated with Socrates.[8]

So why did Socrates invoke the image in this situation? What was he trying to achieve?

In proposing an answer to these questions, I suggest that, rather than coming straight to the point, it is more helpful to approach it like flies of all kinds: in loops and circles. For this is how cultural meaning emerges– sidelong, by association, echoes, and detours. We do so on the assumption that the kind of attributes Socrates claimed for himself as the gadfly will have emerged from the associations blood-sucking flies evoked in the ancient audience.

CIRCLING THE GADFLY

We start off with a brief detour into the realm of philology as a pathway into culture. The ancient Greek *myōps* is an interesting choice of word because 'gadfly', the preferred translation in the English-speaking world, is by no means the only possible translation. Besides 'gadfly' or 'horsefly', as unambiguously attested in Greek literature, it can also denote a 'spur' or a 'goad' and so metaphorically speaking any kind of incentive or motivating force.[9] It is in this sense that Xenophon, in his treatise *On the Art of Horsemanship*, recommends using a *myōps* (a spur) to make horses leap over obstacles.[10] To make things even more complicated, *myōps* as an adjective denotes 'short-sighted' – the root of the English word 'myopic'.

So how do we know which meaning is relevant here?

In a recent article, Laura Marshall has made a strong case for 'spur' as the intended meaning of the word in the *Apology*.[11] Based on contextual considerations, she has shown that the reading of *myōps* as 'spur' or 'goad' resonates throughout Socrates' speech in court. However, so does the reading of *myōps* as 'gadfly' or 'horsefly'.[12] While Marshall's considerations are astute, the conclusion she draws from them – that the proper meaning of *myōps* in the *Apology* is 'spur' and that to render it as 'gadfly' a mistranslation – seems unnecessarily limiting.[13] Instead, I suggest that Socrates used the ambiguous *myōps* on purpose. Had he aimed for clarity, he could have used the straightforward *oistros* for gadfly or the less ambiguous (at least in juxtaposition with the horse) *kentron* for spur.[14] Socrates chose *myōps* because at least two and perhaps even all three meanings of the word – gadfly, spur, and short-sightedness – resonate with his persona. And not just that. The three meanings of *myōps* point to and reinforce each other. So, the loops and circles of the *myops* reveal different aspects of Socrates' personality and the role of the politically active citizen at Athens.

To start with short-sightedness: this meaning is not usually considered to apply to Socrates, for the simple reason that there is no evidence whatsoever to suggest the philosopher was myopic. And yet we variously hear that Socrates was affected by a peculiar condition of the eyes. In a passage in Plato's *Theaetetus*, for example, one Theodorus sets out to tell Socrates about another young man.

> If he were handsome, I should be very much afraid to speak, lest someone should think I was in love with him. But the fact is – now don't be angry with me – he is not handsome, but is like you in his snub nose and protruding eyes, only those features are less marked in him than in you.[15]

This passage resonates with various others which also report that Socrates' eyes, quite literally, stood out.[16] Combined with the snub-nose mentioned above, they would have given the ancient philosopher a piercing gaze.

Did Socrates suffer from a disorder called *exophthalmia*, a thyroid condition, one notable symptom of which is protuberant eyeballs?[17] Whether this is the right diagnosis or not, Socrates' insect-like, bulging eyes point to the gadfly as one of the other meanings of the word *myōps*. Moreover, before the invention of optical lenses, in order to see clearly a myopic person would have to get a lot closer to an object than an ordinary person. And Socrates indeed tended to 'look' closely at things, much more closely than the average person. And then he would turn around to make others see them too.[18] So there may, after all, be a link between his eyes and the deeper form of 'seeing' promoted by Socrates.

Yet it is not just the gadfly and the ocular condition that resonate with each other. The same applies to the spur and the gadfly as further meanings of *myōps*: both describe a piercing force capable of inspiring action in a much bigger beast. Indeed, the very word that Aristotle uses to describe the body part that the gadfly, horsefly, and gnat use to elicit sustenance from their victims is *kentron* which (as pointed out above) doubles as the word for 'goad'.[19] The ancient Greek verb *kentroō* thus means both 'to furnish with a sting' and 'to strike with a goad'.[20] So there are multiple references between the individual meanings of the words and the images and associations evoked by them, all of which resonate with Socrates.

As far as the goad and the gadfly are concerned, differences between them spring from the kind of force we assume to be at work and its effects on those at the receiving end. The spur is a disciplinary device used by a rider.[21] This makes it well suited to point to the similarly educational Socratic method of teaching. The gadfly, by contrast, serves no obvious pedagogical purpose. And yet, the response evoked by the gadfly describes better than the spur those shifts and transformations Socrates' teaching inspired. The spur's purpose is to make a horse move in a certain direction (e.g. to vault obstacles, as in the example from Xenophon above). The gadfly, by contrast, prompts a much more unpredictable response. Anyone who has witnessed or experienced a gadfly, horsefly, mosquito, or gnat in action knows that these insects can make their prey move quite suddenly and in unexpected ways.

As the Greek author Oppian observed during the second century CE:

> Yea, for oxen also, when the cruel gadfly (*oistros*) attacks them and plunges its arrow in their tender flanks, have no more regard for the herdsmen nor for the pasture nor for the herd, but leaving the grass and all the folds they

> rush, whetted by frenzy; no river nor untrodden sea nor rugged ravine nor pathless rock stays the course of the bulls, when the gadfly hot and sharp impels, urging them with keen pains. Everywhere there is bellowing, everywhere range their bounding hoofs: such bitter tempest drives.[22]

This capacity of the gadfly to instigate a sudden and unpredictable departure seems to fit the outcome of the Socratic method, which encourages leaps and associations, and which, more frequently than not, ends in *aporia* (an impasse), with no clear answer or outcome in sight.

The sudden and unpredictable lurch that the gadfly can inspire in much larger creatures is also on prominent display in the myth of Io, in which the effects of the gadfly – referred to as *myōps*, sometimes as *oistros* – are so harrowing it has its own adjective: the ancient Greek word *oistroplex* means 'stung like a gadfly', and metaphorically speaking 'driven wild'.[23] This myth revolves around a young maiden who was unfortunate enough to trigger the fancy of Zeus. Transformed by her lover into a white cow to conceal his extramarital affairs, Io is driven on – and driven mad – by a pesky gadfly inflicted on her by the goddess Hera.[24] She wanders the world with an increasing sense of doom and desperation until Zeus finally returns her to human form so he can liaise with her once again. Here, too, the gadfly stirs another creature to move about with no clear sense of direction.

The panic this tiny creature can instil in others and the link between the gadfly and the divine are even more prominent in another ancient story. In the *Odyssey*, the effect of the goddess Athena on Penelope's suitors is likened to that of a gadfly on cattle. Odysseus and his son Telemachus have just despatched their share of the suitors when the focus moves to the presence of the divine in the following simile: 'Athene held up her aegis, the bane of mortals, on high from the roof, and the minds of the suitors were panic-stricken, and they fled through the halls like a herd of cattle that the darting gadfly (*oistros*) falls upon and drives along in the season of spring, when the long days come.'[25] This is the earliest example in which the gadfly serves metaphorically for someone able to instigate action. Cattle and suitors alike disperse in panic as soon as they make out the identity of their pursuer – the gadfly and Athena, respectively.

So, it seems Socrates was not the only or even the first person in the ancient world to invoke the metaphorical gadfly. In claiming the image for himself, he drew on an existing tradition. Moreover, like the god-sent gadflies of Greek thought and literature, Socrates considered himself to be on a divine mission. He makes this point in the same breath as he refers to himself as a *myōps*, (see the quote in the beginning of the chapter). The point is reinforced when he reminds the jury: 'The god has attached me to the city – the kind of person who wakes you up, prevails upon you and reproaches each one of you and never stops landing on you all day long all over the place.'[26] The god in question here is Apollo, who inspired Socrates through an oracle to examine his fellow Athenians in order to find out whether any were wiser than he.[27] The role of the gadfly is to stir up the horse (read: the *polis*) which, albeit a noble ('well-bred') creature, is always at risk of becoming too set in its ways. In other words: whenever there is the risk of the city becoming too complacent, the gadfly swings – or buzzes – into action.

But that's not all that can be said about the cultural meanings of the pesky insect. Further potentially relevant associations emerge if we consider not only gadflies but blood-sucking flies more generally. As has already become clear from some of the examples above, there seems to have been confusion in the ancient world as to which flies sting and which merely buzz. The ancient Greeks seem to have used different words to refer to essentially the same or similar animals. Despite Aristotle's attempts to distinguish between two separate animals, *myōps* and *oistros* were sometimes used interchangeably to refer to the gadfly in particular; and sometimes even the common fly (*muia*) was credited with the capacity to sting.[28] In catching contemporary associations of the gadfly, we can thus cast our net a bit wider and consider blood-sucking flies more broadly. One more loop around the ancient evidence in another direction reveals a further dimension of blood-sucking flies which may be relevant to Socrates' gadflyism: in the ancient world, they were sometimes ascribed certain character traits.

In his treatise *The Fly*, the satirist and rhetorician Lucian of Samosata (ca 120–180 CE) has astonishing things to say about this tiny insect.

> Of her courage and bravery it is not for me to speak, but for Homer, the most mighty-mouthed of the poets; for when he seeks to praise the

> foremost of the heroes, he does not compare his bravery to a lion's or a leopard's or a wild boar's, but to the fearlessness of the fly and the daring and insistency of her attack.[29]

Given that he speaks of the fly's offensive capacities, it is clear that Lucian here does not mean a regular fly, but a biting fly. And as a small and vulnerable animal that takes on much bigger prey, its characteristics are decisive: courage and bravery.

A quick look to Homer confirms that Lucian here is not just offering a comical aggrandisement. In the *Iliad*, a blood-sucking fly could indeed serve as the animal of choice to illustrate daring and audacity in humans. When the goddess Athena intervenes to instil more courage in the Greek hero Menelaus, for example, this occurs not, as one might expect, with reference to lions or tigers but to the humble fly: 'And she put strength into his shoulders and his knees, and in his breast set the daring of the fly (*muia*) that, though it be driven away often from the skin of a man, ever persists in biting, and sweet to it is the blood of man; with such daring she filled his dark heart within him, and he stood over Patroclus and hurled with his bright spear.'[30] Again a biting fly features here and again it represents human courage. This small and relatively powerless animal, it seems, has the capacity to show more strength and daring than a big and powerful beast.[31]

In using the image of the gadfly, was Socrates making a point about his own courage in fulfilling this important role for the state? Did he suggest that he, too, was ultimately small fry, but that he had the capacity to see off a much bigger beast? Of course, we do not know whether Socrates had Menelaus and the *Iliad* in mind when he referred to himself as a gadfly; nor do we know whether he intended to reinforce the point that he, too, was on a divine mission like other famous gadflies of Greek thought and literature; nor, indeed, can we tell for sure whether he made the point that like those of the hapless Io, the 'wanderings' of those he taught had no clear direction and obvious destination. Yet at least some of the more overt cultural references to the fly provided the background to Socrates' use of the image to describe his own teaching and his relationship to the city.

By choosing the word *myōps* to refer to himself in his speech at court, Plato's Socrates invoked an image that related to his situation in more ways than one. Such ambiguity, and the puzzlement it may have engendered in the ancient audience, is not at all out of character for the famous philosopher. It fits well with the tongue-in-cheek Socrates we know from other parts of the Platonic corpus: a figure on record elsewhere as using wordplay and the ambiguities of language to tease and challenge his interlocutors in more ways than one.[32]

At this stage, we extend the scope of our investigation to include the modern world and, in particular, the modern cousins of the Socratic gadfly. Bringing them into the picture helps us to see the significance of the figure of the gadfly in modern politics. It also allows us to see more clearly what is at stake in its ancient, Socratic impersonation.

ON ANCIENT AND MODERN GADFLIES

If the ancient figure of the *myōps* allowed for different readings, pointing to different aspects of the ancient philosopher's personality, vocation, and in particular his relationship to the city, the modern reception has been much more definite: The English-speaking world in particular has consistently favoured the gadfly over other possible translations of the word, to the extent that outside classical scholarship, the other meanings of *myōps* are rarely, if ever, considered.[33]

This is because in the figure of the gadfly, Socrates has evoked a creature that has lost none of its original sting 2,500 years on. Fast-forward into the present, it appears that the role is as relevant as ever. In the media, the gadfly brand is currently extended to a number of high-profile public figures, including (but not limited to) the Turkish author and Nobel prizewinner Orhan Pamuk, the American screenwriter and filmmaker Michael Moore, the Australian activist Julian Assange, and the American whistle-blower Edward Snowden.[34] These days, gadflies clearly come from different walks of life: literature and filmmaking, journalism and information technology – a point which is in itself revealing. It is not so much that at present the gadfly's natural habitat has expanded beyond politics; rather, these days *everything* has become political.

Perhaps it has always been that way.

Like Socrates, all these individuals continue to goad the status quo by exposing truths unwelcome to some. They challenge authorities of different kinds and question long-established certainties. Like their ancient predecessor, these gadflies take issue with a variety of different themes and topics. Some of them are pursued with the force of the law and find themselves imprisoned. For ancient as for modern gadflies, speaking up comes at a stiff price.

Can these modern impersonations of the gadfly help us understand the ancient figure? What (if anything) do they reveal about the figure of the gadfly as such? And what deeper truths do they expose about the political systems of which they are part?

THE GADFLY: AN AMBIGUOUS FIGURE

The look at the gadfly in the current social and political milieu points to what is arguably its defining feature: inherent ambivalence. Moore, Snowden, Assange – the public give starkly different appraisals of their role and function in society. Some praise them for upholding important democratic values such as transparency and accountability; others decry them as traitors and seek to throw the book at them. To call someone a gadfly can be either compliment or slur. The gadfly polarizes.

It may be tempting to conclude that this polarizing quality is a symptom of the deep ideological polarity and partisanship that have come to define many Western democracies in the first quarter of the twenty-first century. After all, these days we disagree fundamentally on many far less weighty matters, so why not on a figure that targets the centre of the political sphere, broadly defined? And yet if we look back at the ancient world and the way in which Plato presented Socrates in the *Apology*, it becomes evident that this very same polarizing quality is already present in the ancient creature itself. Some Athenians found Socrates' way of looking at the world intellectually stimulating, others deeply unsettling. In particular, members of the younger generations seem to have enjoyed engaging in conversation with him – hence, the accusation of 'corrupting the youth'. To them, the gadfly served as a perpetual motivating force which, like a goad to a horse, prompted them to make the leap and investigate the principles and practices of human existence. The more traditional segments of society, however, found his questions and his inclination to challenge existing positions abrasive and unhelpful.

The Greek author Diogenes Laertius (first half of the third century CE), for example, describes the response of some to Socratic teaching as follows: 'Owing to his vehemence in argument, men set upon him with their fists or tore his hair out.'[35] If Socrates here elicits violent reactions, other authors depict him as propagating knowledge that is at best specious, and at worst dangerous. Socrates' contemporary, Aristophanes, got considerable traction by depicting the philosopher in pursuit of absurd knowledge. In his comedy *Clouds*, staged at Athens in 423 BCE, he has Socrates and his pupils explore the question how many feet a flea can jump and whether gnats hum with their mouthparts or their backsides.[36] This is certainly comic licence. And yet it shows that some at least found the gadfly's presence in the city pointless and unhelpful, and his teaching annoying.[37] It also put Socrates dangerously close to those who came to be known as 'the sophists': a group of philosopher-teachers accused of teaching the power of persuasion without moral conscience – for a fee. In *Clouds*, Socrates is depicted as the go-to man to render a weak argument stronger.

The image of the gadfly, as used by Plato's Socrates, includes a critical dimension. Indeed, Socrates' speech in court is fundamentally shaped by the desire to acknowledge the antipathy of some to the gadfly's presence in the city on the one hand *and* to present this very presence in a more positive light on the other. The first dimension becomes evident when he points out that to slap the gadfly would be a grave mistake: 'It may be perhaps because you are irritated, like people in a half sleep being woken up, you would swat me ... and easily put me to death.'[38] In raising the possibility of finishing off the insect by force, the image of the gadfly anticipates the outcome of the trial. Gadflies are relatively easy to swat: anyone can do it with no great consequence. Yet, as Socrates is suggesting further: why would anyone want to, given its great benefit to the city? As he himself remarks: 'Then you'd spend the rest of your lives asleep, unless the god were to send you someone else, in his care for you.'[39] Put more succinctly: no pain, no gain! The gadfly is an asset to the city rather than a liability; its sting is a necessity, a divine gift, that fulfils an important function.

Given the gadfly's polarizing effects, Socrates' pitch to the Athenians for free meals rather than punishment is less outlandish than it first appears. It can be taken to be a desperate (and ultimately unsuccessful) attempt, argued from a defensive position, to counter the negative image of him sketched by his accusers by presenting himself in a more positive light. Socrates tries to go on the offensive and turn things around by convincing the judges that a different, more generous view of his role is warranted.

Of course, today we might wonder whether it was really necessary to kill the fly and despatch it to the underworld? Why not simply shoo it away? Unfortunately, the great Athenian institution of ostracism – exiling a citizen deemed dangerous to the community for ten years with no loss of reputation or assets – was apparently not an option, having fallen out of fashion a few years earlier.[40] Even though Athenians still voted every year on whether to hold an ostracism, no one was exiled after 417/416 BCE. Socrates may simply not have been important enough to warrant an ostracism. An indictment, especially for a vaguely defined offence such as impiety, might have seemed the best solution.

Moreover, making Socrates leave the city would have stripped the gadfly of its sting – a punishment he might have considered worse than death. The relationship between the gadfly and the horse is symbiotic: horse sustains gadfly just as much as gadfly supports horse.[41] Socrates needed Athens just as much as – or perhaps even more than – Athens needed Socrates.

Once he was on trial, however, events ran their course. Athenian court procedures in the late fifth and early fourth centuries BCE typically followed a two-step process: first, the judges decided whether Socrates was guilty or not. Once he had been found guilty, they were asked to vote again on the appropriate punishment, of which the only two options were a modest cash penalty, or death.[42]

Facing a choice between such extremes, the majority of the judges chose the death penalty.[43] In doing so, however, they set a precedent that resonates to this day. The way in which many gadflies of the modern period are pursued relentlessly – some receiving death threats, some leaving home to seek refuge – recalls the fate of the Socratic gadfly: the famous trial, and its infamous outcome.

THE GADFLY IN MODERN POLITICAL PHILOSOPHY

The comparative perspective on the gadfly in the ancient and modern worlds has revealed a polarizing quality as its defining feature. Even though the traces of this polarity are, as I have shown, deeply engrained in the ancient evidence itself, Plato's Socrates nowhere explores it further. He is too deeply involved to make it the subject of explicit considerations.

Can a modern political thinker's attempts to theorize the role of the gadfly in society illuminate this feature further?

Before we set out to answer this question, it remains to be said that the Socratic gadfly's post-classical life was directly linked to the reception of Plato. What facilitated the flight of the gadfly from the ancient into the modern world was the fact that it came to inhabit the writings of those who theorized the social, political, and intellectual milieus of the modern area. Socrates appears in the works of such important thinkers as John Stuart Mill (1806–73), Friedrich Nietzsche (1844–1900), and Max Weber (1864–1920), to name just a few.[44] Together with Socrates, the gadfly has retained a presence in later periods and in areas that transcend the setting in which it first appeared.

One person in particular can help us understand what is at stake in the polarizing quality of the gadfly: the political theorist Hannah Arendt (1906–75). Her interpretation of Socrates and the gadfly contributes to a deeper understanding of a fundamental conflict faced by all gadflies, past and present. Moreover, Arendt's work helps to explain why the political gadfly remains important in the current climate and why it is worth saving the species from extinction.

Arendt is primarily interested in explaining the political and moral atrocities that shaped the first half of the twentieth century. And yet, the ancient world is a constant presence in her oeuvre. Arendt sketches her assessment of twentieth-century politics against the background of the ancient past. Classical Athens and Republican Rome, in particular, provided Arendt with an alternative reference point from which the maladies underlying the present come into clear focus. They served an instructive and a didactic role: instructive in that the ancient world provided insights into the very beginnings of the political tradition that shaped the history of the West; didactic in that ancient Greece and Rome provided models of the political different from those of modernity.[45] The figure of Socrates is central to this endeavour. Periclean Athens was a time when politics and philosophy, the 'vita activa' and the 'vita contemplativa' – two core concepts of Arendt's work – had not yet separated. Arendt considers this separation to be the direct outcome of Plato's portrayal of Socrates' trial.[46]

Central to Arendt's depiction of Socrates are three images that are applied to Socrates in Plato's dialogues: in addition to the gadfly, these include the midwife and the torpedo fish (or electric ray).[47] To Arendt, the gadfly, the midwife, and torpedo fish do not describe alternate views of the ancient philosopher; rather, they bring out different aspects of how Socrates interacted with his fellow citizens. The gadfly illustrates the original impetus that Socratic teaching provides. As Arendt (quoting Plato) states, 'Socrates is a gadfly: he knows how to arouse the citizens who, without him, will "sleep on undisturbed for the rest of their lives," unless somebody else comes along to wake them up again.'[48] The role of the gadfly is 'to disturb' – that is, to arouse the citizens to a level of alertness necessary for the practice of politics. Yet that is not all. Arendt asks further: 'And what does he arouse them to? To thinking, to examining matters, an activity without which life, according to him, was not only not worth much but was not fully alive.'[49] So the gadfly forces the citizens to slow down, to think things through, and to examine their world in conversation with Socrates. Or, in other words: the gadfly induces the citizens to give birth to their own views, which is where the midwife comes in.[50]

To Arendt, the image of the midwife draws on the specific tasks associated with this role in ancient Greece. In Classical Athens, midwives typically were older women past their childbearing years and no longer able to have offspring of their own.[51] Arendt observes that this reflects Socrates' own 'sterility' in that he had no doctrines of his own to offer but merely helped deliver the views of others. At the same time, the midwives of ancient Greece also played a crucial role in deciding whether an infant was fit to live, thus pointing to Socrates' role in deciding whether a newborn idea was viable or should be dismissed.

Finally, the torpedo fish. Arendt draws on the image to put the focus squarely on the possible effects that the death of an idea could have on those who have just brought it to life. In doing so, she shortcuts the ancient conversation in which the image occurs: in Plato's *Meno*, it is Meno himself (a politician from Thessaly) who applies the image to Socrates. It is instantly rejected by the philosopher who states that the comparison only makes sense if the torpedo fish would stun itself too – which it does not.[52] For Socrates shares in the numbness. Further disagreements then concern the question of what follows next. Meno clearly thinks that once the numbing has occurred, the conversation is over. Socrates, by contrast, insists that this numbness should not be the end of the story. Rather, it should induce those affected to seek answers more vigorously than ever. So, as far as the ancient evidence is concerned, Meno's understanding of the image is rejected at least in so far as the effects of the torpedo fish on society (the numbing) seems to be in opposition to that of the gadfly. Arendt does not engage with this part of the story. She merely uses the image of the torpedo fish to convey the idea that, more often than not, to have an idea refuted renders those who promoted it numb. And she acknowledges that Socrates shared in the resulting stasis.[53] In Arendt's account Socrates' own puzzlement was an important dimension of his teaching, something he passed on to or shared with those with whom he conversed.[54]

So, at least as far as Arendt is concerned, the gadfly prompts the citizens to go into labour, the midwife helps to deliver their views, and the torpedo fish stuns them when these views prove unviable. This description of the three images remains fairly consistent throughout Arendt's work. Significant differences then emerge in Arendt's views of the impact of these figures upon the city. These differences matter because they reveal a perspective on the Socratic gadfly we have not considered so far because it is not developed in the ancient evidence: its particular relationship to the city and her institutions.

Take, for example. the way in which the Socratic gadfly features in 'Philosophy and Politics'.[55] Even though the dominant metaphor in this article is Socrates as midwife, the gadfly does make an appearance too.[56] Arendt introduces the metaphor by making a point about the place of the philosopher within the city. She states that 'The role of the philosopher ... is not to rule the city, but to be its gadfly, not to tell philosophical truths but to make citizens more truthful. ... Socrates did not want to educate the citizens so much as he wanted to improve their *doxai* [opinions], which constituted the political life in which he too took part.'[57] The gadfly here is directly connected to Socrates' relationship to the citizens. Its aim is neither to dominate nor to rule – a role Plato later attributed to the philosopher – but to help the citizens reach and recognize their potential. The gadfly shows itself not only as a deeply political figure, but, as in the ancient world, beneficial and helpful.

Arendt understood perfectly well that this sort of interaction harboured the potential for conflict: she observes that 'nobody can doubt that such a teaching was and always will be in a certain conflict with the polis, which must demand respect for its laws independent of personal conscience, and Socrates knew the nature of this conflict full well when he called himself a gadfly'.[58] So, the Socratic method of arousing people to deliver their opinions potentially came into conflict with the city's insistence on the universal validity of its laws – an irresolvable tension at the heart of the political.

We should not underestimate the significance of this point. The friction Arendt observes here between gadfly and *polis* sets two conceptions of the city against each other: that of the *polis* as the place ruled by law and that of the *polis* as the sum of its *politēs* (citizens). It springs from a genuine conflict of interest between those *polis* institutions that propagate the binding nature of the law on one hand and, on the other, the individual who relies on personal conscience to help his fellow citizens attain truth and freedom.[59]

Possible disagreements between the city and the Socratic gadfly are also at stake in the way in which the gadfly features in 'Thinking and Moral Considerations'. This time the nature of the conflict involves the very core of what Socratic teaching is able to achieve. From the start, Arendt adopts a position much more critical towards the gadfly and its effects on society. Referring to thinking as wind (a metaphor Xenophon attributes to Socrates), she states:

> The trouble – and the reason why the same man can be understood and understand himself as gadfly as well as electric ray – is that this same wind, whenever it is aroused, has the peculiarity of doing away with its own previous manifestations. It is in its nature to undo, unfreeze as it were,

what language, the medium of thinking, has frozen into thought – words (concepts, sentences, definitions, doctrines).[60]

As the human activity the Socratic gadfly inspires, thinking dissolves orthodoxies of all kinds and can have either an empowering and liberating effect, or a debilitating and cataclysmic one. In short: thinking is in itself neither good nor bad but can be used to either end.

Accordingly, the effects of thinking on those engaging in this practice – and thus indirectly of the gadfly as the creature that instigates this activity – are not always beneficial to society. 'The consequence of this peculiarity is that thinking inevitably has a destructive, undermining effect on all established criteria, values, measurements for good and evil.'[61] The gadfly here is an ambivalent creature. 'Thinking and Moral Considerations' speaks to the question of whether evil springs from a lack of thinking.[62] Arendt answers it by suggesting that in certain situations Socratic teaching is important because it creates new space for pluralities whenever rigidities have evolved; in other situations, it may well be of greater harm than benefit.

To what kind of situations is Arendt referring? Arendt is uncharacteristically reticent here. She merely refers to 'certain moments when the chips are down'.[63] But from the context and other parts of her oeuvre, it becomes clear that she sees Socratic teaching as an effective tool to break up the inflexibilities surrounding the emergence of totalitarianism.[64] It is at these moments that the Socratic way of thinking things through is of real benefit to society because it compels the citizens to pause and consider what is at stake. As the political philosopher Adriana Cavarero has pointed out, at the core of Arendt's oeuvre there is a fundamental reconsideration of what it means to be human in itself and, in particular, in its relationship to the political.[65] Arendt's engagement with the classical past and the figure of Socrates in particular is central to this endeavour. The experiences of totalitarianism and the mass atrocities that came with it prompted her to inquire into the kinds of forces that lead to the elimination of plurality, to dehumanization, and ultimately, destruction. In Arendt's oeuvre, the figure of Socrates served as an 'example or the paradigm of a disposition in life and in thought that constitutes ... the only effective antidote against the evil of the twentieth century, namely: "total domination."'[66] So much for the living, thinking, and examining Socrates.

But what about his execution at the hands of the Athenians? Does it exemplify the kinds of forces at work which seek to eliminate this plurality? Arendt does not say so directly. But it is telling that elsewhere she demonstrates the dehumanizing, lethal effects of totalitarianism by using an image that seems to resonate with Socrates and his execution at the hands of the Athenians. In *The Origins of Totalitarianism*, she states: 'The real horror of the concentration and extermination camps lies in the fact that the inmates, even if they happen to keep alive, are more effectively cut off from the world of the living than if they had died, because terror enforces oblivion. Here, murder is as impersonal as the squashing of a gnat.'[67] Even if the gnat is not the gadfly, the image is close enough to point back to Socrates' life and death at Athens.

To illustrate the other point, that Socratic thinking can corrupt, Arendt returns to the ancient world. Examples of the negative, destabilizing effects of the gadfly are readily found in the philosopher's immediate vicinity. Arendt cites those students of Socrates who earned themselves a reputation in the temporary overthrow of democracy at Athens in 411 and 404 BCE, respectively. 'In the circle around Socrates, there were men like Alcibiades and Critias ... and they had turned out to be a very real threat to the polis and this not by being paralyzed by the electric ray but, on the contrary, by having been aroused by the gadfly. What they had aroused to was license and cynicism.'[68] What Arendt is referring to here is that group of demagogues who played a significant role in the coups that destabilized Athenian democracy during the last quarter of the fifth century BCE. By associating these men with Socratic teaching and the impact on the gadfly in particular, Arendt in effect accuses Socrates of having created – through his actions as a gadfly – an intellectual milieu that contributed to the temporary overthrow of democracy at Athens.

So, in one instance, the Socratic gadfly is helpful and beneficial, in the other not as much – or at least not always. Both depictions, however, set the individual against the collective; both acknowledge that there is potential for genuine friction between gadfly and city. It is just that the frictions are of a different nature. In one instance the tension occurs between the personal conscience of the gadfly and the necessity of obeying the city's law; in the other they arise from the fact that thinking can be used in support of the political as well as in its destabilization.

Arendt's interpretation of the role of the Socratic gadfly in society has exposed a latent conflict between two definitions of democratic polity: the city as the sum of its citizens (*politēs*) and the city as a form of the political grounded in the rule of law.[69] Arendt's reading of Socrates thus puts the focus squarely on a question that remains a touchstone in political philosophy up to this day: the relationship between the individual and society. In the idealized and idealizing space of theory, there exists no conflict between them: one constitutes the other. In practice, however, it turns out that all institutions, including those associated with the political, experience moments when certain laws, regulations, or conventions stand in the way of the individual acting on their conscience. The frictions between political communities considering vaccination mandates and those who insist on individual decision-making during the Covid-19 pandemic can serve as a case in point.

This conflict explains the deep polarity in the current public perception of the gadfly. Assange or Moore, Pamuk or Snowden: whether we consider these 'gadflies' to be upholders of the common good, nuisances, or outright threats depends on where exactly we draw the line between individual conscience and the rule of law in their particular milieu. Champions of traditional civic values, who typically favour loyalty over scepticism and individual conscience, and subordination over dissent, will prefer the rule of law over individual conscience. More progressive types, by contrast, will place greater value on the importance of the individual as a moral agent whose role may well include the exposure of corruptions of all kinds.[70] Of course, it matters whether this conflict plays out in an inhumane and inherently unjust political system (such as those created by fascism) or in a modern liberal democracy. In this point the moral stance of the anti-vaxxers who prioritise their own physical integrity differs fundamentally from that of the gadfly who takes aim at the injustices of the system as such.

AND FINALLY ...

We return once again to the question with which we started: what did Socrates mean when he called himself a gadfly? Tracing the gadflies, horseflies, and other blood-sucking insects in Greek thought and literature has shown that in evoking the image of the gadfly Plato's Socrates created a complex image which, highly ambiguous in itself, has the capacity to point to different facets of his persona, teaching style, and role at Athens. By invoking the image in court, Plato's Socrates also seems to acknowledge the fact that several of his contemporaries found him annoying and an abrasive presence in Athenian public life – irritating enough to choose his execution when the possibility presented itself.

The reception of this figure in the modern political landscape and beyond has cast more light on the ancient one, revealing a polarizing quality as its defining feature. The Socratic gadfly, as presented in Plato's *Apology*, acknowledges adverse reactions to its presence in and impact on society and seeks (unsuccessfully) to replace them with a positive image of its service to society. A polarizing quality also defines the modern gadfly – lauded as indispensable to democracy by some, dismissed as treasonous by others.

Hannah Arendt's interpretation of the Socratic gadfly helps to explain the nature of this polarity by placing it in divergent definitions of the democratic city: that between the *polis* as the sum of its citizens and that of the *polis* as a collective entity ruled by law. It identifies the milieu of the gadfly as those moments in time when individual conscience clashes head-on with the rule of law, when different aspects of the city and different views on what constitutes the common good are at stake. It is in these moments that the figure of the gadfly finds itself at the heart of an important conversation about the place of individual conscience and the scope and limits of dissent in society. This conversation is its ultimate contribution.

The Socratic gadfly, then, is a very special creature connecting us with the ancient world. Originally describing a particular person at a particular point in time, it has come to define a certain kind of political identity: the politically engaged, critically inclined citizen able and willing to expose truths, however unwelcome. As such, it is an essential part of the kind of democracy we (like to convince ourselves that we) have inherited from the ancient Greeks.[71] Given its uniqueness, rarity, and contribution to society, it is high time we protect it. In the twenty-first century, as in the fifth and fourth centuries BCE, our democracies cannot afford its extinction.

So, next time you hear it buzzing, don't panic, don't run – and definitely don't swat. Stop and take a good, hard look. Whether you like it or not, chances are something requires questioning and investigation.

CHAPTER 9

In the final two chapters we return from the thinking of particular human identities to conceptions of the human more generally, picking up the thread from the beginning of the book. But the specific human identities featured in the previous pages remain relevant here too. Every so often they play into the stories under investigation.

The figure at the centre of Chapter 9 is the Minotaur; the larger theme explored through his presence is hybridity. The specific allure of his hybrid existence emerges against the background of similar creatures, such as the centaurs and satyrs, and of the god of shepherds, flocks, and the wild: Pan.

The peculiar hybridity of the Minotaur and the ancient story explaining his genesis raise questions about the scope and limits of human intervention into the realm of nature. Rather than exploring the limits of the human in positive ways, the figure of the Minotaur manifests the monstrous consequences of human transgression.

It is this dimension of the ancient figure that carries on from the ancient into the modern world, where we find it developed by the Spanish painter Pablo Picasso. His adaptations of the Minotaur resonate with the themes of the ancient story in ways that put the focus squarely on modern conceptions of the human and the role of Classicism in shaping them.

9.1. Attic black-figure kylix by the Painter of London E4 (ca 515 BCE) showing a running minotaur. Museo Arqueológico Nacional, Madrid, 1999/99/80. © Werner Forman/Getty Images.

The Minotaur (*Hybrida minotaurus*)

THIS STORY TAKES US TO THE BEAUTIFUL ISLAND OF CRETE and that very early period in the history of the ancient world usually referred to as 'Minoan Greece' (ca 3500–1100 BCE).[1] At this time, long prior to the arrival of the Greek city-states (*poleis*), Crete was the cultural and economic centre of a palace culture whose influence reached throughout the Mediterranean world. Its largest settlement, Knossos, housed the palace of Minos, the legendary king of old after whom the whole period is named, and who was said to have reigned over Crete about a century before the Trojan War.[2] The creature at the core of this chapter, the Minotaur, is inextricably linked to the king not least by its name: he is the bull (ancient Greek: *tauros*) of Minos.

But the creature in question is not your average bull. The Minotaur combines the body parts of man and beast: specifically, the head of a bull and the body of a man, often adorned with a bovine tail as in the Attic black-figure eye cup dating from the late sixth century BCE, shown in Figure 9.1.[3] So in the case of the Minotaur, the line between human and non-human animal that is in play in one form or another in *all* the creatures populating this book here runs – literally – through an individual body.

How does one end up with such an extraordinary physique?

An ancient story explains how this peculiar creature came into being. King Minos once prayed to Poseidon, god of the sea and progenitor of the Cyclops Polyphemus, to send a bull from the depths of the ocean.[4] The reason for this unusual request is that Minos' claim to the kingship over Crete is contested. To prove it is rightfully his, Minos seeks to showcase his special relationship to the gods.[5] The bull is then to be sacrificed to Poseidon, to return the favour.

However, as so often the case in Greek myth, things do not go as planned. When the bull ascends from the depths of the sea, it proves so magnificent that Minos finds him impossible to sacrifice. Yielding to temptation, he keeps the handsome bull for himself and instead offers up an inferior specimen. Needless to say, this charade does not go down well with Poseidon. The god's response to the sleight of hand targets Minos where it hurts most: via his wife Pasiphaë.[6] More precisely, Poseidon inspires in Pasiphaë a strong passion for the beast.

This might have been the end of the story but for the intervention of a certain Daedalus. The skilful craftsman, who later famously seeks to escape from Crete together with his son Icarus on artificial wings, facilitates the unlikely union between human and animal. As Apollodorus (second century CE) put it: 'He constructed a wooden cow on wheels, took it, hollowed it out in the inside, sewed it up in the hide of a cow which he had skinned, and set it in the meadow in which the bull used to graze. Then he introduced Pasiphaë into it.'[7] The unspeakable or, perhaps, inevitable occurs.[8] Later, the Minotaur is born, the biological offspring of the union between the bull and the woman.[9] According to some ancient sources, he went by the name of Asterion ('Starry').[10]

It would be easy to dismiss this story as an amusing (if somewhat disturbing) but ultimately inconsequential ancient tale. Yet this would be to throw out the baby with the bathwater – or perhaps better, the calf with the dung? In many ways, the story itself provides clues to the nature and meaning of the creature at its core. It puts the focus squarely on the extraordinary circumstances leading up to the making of the Minotaur. More specifically, it presents, and thus accounts for, the Minotaur's hybridity as the product of the sexual union of woman and bull. Sexual intercourse here provides a pathway for Pasiphaë to breach the boundary between human and non-human animal.

The Minotaur's hybrid biology raises a set of fundamental questions: how do human and animal entities and identities intersect in this figure? Does the Minotaur transcend the boundary between man and beast – or does he ultimately affirm it? And what kinds of principles – of nature, justice, and morality – apply? Human principles, or those pertaining to animals (and bulls in particular)? Or perhaps a different set of principles altogether? These questions are by no means peripheral. Nor are they merely a trivial pursuit; they strike at the centre of human identity. The Minotaur, through his mere existence, reveals a question central to our humanity – a question pre-dating Darwin and the advent of evolutionary theory – a question as revealing as it can be unsettling: what if we really *are* animal, at least in part?

HYBRIDITY AND MONSTROSITY: THE MINOTAUR AMONG CENTAURS, SATYRS, AND PAN

The Minotaur belongs to a larger group of hybrid creatures that populate Greco-Roman mythology. Indeed, the 'bull of Minos' is part of a sizeable group of mythological figures that combine not merely the body parts of different *kinds* of beings – as, for example, the Chimera, a fire-breathing beast comprising a goat's head, a lion's body, and a tail sporting a serpent's head – but those of humans and animals as different *categories* of being. As such, he is related to a number of other mythological creatures that also combine human and animal parts. These include: the centaurs, a combination of horse and human rider; the satyrs, creatures sporting the ears and tail of a horse grafted onto an otherwise fully human body (featuring a permanent erection); and Pan – the legendary minor Greek deity of the rustic and wild, whose otherwise human physique is adorned with the legs, horns, and ears of a goat.

These creatures have in common that they inhabit spaces at the margins of human society. As the god of the wild, shepherds, their flocks, and music, Pan is closely associated with the rustic countryside, in particular the quintessentially pastoral region of Arcadia. The playful satyrs inhabit remote locations outside of the settled space of the Greco-Roman city as do their more violent and threatening counterparts, the centaurs.

While all of these hybrids have a veritable storied life (both literary and in the form of iconographic representations on pottery and monuments), it is in particular the centaurs whose feats and problematic interactions with humans have been the subject of a rich body of mythological tales. One of these tales tells us about one Pirithous, king of a legendary people called the Lapiths, who made the fatal mistake of inviting the centaurs to his wedding party. He came to regret it soon after, when his non-human guests bust the party by resorting to alcohol-infused violence.[11] Since then, so the story goes, the centaurs have been in conflict with humans.[12] With the exception of two particularly well-adjusted, wise, and cultured specimens (Chiron and Pholus), they stand for sexual exuberance and uncontrolled violence and thus the absence of societal norms. Their subjugation by Heracles is cast as the ultimate victory of humanity over animality and of the good order.

So the Centaurs bust a wedding to rape the bride and must be killed. The satyrs chase maenads (frenzied female followers of the god Dionysus) and have sex with any object they can no matter whether animate or inanimate. And Pan is associated with masturbation and sexual seduction. It is obvious that in Greco-Roman myth these creatures bring out the animalistic side of human sexuality. Their excesses and transgressions raise fundamental questions about procreation as an activity we share with non-human creatures: just how physical, how animal-like, how violent is it? As human/animal hybrids these creatures are particularly suited for an exploration of these issues. Taken together, they illustrate that already in the ancient world, humans resort to the animal realm to make sense of human sexuality.

We will return to these questions and the way in which the Minotaur relates to them in due course. Here, we merely add that in contrast to the centaurs, which procreate with each other to make more centaurs, the Minotaur stands out: he is a one-off, an individual creation, begotten by extraordinary circumstance, and therefore not part of a larger group (what we might call a 'species'). This puts him on par with Pan, the rustic deity of the wild already mentioned. And yet, in contrast to Pan, whose head is human (if we disregard the goat horns and ears), the Minotaur sports an animal rather than a human head. This is an outstanding feature only shared by a handful of other mythological creatures[13] Most other human/animal hybrids have a human head atop various animal parts. That the Minotaur features an animal head matters because it goes against the traditional view, variously on show throughout this book, which associates the 'human' firmly with the mind and all its capacities and intricacies, and the 'animal' with the physical dimension of existence. The Minotaur's humanity is restricted to certain physical parts, while the head and mind are fully that of a bull. This peculiarity puts him in a category of his own.

How deeply the ancient Greeks and Romans engaged with the concept of the Minotaur's hybridity becomes clear from the way in which this creature is presented in the ancient evidence. In the ancient world, the Minotaur's extraordinary physique warranted extensive comment. The Greek philosopher Plutarch quotes the Greek playwright Euripides as speaking of 'a mingled form and hybrid birth of monstrous shape . . . two different natures (*diplai physeis*), man and bull, were joined in him'.[14] Diodorus of Sicily refers to him as being of 'double form' (*diphuē*): 'the upper parts of the body as far as the shoulders being those of a bull and the remaining parts those of a man'.[15] And Pausanias, relating to the myth (re)told in the beginning of this chapter, wonders 'whether this was a man or a beast of the nature he is said to have been in the accepted story'.[16] In Latin literature he is referred to variously as *biformis* ('double-formed'), *mixtum* ('mixed'), and *geminus* ('double').[17] The ancient authors clearly define the Minotaur as the quintessential hybrid and, as such, they frequently include him in the category of the monstrous which also includes the Sphinx and the Cyclops.

As we will see below, the Minotaur's extraordinary physique puts the focus squarely on hybridity both as a physical fact *and* as a problem of categorization. And hybridity – the product or combination of two different (id)entities – always raises questions of belonging. It melds a perspective on life in all its confusing diversity with a more general focus on the blending of two distinct types. Hybridity is thus ultimately an acknowledgement of the fact that the world is more complex than the categories we have created to describe, contain, and control it.

GROWING THE BIOLOGICAL HYBRID

In highlighting the generation of the Minotaur, the myth frames the hybrid presence through the lens of biology. At a time of only limited insight into the principles and practices of heredity and descent, it seems extraordinary that the ancients already conceived of hybridity as the product of the biological crossing of two different kinds.

So where could this knowledge come from?

To answer this question, it is worth looking beyond Greek mythology to consider where the ancient Greeks will have encountered hybridity in real life. The ancient world allowed for various observations of mixed types. Ancient agricultural practice was well advanced and included the cross-breeding of different animals and plants to enhance production of livestock, fruit, and vegetables.[18] In the animal realm, the mule constituted a ubiquitous example of biological hybridity.[19] The offspring of a jackass and a mare was a popular domestic animal used for travel and transport, and as a source of milk.[20] By contrast, the crossing of a stallion with a jenny, the so-called 'hinny', was far less popular, ostensibly because it is more difficult to breed, smaller on average than the mule, and said to be of an uncooperative, stubborn character.[21]

In the realm of plants, we likewise find various hybrid crossings. Grafting was widely practised in the ancient world to produce new plants.[22] The ancient author Pliny the Elder, for example, mentions in his discussion of fruit trees: 'The rest of the fruits produced by trees can scarcely be enumerated by their appearance or shape, let alone by their flavours and juices, which have been so frequently modified by crossing and grafting (*totiens permixtis atque insitis*).'[23] Apparently, in this case at least, the resulting hybrids looked and tasted sufficiently different from the plants from which they were originally derived that they no longer resembled them in any meaningful way.

If hybrid plants seem worlds apart from the hybrids of Greek and Roman mythology, we find them directly linked in a passage from Plutarch's *Table Talk*: when a certain Soclarus treats his guests to a brief tour of the lavish grounds of his estate, at first everything seems to stay firmly in the realm of the botanical.

> Soclarus, while entertaining us in his gardens bordered by the Cephissus River, showed us trees which had been fancified in all sorts of ways by what is called grafting; we saw olives growing upon mastic trees and pomegranates upon the myrtle; and there were oaks which bore good pears, plane trees which had received grafts of apples, and figs grafts of mulberries, and other mixtures of trees mastered to the point of producing fruit.[24]

The response of the guests to the unusual plant crossings – the grafts in question are not just regular hybrids but combinations of biologically unrelated plants (modern epiphytes) – soon prompts a surprising imaginative turn: 'Then the rest of the company began to tease Soclarus for raising, as they said, classes (*genē*) and specimens (*thremmata*) more marvellous than the sphinxes and chimaeras of the poets.'[25] This observation is invariably revealing. The grafted plants with their propped-up parts recall the marvellous physical combinations of the mythological hybrids.

Even though this is certainly a light-hearted leap from biology to mythology, it is informed by the understanding of grafting as a quasi-sexual process. And on this point Plutarch is not alone: various ancient authors also convey a sexualized conception of grafting.[26] It is articulated, for example, in a passage in Theophrastus' treatise on all things botanical, *Enquiry On Plants*, in which the author concludes: 'Trees then grow and come into being in the above-mentioned ways; for as to methods of grafting (*emphuteiai*) and inoculation (*enofthalmismoi*), these are, as it were, combinations (*mixeis*) of different kinds of trees.'[27] The ancients clearly included plants in how they thought about the technicalities of sexual reproduction.[28]

The sexualized conception of grafting matters because it puts this practice on a par with the breeding of mules as another example of an artificial sexual union between different species. It sets up the hybridity of grafted plants to synchronize with the crossbreeding of animals and the biological hybridity of the Minotaur. As we have seen in the case of the latter here, too, detail matters: the ancient myth goes to great lengths to account for how the unusual sexual union between the bull and the woman is achieved.

And yet, the very boundary that the sexual act sought to overcome with the help of the technical device – the faux cow – remains all-too-visible in the offspring of this union. As with certain grafted plants, the Minotaur's constitutive parts remain recognizably distinct, visually underlining the hybridity of the creature. In this case at least, a real union seems impossible. A full blending of a human and non-human animal, in which the two generating parties are no longer visible as separate entities in the offspring, cannot be attained.

ON HYBRIDS AND HUBRIS

The biological understanding of hybridity raises the issue of the reproductive processes of nature only to let it drop: the kinds of hybrids paraded here are not the result of natural processes at all. Rather, in biology and mythology, the focus is firmly on human interference. What brings together the breeding of mules, the grafting of plants, and the generation of the Minotaur is that they are all *human* (cultural) practices. In all instances, humans are the driving force.

That these kinds of hybrids were seen as instances of human intervention into the order of nature becomes clear from a passage in Aelian's *On Animals.* It refers to the philosopher Democritus, who observed that 'the mule is not the product of nature but a surreptitious contrivance (*epitechnēma*) of the ingenuity and, so to say, adulterous daring (*tolmēs moichidiou*) of man'.[29] The point here is that jackasses and mares do not usually mate due to a distinct dislike of each other. To produce the mule, they must be brought together by humans. The reference to adultery leaves no doubt that this act is conceived of as a form of transgression. It casts the breeding of the mule in terms of a violent human intervention into the order of nature.

The evaluative dimension of hybridity comes out even more strongly when Aelian quotes Democritus' explanation of the origins of this human practice: 'And I fancy, said Democritus, that a mare became pregnant from being by chance violated by an ass, and that men were its pupils in this deed of violence, and presently accustomed themselves to the use of the offspring.'[30] This observation leaves no doubt as to how we are meant to view the origins of the mule. Its breeding is a violent and transgressive act which first happened as an extraordinary occurrence, an aberration of nature, later copied by humans who then applied it to their own advantage.

This passionate dismissal raises questions: what kinds of considerations motivate it? What kinds of evaluative frameworks apply?

The violent sexual act described here evokes a Greek concept that we have already variously encountered throughout this book and that the Greeks applied to transgressions of all kinds: that of hubris. In ancient Greece, hubris denotes the crossing of a boundary of what was regarded proper and appropriate in different realms of the human experience.[31] Hubris is in play when Creon (in Sophocles' drama) refuses to bury Antigone's brother and when Antigone refuses to obey Creon's orders.[32] Hubris is also paraded when, in 480 BCE, the Persian king Xerxes and his army crossed the natural boundary of the Hellespont from Asia into Greece during the Persian Wars with the help of a bridge made of ships.[33]

These notable instances of hubris resonate with the modern use of the word. In the ancient world, however, the core meaning of the term covered much narrower ground. It emerged from a gendered and sexualized context involving the breach of rules and conventions applying to relations between men and women. In Classical Athens, for example, rape featured as a form of hubris, as did seduction and – intriguingly, given the reference in the passage above – adultery.[34] All of them incurred shame in the public eye.

The circumstances of the Minotaur's creation points to the concept of hubris in more than one way. In the attempt to cross the human/animal boundary in a sexual union conceived of by man, the myth parades exactly the kind of sexual transgression that is at stake in the ancient Greek conception of hubris (narrowly defined). At the same time, the actual sexual encounter between human and non-human animal is the consequence of other acts of hubris. It is, for example, already anticipated in Daedalus' construction of the wooden cow. This is because in the myth of the Minotaur, conception does not remain a biological process. The story also parades 'conception' in a wider sense, as a process of the mind – a cognitive feat. The physical act of the Minotaur's making is anticipated in the creation of the artificial cow as the material device that enables the unusual union. The cow provides the link between both types of 'making', one biological, one technical. It is a human conception and a technical production on the one hand *and* a facilitator for the biological union between human and animal on the other. As a device, it gives Pasiphaë's longing a physical presence and enables the transition from merely desiring to actual doing. As a device built to present and contain the human body in animal form, the cow also anticipates the hybridity of the Minotaur as the physiological offspring of the connection it makes possible. It is both human and animal and thus, in effect, *neither* (fully) human *nor* animal.

In other words: Daedalus, the quintessential craftsman and technology buff of the ancient world, hatches a plan to put Pasiphaë's desire into action and constructs a technical device facilitating it. Before Pasiphaë and the bull physically cross the line, Daedalus crosses it in his mind first. Moreover, both transgressions emerge as a consequence of Minos' primordial hubris towards the gods when he withholds the prize promised to

Poseidon. Hubris is in play at different levels throughout the story; the Minotaur emerges as a consequence.

That this is by no means an anachronistic reading of the myth becomes clear if we listen to a creature from earlier in this book: Grunter, the philosophically inclined pig and unlikely hero of Plutarch's treatise *Beasts Are Rational* (see Chapter 2). Just to recall: the pig is one of the Greeks that the sorceress Circe had turned into animals on a remote island somewhere in the Mediterranean. The pig makes the case for why it is better to remain an animal rather than be turned back into a human being.[35] And one argument in favour of the porcine condition sets the transgressive promiscuity of the human against the apparent constraint of animals. The pig asserts:

> On this basis even men themselves acknowledge that beasts have a better claim to temperance and the non-violation of nature in their pleasures. Not even Nature, with Law for her ally, can keep within bounds the unchastened vice of your hearts; but as though swept by the current of their lusts beyond the barrier at many points, men do such deeds as wantonly outrage Nature, upset her order, and confuse her distinctions.[36]

The natural constraint of animals is directly contrasted here with the apparent willingness of humans to cross the human/animal boundary. Human promiscuity sidesteps the order of nature, which does not usually accommodate such transgressions. That a pig is making this point is deeply ironic: it reveals a claim to human exceptionalism that turns *against itself* the dynamics of the 'man-only *topos*' – the claim that humans stand out among all beings because they have certain features (see Chapter 2).[37] Here, human exceptionalism features as part of an argument designed to discredit the human capacity to show temperance and constraint.

If these claims still remain somewhat abstract and academic, what follows leaves no doubt as to what the pig is talking about: 'For men have, in fact, attempted to consort with goats and sows and mares, and women have gone mad with lust for male beasts. From such unions your Minotaurs and Aegipans, and, I suppose, your Sphinxes and Centaurs have arisen.'[38] This is to say that humans sometimes know no natural restraint in coupling with beings of another order – and with the obvious hybrid consequences. Animals, in turn, do not usually cross that line. As the pig is quick to point out:

> Yet it is through hunger that dogs have occasionally eaten a man; and birds have tasted of human flesh through necessity; but no beast has ever attempted a human body for lustful reasons. But the beasts I have mentioned and many others have been victims of the violent and lawless lusts of man.[39]

The pig here compares and contrasts interspecies mating with carnivorous animals feasting on human flesh. In both instances, the physical barrier between human and non-human animal is crossed and different kinds of bodies morph into one. Yet while meat-eating as another form of interspecies transgression ultimately constitutes a necessity of life for many animals, interspecies coupling stands as an unnatural, violent, and pointless human intervention into the order of nature. That humans consume the flesh of animals for mere gluttonous enjoyment is, of course, another criticism implicit in the pig's observations (see Chapter 5).

The myth of the Minotaur, with its emphasis on man's multiple transgressive initiatives in the creation of the hybrid creature, lends itself to such readings. It provides a prime example of the intervention of man into the order of nature in ways which recall the complex meanings of the Greek concept of hubris. It presents humanity as the prime violator of the boundary separating human from non-human animals by instigating – even forcing – a union between them.

THE SLAYING OF THE MINOTAUR

In Greek thought and literature, *hybris* ('hubris') is often followed by *nēmēsis* ('retribution'). To restore the order of nature, human transgressions warrant a corrective response. And more often than not, the Greek gods are in charge of settling the balance. Zeus, Apollo, and their like routinely punish those who overstep the mark by sending all sorts of calamities. Infertility, disease, especially blindness, even death, the loss of political power or of beloved family members – all these afflictions could be seen as forms of divine punishment.

The Minotaur's hybrid body stands for the transgressions that generated it.[40] It is a constant physical reminder of the hubris that brought it into being. It thus comes as no surprise that King Minos of Crete has him locked up in another construction of the now (in)famous Daedalus: a labyrinth 'in which he who entered could not find his way out; for many a winding turn shut off the secret outward way'.[41] Yet as contained as the creature may be, it is not controlled. For even there, in the labyrinth, the Minotaur wields his destructive powers. Every nine years he devours seven boys and seven girls the Athenians send to Crete as a tribute to Minos.[42] Man-eating becomes the Minotaur's defining feature.

The Minotaur's man-devouring habit cannot be explained with reference to his human nor his animal parts. In the human realm, man-eating ('anthropophagy') is a dehumanizing feature attributed to a handful of people at the margins of the civilized world (and the margins of the human, see Chapter 4). At the same time, while bulls may occasionally attack humans, they do not consume them. Moreover, bulls (as well as cows and oxen) are one of the quintessential sacrificial victims of ancient Greek religion and not normally the executors of sacrifice. Here the usual roles of sacrificer and sacrificed are reversed – a further compelling image of the conceptual challenges represented by this creature.

The Minotaur thus inhabits a third space beyond the parts that constitute him. He lives out his life according to his own laws which pertain neither to humans nor to animals. So, to answer the question raised at the beginning of this chapter: in the end, this figure does not transcend polarities but carries them to extremes. The violence it commits – devouring young humans – serves as an extension of the conceptual violence that generated it: both rock the very fundamentals of what it means to be human.

The labyrinth accommodates and contains the violence for which the Minotaur stands. At the same time, it reflects his paradoxical existence. The maze is both open and closed, accessible and inaccessible, liminal and central, somewhere and nowhere. It is itself a hybrid space in which boundaries variously extend into pathways and vice versa, a confusing space in which new openings emerge that, more often than not, lead nowhere. Moreover, as Apollodorus asserts, if it is hard to find one's way into it, it is even harder to leave: 'Now the Labyrinth which Daedalus constructed was a chamber "that with its tangled windings perplexed the outward way".'[43] It is a space where a life-threatening force can lurk in every corner – a space hard to access and even harder to come back from.

The one who finally pulls off this feat is Theseus.[44] His success in locating the monster, slaying it, and exiting the maze unharmed rests on a particular blend of daring, physical strength, and human ingenuity that is typical of the quintessential Greek hero. But this time the physical object assisting this ingenuity has nothing to do with Daedalus and is decisively low-tech: a thread, given to Theseus by Ariadne, the daughter of King Minos and half-sister of the Minotaur, ultimately allows him to re-emerge from the labyrinth after overpowering a force which had previously proved insurmountably destructive.

And so, the story ends . . .

PICASSO'S MINOTAUR

Except that it does not. The Minotaur has a veritable post-classical afterlife in numerous artistic, literary, and other forms.[45] The second part of this chapter considers one such modern rendering of the ancient figure. It follows the Minotaur's human footsteps into the works of the Spanish painter Pablo Picasso (1881–1973).

Inspired, perhaps, by the recent publication of the archaeological discoveries on Crete by Sir Arthur Evans, Picasso engaged with the ancient figure widely and creatively.[46] The Minotaur features particularly frequently in works he created during the mid-1930s.[47] These include a collage that he assembled in 1933 for the first edition of *Minotaure*, a magazine dedicated to all things Surrealist, as well as numerous etchings, drawings, and paintings including the so-called *Minotauromachy* ('Minotaur Battle'), a 1935 work that, in many ways, represents the apex of Picasso's Minotaur-themed works (see Figure 9.12). The Minotaur also has a strong presence in the so-called Suite Vollard – a collection of 100 etchings that Picasso created between 1931 and 1937.[48] The bull-man from Greek mythology obviously struck a chord with the artist.[49]

What motivated Picasso to explore the ancient figure in some of his artistic productions beyond his obvious interest in bulls and bullfighting?[50] What kinds of human and non-human identities, come, quite literally, into the picture in this modern adaptation of an ancient creature? And *whose* humanity is at stake in this modern rendering of the ancient figure? The answer to these questions brings us right back to the peculiar kind of hybridity of the Minotaur from the first part of this chapter. Picasso developed it in ways that focus squarely on the perils of modernity and its problematic and fragile conceptions of the human.

HYBRIDITY RECONCEIVED

A quick look at several of his Minotaur-themed works reveals that in Picasso's oeuvre the creature's hybridity takes on ever new forms. Many of his works follow the classical lead by attributing the Minotaur with the full head of a bull.[51] Yet other works feature a more human-like head. Nowhere is this more evident than in some of the portraits Picasso sketched of the figure (Figures 9.2, 9.3, and 9.4).

9.2. Pablo Picasso, *Tête de minotaure/ Head of Minotaur* (1937). Staatsgalerie Stuttgart. Photo © Bpk/ Staatsgalerie Stuttgart. © Succession Picasso/Copyright Agency, 2023.
9.3. Pablo Picasso, *Minotaure/ Minotaur* (no date). Picasso National Museum, Paris. Photo © RMN-Grand Palais (Musée national Picasso-Paris)/Rachel Prat. © Succession Picasso/ Copyright Agency, 2023.
9.4. Pablo Picasso, *Minotaure/ Minotaur* (1958). Picasso National Museum, Paris, MP1117. Photo © RMN-Grand Palais (Musée national Picasso-Paris)/ Mathieu Rabeau. © Succession Picasso/Copyright Agency, 2023.

It is difficult not to look for human sensitivities in the facial expressions of these close-up frontal depictions. In each, Picasso humanizes the Minotaur by giving him human facial features while still retaining the otherwise bullish contours of the head. The Minotaur in Figure 9.2, for example, seems to charge (at) the viewer directly with a penetrating, piercing stare as if to say 'Look away! Nothing to see here.' And yet, there is something unmistakably human – and specifically male – about the way he looks (on). Is it the absence of excess facial hair and other overtly animalizing features? Or is it the intensity of his (fully frontal and hence humanizing) glare that suggests it is driven by human thoughts and emotions? Or something different altogether?

The Minotaur shown in Figure 9.3 does not face us directly. His pose is not confrontational. Rather, this particular Minotaur seems astonished or taken aback. His mouth is slightly open and his eyes are focused on something beyond the frame of the image. What stands out in this specimen is the fully human features of the face. It is only the horns and the pointed ears which give away his pedigree. This Minotaur is clearly a more sophisticated, more civilized and, perhaps, more fragile specimen than the one depicted in Figure 9.2. The Minotaur shown in Figure 9.4, finally, is not facing the viewer directly. He is portrayed half-frontally, looking at a point beyond the viewer/painter. This Minotaur has a prominent, determined face featuring fiery nostrils, a pair of strong, assertive jaws, and sensuous lips. A vigorous, assertive human masculinity is on display here underscored by the bullish curves.

Picasso obviously took an interest in developing the hybridity of the Minotaur.[52] In distinct contrast to ancient representations of the figure, which keep the human and animal parts clearly separate, here they blend seamlessly into each other. In all three examples, it is impossible to tell where exactly the animal ends and the human begins.

Picasso does not merely provide a modern rendering or retelling of the old story. There is no wooden cow, no Theseus, no labyrinth. Nor does he provide ever new depictions of the same figure. Rather, his Minotaurs vary in the extent and nature of the humanity attributed to them. In some of his works, Picasso draws on the traditional association of the human with the mind to inscribe human sentiments in the Minotaur's face while still maintaining a distinctly bullish streak. In others, this dimension remains unrealized with the Minotaur retaining the head of a bull without any overtly humanizing features.

What could warrant such different representations? What might have inspired Picasso to explore the Minotaur's hybridity in this way?

AUTOBIOGRAPHICAL RENDERINGS

Various modern commentators have suggested that Picasso drew on the figure of the Minotaur in order to articulate aspects of his own identity.[53] This suggestion is not merely a matter of conjecture: Picasso himself once famously remarked: 'If all the ways I have been all along were marked on a map and joined up with a line, it might represent a Minotaur.'[54] This is a remarkable statement in more ways than one: it presents the Minotaur as the personification of the sum of Picasso's past experiences ('all the ways I have been'). At the same time, it highlights the symbolic nature of a figure that emerges, not entirely unlike a drawing, by connecting the biographical dots of Picasso's life. The contours of the resulting figure point to the man who created ever new representations of the ancient creature.

Two aspects in particular are frequently invoked to explain how the figure of the Minotaur resonates with Picasso: making art and making love. In the realm of love-making the Minotaur is thought to represent Picasso's problematic entanglements with his romantic partners in general and Marie-Thérèse Walter in particular. Picasso started a relationship with Walter, a woman twenty-eight years his junior, in 1927 when he was still married to the Russian ballet dancer Olga Khokhlova.[55] In 1935, when Walter became pregnant, he started a new relationship with Dora Maar, the artist, photographer, and poet. The popularity of the Minotaur in Picasso's works of the 1930s, together with the fact that the ancient creature is frequently depicted in interaction with women (many of which show a striking resemblance to Walter), has been taken to suggest that Picasso used the Minotaur to come to terms with this turbulent situation.[56] It has prompted at least one commentator to speculate that it was Walter's pregnancy that brought out the Minotaur in the works of Picasso.[57] And even as most have shied away from linking the Minotaur to any specific event, similar psychological and biographical interpretations abound.

The Minotaur's relationship to Picasso's art-making is hardly ever explored in any detail. This line of interpretation seems to be driven by the desire to locate a deeper dimension in Picasso's work that transcends his personal relationships and warrants his standing as a grand master. Yet, existing explanations rarely move beyond vague remarks about Picasso's engagement with the classical tradition both in style and content.[58] How exactly the Minotaur emerges from the way in which the ancient and the modern worlds come together in his work is not made explicit. It remains unclear how the Minotaur relates to Picasso's role as an artist.

And yet, we may wonder: should we really assume that the complexity of Picasso's artistic interventions emerges through a sole (or primary) focus on the life of the artist that created them?[59] The biographical dimension has sometimes led to a somewhat flat interpretation of Picasso's artistic interventions, as if artworks were merely a representation of a particular aspect of reality by indirect means. More recently, such overtly biographical readings have thus become subject to criticism.[60] In pursuing the Minotaur into the works of Picasso, we will thus take the biographical dimension only as a springboard for deeper considerations about the place of the ancient creature in Picasso's oeuvre.

THE MINOTAUR AS LOVER

Several of the Vollard etchings take the viewer into what is arguably the most intimate of all settings: the bedroom. They show the Minotaur in a private and amorous tête-à-tête with a fully human – and distinctly nude – female (see, e.g., Figures 9.5 and 9.6).

9.5. Pablo Picasso, Vollard Suite, plate 83 (17 May 1933). Museum of Modern Art, Paris, SAME 1104. Photo © RMN-Grand Palais (Musée national Picasso-Paris)/Thierry Le Mage. © Succession Picasso/Copyright Agency, 2023.

9.6. Pablo Picasso, Vollard Suite, plate 93 (18 June 1933). Picasso National Museum, Paris, MP1982-152. Photo © RMN-Grand Palais (Musée national Picasso-Paris)/Mathieu Rabeaum. © Succession Picasso/Copyright Agency, 2023.

In Figure 9.5, the Minotaur holds a goblet in his upraised hand – an echo of the glass of red wine consumed as a symbol of civilization and humanization by Kafka's ape Red Peter (Chapter 2) and, perhaps, an allusion to the potential for alcohol-infused violence in the hands of the centaurs. But this Minotaur is not charging at the viewer. The atmosphere is relaxed, perhaps even 'celebratory'.[61] The focus of this image is quite clearly on looking rather than doing: the female figure seems to point at her own eyes while looking sideways into the Minotaur's face. The Minotaur's own gaze rests on the goblet. And yet, it is not just the Minotaur and his female companion who are doing the gazing here. We as viewers of the image share in this activity. We, too, are invited into the bedroom to gaze – in quasi-voyeuristic fashion – at the two bodies spread out alongside each other.

Gazing or staring – a more directed, focused, intentional from of looking – is also in play in Figure 9.6. But here, it is only the Minotaur who does the staring while the eyes of his female human partner are firmly closed.[62] She is peacefully sleeping while he bends over her, his heavy bullish head hovering directly over her delicate features. Again, we notice that his mouth is slightly open. As a gesture, the open mouth is hardly innocent. It is deeply ambiguous, referencing the mouth as the organ of both speaking *and* eating.[63] The open mouth thus points at once to the human as the (only) creature capable of speech and to the animal as a being associated with the physical aspects of existence. It underlines the creature's hybridity and makes us wonder: is this what it looks like if a monstrous creature whispers tender words into its lover's ear? Or is there something more sinister in this situation?[64]

In both images our eyes ultimately come to rest on the two heads, the two faces, one female and human and one male and animal. It is here that we look for clues about the kind of relationship that brings together the two figures represented here. And yet this proves surprisingly difficult. It is impossible to move beyond the fundamental divide that separates the hairy head of the bull from the delicate female and fully human features. With the taurine and human heads directly side by side, the chasm that separates them comes fully to the fore – despite the intimacy of the two human bodies stretching out alongside each other.

Despite the apparent peace and affection between the Minotaur and his human lover, one cannot fully shake off the uneasy feeling that the monster's caring tenderness may lapse into violence at any time.[65] We may wonder: which side of the Minotaur will ultimately prevail: the gentle caring or the bestial one?

The themes of sexuality and transgression that we found embedded in the ancient myth discussed in the first part of this chapter are all at play here too, even though – or perhaps *exactly because* – they are not realized. It is just that in Picasso's rendering the Minotaur is not the product of a transgressive union between human and animal but himself engaged in this kind of boundary-crossing.

In Figure 9.7, our reservations and premonitions about the Minotaur's relationship to his female partner seem to have become realized. Gazing has clearly given way to touching in what amounts to a much more aggressive and transgressive scene. The etching has frequently been taken to show the Minotaur raping a woman.[66] However, this is clearly not what is

9.7. Pablo Picasso, Vollard Suite, plate 87 (23 May 1933). Photo © RMN-Grand Palais (Musée national Picasso-Paris)/Thierry Le Mage. © Succession Picasso/Copyright Agency 2023

going on. Rather, to showcase the Minotaur's violence, Picasso here again references the human/horse hybrids of Greco-Roman thought and literature mentioned in the beginning of this chapter: the centaurs. It is a female centaur (human/horse combination) that is subjected to the Minotaur's sexual overtures here, not a human being. Picasso displaced the most violent articulation of the Minotaur's transgressions into the realm of myth. The focus here is entirely on the two bulky bodies hopelessly entangled with each other as well as the force with which the Minotaur thrusts himself onto his female counterpart.

It thus seems that the physical hybridity of the Minotaur extends into a profound behavioural and moral ambivalence. In all these instances, it is unclear whether we are meant to be scandalized by what is happening right here in front of our eyes. Picasso refers to the ancient figure of the Minotaur and his problematic hybridity to question male sexuality. Here, too, the question is: how bodily, how animal-like, how violent is it?

In the first (classical) part of this chapter, we have shown that the ancient figure of the Minotaur does not transcend polarities but carries them to extremes. In this aspect he differs from the satyrs which represent a more gentle version of how men become like animals when drinking, hunting, and having sex. This dimension of the Minotaur is particularly brought to the fore in Picasso's renderings of the ancient figure.[67] He is represented alternately as a gentle and loving creature, then as a raping, violating monster; he parades a potent masculinity in one rendering, but a fundamental fragility in the next. Its most evocative articulation comes in the figure of the suffering, wounded, blind, or dying Minotaur – a subject that features prominently among Picasso's Minotaur-themed works (see, e.g., Figure 9.8).[68] And, again, the mouth of this Minotaur is slightly open, thus referencing his human and animal sides.

In the ancient myth, the Minotaur is the personified offspring of human hubris, the boundary-crossing between human and animal made flesh. As such, he also comes to impersonate the notion of *nēmēsis* ('retribution') that befalls those who cross the boundary. In Picasso's renderings of the ancient figure, it is the Minotaur himself who appears at least occasionally as a suffering and tormented figure. It is he himself who transgresses and he himself who comes to harm.

9.8. Pablo Picasso, Vollard Suite, plate 90 (30 May 1933). Photo © RMN-Grand Palais (Musée national Picasso-Paris)/Thierry le Mage. © Succession Picasso/Copyright Agency 2023.

He is at once potent lover and conqueror of women, then destitute subject of a female helping hand (as in the representation of the blind Minotaur led by a little girl shown in Figure 9.9).

What could warrant such stark contrasts? The second dimension in which the figure of the Minotaur is thought to resonate with Picasso – making art – helps to answer this question.

THE MINOTAUR AND THE ARTIST

It might be tempting to think that the domains of love-making and art-making constitute different aspects of life. After all, one is intimate and private, the other professional and public. But in Picasso's case, there is a deeper connection between them. He frequently chose his female partners as both a source of artistic inspiration and as the subject of his creative

9.9. Pablo Picasso, Vollard Suite, plate 96 (23 October 1934). Photo © RMN-Grand Palais (Musée national Picasso-Paris)/Thierry le Mage. © Succession Picasso/Copyright Agency 2023.

works.[69] A closer look reveals that in Picasso's oeuvre the Minotaur inhabits a deeper ground in which art-making and love-making converge. And, again, this convergence points us back to the themes we found in the ancient myth: boundaries, transgression – and ultimately destruction.

In the Vollard etching shown in Figure 9.10, the intimacy of the bedroom scene has given way to a more 'communal' setting with two nude young women sitting by, one playing a flute. The bodies of the Minotaur and his female partner that were so carefully draped alongside each other in Figure 9.5 are now reaching into each other. The hairy hands of the Minotaur fondle the woman's right breast. Some nibbles and drink are presented on a small table on the right. Flute-playing, wreaths, food, and drink make the scene loosely reminiscent of the ancient Greek male drinking party ('symposium'). At the same time, the presence of the classicizing bust in the far-left corner also points to the studio as a setting featured in many of Picasso's artworks;[70] likewise the disembodied, oversize face looking directly at the viewer from the back through what appears to be a window.

9.10. Pablo Picasso, Vollard Suite, plate 84 (18 May 1933). Photo © RMN-Grand Palais (Musée national Picasso-Paris)/Thierry le Mage. © Succession Picasso/Copyright Agency 2023.

The same handsome, bearded, male face also features elsewhere in the Vollard Suite and is generally accepted to represent the artist himself.[71]

The presence of the artist's face in the background of the etching puts the focus again on the faculty of sight. More specifically, it draws attention to the role of seeing in the creation and reception of images. And yet, his is a disembodied gaze. If it is focused on anything at all, it is on *us* as the viewers of the image and not on the events right in front of him. He seems to have no stake whatsoever in what is happening in the picture.

This way of looking on points to the idea(l) of the impartiality of the artist as someone who creates a realistic representation of a slice of the world as if he was – literally! – looking in a window.[72] The dominant mode of representation here and in all the previous images featuring the Minotaur is that of Classicism.[73] The subject alludes to what is arguably a core theme in Western artistic representations from antiquity to the present: the (fully nude) female body presented as an object of erotic desire. Here it is rendered in typical classicizing fashion through a set of simple, fine lines evoking ideal proportions. The artist's head is rendered in the same style: his harmonious lineaments, which recall representations of Zeus on Classical Greek pottery, present the most explicit presence of the classical ideal of the human body in the picture.

The Minotaur's presence sustains and interrupts the realism of Figure 9.10. As an ancient mythological figure, he blends seamlessly into the classicizing setting. His monstrous and imposing physique either scandalizes or, indeed, animalizes the nude female body. In other words, the Minotaur's presence here challenges the principles and practices of Classicism and of realistic representation *from within that tradition* and

9.11. Pablo Picasso, *Tête de femme/Head of a Woman* (Jacqueline) (1961/2). Los Angeles County Museum (LACMA) M.2005.70.110. Photo © RMN-Grand Palais (Musée national Picasso-Paris). © Succession Picasso/Copyright Agency 2023.

exposes them for what they really are: a form of artistic fiction-making among others, but one claiming to be grounded in the real. At the same time his amorous intervention brings out the idea of art as transgression, as the pushing of boundaries, as an act of creation, and as an act of violation.

Transgressions, violations, and boundary-crossings are central to some of Picasso's preferred forms of artistic representation. As he famously pointed out, the act of creation necessarily involves destruction.[74] The violence is no coincidence. By the first half of the twentieth century, the realism inherent in Neoclassicism had been largely replaced by other modes of artistic representation. They no longer idolized the artist looking onto the world from the impartial vantage point of Zeus. Instead, they cast artistic creation as a form of intervention and violation with the ultimate aim of bringing out a deeper essence of that which is represented.

Does the presence of the Minotaur in works to do with art and representation reflect such considerations? The freedom of composition and representation opened up and afforded by Cubism as an artistic movement which adopted several perspectives at once and which broke down objects into simple geometric shapes. It frequently led to the destruction of the physical integrity of the subjects represented. This applies in particular to the bodies of the female companions who inspired Picasso's artwork (see, e.g., Figure 9.11).[75]

Is to imagine the Minotaur as the alter ego of the artist perhaps also a nod to the – sometimes violent – dismantling this involves?

THE *MINOTAUROMACHY* AND THE PERILS OF MODERNITY

At this point we move on to the 1935 work that is generally regarded as the culmination of Picasso's Minotaur-themed works: *The Minotauromachy* ('Minotaur Battle', see Figure 9.12). It is here that Picasso generalizes from the experiences of human relationships at play in the works discussed above to comment on the human condition. And he does so by referencing once again the centaurs: he renders the more common Centauromachy into a Minotauromachy – and thus replaces the fight for

9.12. Pablo Picasso, *The Minotauromachy* (1935). Photo © RMN-Grand Palais (Musée national Picasso-Paris)/Béatrice Hatala. © Succession Picasso/ Copyright Agency 2023.

civilization with a more complex sense of what is being fought over and why.

The picture brings together a number of themes and figures that also feature elsewhere in Picasso's oeuvre. What is new is the Christ-like figure on the ladder to the left.[76] Everything else is familiar. Again, there is the little girl with flowers, here also holding a candle; there is the fragmented upper torso of a woman (frequently taken to be a matadora, a female matador) with her breasts exposed, hopelessly entangled with the body of a white mare (another frequent motif of Picasso's oeuvre);[77] and there are two young female spectators with doves (or pigeons) overlooking the scene this time from a window above.[78] The Minotaur with a mighty bullish head and mouth, again slightly open, is walking into the picture from the right. He dominates the scene with an outstretched right arm taking up the middle section of the picture. He is clearly the visual and logical centre of the relationships depicted here. All other figures relate to his presence.

The *Minotauromachy* stands out in the depth of its composition. The figures are brought together in a series of contrasts that extend almost seamlessly from the subject of the picture to the mode of its composition: there is darkness and light, proximity and distance, stagnation and movement, land and sea, sky and earth, male and female.[79] The Minotaur's human and animal components, including once again its ambiguously open mouth, are part of this blending of contrasts. Moreover, the etching features symbols of peace (the white dove) and innocence (the girl holding the candle and flowers) alongside representations of violence and destruction (the sword, the entangled and exposed bodies of the woman and the mare). There are no obvious clues about how to reconcile them.

Has the Minotaur made the horse buckle? Has he exposed and broken the female body?[80] If so, why? Picasso here chose the traditional human/bull combination with the human features strictly limited to the beast's brawny, masculine body and the head fully that of a bull. As we have seen above (in Figures 9.2–9.4), this combination, this rendering of hybridity, makes it difficult to discern the motivations of the Minotaur.[81] There are no humanizing features that allow us to deduce such information. What stands out is his grand, imposing gesture.[82]

Given the etching's title of 'Minotaur battle', we may wonder who is fighting here? And whom? The answer to these questions brings us once again face to face with the centaurs as another group of hybrid creatures from the ancient world. The Minotaur-battle references the more common centaur-battle ('Centauromachy') – a popular theme of ancient Greek art from the Archaic period onwards. Represented prominently in the metopes of the Acropolis, the Centauromachy visualizes the quintessential human battle for civilization against wild, violent, and animalistic forces. As far as the depictions on the Acropolis are concerned, the centaurs put on a strong fight against the legendary people of the Lapiths. They may even momentarily have the upper hand even though (according to the myth) they will ultimately loose. Picasso's *Minotauromachy* recalls this paradigmatic battle but replaces the centaurs as forces that stand outside of human culture with the Minotaur as a figure which represents human hubris and transgression. Picasso thus generalizes the themes of the Centauromachy. In the *Minotauromachy*, it is no longer the specific Greek (male) political identity and its civilizing presence that is at stake but human nature more generally.

The *Minotauromachy* depicts, I believe, the human at war with the self. The Minotaur's imposing presence exposes destructive forces deep within the human that defy domestication and stand in sharp contrast to culture and civility. As in all successful works of art, the subject points in different directions, referring to Picasso's experience as a lover *and* to the way in which it inspired his artistic vision.[83] It alludes to the historical situation as much as the human condition more broadly.[84] The figure of the Minotaur is central to this perspective: the picture places him firmly within a realm that brings together symbols of war and peace, destruction and resurrection, hope and despair, thus highlighting the volatility of the human condition as an experience that defined both his personal life and the larger historical situation. The Minotaur and the figure of Christ bring together Classicism and Christianity as formative strands in Western conceptions of the human. Both bring out notions of death and destruction *and* (the possibility of) resurrection. The candle and dove also allude to Christian symbolism. Picasso draws selectively on some of the formative forces of the Western tradition to critique its underlying conceptions of the human from within by exposing its contradictions and inconsistencies.

Only two years after the *Minotauromachy*, Picasso conceived of another work that resonates with the Minotaur-themed masterwork in theme, composition, and ambition. Arguably Picasso's most significant work, *Guernica* is a large oil painting (349 x 776 cm) named after the Basque town which, in 1937, during the Spanish Civil War, was bombed to oblivion by Nazi Germany and Fascist Italy (see Figure 9.13).[85] *Guernica* depicts human suffering and the terrors of modern warfare in all its cruelty through a focus on mangled bodies, stretched out arms, and gaping open mouths. The *Minotauromachy* is frequently seen as anticipating *Guernica* even though the overall mood in the latter is distinctly more grim than in the former: in *Guernica,* the space of the Minotaur has been taken by a bull and there is no longer a little girl with a candle that provides hope: just a cold, industrial light.[86]

AND SO?

In Picasso's oeuvre, the Minotaur represents a counterforce from within the classical tradition that challenges the aesthetics of Classicism and its formative modes of thinking and representing the human. Picasso's Minotaur, through his mere presence, takes aim at Western humanism in terms of body *and* mind. He does not stand for the physical integrity and aesthetic ideal of the classical body and its many impersonations in Neoclassicism; nor does he represent the power of *logos* and its claims to represent or shape a world that is rational, realistic, and devoid of contradictions. Instead, he personifies the intervention of the irrational, the physical, and the unconscious into the rational, cerebral, and reasoned.

His hybridity – elaborated so carefully in the ancient myth – is central to his modern presence. In his violent and destructive streaks, he shows the human (and human sexuality) at its most animal-like. And yet, at the same time, he shows an existential vulnerability shared by human *and*

9.13. Pablo Picasso, *Guernica* (1937). Photo © BPK, Berlin, Dist. RMN-Grand Palais/Alfredo Dagli Orti. © Succession Picasso/Copyright Agency 2023.

non-human animal alike. In his – now more, now less – humanized impersonations, Picasso's Minotaur exposes a painful insight underlined by the volatile events of the early twentieth century: our humanity is only ever a thin veneer on a deeper animality that may break through at any time.

Overall, then, the figure of the Minotaur, in both its ancient and its modern manifestations, presents a test case for what happens if human and animal identities come together, a testing of the boundaries of the human condition, as well as a further example of the appropriation of the animal in thinking the human. At the same time, the questions raised by his hybrid existence anticipate some of the themes and problems that will play a central role in the next chapter on metamorphosis.

And it is to a new story – the last in this book – that we now turn.

CHAPTER 10

The final chapter revolves around metamorphosis – the idea that in the realm of myth and storytelling, humans can transform into non-human animals and, sometimes, back again. The lead creatures here are the shearwaters of Diomedea – a group of seabirds. The back story explaining their presence on a small island in the Mediterranean Sea presents metamorphosis as the ultimate test case for thinking the human.

This chapter shows that tales of metamorphosis draw on the same notion of hybridity discussed in the previous one. Many of the ancient and modern creatures affected by it are, in effect, hybrids: they retain part of their human identity while also sporting the body of an animal. The traditional association between the mind with the human and the body with the animal side of our existence again plays into the picture here.

We put the shearwaters in conversation with other humans-turned-animals, both ancient and modern, and investigate how they reflect on the experience of transformation. It is on this point that a fundamental difference between ancient and modern ways of thinking the human becomes apparent. Modern tales of metamorphosis tend to explore the dissolution of the boundary that separates the human from all other animals. The ancient conversation, by contrast, returns to – and ultimately affirms – some of the positions of the philosophical debate and the case for human difference made over its course.

10.1. Mank's Shearwater Robert Havel after J. J. Audubon (1836) © Wikimedia Commons.

The Shearwaters of Diomedea (*Calonectris diomedea transformata*)

THE SCOPOLI SHEARWATER (CALONICTRIS DIOMEDEA) IS a medium-sized seabird still common today in the Adriatic Sea and in other parts of the Mediterranean.[1] It feeds mainly on small fish, crustaceans, squid, and zooplankton. Migratory and pelagic, it comes ashore to breed on rocky cliffs. Its calls are surprisingly similar to the sounds of a crying baby. One modern naturalist aptly describes them as a 'harsh, snoring, repeated wail'.[2] No wonder, then, that in the ancient imagination the cry of these birds reminded some of human lamentations.[3]

In *On Animals*, Aelian describes the curious behaviour of a shearwater population inhabiting a remote island in the middle of the Adriatic Sea:[4]

> These (shearwaters), it is said, neither harm the barbarians nor go near them. If, however, a stranger from Greece puts in to port, the birds by some divine dispensation (*theia tini dōrea*) approach, extending their wings as though they were hands, to welcome and embrace the strangers. And if the Greeks stroke them, they do not fly away, but stay still and allow themselves to be touched; and if the men sit down, the birds fly on to their lap as though they had been invited to a meal.[5]

Surely, it seems, the local shearwaters stand out not only in the uncanny capacity to distinguish between Greek and non-Greek members of the species *homo sapiens* but also in the human-like way they welcome visiting Hellenes with outstretched wings and a large dose of trust.

So, what is the story here? What is it about the island and its avian population that these birds seem unafraid of certain human visitors – even seek physical contact with them – but show no interest whatever in others?

Aelian's explanation of why the birds extend this special welcome to Greeks visiting their shores departs from the seemingly impartial tone of naturalistic observation and enters the realm of myth and storytelling:

> They are said to be the companions of Diomedes and to have taken part with him in the war against Ilium (Troy); though their original form was afterwards changed into that of birds, they nevertheless still preserve their Greek nature and their love of Greece.[6]

According to Aelian, the local shearwaters had once been human – and specifically, Greeks – the comrades of Diomedes, the king of Argos who had fought alongside Achilles, Odysseus, and the other Greek heroes at Troy.[7]

A quick look elsewhere in Greco-Roman mythology confirms that there is indeed an extended back story to explain the curious behaviour of the birds: one of Diomedes' questionable achievements in the Trojan War was wounding Aphrodite, the Greek goddess of love and passion.[8] That it was ill-advised to do so became painfully clear to Diomedes on his return home, where he learnt that his wife had been unfaithful and was plotting his demise.[9]

So, Diomedes set off again to sail the Mediterranean. In the following years, he is said to have founded several cities in southern Italy, until finally – according to one tradition – he died on the very island now inhabited by the birds.[10] At his death, his comrades grieved so deeply that the goddess Aphrodite – either from compassion or the desire for further retribution – turned them into birds.[11]

METAMORPHOSIS AND THINKING THE HUMAN

At first glance, this story reads as another touching example of outstanding animal loyalty. The birds' cries forever recall the death of Diomedes, while their favouring of Greeks appears to acknowledge their former ethnicity. Yet there is more to this tale. The shearwaters of Diomedea embody the result of a process that is perhaps the most spectacular, complex, and significant form of human/animal entanglement that connects us with the ancient world: metamorphosis.

The Greeks and Romans entertained the idea that, in certain situations and under certain conditions as paraded in ancient myth and storytelling, it was possible for humans to change shape and to take on animal form. While tales of human/animal transformation are also well known from other cultural traditions, the ancient world contributed some of the most famous accounts of metamorphosis of all time – accounts that continue to resonate in the literary tradition to this day.[12]

In Greco-Roman thought and literature, the transformation of humans into non-human animals constitutes just one facet of a much larger spectrum of possible metamorphoses.[13] We also encounter dramatic (self-)transformations of some gods and goddesses from their predominantly human form into animals, or different features of the natural environment (plants, water, stones, islands, or mountains), or the likeness of particular humans. The same gods could also effect the transformation of humans into an equally impressive array of animals or environmental features. All things considered, Diomedes' comrades got off lightly: their avian form was certainly preferable to the fate of the deplorable Niobe, who was turned to stone after angering some Greek gods, thus crossing not merely the boundary from human to non-human animal but, arguably, the more consequential one from animate to lifeless.[14]

ANALOGIES AND CONTINUITIES

Aelian's account does not give many particulars of the transformation of Diomedes' comrades into birds. His focus is entirely on the outcome once the transformation is complete and the way in which the local shearwaters conduct themselves vis-à-vis visitors to their island. In order to find out more about the specifics of metamorphosis as a process rather than a fait accompli, we turn to another ancient author.

About two centuries before Aelian, the Roman poet Publius Ovidius Naso (43 BCE–17 CE), better known as Ovid, wrote his *Metamorphoses* – one of the most influential texts from classical antiquity. This extended narrative poem combines an account of the world from its creation to the deification of Julius Caesar in 42 BCE. It is an invariably complex and many-layered text that playfully performs in its own narrative the kind of metamorphoses it depicts, and which transforms the reader in the course of it. With the swirl of mythological stories at its core, it provides a contrast to the strict and all-encompassing imperial epistemology of the Augustan Age.[15] It draws on narrative to subvert the very certainties – be they religious, ideological, or political – that it seems to embrace elsewhere. The concept of metamorphosis is central to this endeavour. Ovid takes a broad view of the topic; his description of human/animal metamorphosis is grounded in a larger account of change and transformation in the natural world.

Metamorphoses includes a detailed account of the very moment Diomedes' comrades turn into birds. A man called Acmon from the city of Pleuron in Aetolia in northern Greece, who had himself roused Venus/Aphrodite's ire, is the first to change shape:

> [H]is voice and throat together grew thin; his hair was changed to feathers, and feathers clothed a new-formed neck and breast and back. His arms acquired large pinion-feathers and his elbows curved into nimble wings; his toes were replaced by webbed feet and his face grew stiff and horny, ending in a sharp pointed beak.[16]

In the face of such dramatic events, Diomedes' remaining comrades are left with the very sense of wonder and astonishment (Greek: *thambos*, Latin: *mirabilium*) that Richard Buxton has described as the typical human response to the metamorphotic experience in the ancient Greek world: 'Lycus viewed him in wonder, so also Idas, Rhexenor and Nycteus and Abas too' (*hunc Lycus, hunc Idas et cum Rhexenore Nycteus, hunc miratur Abas*).[17] And yet, they soon turn from witnesses of metamorphosis to subjects and undergo the same changes as Acmon.

If the reader is still in doubt as to what the new creatures looked like, Ovid, or rather the internal narrator of his text, provides an analogy: 'If you ask the shape of these birds so swiftly formed, while they were not swans, they were very like snowy swans.'[18] This is odd because shearwaters don't really look like swans at all. However that may be, with this observation, the focus of the narrative has changed: from the description of individual body parts and the process of transformation as such to its final outcome and (pun intended) a bird's-eye view of the animal bodies generated in this way. The transformation is complete; the shearwaters are ready to stretch their wings and fly off.

Here and elsewhere, Ovid foregrounds the process of transformation with a focus on the changes affecting individual body parts: human hair turns into feathers covering the whole torso, elbows bend into wings.[19] Human feet morph into the webbed feet of seabirds that can navigate on land and in water. The face becomes hard and stiff, as does the mouth, which transforms into a beak. The specific steps necessary to turn a human body into that of an animal are described in minute detail. The vivid and confronting description visualizes the transformation in all its startling detail.

Yet are the particulars of this transformation merely accidental, due perhaps to the predilections of the supernatural that enacts it? Or is there a deeper logic behind it? At least in this particular story, there is nothing bird-like about Diomedes' comrades to suggest that their conversion into shearwaters is anything but random. Indeed, it is probable that the birds' human-sounding cries inspired the shaping of the tale, not the other way round.[20] We also do not hear of any physical or behavioural characteristics that carried over from their human into their animal states – the birds' wailing cries notwithstanding. But in other sections of *Metamorphoses*, Ovid goes further and suggests that there are not just general physical analogies between humans and other animals, but overt individual continuities.[21]

A single example among many to illustrate this point: that of the hubristic, obnoxious king Lycaon of Arcadia with his apposite name (Greek *lykos* means 'wolf') and insatiable appetite for contemptuous behaviour towards gods and humans alike. When he finally sets out to put Zeus/Jupiter's divinity to the test by trying to kill him in his sleep and serving up roasted human flesh, the most powerful of the Greco-Roman gods has enough and punishes one boundary transgression with another: 'His garments change to shaggy hair, his arms to legs. He turns into a wolf.'[22] This is not very different from the description of the transformation of the shearwaters. There is, however, more to this metamorphosis than meets the eye. The wolf's behaviour reflects Lycaon's when human: 'His mouth of itself gathers foam, and with his accustomed greed for blood he turns against the sheep, delighting still in slaughter.'[23] This aspect of the transformation implies a closer, more individual, more intimate connection between Lycaon, the human, and Lycaon, the beast, in particular as such behavioural continuities extend on the physical level: 'And yet (he) retains some traces of his former shape. There is the same grey hair, the same fierce face, the same gleaming eyes, the same picture of beastly savagery.'[24] These observations focus on individual features that carry across from human to animal. They suggest that the ferocious, wolf-like nature already present in Lycaon comes fully to the fore in his animal incarnation.[25] In other words, his bloodlust, violence, and general ferocity – all traits that already defined Lycaon as a human being – become somatized when he is transformed into an animal. So, this human was already a 'wolf', not just in name but in character as well, long before he drew the ire of the gods. The example of Lycaon shows that some accounts of metamorphosis present mind and body as connected dimensions of identity. The body serves as a canvas for the inner animal nature to take physical shape.

The example of Lycaon illustrates the closeness of metamorphosis to a figure of speech, which likewise presupposes two things separate in principle and sets them in relation to each other: that of metaphor.[26] Metaphor brings two seemingly disparate entities together by highlighting a single, real, or imagined common feature.[27] Intriguingly, perhaps, humans *and* animals often feature in pairs between which we make such connections. To call a woman a 'bitch', a man a 'snake', and someone pulling a string of all-nighters a 'night owl', we – or at least those of us inclined to label our fellow humans in such unfavourable terms – imply that there is some internal connection, some central feature or characteristic that brings together the human and non-human in question. Metamorphosis tells the story of a real, sudden, and catastrophic intervention into the human condition that leads to the transformation into animal. And yet, in many instances it also alludes to the possibility of a deeper metaphorical connection between those human and animal identities – a connection that the process of transformation brings to the fore.

Such metaphorical associations between humans and animals feature already in the earliest examples of classical literature. Fragment seven of the ancient Greek poet Semonides, for example, dating from the seventh century BCE, kicks off in the manner of a grand revelation: 'In the beginning the god made diverse the female mind.'[28] The real flavour of this 'revelation', however, emerges in the next line: 'One woman he created from a long-bristled sow. Throughout her house everything lies in disorder, befouled with mud, and rolls about on the floor, and she herself unwashed, in clothes unwashed, sits in the dung and grows fat.'[29] This is hardly a flattering description. What comes next is no better: Semonides goes on to distinguish a number of female types by associating them with animals (the vixen, the bitch, the monkey, etc.).

Semonides' poem reverberates with human/animal metamorphosis in interesting ways: As in metamorphosis, the power to overcome the human/animal divide and to form one out of the other is attributed to the gods (*theos empoiēsen*). And here, too, there is continuity of character between the human and animal in question. Yet, in this instance, it is the human that morphs out of the animal – not the other way around. Moreover, this transformation does not occur on the individual level (as in metamorphosis) but affects a whole type. The poem thus plays with the very assumptions and conventions that also inform the idea of metamorphosis. Above all, it establishes a connection between the human and the non-human animal that at first seems to tell a temporal story of creation by divine intervention but soon moves beyond, to the timeless level of metaphor and analogy. By highlighting the act of creation, Semonides' poem draws attention to the transfer of meaning at the heart of all metaphorical typecasting. Quite literally, it parades metaphor in the making.

Here and elsewhere, the charades resulting from this kind of typecasting prove good to laugh with. In Aristophanes' comedy *Acharnians* (425 BCE), an impoverished Greek from Megara (a *polis* infamous for the crude humour of its inhabitants) tries to sell off his two daughters as little pigs to be sacrificed at an upcoming festival. But his efforts carry a not-so-subtle subtext: the ancient Greek word for little pig – *choiros* – doubles as a slang word for female genitalia. Both meanings of the word remain at play in the ensuing conversation and the resulting double entendre is tangible even in English translation:

MEGARIAN: Is that a piggy (*choiros*)?
DICAEOPOLIS: It looks like a piggy now, but all grown up it'll be a pussy!
MEGARIAN: Rest assured, in five years she'll be just like her mother.[30]

We should not kill the joke here by overthinking it. Suffice it to say that the semantic space in which piggy and pussy converge is invariably fertile: it houses a mother sow and her offspring and carries the stench of fertility, shameless sexuality, and innocence lost. It is a space in which literal and metaphorical meanings seamlessly blend into each other.

Occasionally, however, the relationship between metaphor and metamorphosis is literal. In his satirical novel *The Golden Ass* (second century CE), Apuleius tells us about a certain witch who, as a form of punishment, turned her unfaithful lover into a beaver (*castor*). If this seems an unusual choice, the explanation is even more arresting: '[B]ecause when that animal is afraid of being captured it escapes from its pursuers by cutting off its own genitals, and she wanted the same thing to happen to him since he had intercourse with another woman.'[31] As in the case of animal metaphors applied to humans, it is a single behavioural feature which carries over from animal to human.

In other instances, there is no such literal transfer of meaning, and the relationship is analogical. It is at this point that Aelian's shearwaters come into the picture again. Written by a Roman in the ancient Greek language during the first/second centuries CE, *On Animals* (a naturalistic account of animal lore) is deeply grounded in the ideological concerns of the 'Second Sophistic', a period we already touched upon in Chapter 2 that witnessed a reorientation towards Classical Greek learning and an understanding of Hellenicity long after Greece itself had come under Roman rule.[32] Aelian uses the shearwater passage as an opening chapter in order to make a point about the incorruptible essence of Hellenism which continues to exist in the birds post transformation.[33] The shearwaters harbour a veiled reference to the significance and standing of Greek *paideia* (education and learning) among the educated elites of the Roman Empire. In other words: the transformation of human into animal stands for the transformation of Greeks into Romans. Aelian refers to the story to assert that, 'regardless of one's physical appearance, one's central Greek core is unchangeable'.[34] And yet, at the same time, the shearwater story also seems to criticize this 'identity politics': given that the story is set on a Roman island, Aelian also points to the artificial and constructed nature of this Greek identity in Roman lands.

The transfer of meaning from the non-human to the human animal is not exclusive to Aelian and the shearwaters, nor indeed to the animal world: it can also be found in modern accounts of metamorphosis. In Marie Darrieusceq's provocative novella *Pig Tales: A Novel of Lust and Transformation* (1996), for example, it takes the form of an extended allegory in which certain aspects of the human condition become tangible through association with the non-human and animalistic. The story she tells takes literally the same association between human and animal that we already saw at play in Semonides' first type of female: the derogatory reference to a human female as a 'sow'. Set in a dystopian future of uncertain time and place, the novel's female narrator finds herself veering between the human and the animal condition, and several states between. In her case, these identities emerge as the result of both self-identification and the projections onto her by others. Above all, they are formed in interaction with men encountered in her role as escort in a massage parlour. That the result involves a certain amount of dehumanizing is telling. It reveals the prejudices, associations, and slurs that constitute the ugly underbelly of present-day gender politics. It is also a symptom of the modern condition more broadly, in which the female body is commodified, exploited, and abused. The sow thus internalizes the way in which women are degraded and presents the resulting humiliation and loss of self-respect as a malady of modernity. It unmasks aspects of the human condition which would otherwise remain unrepresented – and unnoticed.

Of course, this is a far cry from the shearwaters of Diomedea. The link to their former humanity is much more tenuous and brittle. But there is a strand in the thinking about the human condition that was already present in Aelian's description of the birds and their welcoming outstretched wings: the physical analogies between humans and animals which, occasionally at least, extend into analogies in character and behaviour. So, in some sense, metamorphosis *is* metaphor. In the examples discussed above, the process of transformation stands for a deeper transfer of meaning between human and non-human animal, mind and body.

METAMORPHOSIS, MIND, AND BODY

In many other instances, however, there is no deeper connection between the human character and the species into which a person is transformed. In such instances, there is no transfer of meaning – metaphorical or by analogy – between mind and body and hence between the human and animal modes of existence. In this strand of the tradition, the identities of human and non-human remain largely separated in the creatures that undergo such transformation. This is because in many instances, the metamorphosis from human to animal is not complete. It is the body that turns into an animal; the mind remains human.[35]

Again, the shearwaters are a case in point. Nothing in their physical appearance suggests that they are not proper members of the animal kingdom. And yet, even in their avian form, Diomedes' comrades seem to have retained not just (parts of) their human identity, but more specifically their Greek identity. It is their previous life *as Greeks* that explains the birds' astonishing capacity to distinguish between Greeks and non-Greeks, not to mention their blatant and unapologetic preference of the former over the latter.

These creatures may look and, in many ways, act like birds. And yet, in other ways their behaviour is not at all what one would expect from a bird, in particular from a species inhabiting a remote island free of human habitation and hence with limited human contact. The solution to this curiosity, as offered by Aelian, lies firmly in the past: the shearwaters of Diomedea still appear to be informed by their old human ways, in particular their specific Greek views and experiences – what Aelian himself calls their 'Greek nature' (*to einai Hellēnes*).

What this 'Greek nature' entails is not explicit in Aelian's account but left to us to infer. The shearwaters in question seem aware of their own human origins, and of the conventions of human encounters in general and those between Greeks in particular. They give their Greek visitors a special welcome; they seek physical contact with them as if welcoming old friends or family; finally, they settle with them for that most basic 'staple' of ancient Greek conviviality: a shared meal.

Other authors go further than Aelian in adding a moralizing twist to the story. The ancient Greek geographer Strabo (ca. 64 BCE–after 21

CE) states that the birds continued 'to live a sort of human life, not only in their orderly ways but also in their tameness towards honourable men and in their flight from wicked and knavish men'.[36] The preference of Greeks over non-Greeks in Aelian's account has turned here into an attraction to the morally good and a revulsion at the bad. Both variants of the story attribute to the shearwaters human values and preferences.

In retaining part of their human nature, the shearwaters are by no means exceptional. Again, there is a distinct strand in the metamorphotic tradition from ancient through to modern times that presents the transformation as a partial affair, affecting the body but leaving the mind untouched. That this is yet another instance of anthropocentrism becomes evident if we consider modern research into animal cognition. The growing field of cognitive ethology has variously shown that animals think and act differently from humans and that they do so according to the needs and experiences specific to their own species – an insight that every owner of a cat or dog will readily confirm.[37]

Already, the very first extended account of human/animal transformation in classical literature – the famous story from Homer in which the sorceress Circe turns some of Odysseus' comrades into pigs – highlights the centrality of the human in this way. Although Circe erased their memory of their homeland – in direct contrast to Aelian's shearwaters, who explicitly recall their ethnicity – the first thing we hear about them after their transformation is that 'they had the heads, and voice, and bristles, and shape of swine, but their minds (*nous*) remained unchanged, just as they were before'.[38] Like the shearwaters, the humans-turned-pigs retain their human minds but find their bodies morphed into animal form. The resulting duality between mind and body and human and animal parts adds new meaning to the notion of 'entanglement', as evident in the relationships explored in this book.

And yet, as we will see, the distinction between human and non-human animals, as one between mind and body, does not stand on its own. Further dualities align along the same divide: between physical and the mental dimensions of identity and being, for example, and between doing and thinking as separate yet mutually informative activities. In this part of the tradition, the transformed creatures are hybrids – their human and animal parts continue to exist separately.[39] This brings metamorphosis in line with those parts of the philosophical debate which have argued that humans have *logos* and animals have not, and that it is the presence of mind which defines our humanity.

METAMORPHOSIS AND METAPHOR REVISITED

Even though the shearwaters of Diomedea show the mind/body duality typical of many ancient and modern tales of transformation, Aelian's brief account of the birds' curious behaviour does not devote much space to it. The insight that the birds retain (at least some of) their human outlook and intelligence becomes evident merely in their behaviour and in its explanation provided by Aelian himself. In his naturalistic account of animal lore, the creatures themselves are not given a voice, at least not one intelligible to humans beyond the wailing sounds.

To listen to what humans-turned-animals have to say, then, we turn to some of the extended stories of human/animal metamorphosis from the ancient and modern worlds. We start with Lucius from the Greek city of Corinth, the infamous protagonist of Apuleius' Latin novel *Metamorphoses* (second century CE). Through some magic gone wrong he finds himself transformed into a donkey. His adventures in asinine form constitute the core of the tale until, finally, much later, he is transformed back into a human being with the help of the goddess Isis. The story takes the form of a first-hand account, so we hear what it is like to be an ass in the Roman Empire in the second half of the second century CE straight, as it were, from the donkey's mouth.[40]

Predictably, perhaps, the ass proves a problematic narrator who does not seem to be in full control of the story. This leaves the reader with the difficult task of making sense of it.[41] Despite its light-hearted, rowdy tone, *Metamorphoses* emerges as a surprisingly complex text that raises fundamental questions of credibility and direction without always resolving them. In Lucius' voice, human and asinine experiences, human and asinine concerns, and human and asinine longings blend. What shines through, nevertheless, is the excitement of the human turned animal. It manifests itself in the form of numerous situations in which Lucius, in his asinine form, runs into very human problems. Even though the tale touches on serious topics, such as slavery, exploitation, and suppression (see below), the light-hearted tone prevails. It is driven by a form of wild humour which combines sexual and metamorphic innuendo in a bawdy tale of lust and abuse.

And yet even the most avid reader will be vexed by the last transformation when the racy gives way to the religious. The story seems to end on a more sombre note when Lucius is initiated into the mysteries of Isis and ends up serving as her priest at Rome. And yet, we may wonder, are we really meant to believe that he now leads the respectable life of a religious convert? Or is Apuleius perhaps poking fun at the way in which the gullible Lucius, now restored to human form, still falls short of using his brainpower to make sure he is not exploited once again, this time by falling victim to a bogus religious cult?[42]

No matter what we make of this ending, one thing is clear: the animal form here provides the opportunity for the humorous appreciation of very human vices. This is because, as with Aelian's shearwaters, the ass has retained some of his humanity. Despite sporting enormous ears and gigantic genitals as markers of his new membership to the asinine species, he, too, maintains his *sensus humanus* ('his human intelligence').[43] So while his body may be that of an animal, Lucius' inner humanity persists – and comes to experience the human treatment of animals.

Lucius suffers variously at the hands of those humans with whom he comes in contact. He fears castration, even death, and is beaten regularly.[44] Occasionally such abuse inspires the asinine narrator to reflect on the standing of animals more generally:

> As for my comrades, the animals, what can I say? How can I describe their condition? What a sight! Those old mules and feeble geldings stood round the manger with their heads sunk down, munching through piles of chaff; their necks sagged from the rotting decay of sores; their flabby nostrils were distended from constant coughing; their chests were ulcerated from the continual rubbing of the rope harnesses; their flanks were bare to the bone from everlasting whipping, their hoofs stretched out to abnormal dimensions from their multiple circling, and their entire hide rough with decay and mangy starvation.[45]

As far as Lucius himself is concerned: At several points in his journey, he is treated as a commodity – sold, traded, and stolen.[46] Once he even serves as an unlikely trophy and object of misdirected sexual desire.[47] Of course, the novel never sheds its humoristic tone, and it is absolutely possible to laugh off the humiliation Lucius is experiencing. But behind the comic, the story strikes a more serious tone. It clearly shows that to many humans, animal life is worth only as much as it is of use to us. It has no intrinsic value. Indeed, at some point the asinine Lucius explicitly bemoans that humans see him and his companion, the horse, merely as 'future conveyors of the goods' and with 'no concern for our welfare'.[48] So even when humans appear to care for animals, they actually care only for themselves.

Lucius' existence at the margins of human society draws attention to other disadvantaged and dehumanized creatures in the ancient world, most notably slaves. Just like he himself, most of the other domestic animals he encounters suffer terrible abuse and the exploitation of their labor. In one reading, Apuleius' novel presents itself as a commentary on the institution of slavery.[49] In particular, it puts the focus sharply on the dehumanizing aspects of slavery.[50] The exploitation of slave labour, the physical abuse and maltreatment of slaves, and their status as a commodity are all aspects of Greco-Roman slavery explored through the analogy between animal and human suppression.[51] And yet, at the same time, all of this is contained in a storyline that draws on humour and 'cheap' puns to invite the reader to laugh at the thoughts of its main protagonist and to be entertained by his missteps and misfortunes. The serious and the light-hearted blend into each other to yield a situational comedy that observes rather than evaluates. And yet, serious questions as to the human treatment of other humans lurk just beneath the humoristic surface of the story.

Throughout the novel, different social realities come into play: although prior to his transformation Lucius was part of the elite of a Greek city in the Roman Empire, many of his new owners are not.[52] And, as with slavery, Lucius' social and economic status is linked to that of his owners. If they suffer from starvation, so does he; when they enjoy luxury and abundance he usually fares better, too. The perspective of Lucius, the ass, who takes the reader on this journey, exposes the inequalities in Roman society.[53] His suffering at the hands of his owners becomes representative of the suffering of all those disenfranchised, exploited, and dehumanized in the Roman Empire in the second century CE, no matter whether they are human or animal.

In associating Lucius' animal status with that of slaves, Apuleius develops a line of reasoning that has a long history in ancient thought and literature. The ancient Greek philosopher Aristotle developed his definition of natural slavery in analogy to that of non-human creatures. In *Politics*, he argues that slaves are to masters what domestic animals are to humans: both lack in intellect and are driven by emotions rather than reason. Both support their masters through physical labour.

> For he is by nature a slave who is capable of belonging to another (and that is why he does so belong), and who participates in reason so far as to apprehend it but not to possess it; for the animals other than man are subservient not to reason, by apprehending it, but to feelings. And also the usefulness of slaves diverges little from that of animals; bodily service for the necessities of life is forthcoming from both, from slaves and from domestic animals alike.[54]

The same analogy resonates in different parts of Greco-Roman thought and literature. It informs the writings of Xenophon about how to force slaves into obedience (by feeding them well, like animals), to the agricultural writings of the elder Cato who readily subsumes old or sickly slaves into the same category as 'worn-out oxen, blemished cattle, blemished sheep, wool, hides, an old wagon', to be readily disposed of when no longer useful.[55] In putting the spotlight on the suffering of Lucius, Apuleius reflects on a conversation that was going strong in other areas of Greco-Roman thought and literature.

The way in which *Metamorphoses* prompts the reader to draw analogies between the disenfranchisement of certain humans and animals emerges ever more clearly if compared to another version of the same story by Lucian. In his telling of the tale, he imagined an alternative ending to the story. After his transformation back into his human form, Lucius here returns once again to one of the women he had sex with as an ass . . . only to be outrightly dismissed when she finds out that he is now fully human!

Apparently, it was exactly his animal form which proved seductive, an attraction lost when Lucius is transformed back into human form. As one modern commentator has pointed out, the ending of the story 'wryly implies that a form of animality is in fact inherent in all human beings'.[56] In both Lucian's and Apuleius' rendering of the story, metamorphosis thus instigates a swerving between a literal and metaphorical animality of the human, between serious and humorous undertones. In both cases, the figure of Lucius, the human trapped in the body of an ass, holds up a mirror which shows very clearly that our humanity is on less firm footing than we are inclined to believe.

ESSENTIALLY HUMAN: FOOD

It is high time to point out what has already become obvious from the shearwaters and the other examples discussed so far: Metamorphosis, at least the conception of metamorphosis that emerged from of a specific part of the Greco-Roman tradition, centres the human condition. Rather than leading to a blurring of the conceptions of human and animal (as one may expect), or a deeper engagement with our own animal natures, metamorphosis points back to Greco-Roman conceptions of what is essentially human as they variously came into focus in the previous chapters of this book.

Take food for example. Humans and animals differ not only in their food choices but also in the style and manner of consumption. Accounts of metamorphosis variously dwell on this difference. Indeed, the fact that old culinary habits die hard is one of the first and most frequently commented-upon aspects, post transformation.

Again, the shearwaters prove the point. In their avian bodies, Diomedes' former comrades have retained some of their human appetites. In their apparent enthusiasm for mingling with Greek visitors to their islands for a communal feast, the birds' inner humanity and their Greekness shine through. Another version of the story, by the Hellenistic Greek poet Lycophron, develops the culinary dimension further. He mentions that the shearwaters of Diomedea do not merely welcome those they identify as Greeks (as Aelian has it) or good men (Strabo). Instead, he has them 'eat crumbs from the hand and fragments of cake from the table, murmuring pleasantly, remembering, hapless ones, their former way of life'.[57] The birds here seem to have retained their appetite and appreciation for the baked goods offered by Greek visitors. Their consumption brings them physically and culturally closer to their human origins.[58]

In a similar vein, Lucius, the ass, is delighted when served the leftovers of a lavish feast: 'pork, fowl, fish, and every other kind of meat' and 'breads, cookies, fritters, croissants, biscuits, and many other honey-sweetened dainties'.[59] In the face of such delicacies, he readily asserts that he 'was not such a complete fool nor so truly an ass (*nec . . . tam stultus eram tamque vere asinus*) to pass by those delicious dishes and dine on coarse hay.'[60] A comic self-recognition that turns around the link between certain foodstuffs and human identity.

The delight in certain (human) foodstuffs is one thing. The repulsion against other food items is another. Understandably, perhaps, the piggy protagonist of *Pig Tales* finds herself put off by pork: 'I could not eat ham sandwiches any more, they made me sick'.[61] The prospect of consuming pork triggers a strong feeling of disgust – a physical response typically occurring when one confronts rotten food, faeces, or decay as well as the transgression of moral boundaries.[62] In the revulsion of pig against pork the disgust against food and moral transgression merge and the possibility of cannibalism rears its ugly head again. By abstaining, the female protagonist protests both the human oppression of animals *and* the male domination of women.[63] And yet, at the same time, the repulsion against pork again points to an inner humanity: it is the thinking, rationalizing self that leads to the abstinence. The pig's revulsion thus also articulates a sense of alienation from certain manifestations of the self – something perhaps typical of the modern condition.

One more example: given its role in defining the identities of the human and non-human animal alike, it makes perfect sense that in David Garnett's novella *Lady into Fox* (1922), the choice of food becomes a litmus test for the main character's humanity. Garnett tells the story of a woman from Oxfordshire who, through unexplained circumstance, is transformed into a vixen. At first, the protagonist is reassured of his wife's inner humanity by her continuing taste for a civilized meal: 'She was still fond of the same food that she had been used to before her transformation, a lightly boiled egg or slice of ham, a piece of buttered toast or two, with a little quince and apple jam.'[64] And yet the civilized veneer disappears abruptly later in the tale. When his wife's inner humanity comes more and more into question, the increasingly desperate husband resorts to a simple test. He presents the vixen/wife with a basket containing a bunch of flowers and a rabbit and leaves the room for five minutes. Surely her inner humanity will prevail in her choice of flowers over rabbit? Not so! Upon his return, the shocked husband finds the flowers untouched but what remains of the rabbit splashed all over the floor.[65] The woman's increasing adherence to animal rather than human behaviours tracks her status as changing from human into animal. It might be tempting to read this story as representative of a noxious misogynism. Yet that would be too simple. By the 1920s, when the novella was published, the first wave of feminism had just created enough of a splash to make its effects felt beyond the circles of its key proponents. In one reading of the story, then, the woman's transformation from human into animal allows an escape from traditional gender stereotypes.[66]

But food preferences are only one of the issues highlighted in tales of metamorphosis to parade how human and non-human natures clash. Human and animal sides also rub up against each other in other ways. For example, Lucius, the ass, insists that, despite his donkey form, he once 'slept the sleep of a human being'.[67] In an unguarded moment, he stands up on two legs, giving up the animal gait altogether: 'Away from the road and hidden by the bushes, I could rise once more from the bent gait of a four-footed beast of burden to stand erect as a man, with no one watching.'[68] This latter example is especially telling: it points to the view that the upright posture defines the human – a variant of the 'man-only *topos*' that originated in the ancient world and much later informed such diverse works as Immanuel Kant's *Critique of Practical Reason* and Sigmund Freud's *Civilization and Its Discontents*.[69]

ESSENTIALLY HUMAN: LANGUAGE

Predictably, perhaps, given its status in the philosophical debate (see Chapter 2), language serves as another important marker of human status explored in tales of metamorphosis.[70] And here, too, we will find that mind and body, human and animal aspects of identity clash. This is because language stands at the intersection of the physical and the mental/cognitive. While the thoughts themselves are a matter of the mind, the capacity to express them in spoken words involves coordination between the brain and parts of the body – vocal cords, tongue, teeth, and other parts of the mouth. So, the thinking of thoughts is one thing; the ability to articulate them through spoken language quite another.

The loss of human language is one of the most common afflictions of humans-turned-animals in Greco-Roman literature. And, in some cases, there is again an element of continuity: our shearwaters, for example, certainly find their capacity to articulate limited to distinctive cries. And yet, these cries still retain a distinctly human ring, intelligible to human visitors to the island as expressions of mourning. In most other cases, however, the creatures affected are bereft even of this minimal link to their previous and now fully internalized humanity: they are deprived of all ways to articulate what they have to say, at least through the medium of spoken language.

This is how the unfortunate Argive princess Io fared after her transformation into a cow:

> [A]nd when she attempted to voice her complaints, she only mooed. She would start with fear at the sound, and was filled with terror at her own voice. She came also to the bank of her father's stream, where she used to play; but when she saw, reflected in the water, her gaping jaws and sprouting horns, she fled in very terror of herself ... if only she could speak (*si modo verba sequantur*), she would tell her name and sad misfortune, and beg for aid. But instead of words, she did tell the sad story of her changed form with letters which she traced in the dust with her hoof.[71]

The example of Io, as presented by Ovid, again highlights that it is not an absence of human thoughts that torments the creature in question but the physical inability to articulate them in spoken language. Io resorts to writing to disclose her inner human identity to her father. Other creatures adopt the silence that some philosophers have taken as typical of the animal condition. Lucian the ass finds himself unable to bemoan his fate. Referring to the slave girl Photis who had accidentally transformed him into a donkey, he states: 'I wanted to complain about what Photis had done, but I lacked human gestures as well as words. Still, I did the only thing I could: I hung my lower lip, looked askance at her with moist eyes, and berated her in silence.'[72] This silence stands in stark contrast to the distinctly articulate first-person narrator, who is not shy to share his thoughts both grand and small.[73]

It is deafening.

What the ass *is* able to articulate fails to convince us otherwise. Lucius seeks to voice his admiration for the emperor in this way: 'I tried amidst those crowds of Greeks to invoke the august name of Caesar in my native tongue. And indeed I shouted the "O" by itself eloquently and vigorously, but I could not pronounce the rest of Caesar's name.'[74] The donkey's characteristic braying here passes as veneration but falls short of naming its object.

Metamorphosis as a locus of the ancient and modern *imaginaire* enacts the mind/body duality to revisit the question of what makes us human. For a moment, the possibility of transcending the boundary and experiencing the world from the point of view of an animal seems within reach; and yet, before we really cross over into new, unknown, and potentially disturbing territory, the conversation reverts, once again, to the standard tropes of thinking the human: the capacity to speak, to eat certain foodstuffs in certain ways, to stand upright, and, above all, to thinking, reasoning, and arguing.

THE SPECIAL CASE OF KAFKA'S GREGOR SAMSA

It is against the background of the metamorphic tradition that the experiences of Franz Kafka's Gregor Samsa stand out – arguably the most famous modern tale of a transformation of human into animal. In *Metamorphosis* (first published in 1915), Kafka draws on the features of the ancient metamorphic tradition. Here, too, language, food, and upright posture and an emphasis on the mind over the body serve as markers of humanity. Yet, Kafka presents them in new and distinctly modern ways that convey a fundamental alienation from the self.

Language again serves as a prominent example. In Kafka's *Metamorphosis,* too, we find a divide between human mind and animal body; here, too, the struggle between the main characters' human and non-human sides becomes tangible in the medium of language; and here, too, the ruptures resulting from the transformation are reflected by the affected creature itself:

> Gregor had a shock as he heard his own voice answering hers, unmistakably his own voice, it was true, but with a persistent horrible twittering squeak behind it like an undertone, which left the words in their clear shape only for the first moment and then rose up reverberating around them to destroy their sense, so that one could not be sure one had heard them rightly.[75]

Gregor Samsa, the travelling salesman, who one morning finds himself transformed into a 'monstrous vermin' ('ein ungeheures Ungeziefer'), perceives the sound of his own voice as being both human and animal.[76] More specifically, his animal sounds interfere with his human voice 'from below', making it impossible for Samsa to express himself clearly and intelligibly. At first, he dismisses the change as the lingering effects of a cold, but soon enough it becomes clear that he is increasingly incapable of human language.[77]

In Kafka's radical rendering of metamorphosis, there is thus more at stake than a mere disconnection between mind and body. *Metamorphosis* tells the story of both a sudden transformation from human into animal and a slow, processual one. While the initial, physical transformation of the travelling salesman into a verminous bug is sudden and presented as a fait accompli at the beginning of the story, its core consists of the gradual adjustment of Samsa's reflective human self to his new physical reality. So, mind and body, human and non-human sides of identity do not remain separate and separable entities but variously interfere with each other, with the mind gradually adjusting to the new realities of the body.

At first, Samsa carries on with his usual human routines. Yet, he soon realizes that they no longer satisfy him. His attempt to walk upright, for example, results in him falling over; soon he finds more comfort in using all his little legs.[78] Later on, he embraces the fact that creeping is the new walking and crawls over the walls and the ceiling. Similarly with food: he is excited at first to be served milk, a favourite drink prior to his transformation – but finds that he no longer likes it.[79] He is disgusted by fresh food but fancies the very same cheese he had previously deemed inedible.[80] In Samsa's experience, the traditional markers of humanity (food, language, upright posture, etc.) are evoked only for the protagonist to realize that they no longer fit his new physical reality. As a result, it is impossible to tell where Samsa's humanity ends and where his animal nature begins.[81]

It matters that it is not just any animal body that Samsa assumes here but one which ends up mute, which is monstrous and disgusting – even to the affected creature itself and which, from its very inception, flags the possibility of eradication. This possibility is realized by the death of the vermin at the end of the story. Before that, however, we find that Samsa's inner humanity does not remain unaffected by his body but gradually fades away. It is this experience which makes Samsa's story one of the most profound instances of debasement in the whole metamorphic tradition.

What drives this process?[82] What kind of force shapes this particular transformative experience? Could the transformation stand for the wish to escape from the confines of a close-knit domestic situation and its problematic family relations?[83] Is Kafka here fictionalizing very real questions of exploitation and subservience?[84] Is Samsa's transformation 'a form of punishment for a failed existence'?[85] Or is this ultimately 'a tale of stigmatization and societal exclusion'?[86] All these different interpretations take the figure of the verminous bug to be an image that reveals certain aspects of the human condition. From the wish to escape from the present, as an expression of solitude, or as a rejection of the exploitation of labour, the creature's experience points by analogy to the human realm. In Kafka's account, too, metamorphosis draws on metaphor, a feature that again points back to some of the famous metamorphoses in the ancient world.[87]

Ever since Darwin's theory of evolution, it has become clear that humans are, in effect, animals. This applies not merely to the physical but to behavioural and cognitive aspects as well, making it increasingly hard to tell what (if anything) sets the human apart. At the same time, the gods are mostly absent from modern tales of metamorphosis. They are no longer attributed with the power to initiate the transition from human to animal. Instead, the transformation seems more accidental or fortuitous – motivated by forces in ourselves or the company we keep. To bring these forces to the fore, modern tales of metamorphosis tend to focus on transformation as a process rather than a one-off event, thus opening up space for the intermediary stages. The affected creatures can veer back and forth between the human and the animal condition, as in the case of the female protagonist of *Pig Tales*, or undergo a period of inner adjustment to their new physicality like Gregor Samsa. This oscillation between the human and the animal condition seems to be a feature of the modern metamorphic literature. In the wake of Darwin's theory of evolution, it reflects a new level of uncertainty about where our human sides end and where our animal natures begin.

PLACE, TIME, AND RITUAL

In the final section of this chapter, we return once more to the ancient world and, in particular, the power of the gods to instigate the transformation from human to non-human animal. To revisit the shearwaters, we listen to one more voice commenting on their behaviour. It belongs to the Christian theologian Augustine of Hippo in northern Africa (354–430 CE), a decisive force in the early history of Christianity.[88]

In *City of God*, he too touches upon the shearwaters' curious behaviour. By his account, the birds do not merely spurn non-Greek visitors to their island but actively abuse them:

> [I]f any Greeks or men of Greek descent happen to visit the spot they not merely keep the peace, but even fawn upon them, whereas if they see men of other races, they fly up at their heads and wound them with such heavy blows as even to kill them. For they are said to be well armed for these battles with huge, hard beaks.[89]

We are back to the shearwaters distinguishing between Greek and non-Greek visitors, as in Aelian's account. Yet, rather than merely ignoring non-Greeks, the birds attack them for no apparent reason other than their ethnic difference.

The birds' aggressive behaviour is not explained here; nor is their motivation to distinguish between Greek and non-Greek visitors to their island as in Aelian's account. Yet, in evoking this behaviour of the birds, Augustine's story recalls another variant of the tale that expands on some of Diomedes' experiences after the Trojan War. According to one tradition, invading Illyrians killed the followers of Diomedes on the island of Diomedea while they were conducting sacrifices, resulting in their subsequent transformation into birds by Zeus. This would afford a motivation for the birds' discriminatory behaviour.

Augustine's references to the story stand out for their distinctively religious twist, presenting the birds as devout worshippers in avian form. Referring to the fact that Diomedes was – post-mythological-mortem – venerated as a semi-divine figure on the island, he states: 'In fact, they say that his temple is situated on the island Diomedea not far from mount Garganus in Apulia, and that these winged creatures fly about the temple and dwell there, showing such marvellous veneration that they fill their beaks with water and sprinkle the temple with it.'[90] This time, the shearwaters are not merely lamenting the death of their former comrade but are actively involved in his worship.

There is one dimension of the ancient metamorphotic tradition which we have not yet considered that the shearwaters can help to explain: in addition to their transformation, the affected creatures seem to step outside of time.[91] The local shearwaters will forever discriminate between honest and dishonest men (Strabo); they will carry on with their wails, forever bemoaning the death of Diomedes (Aelian); they will carry on venerating him and participating in his cult in perpetuity (Augustine). There is nothing in any of these authors to suggest that subsequent generations of these birds are in any way different from the first. Indeed, Augustine himself acknowledges this peculiar feature of the birds when he points out that 'their type is said to persist through successive generations'.[92] The local shearwater population remains connected to the story of Diomedes for all time. His life and death remain the sole and eternal point of reference for how these birds feature in Greco-Roman thought and literature.[93]

Their timelessness makes these birds superbly suitable for their role in the cult of Diomedes. Ritual practice is deeply grounded in the idea of repetition and of keeping the past present. So, the birds' curious behaviour, in particular their involvement in worship, sustains the cult of Diomedes in more than one way: the shearwaters provide the cult with a story that links the island with the figure of Diomedes and keeps the mythical past alive and relevant through the presence of the birds.

In this function, the story of the shearwaters is by no means unique. The link between metamorphosis and features of the natural environment is well established.[94] Typically, accounts of metamorphosis give an explanation for certain natural features by presenting them as the result of a transformation that occurred in the mythical past. The stories surrounding the shearwaters of Diomedea constitute a variant of such tales. While they do not explain a feature of the natural environment, they do explain the island's special connection to Diomedes. Moreover, the extraordinary behaviour of the local birds sustains the claim of the extraordinary, supernatural status of Diomedes himself, thus sustaining and legitimizing his cult on the island.

Recent archaeological research has revealed evidence of cult activity centred upon the figure of Diomedes in different parts of the Adriatic Sea, including on several islands and in Greek coastal settlements.[95] This evidence supplements the literary evidence from the ancient world associating Diomedes with the foundation of various coastal cities in southern Italy.[96] It shows that there was a lively cult of Diomedes among the seafaring Greeks of the Adriatic Sea that probably started during the Archaic period but reached its peak in Hellenistic times.[97] The Greek cities in question invoked the figure of Diomedes as both explanation and affirmation of their Greek identity as well as protector of seafaring, shipping, and trade. That the birds distinguish between Greek and non-Greek visitors to their shores and otherwise affirm their Hellenist credentials is thus central to their purpose.

The stories surrounding Diomedes and the shearwaters are thus part of a larger network of tales that help to place and define local identities.[98] The story of Diomedes, his successful return after the Trojan War, and his subsequent adventures bestow particular religious importance to certain places. The theme of metamorphosis, in turn, anchors these tales in larger questions of identity and difference, including those between Greeks and non-Greeks, and among gods, humans, and animals.

And this is exactly the point at which Augustine's comments on the shearwaters become relevant. With the ultimate aim of advancing his Christianizing agenda and to replace the traditional polytheism with the idea of a single, powerful God, Augustine attempts to dismantle the ancient beliefs by dismantling the stories connected to them.[99]

To do so, Augustine takes aim at accounts of human/animal metamorphosis in general and that of Diomedes' comrades in particular. He starts from traditional beliefs in the supernatural powers of divinity and the gods' role in instigating human/animal metamorphosis and tries to deflect them by exposing them as false. He argues that Diomedes could not really be divine because he was unable to turn his comrades back into humans either through his own intervention or by asking this favour from the even more powerful Jupiter.[100] The idea of the divinity of Diomedes is thus untenable because it contradicts the notion of divine omnipotence.

As for the shearwaters of Diomedea: Augustine asserts that no metamorphosis whatsoever occurred on the island. He argues that the existence of the birds can be explained as a simple sleight of hand. The comrades of Diomedes were destroyed by 'avenging evil angels' (*ultoribus angelis malis*) and vanished from the island altogether. They were swiftly replaced by birds introduced from another location by demons – a lowly category of supernatural beings – to sustain the credibility of the story of their transformation.[101] It is the credulity of the people, and their willingness to accept unquestioningly what is presented to them, that allows for the belief in the traditional pagan gods. What Augustine promotes instead is a deeper engagement with the one and only God.

Reaching out from the example of the shearwaters to look at ancient accounts of metamorphosis more generally, Augustine goes on to argue that there is no truth to such stories. To him, the famous accounts of metamorphosis do not involve real transformations but optical illusions created by demons: 'It is merely in appearance that they change beings that are created by the true God, so that they seem to be what they are not.'[102] Drawing on the ancient conception of the phantom, a figment of the imagination that deceives the human eye, he states: 'This phantom, I hold, can in some inexplicable way present itself to the senses of others in bodily form, when their physical senses are dulled or blocked out.'[103]

The implied criticism here is again that those who believe in metamorphosis are guilty of letting themselves be deceived. In conclusion, Augustine points back to the distinction between mind and body and the way this is presented in ancient accounts of metamorphosis: 'Therefore, I should by no means believe that the soul, or even the body, can be really changed by the craft or power of demons into the members and features of beasts.'[104] For him, humanity is unique and irreducible, and created by the one and only God. It is a matter of both mind *and* body; neither can change into animal. In emphasizing this point, Augustine practically squashes the duality between mind and body on which many ancient stories of metamorphosis rest.

AND SO?

Metamorphosis, the idea that in the realm of myth and storytelling humans could turn into animals and back again, speaks to the question of what makes us human. It allows for the possibility to temporarily experience the world through the eyes of another being and thus, in principle, at least, opens up space to bridge the gap between human and non-human animals. And yet, in Greek thought and literature, this experience seems to have been available to (gods and) humans only: while they are frequently transformed into animals, it is pretty well unheard of for an animal to become human.[105] There is no Puss in Boots in antiquity. In the ancient Greek and Roman worlds, you could not kiss a frog and get a prince.

This matters because it tells us something important about ancient conceptions of the human and the non-human and the hierarchies among different kinds of being. As in the case of the shearwaters of Diomedea, ancient stories of transformation remain indebted to the idea that it is the mind, and its associated cognitive functions, that contains our humanity, while the body contributes little, if anything, of substance.

In this view, mind and body remain largely separate entities. Many accounts of metamorphosis, both ancient and modern, then go on to explore the frictions and fault lines between our human and our animal sides through the frictions and fault lines between mind and body.

Analogies between human and animal forms of being in the world then emerge merely as a result of the closeness of metamorphosis to metaphor. The human remains firmly at centre stage.

This conception of metamorphosis is in stark contrast with current critical idioms that do not conceive of mind and body as different dimensions of our identity, but which explore how they shape human identities together and in interaction with each other.[106] Current research in the cognitive sciences and the philosophy of mind has shown that the physical side of our existence is much more than a mere container; it fundamentally influences our thinking in a number of ways, giving raise to the notion of 'embodied cognition' as an umbrella term for all the different ways in which cognitive processes are shaped by the body as a moving, acting, and perceiving presence.[107] As one of our most central organs, the mind itself is part of our physiological makeup. In short: today we tend to think that it matters that we are in human bodies, and the ways in which these bodies do and do not resemble the bodies of other animals shape the way we think about the world, about ourselves, and about others.

The metamorphoses discussed in this chapter, by contrast, draw and continue to draw on the traditional view by which mind and body are separate and separable entities; they do not entertain the possibility of whether a creature's new animal body enables a whole set of new experiences of being in the world.[108] Nor do they explore the impact such experiences would have on the mind. So, at the very moment when the ultimate crossing (and dissolution) of the boundary that separates human from animal seems within reach, the conversation shies away from imagining the unimaginable.[109] It turns and remains strictly within the limits of thinking the human set by the philosophical debate.

Conclusion

WE HAVE (NEARLY) REACHED THE END. OUR WAY through this book has brought us face to face with many weird and wonderful creatures: from the humanized lion of Androclus, to the questionable humanity of the Cyclops. From Achilles' speaking horse Xanthus to the peculiar cries of the searwaters of Diomedea. From monarchic bees to their democratic counterparts. In the course of exploring these and other creatures in their select ancient and modern habitats, the journey has taken us to many fascinating places: the gates of Troy, the labyrinth of Knossos, a dinner party on the gulf of Naples, Sigmund Freud's consulting rooms, the political philosophy of Hannah Arendt, and the works of Pablo Picasso. I hope you enjoyed the ride.

What remains to be done now is to summarize what we have found, to pull out some strands of argument that emerge (only) between the individual chapters, and to offer some concluding remarks about their relevance within the larger picture.

In other words: what have we discovered? And why does it matter?

This book explored ways of 'thinking the human' in select examples from antiquity and the modern era (up to the present). More specifically, the focus was on the role of non-human creatures in the negotiation of human identities in classical antiquity and today. I showed that the animal is invoked whenever the category of the human as such, or particular human identities, are at stake. In this sense, Argos, the loyal dog of Odysseus, featured in the introduction to this book, indeed pointed the way. It was *his* capacity to sniff out the human camouflaged in animal clothing that first put us on the trail leading through its individual chapters.

To break down a large and complex topic, we explored the question of what it means to be human through the lens of ten ancient creatures which, all in their own ways, exist between the categories of human and animal. At the same time, the creatures that lent their names to the individual chapters exemplified different ways in which we, as humans, engage with non-human creatures. They parade different facets of what I have referred to as our 'entanglement' with animals: the way in which our notions of self (and other) – our sense of humanity in the abstract, and of particular human identities – are entangled with non-human animals. The scope and meaning of the human takes shape in the kind of negotiations that take place in the myriad different ways we encounter, interact with, and appropriate non-human animals: by eating some of them or by consciously abstaining from their consumption; by using them as metaphors and symbols for how we engage with ourselves, each other, and those we seek to relegate to the category of 'the other'; by highlighting those aspects of being in the world that we share with animals or playing up the ways in which we differ. Individually and as a group, the creatures featured in this book expose different aspects of our humanity. At the same time, they remind us that the human animal remains intricately bound up with non-human animals and in more ways than we are usually prepared to admit.

The fundamental conflict at the core of this book, then, is, perhaps, most sharply put like this: to save a puppy rather than a baby from a burning house would rightly be regarded as morally wrong. And yet, at the same time, to justify cruelty towards animals is also morally wrong and a form of speciesism. This is because human life remains deeply tangled up with non-human creatures in more ways than our joint biological heritage suggests. How to reconcile these two positions is the problem. To simply favour the first over the second without further thought is merely evading the problem rather than facing it upfront.

***

Many of the animals included in this book belong to the class of *Mammalia.* This is no coincidence. Owing to their biological closeness to humans, horses, lions, boars, and bulls particularly lend themselves to play a role in human efforts at self-definition. But occasionally at least, we went beyond such culturally prominent four-footed mammals to consider the cultural meanings of other classes of animals such as insects ('The Political Bee' and 'The Socratic Gadfly') and birds ('The Shearwaters of Diomedea'). It seems that sometimes at least, qualities other than their mere biological closeness to humans mattered.

The tool that allowed the conversation to occur, and that in many ways carries and drives it, is storytelling. Storytelling is not only the stuff of literature and history – and that most enticing of all spaces where they meet; it is also the tool that allows us to make connections, to establish cause and effect, to compare and contrast, to enchant, and engage. Throughout this book, I have variously traced the way in which stories were told and retold by different authors, in different times and places, in different forms and media, and to different ends. Many of the stories that sustain the creatures included in this book also reveal the enduring power of myth to reinvent itself in order to comment on the big questions concerning the human condition, including that of what this condition entails. Far from being 'mere' fiction, these stories have the unnerving capacity to call into question truths long accepted and to reveal the kinds of issues at stake in a given situation. They cast a light on the animality of the human and the humanity of the animal as they present themselves in ever new ways. And yet, this is not the only way in which narrative came into the picture here. Throughout this book, I have also used the power of the story myself to point to certain connections and to draw multiple lines between past and present.

This juxtaposing of past and present becomes possible because, even though the creatures included in this book originate in classical antiquity, they do not remain confined to it. They themselves, or the larger themes they represent, show an astonishing persistence, variously crossing from the ancient into the modern worlds and sometimes – whenever the modern informs our understanding of the ancient – back again. The links between past and present that emerged in this way are sometimes the result of a general humanity that we share with the ancients and that persists throughout time and space despite all the differences that separate us from the ancient world. This was, for example, the case in the remarkable ways in which ancient stories of human/animal cooperation resonate with modern ones. Both draw on fundamental aspects of the human condition.

At other times, however, such links are a direct consequence of the formative role attributed to the classical past in shaping modern (Western) conceptions of the human. Or, as in the case of Freud's use of the Sphinx, their modern appeal is part of an appropriation of the ancient past in the attempt to present certain concepts ('the Oedipus complex,' the unconscious) as universal. And yet it would be wrong to limit the story told in this book to one of the ongoing power and appeal of classical humanism: sometimes – as in the case of Picasso's reception of the Minotaur – the ancient and the modern come together exactly through a critical engagement with the formative role traditionally attributed to the classical past.

Moreover, the differences that emerged between the ancient and the modern worlds are as revealing as the continuities and resonances between them. To single out just one of them: a recurrent theme featuring in several chapters was the role the ancient Greek and Roman authors attributed to the divine in the ways in which humans and animals come together. No matter whether it is the capacity of certain animals to speak in human language, or the fashioning of the Trojan horse, or, indeed, the politico-philosophical mission of the Socratic gadfly: the Greek and Roman gods are at the table whenever human identities are at stake. As far as the ancient world is concerned, they provided a second point of reference in the negotiation of human identities, besides the animal.[1]

Nowadays, the influence of religion (at least of the Judaeo-Christian kind) is much more contested. This is why, in the modern forms of entanglement discussed in this book, the divine has sometimes been substituted by other forces, such as Freud's conception of 'the unconscious' (see Chapter 1, 'The Sphinx'). In other instances, the void has not been filled. In Kafka's *Metamorphosis*, for example, it is unclear what exactly instigated the transformation of Gregor Samsa into a verminous bug (discussed in Chapter 10, 'The Shearwaters of Diomedea'). This openness reflects a greater uncertainty about the human condition in some of the modern stories considered in this book. In the wake of the arrival of evolutionary theory as well as the mass atrocities that shaped much of the history of the twentieth century, what it means to be human remains more open, more problematic, more contested – and more pressing a question than ever.

Any differences between ancient and modern conceptions of humans and animals, then, also reflect fundamental shifts and transformations in the way in which we relate to *real* animals. In the ancient world, animals lived in close proximity to humans. In the modern (Western) world, this is no longer the case. As the cultural critic John Berger rightly pointed out in his influential essay 'Why Look at Animals?', the nineteenth and twentieth century brought about a deep rupture in the way we relate to animals.[2] The previously close relationship gradually gave way to one in which the exposure of most people to animals, both domestic and wild, is extremely limited. Berger suggested further that the absence of animals from our daily lives has been compensated by the ubiquity of animal representations and animal appropriations in the form of stuffed animals, in comics, in advertising, and as various icons. Berger is certainly right to point to fundamental differences in human/animal relations over time. And yet, as I have argued elsewhere, the appropriation of the animal for the sake of human self-definition is not primarily a symptom of modernity.[3] As the individual chapters in this book have shown, right from the beginning of the conversation in classical antiquity, animals and the concept of animality as such were drawn into human efforts to make sense of the human condition.

Indeed, the stories told and retold in this book show how widely the question of the human (and that of the animal) reached into areas beyond the confines of the philosophical debate. From the choices of what we do or do not eat to the way we fit out the human at war; from the naturalizing of political systems to the modelling of the individual politically engaged citizen: in all these instances the question of the human is tied up with the question of the animal. The way in which the human features in these and other areas relates to the philosophical conversation, without being identical to it. There is a much larger array of sources that implicitly or explicitly speak to the question of the human. To see the full picture, the voices of the creatures included in this book and the stories sustaining them deserve to be heard. They are an integral part of the story of Western conceptions of human *and* animal.

So, what do these voices have to say? What kind of positions come to the fore?

The conversation is still largely driven by a profound anthropocentrism. In the attempt to define 'the human', the ancient and modern texts and images appropriated the category of 'the animal' as such. Or they drew on the features of specific animal species to articulate specific human identities. Some of these identities are political (the Socratic gadfly, the political bee); others gendered (the "Trojan" boar); others again concern the margins of the human as mapped onto the ethnographic landscape (the Cyclops); or they describe the human at war (the Trojan horse). Some found the human in the animal (the Trojan horse, the lion of Androclus), or, indeed, the animal in the human (the shearwaters of Diomedea, the Trojan boar). But no matter how they negotiated their particular human and animal parts: All the creatures included in this book both challenge and reaffirm the category of the human in various ways. All of them draw on notions of the animal, animalistic, and wild to speak to the question of what makes us human, and they do so in ways that have little to do with mere 'othering'.

In many instances, this involved the outright anthropomorphizing of non-human animals. In order to perform their various roles in the story at the core of this book, animals were frequently attributed with human-like feelings, behaviours, and desires. Lions do not usually save humans from death, horses do not speak, and honeybees do not really care about the political qualities of their leaders. And yet, there is something to be gained from entertaining the idea that they might. By giving them the space and capacity to do so, storytelling affords us visits to territory not otherwise open for exploration.

It may be tempting to dismiss such efforts as another form of appropriation of the non-human for the sake of human self-definition – and to some extent they certainly are. And yet, there is also another way of looking at the human tendency to anthropomorphize.[4] In some instances at least, the locating of human features and sentiments in animals also allows for the highlighting of real communalities between human and non-human animals. Central to the tall story about Androclus' lion, for example, there is the very real insight that animals are sentient creatures too and that they share with us certain physical attributes as well as a fundamental set of needs: for safety, food, and companionship, for example. In other words: anthropomorphism is not always necessarily a form of appropriation, misunderstanding, and distortion. It can also be a pathway to real sympathies, real communalities between the human and the non-human.

And yet, despite such moments of communality and understanding, we touched upon many more instances in which the idea of an insurmountable difference between the human and all other animals prevailed. The view that humans stand out from all other creatures due to the presence of certain features, skills, or capacities – a view that gave rise to the so-called 'man-only *topos*' in Greco-Roman philosophy – can also be found in other areas beyond the philosophical debate. It informed ancient conceptions of hybridity and metamorphosis. It was also at play in the marginal or questionable humanity of the Cyclops. In so far as they parade human exceptionalism and essentialism, the stories discussed here resonate with views articulated in more abstract terms by the Greek and Roman philosophers.

But, again, this is only part of the picture: we also encountered a set of other voices that push back against notions of human exceptionalism and the idea of human superiority derived from it. These voices include Grunter, the philosophically inclined pig, who spoke up in defence of the animal in several chapters, a nameless rooster who claims to be Pythagoras reincarnated and who shows an equally surprising tendency to beat his human interlocutor at their own game, the lion of Androclus and a number of other major and minor figures. Individually and as a group, they challenge the anthropocentrism evident in other parts of the conversation. They do so by highlighting the communality of humans and animals, by reminding us that not all animals – and certainly not all *human* animals – are 'created equal', by illustrating the (at times astonishing) things certain animals can do. Finally, they also expose the circular argument we engage in whenever we base our claims to human superiority on the presence or absence of certain uniquely human features, skills, or capacities.

These voices matter not least because they challenge the traditional story that has associated the ancient world firmly with the origins of the idea of the human as the measure (and pinnacle) of all things. By showing that the idea of human essentialism and superiority did not go uncontested, they illustrate that from the very beginning of the conversation in classical antiquity other ways of conceiving of the categories of 'the human' and 'the animal' were put forward and circulated in Greco-Roman thought and literature. The story of how these views came to be supressed to the extent that they were almost forgotten (at least outside of the realm of storytelling) is beyond the scope of this book. Here it merely matters that they did exist and that they conveyed their perspectives as part of a set of influential stories that engaged human audiences well beyond the confines of classical antiquity.

Their presence confirms that even though the ancient Greeks and Romans are frequently still invoked as the origin of stories that lead up to us today, they have always also resisted such appropriations. Greco-Roman antiquity has always been more (and less) than what we have made of them. This is because the ancient Greeks and Romans had the unnerving capacity of questioning the very foundations of their way of looking at the world. That this questioning could take the form of a talking pig is both an acknowledgement and a critique of the formative role of logocentrism in ancient conceptions of the human.

This point brings us back to the critical engagement with the formative role that has traditionally been attributed to the Greco-Roman past. There has recently been a groundswell of voices from within classical scholarship that has sought to reposition the way in which we look at the ancient world, its histories, and literatures. Parallel to similar efforts in a number of other disciplines, this move has sometimes been linked to the shorthand of 'decolonizing the Classics'. What is at stake here is the desire to examine and, as much as possible, correct the traditional association between classical studies on the one hand and notions of Western elitism, superiority, and dominance on the other. More often than not this involves the attempt to move beyond the dividing lines that we have created around and out of the Greco-Roman world, including those of West vs. East, civilized vs. primitive, male vs. female – and, we may add, human vs. animal. This dissolving of dividing lines takes predominantly three forms: first, a direct critique of the notion of classical antiquity as a preferred point of reference and the insistence that it is just one past among others of concern to us. Second, a stronger emphasis on the voices, perspectives, and viewpoints of those who were suppressed and disenfranchised in the societies of the ancient world themselves (women, slaves, foreigners, etc.). And, finally, a stronger drive to assure that it is a diverse cast of scholars who gets to (re-)write the history of the ancient world today.

That Western conceptions of the human have long centred (on) the white, male, and logocentric position (and marginalized others) is by now well known. And yet, there is another dimension to this centring which has not yet received the same level of attention: that logocentrism and andro-centrism feed into and are sustained by a fundamental anthropocentrism that is grounded in the idea of the human as fundamentally different from, and superior to, all other beings. The same normative forces that foreground the mind over the body, the rational over the emotional, the civilized over the uncivilized, the male over the female, are also those that set the human in opposition to the animal and place the former above the latter. Indeed, various chapters of this book have shown that they play directly into it. And this distinction (like the others) has had devastating consequences for all those that do not fit under the umbrella of the human so defined.

To bring different ancient positions on the question of the human more firmly into the picture thus aligns with recent efforts in 'decentring' notions and concepts that we have long taken for granted. It appears that classical scholarship can make a meaningful contribution to such efforts by drawing attention to those voices that have remained silent, to those stories that have remained untold, and those histories that have remained unwritten. Doing so allows us to examine and, in part at least, challenge a series of views and conceptions that have been derived out of its study in the past. In this sense, too, the stories told and explored in this book throw light on a dimension of Western thought and literature that resonates well beyond the rather small circle of those with an academic interest in such issues. All of them reveal how deeply the animal is entangled in our efforts to answer the questions of who and what we are.

One final thought: in the face of human suffering, disenfranchisement, and oppression, it might be tempting to think that there are more pressing issues than the way in which we relate to animals. But that would be to disregard the fact that both strands of thinking invariably intersect.

In other words: whenever questions of human identity are at stake, the animal is never far away. If this book has shown anything at all, it is that 'the human' as such is a fragile creature. *Homo sapiens* may exist as a biological entity, or in other words, a species. Yet, as soon as we try to fill this biological entity with further meanings, we are on shaky ground. This is because there is ultimately little that sets us apart from our non-human cousins. What it means to be human emerges as the product of a set of complex negotiations and conversations we have with ourselves and the other animals we encounter.

In the end, then, it appears that it is this process, the process of negotiation, that matters. The end-product – a hard-and-fast definition of the human as different from all other animals – not so much. It is this process that makes us human.

Notes

INTRODUCTION

1. Homer, *Odyssey* 17.291–4.
2. Homer, *Odyssey* 17.300–4.
3. Homer, *Odyssey* 17.304.
4. Homer, *Odyssey* 17.326–7.
5. On dogs as loyal companions in the ancient world, see Franco 2014: 17–27, 123–5. On ancient companion animals, see MacKinnon 2014b (for dogs see 270–4). On human/canine relations in general, see Garber 1996.
6. See Goldhill 1988: 9–19 for a reading of the recognition scene as an example of how Homer builds complex meaning by juxtaposing themes throughout the narrative.
7. Homer, *Odyssey* 17.294–8.
8. Homer, *Odyssey* 17.313–15.
9. Here and below see Goldhill 1988: 14–15.
10. See, e.g., Xenophon, *On Hunting*, in particular 7; Arrian, *On Hunting*.
11. Goldhill 1988: 13–14. See also Goldhill 1991: 12–13.
12. Redfield's comments (1994: 194) on pity arising from the gap between a man's attributes and the situation he finds himself in are relevant here as they apply to both Odysseus and the dog.
13. The 'metonymic relationship' between domesticated dogs and their owners in Homer: Redfield 1994: 194.
14. Goldhill 1991: 13.
15. Argos as 'faithful *philos*': Goldhill 1991: 13.
16. Homer, *Odyssey*, 17.307, as pointed out by Strauss Clay 1974: 129, note 2. The only other exception is in 10.240 in reference to Odysseus' comrades turned pigs.
17. Darwin 1859.
18. See e.g. Murthy 1985; Foster 2009.
19. E.g. the material discussed in de Castro 1992; Descola 1994.
20. The Christian contribution to the conversation as it emerged out of Greco-Roman views on humans and animals is discussed in detail in Gilhus 2006.
21. For introductions to the field of human/animal studies, see e.g. Waldau 2013; Taylor and Twine 2014.

22. But see the scholarly interest in the classic tripartite scheme of living beings as including gods, humans, and animals as developed by Jean-Paul Vernant 1990c.
23. Important studies in this area include: Dierauer 1977; Sorabji 1993; Cassin and Labarrière 1997; Wolff 1997; J. Heath 2005; Newmyer 2006; Gilhus 2006; Kalof 2007; Alexandridis, Wild, and Winkler-Horaçek 2008; McInerney 2010; Calder 2011; Campbell 2014; Newmyer 2014; Korhonen and Ruonakoski 2017; Fögen and Thomas 2017, and the titles included in note 24. See also the area review by Kindt 2017.
24. But see the pioneering works of Osborne 2009; Payne 2010; and Newmyer 2017 which have shown just how productive such connections can be for our understanding of past and present.
25. On which see Newmyer 2017.
26. See, e.g., Aristotle, *Parts of Animals* 1.1 (641b7), *Nicomachean Ethics* 1.7 (1098a3–5) with Sorabji 1993: 12–6 (and further references); Newmyer 2017: 44–51.
27. Aristotle, *Politics* 1332b4–5.
28. Galen, *On the Usefulness of Parts* 1.3.
29. Pliny, *Natural History* 7.5.
30. See Aristotle, *Parts of Animals* 656a7–8 and Galen, *On the Usefulness of Parts* 1.2 on the related observation that man only has a share in the divine.
31. Socrates in Xenophon, *Memorabilia* 1.4.12.
32. On the ancient 'man-only *topos*' and its reception in modern philosophy, see Newmyer 2017 (with further examples) as discussed in Chapter 2.
33. For the ancient conception of a *scala naturae*, see Akinpelu 1967; Wolff 1997; Bénatouïl 2002; Wildberger 2008.
34. On the notion of human 'entanglement' in cultural theory today, see, e.g., Giraud 2019 (with further literature).
35. The sympathy of humans and animals as featured in parts of Greek literature was first brought to the fore by Korhonen and Ruonakoski 2017.

1 THE SPHINX (*SPHINX AENIGMATICA*)

1. There were different kinds of sphinxes in the ancient world, some male, some female, some benevolent protectors of certain sites (such as graves), others malevolent agents of death. For an overview see Demisch 1977.
2. Apollodorus, *Library* 3.5.8. See also Diodorus Siculus 4.64.3.
3. Apollodorus, *Library* 3.5.8.
4. According to Apollodorus, *Library* 3.5.8, the sphinx killed Haemon, the son of Creon, who was the brother of Jocasta who ascended to the throne after Oedipus' departure from Thebes.
5. On the complex of afflictions coming together in the so-called '*loimos* motif', see Parker 1983: 271–5.
6. This part of the story is dramatized in Sophocles' *Oedipus at Colonus* which recounts the events leading up to Oedipus' death.

7. See Padgett 2003: 78–83. On the Sphinx at Giza, see Hawass and Lehner 1994; Coche-Zivie 2004.
8. Hesiod, *Theogony* 326–9. Other ancient authors give her a different pedigree. According to Euripides (*Phoenician Women* 1019–25), she is the offspring of Earth (Gaia) and the Echidna. Some ancient authors (falsely) explain the etymology of the Greek word as a derivation from ancient Greek *sphingein*, 'to bind tight', 'to bind fast', a possible reference to her captivating presence at Thebes (see Chantraine 1977 with references).
9. Diodorus of Sicily 4.64.3 thus refers to the Theban Sphinx as 'a beast of double form' (*dimorphon thērion*). On these monstrous hybrids, see, e.g., Aston 2011.
10. For monumental representations of sphinxes in Greece and Rome, see Lesky and Herbig 1929: 1726–49. On iconographic representations of the Sphinx in the context of the Oedipus myth (and beyond), see Moret 1984; Krauskopf 1994: 3–9.
11. But see Delcourt 2020b: 135–6 on ways in which the myth reverberates with popular story types that can be found throughout world literature.
12. The ancient authors telling the myth do not specifically elaborate on this detail. In terms of her function in the narrative, her role is to provide a reason why Oedipus is allowed to marry Jocasta (as argued by Edmunds 1981: 18).
13. See, e.g., Euripides, *Phoenician Women* 810–1 (Hades) with Edmunds 1981: 12–13 (with further evidence); Dio Chrysostomus, *Oratores* 11.8.1 (Hera); Apollodorus 3.5.8 (Hera), Scholium on Hesiod, *Theogony* 326 and Euripides, *Antigone* frag. 178N (Dionysus); Euripides, *Phoenician Women* 810–1 (Hades) with Lesky and Herbig 1929: 1706–8.
14. As pointed out by Edmunds 1981: 18.
15. See also Krauskopf 1994.
16. For a list of references to ancient authors featuring the actual words of the riddle, see Lesky and Herbig 1929: 1718–22.
17. See, e.g., Sophocles, *Oedipus the King* 391–2 (a 'versifying hound' – *rapsōdos kuōn*) with Finglass 2018: 296 suggesting that this might align the Sphinx with the Erinyes who are also sometimes referred to as dogs. Sophocles, *Oedipus the King* 508 (a 'winged maiden' – *pteroessa kora*). Sophocles, *Oedipus the King* 1199–1200 ('a prophesyung maiden with hooked talons' – *gampsōnux parthenon chresmōdon*) with Finglass 2018: 530–1 suggesting that this highlights the Sphinx's bird-like nature.
18. Sophocles, *Oedipus the King* 1524–30.
19. This view features prominently in Herodotus' *Histories* 1.30–33 in which it is attributed to the Athenian statesman-philosopher Solon (see, in particular, at 1.32).
20. Sophocles, *Oedipus the King* 1186–96.
21. On this aspect see, e.g., Vernant 1990a: 92: 'Tragedy's true domain is that border zone where human actions are intermeshed with divine powers and reveal their true meaning.'
22. See Segal 2001: 73–87 ('The Crisis of the City and the King').
23. Personal crisis as a collective (political) crisis: Zak 1995: 200; Ahrensdorf and Pangle 2014: 1–13.

24. Sophocles, *Oedipus the King* 1065. The quest for truth in the *Oedipus the King*: Vernant 1990b: 116–17.
25. Sophocles, *Oedipus the King* 390–8.
26. See in detail Goldhill 1986: 199–221; Segal 1995: 138–60 (both with references).
27. See, e.g., Sophocles, *Oedipus the King* 397. On the meanings embedded in Oedipus' name, see Goldhill 1986: 216–19 and below, note 32.
28. Finglass 2018: 296 points out that ancient Greek prophecy involved knowing the past, present, and future 'and so solving a riddle was an appropriate task for a prophet'. One may want to add that this applies in particular to a riddle of which the imagery spans across the different stages of human life – some already in Oedipus' past, some currently present, and some still in the future.
29. The inability to understand the enigmatic oracular words is also a popular theme of oracle stories (on which see, e.g., Kindt 2016, in particular 153–68). On Oedipus, the Sphinx' riddle, and Delphi, see Cameron 1968: 21; Goldhill 1986: 212–13; Segal 1995: 140–50.
30. As Vernant 1990b: 138 has pointed out, Oedipus' actions blur the succession of generations within his family – another way in which the riddle's imagery applies to him personally. On this point see also Goldhill 1986: 212.
31. Ahrensdorf and Pangle 2014: 9 argue that Oedipus' hubris consists in favouring 'a form of rule that is purely rational and hence free from constraints imposed by convention, tradition, and law – human or divine .... The "tyrannical" rule of Oedipus ... represents the elevation of reason over blood, age, and above all, (ostensibly) divine wisdom and law.'
32. See Sophocles, *Oedipus the King* 517–19, 717–19, 1033–6, 1349–55. See also Diodorus of Sicily 4.63.1.
33. Vernant 1990b: 123.
34. As pointed out by Goldhill 1986: 216. On this point see: Delcourt 2020b: 137.
35. See, e.g., Aristotle, *Metaphysics* 1037b11–13 (7.12) with Kietzmann 2019: 26–9; Plato, *Cratylus* 399c; Cicero, *On the Nature or the Gods* 2.134–5; Ovid, *Metamorphoses* 1.85–6, Manilius, *Astronomica* 4.905–7 with Newmyer 2017: 108–12.
36. The 'downward gaze' as an 'orientational metaphor' in human/animal relations: Danta 2018: 10.
37. Athenaeus, *The Learned Banqueters* 10.83 (456b). See also *Palatine Anthology* 14.64.
38. The distinction between terrestrial and maritime animals is, for example, at work in Plutarch's dialogue 'Whether Land or Sea Animals are Cleverer' (*Moralia* 959B–985C). On ancient taxonomies, see Lewis and Llewellyn-Jones 2018: 8–31.
39. See Sorabji 1993: 20–2.
40. As Tiresias anticipates in the later part of the tragedy, in the end it will be the three-footed Oedipus who will 'travel over strange land blind instead of seeing, poor instead of rich, feeling his way with his stick' (455–6). See also Hesiod, *Works and Days* 533–5 who refers to an old man using a walking stick as 'three-footed' (*tripous*) with Delcourt 2020b: 138 who suggests that 'the conundrum might have long been in circulation before being incorporated in a fictive context'.

41. In the drama, this ambiguity pervades every level of the plot and is reflected on the linguistic level in words changing their meaning throughout the play. See Vernant 1990b: 113–25 in particular.
42. See, e.g., Segal 2001: 73–107 ('Discovery and Reversal').
43. See Vernant 1990b: 117–19.
44. One way in which the transformation of Oedipus is articulated in the drama is through the metaphors of sight and seeing: as Tiresias, the seer, succinctly put it with regard to Oedipus himself: 'I say that you have sight, but cannot see what trouble you are in' (412–13). Later on, when Oedipus has taken his own eyesight as a form of self-inflicted punishment, the situation will be reversed: bereft of the physical capacity to see, he will have gained a much deeper level of understanding (see in more detail Vernant 1990b: 118–19).
45. The riddle appeals to human *logos*, yet the Sphinx herself remains unavailable to human reasoning. By combining the body parts of human and beast, the Sphinx defies the usual categories of being and the modes of sense-making that come with them. Like other monstrous creatures in Greco-Roman mythology (e.g., the harpies, the Minotaur, the Echidna), she inhabits her own monstrous plane which is situated somewhere between the physical and the spiritual worlds. Inhabiting a rocky mountain just outside of Thebes, she lives outside the laws of the city and the laws of nature.
46. Vernant 1990b: 138: 'Oedipus is discovered, at the end of the tragedy, to be identical to the monstrous creature referred to in the riddle'; Moore 1980: 3: 'Initially portrayed as alien, as Other, as absence, the Sphinx gradually merges with Oedipus, and, by the conclusion of the Oedipal cycle, becomes identified with him ... he becomes the Plague of Thebes, the Shpinx.'
47. On Freud and Oedipus see in detail Rudnytsky 1987; Leonard 2015: 108–30.
48. But see now Leonard 2021. See also Rudnytsky 1987: in particular 264–6; Armstrong 2005: 52–9.
49. See Hegel, *Lectures on Fine Art* (1835); Propp, *Oedipus in the Light of Folklore* (1944), Lévi-Strauss, *The Structural Study of Myth* (1955) with Edmunds 2006: 100–5, 121–8. On the modern reception of the sphinx more generally, see Edmunds 2006: 100–28 (with further examples).
50. Freud, *Standard Edition* (*SE*), 4: 261 (*The Interpretation of Dreams*), 7: 194–5 (*Three Essays on the Theory of Sexuality*), 9: 135 (*The Sexual Theories of Children*), 10: 133 (*Analysis of a Phobia in a Five-Year Old Boy*), 16: 318 (*Introductory Lectures on Psychoanalysis*), 20: 37 (*An Autobiographical Study*).
51. On the 'inward turn' in the reading of the Oedipus myth: Edmunds 2006: 100–28.
52. See Gamwell and Wells 1989: 50, 93 (on sphinxes) and 95 (on the *hydria*). On Freud's antiquities and their link to his method, see also Lane and Weihs 2010 with Trustram 2011. On Freud's travels to Athens and Rome, see, e.g., Freud, *SE* 22: 239–48 (*A Disturbance of Memory on the Acropolis*) with Armstrong 2005: 1–7.
53. On Freud's Classicism see, e.g., Armstrong 2005; Leonard 2013, 2015: 108–30. On his interest in ancient Egypt and its impact on his work, see Goldhill 2021; Leonard 2021.
54. See Freud, *SE* 4: 261–4 (*The Interpretation of Dreams*).

55. Freud, *SE* 4: 260 (*The Interpretation of Dreams*).
56. For substantial references to the Oedipus complex in later works, see, e.g., Freud, *SE* 13: 129–32 (*Totem and Taboo*), 14: 62–4 (*On the History of the Psycho-Analytic Movement*), 16: 329–38 (*Introductory Lectures on Psychoanalysis*), 23: 192–4 (*An Outline of Psychoanalysis*). For a complete list see the index in Freud, *SE* 24: 337–8.
57. Freud, *SE* 4, 261 (*Material and Sources of Dreams*).
58. Freud, *SE* 7: 56 (*A Case of Hysteria*).
59. See, e.g., Freud, *SE* 4: 262 (*The Interpretation of Dreams*).
60. See, e.g., Freud, *SE* 16: 318 (*Introductory Lectures on Psycho-Analysis*), *SE* 7: 194–5 (*Three Essays on the Theory of Sexuality*), *SE* 9: 135–9 (*The Sexual Enlightenment of Children*), 10: 133 (*Analysis of a Phobia in a Five-Year-Old Boy*), 20: 37 (*An Autobiographical Study*).
61. See, e.g., Segal 1995: 161–79. Vogt 1996; Rohde-Dachser 2003: 144.
62. See, e.g., Freud, *SE* 9: 134–9 (*The Sexual Enlightenment of Children*).
63. About the paintings and their place in Ingres' oeuvre, see Siegfried 2009: 26–41. For a psychoanalytical reading of the paintings in terms of the artist's own relationship with his father, see Posèq 2001. On Ingres' Classicism, see King 1942; Mongan 1947.
64. Armstrong 2005: 52; Renger 2013: 47–59; Leonard 2021: 131–3.
65. As suggested by Leonard 2021: 131–44 extending the work of Said 2003: 13–55.
66. A rendering of the scene of Oedipus facing the beast also decorated one side of a celebratory medal the doctor's friends had given him in 1906, on his fiftieth birthday, together with the slogan 'he who unravelled the great riddle, and was first in power' – a direct, if misappropriated, quote from Sophocles (see Rudnytsky 1987: 4–6). Again, it is Freud himself who is addressed and clearly celebrated here as the solver of riddles – the inquirer into the secrets of the psyche and the mysteries of the human condition. The same association of Freud with the figure of Oedipus as the solver of the Sphinx's riddle also motivated what became the official logo of the International Psychoanalytical Association (IPA). Founded in 1910 by Freud and Carl Jung, it is now 'the world's primary accrediting and regulatory body for the profession' of psychoanalysts, with over 12,000 members.
67. On this point see Rohde-Dachser 2003: 144.
68. Female psychology as a 'dark continent': Freud, *SE* 20: 212 (*The Question of Lay Analysis*): 'the sexual life of adult women is a "dark continent"'. On women as a riddle, see, e.g., Freud, *SE* 22: 113 (*New Introductory Lectures on Psycho-Analysis*). See also Young-Bruehl 1990; Khanna 2003 (on psychoanalysis as 'a masculinist and colonialist discipline'); Raphael-Leff 2007.
69. See, e.g., Mitchell 1974.
70. Freud, *SE* 21: 103–4 (*Civilisation and Its Discontents*).
71. Oedipus' 'universality': Rudnytsky 1987: 6–7, 62–4, 264. On the gendered dimension of Freud's universalism, see also Leonard 2013.

2 XANTHUS, ACHILLES' SPEAKING HORSE (*EQUUS ELOQUENS*)

1. This idiom points to the practice of evaluating a horse's health and age by inspecting its teeth. It is used in horse racing by bettors who do not want to reveal their source of information on promising horses and who claim that it is 'straight from the horse's mouth' (Palmatier 1995: 371).
2. The speaking animal is a popular literary motif included in Stith Thompson's *Motif-Index of Folk Literature* (1989: 396–401).
3. Homer, *Iliad* 19.408–17.
4. See Homer, *Iliad* 9.410–4.
5. Homer, *Iliad* 19.420–3. As Korhonen and Ruonakoski (2017: 82) point out, it is not unusual for Homeric heroes to address their horses directly (see p. 214, note 27 for references).
6. A little published Attic red-figure vase from ca. 460 BCE shows Apollo guiding Paris' arrow against Achilles' heel (see Bochum, Ruhr-Universität S1060; *Lexicon Iconographicum Mythologiae Classicae* (*LIMC*) I.1, s.v. 'Achilleus' nr. 851 = *s.v.* 'Alexandros', nr. 92). I would like to thank Jan Bremmer for pointing this out to me. The story about the arrow piercing Achilles' ankle also features in some later literary sources such as Apollodorus, *Epitome* 5.3 and Hyginus, *Fabulae* 107 dating from the second century BCE and the first century CE respectively. On the death of Achilles, see also Burgess 1955; 2009: 27–42, 72–92.
7. On speaking animals in Greco-Roman thought and literature, see Hawkins 2017; and the contributions to Mordeglia and Gatti 2017; 2020 and to Schmalzgruber 2020. On ancient views on animal communication, see Fögen 2007, 2014.
8. Gnat: Ps.-Virgil *Culex*. Eel: Oppian, *On Fishing* 2.301–7 with Kneebone 2020: 328. Pig: Plutarch, *Beasts Are Rational* 985D–992E. Rooster: Ps.-Lucian, *The Dream or the Cock*.
9. This debate is discussed in detail in Newmyer 2006.
10. On the question of language in the ancient philosophical debate, see Fögen 2007 (with extensive bibliography), 2014; Newmyer 2006: 45–7 (and 10–17 on modern forms of this debate). See also Sorabji 1993: 78–96; J. Heath 2005: 39–78;Osborne 2009: 64–97.
11. Aristotle's position: Sorabji 1993: 12–16; Glock 2019; Kietzmann 2019; Lennox 2019; McCready-Flora 2019.
12. Danta 2018: 1–3.
13. The ancient fable: Holzberg 2002. Representation of animals in the ancient fable: Lefkowitz 2014; Gärtner 2020; as well as the chapters collected in Schmalzgruber 2020: 55–102.
14. As argued in detail by J. Heath 2005: 39–40, 51.
15. See J. Heath 2005: 51 following Bologna 1978.
16. Bologna 1978: 306–17 with J. Heath 2005: 51.
17. Here and below see J. Heath 2005: 39–42.
18. Hawkins 2017: 1 referring to Fögen 2007, 2014.
19. See Homer, *Iliad* 19.407. Johnston 1992: 87–8 argues that there is nothing in Homer that suggests that Hera merely bestowed human speech on the horse right before the moment it responds to Achilles and that she inspired the horses' prophecy. Rather, she

suggests that Hera gave Xanthus the capacity to speak before he was gifted to Peleus/Achilles.

20. As pointed out by J. Heath 2005: 40. On the reading of divine signs in the ancient world, see, e.g., Johnston 2008. On Greek divination and oracles involving animals in particular, see Kindt 2020b.
21. See, e.g., Herodotus, *Histories* 3.84–5 (Persians), Tacitus, *Germania* 10 (Germans), Isidore, *Origins* 1.1.44 with Johnston 1992: 90 and Dietrich 1962.
22. See Homer, *Iliad* 19.418. See Johnston 1992 on the different mythical traditions that underpin the Homeric passage that explain the presence of Hera and the Erinyes.
23. Johnston 1992 argues that there is no evidence to suggest that the Erinyes removed Xanthus' capacity to speak as such, rather than just ending this particular prophetic streak from the horse. While there is nothing in Homer's text to suggest such a final removal, there is also nothing to suggest the horse still has the capacity to speak later on.
24. The fundamental alignment of Xanthus and Achilles: Willey 2021: 82–8; J. Heath 2005: 39–42.
25. In this role, the figure of Xanthus resembles the Homeric animal similes, which also align human and animal states of being and use the latter to reflect on the former. On the Homeric animal simile, see also Chapter 5, notes 111 and 116 (with further references).
26. Here and below see Hawkins 2017: 1–5. Humans and animals sharing a common language during the Golden Age: Plato, *Laws* 713A-714A; *Statesman* 272B-C with Dillon 1992. See also Callimachus, *Iambi* 2.192; Babrius, *Fables* – Prologue 1.5–16. The so-called Orphics, a philosophical-religious movement revolving around the legendary poet and singer Orpheus, entertained a similar notion. Allegedly Orpheus' song and playing of the kithara entranced not only humans, but animals and even plants as well (see, e.g., Euripides, *Bacchae* 560–4; Diodorus 37.30.3; Seneca, *Medea* 625–633; Pausanias, *History of Greece* 6.20.18, 9.17.7, 30.4). On Orpheus and Orphism, see Blundell 1986: 11–20; Segal 1989; Guthrie 1993.
27. See, e.g., Hesiod, *Works and Days* 109–26; Ovid, *Metamorphoses* 1.89–112. See also Blundell 1986: 135–64 (with references) and Vidal-Naquet 1983: 285–301.
28. See Aesop, *Fables* 431 (Perry) (= 383/Halm); Philo, *On the Confusion of Tongues* 3 (6–8).
29. On the difference between human and divine language, see Kindt 2016: 159–64.
30. As argued by Hawkins 2017: 5.
31. Xanthus' anthropomorphism is also evident in the fact that he has a proper name and that (in *Iliad* 17.426–40) he is depicted as having the capacity to mourn in human ways.
32. Ancient agriculture and farming: Howe 2014; Kron 2014.
33. E.g. Pliny, *Natural History* 8.1–34, 8.41–58; Aelian, *On Animals* 8.19, 11.25, 13.121 with Fögen 2014.
34. Porphyry, *On Abstinence* 3.192 (trans. G. Clark 2000).
35. See, e.g., Pliny, *Natural History* 10.117–24; Aelian, *On Animals* 6.19, 7.22, 16.3 with Fögen 2014: 223–5; Kitchell 2020.
36. Aelian, *On Animals* 12.3.

37. Aelian, *On Animals* 12.3.
38. Aristotle, *Politics* 1.1253a.
39. In his zoological writings, Aristotle distinguishes between voiceless animals, animals with a *phōnē* (voice), and animals capable of articulate speech (*dialektos*). The last category consists of those animals which, like humans, are capable of articulating vocals and consonants thanks to flexible tongue, lips, and other physical features. *Logos*, however, is specific only to humans. See Aristotle, *History of Animals* 4.9. (535a31–b3), *Parts of Animals* 2.16–17 (659b27–660a29) with Fögen 2007: 46–9.
40. See, e.g., Democritus 164; Plato, *Protagoras* 321c; Xenophon, *Hiero* 7.3; Aristotle, *Nicomachean Ethics* 3.1.27 (1111b).
41. On the Stoic position on human and animals, see, e.g., Akinpelu 1967; Bénatouïl 2002; Steiner 2008.
42. Oppian, *On Fishing* 2.167–79.
43. The intellectual difference between humans and other animals: Aelian, *On Animals* Praef. 1.8. Storks: 3.23. Wolves: 3.6. Bees: 5.13. The story of the bees is also told by a number of earlier authors (see Kitchell 1988 with further references).
44. Sextus Empiricus, *Outlines of Pyrrhoism* 1.68.
45. See Plutarch, *Beasts Are Rational* 989B with Fernández-Delago 2000: 181; Herchenroeder 2008: 361 and Lucian, *The Dream, or the Cock* 4 respectively with Jazdzewska 2015: 146.
46. See Homer, *Odyssey* 10.134–405.
47. See Homer, *Odyssey* 10.388–99 invoked as a matrix for philosophical reflection.
48. Plutarch, *Beasts Are Rational* 985D. Casanova 2005 has argued Grunter is not one of Odysseus' comrades but another Greek unknown to Odysseus and the conversation probably takes place when Odysseus returns to Circes' island later on in the *Odyssey*.
49. Plutarch, *Beasts Are Rational* 985E.
50. Plutarch, *Beasts Are Rational* 985E.
51. Ancient Greek *gryllizō* is 'to grunt'. On different possible connotations of Grunter' name see Herchenroeder 2008: 348–59.
52. The dialogue combines elements from various philosophical traditions, most notably those of Platonism, Cynicism, and Epicureanism (see Jazdzewska 2015, note 2 for references). On the cynic dimension see also Fernández-Delago 2000.
53. Plutarch, *Beasts Are Rational* 987 B–C.
54. As Konstan 2010/2011: 376 and 380 has rightly noted, Plutarch's dialogue seems to follow the order in which the virtues are presented in Aristotle's *Nicomachean Ethics*.
55. Courage: Plutarch, *Beasts Are Rational* 986F–988E. Temperance: 988F–991D.
56. Plutarch, *Beasts Are Rational* 988 A–B.
57. Plutarch, *Beasts Are Rational* 989A.
58. Courage: Plutarch, *Beasts Are Rational* 988 B–C. Food restrictions: 991 A–C. Moderation: 989 B–F.
59. On the 'man-only *topos*', see Newmyer 2017 (with further evidence and literature). As Angela Pabst has pointed out, the depiction of humans as lacking certain skills and features is not new but also features elsewhere in Plutarch and other examples of

ancient thought and literature. What the pig contributes here is merely a particularly original variant of this line of reasoning, pointing to their lack of bristles, tusks, and crooked claws (see Plutarch, *Beasts Are Rational* 988E and Pabst 2020: 345–6 with further examples).

60. Plutarch, *Beasts Are Rational* 992C.
61. See, e.g., Aristotle, *Nicomachean Ethics* 1.7 (1098a3–4) with Sorabji 1993, in particular 12–16, 78–96. Some modern commentators have argued that Grunter is an inefficient speaker and that his positions are not to be taken seriously. Konstan 2010–11 maintains that Grunter's examples of animal virtue illustrate only instinctual responses that do not require reasoning and thus morality. He therefore suggests an ironic reading of the dialogue in which the pig's arguments actually confirm the position (going back to Aristotle's *Nicomachean Ethics*) that animals do not have virtue. Herchenroeder 2008: 363 describes Grunter's speech as 'unrestrained, or even rambling'. He argues that there is a gap between Grunter's presentation of 'virtue as a state of radical freedom' attained only by animals and his actual role as 'the pet sophist' of Circe. Both interpretations are problematic because they rely on the reader to take the pig illustrating the opposite of what it actually says. Particularly in light of Plutarch's other two treatises on animal capacities, such an ironic inversion seems unlikely. Moreover, as I argue here, the pig's points are far too elaborate and specifically targeted to refute the notion of human exceptionalism to pass as irony. Plutarch is not going for a quick dressing down of the pig's position.
62. Plutarch, *Beasts Are Rational* 992 C–D.
63. See, e.g., Aristotle, *History of Animals* 588b4–14; *Parts of Animals* 681a10–15. For Aristotle's place in the history of this idea, see the still seminal study by Lovejoy 2001 [1936]: 24–66, in particular 58–9. Aristotle's conception of the *scala naturae*: Franklin 1986; Keil and Kreft 2019a: 5–7.
64. Plutarch, *Beasts are Rational* 992D. On the pig's description of the island of the Cyclops as a reference to the Golden Age, see Herchenroeder 2008: 360, 369.
65. Indeed, the parallels between both texts are so noticeable that some modern commentators (e.g. Wächli 2003: 230–7) have assumed that Lucian offers a commentary on or extension of Plutarch's dialogue.
66. See Marcovich 1976: 332 on the possibility that Micyllus never really woke up and that the cock appears to Micyllus in the dream. As in the opening passage, the rooster's crows feature elsewhere in the dialogue alongside his capacity to speak in human language (see, e.g., 12, 14, 28). It seems that the cock uses his crowing as a corrective force.
67. Lucian, *The Dream, or the Cock* 2.
68. Lucian, *The Dream, or the Cock* 2.
69. As pointed out by Marquis 2020: 363.
70. On Lucian's rooster and *metempsychosis*, see also Korhonen and Ruonakoski 2017: 97–9. Marcovich 1976: 332 points to the possibility that Hermes attributed the cock with the capacity to speak, referring to Lucian, *The Dream, or the Cock* 2: 'I am the friend of Hermes, the most talkative and eloquent of all the gods'.

71. See Lucian, *The Dream, or the Cock* 19–20. On different theories as to why a cock features as an impersonation of Pythagoras here, see Marcovich 1976 (with further literature).
72. The cock's cynicism: Marquis 2020: 365. On Cynicism more generally: Desmond 2006.
73. Lucian, *The Dream, or the Cock* 27.
74. See, e.g., Konstan 2010/11 on Plutarch's *Beasts Are Rational* and Marquis 2020: 269–73 on Ps.-Lucian's *The Dream or the Cock.*
75. Some recent works: Shettleworth 2001; Godfrey-Smith 2018; Suzuki 2021.
76. As explored in detail by Newmyer 2006. See also Fögen 2007, 2014.
77. See, e.g., Newmyer 2017: 1–9 (with examples).
78. I here follow Danta 2018: 1–3.
79. Below, I expand on the discussion of Kafka's text in Danta 2018: 169–74.
80. On the representation of mimesis and adaptive behaviour in this story, see Norris 1985.
81. Kafka 2018: 276–7 (Kafka 1992b: 153). The English translations are by Willa and Edwin Muir (from Kafka 2018, with small adjustments). I have used the German original and give the relevant page numbers to the German edition listed in the bibliography in brackets.
82. Kafka 2018: 277 (Kafka 1992b: 153).
83. See Kafka 2018: 273. Alas, Muir and Muir translate the German *gurren* as 'grunting' which translates better as 'cooing' (see Kafka 1992: 151).
84. Kafka 2018: 277–8 (Kafka 1992b: 154).
85. See Kafka 2018: 270 (Kafka 1992b: 148–9).
86. Kafka 2018: 277 (Kafka 1992b: 154).
87. Kafka 2018: 269–70 (Kafka 1992b: 148).
88. Mundis 1976: 36–8.
89. Mundis 1976: 43.
90. Temerlin 1975: 122–3.
91. S. Anderson 2004: 2.
92. See in detail S. Anderson 2004: 15–37.
93. S. Anderson 2004: 41.
94. Porphyry, *On Abstinence* 3.5.2–3.
95. Thompson 1989: 396 (B210.1).
96. On the problematic ethics of speaking for the animal, see Suen 2015: 7–27.

3 THE LION OF ANDROCLUS (*PANTHERA LEO PHILANTHROPUS*)

1. Aulus Gellius, *Attic Nights* 5.14.
2. Seneca, *On Benefits* 2.19. Another variant of the tale, which differs from Gellius' in several aspects, features in Aelian's book *On Animals* (7.48). A prose variant of the story ('the lion and the shepherd') is included in Babrius' retelling of Aesopic fables (Perry 1952: 609, no. 563) which dates from the first century CE but is generally not considered Aesopic. For a similar fable featuring a lion and a mouse, see Perry 1952: 150. On the different variants of the tale, see Scobie 1977: 18–23.

3. Apion's text was entitled 'History of Egypt' (*Aegyptiaca*) and (according to Gellius) included the story in book 5. Apion was a well-known author and philologist, and was roundly attacked by the Roman/Jewish historian Flavius Josephus (first century CE). Alas, Gellius' reference to Apion here should be taken with caution insofar as the eyewitness accounts of Apion gained a certain notoriety in the ancient world (see Cohn 1894: 2806).
4. See in detail Coleman 1990.
5. Lions – sometimes hundreds of them – were a common feature at these spectacles. See Bertrandy 1987; MacKinnon 2006; Shelton 2014: 466–75.
6. Aulus Gellius, *Attic Nights* 5.14.
7. Aulus Gellius, *Attic Nights* 5.14.
8. Aulus Gellius, *Attic Nights* 5.14.
9. Aulus Gellius, *Attic Nights* 5.14.
10. At that time, spectacles involving exotic wild animals were popular throughout the Roman world and those in charge of sponsoring the festivals were always on the lookout for suitable beasts, some of which became exceedingly rare and expensive. See Coleman 1990: 51–4.
11. For other examples see Shelton 2014: 471–4.
12. Aulus Gellius, *Attic Nights* 5.14.
13. See, e.g., Aristotle, *Politics* 1.1253a with Sorabji 1993: 7–16.
14. Here and below see Sorabji 1993: 107–21; Newmyer 2017: 76–106 (both with further examples).
15. And not just Gellius' version of the story: Catherine Osborne (2009: 135–61) was first to make a connection between the variant of the tale related to us by Aelian and the philosophical debate on the question of the human.
16. Osborne 2009: 137–8 and 152 argues that in Aelian's version of the story, the lion is actually a more successful communicator than Androclus, who repeatedly fails to grasp the situation.
17. Aelian explicitly mentions that the take-away line of the tale was that animals have memory (see *On Animals* 7.48). The presence or absence of memory in the non-human features extensively in Aristotle's writings. He is prepared to attribute some form of memory and some capacity to form universal concepts to some animals (see Aristotle, *Metaphysics* 980b22 (1.1.2–3) and *Nicomachean Ethics* 1147b11 (7.3.11) respectively with Sorabji 1993: 65–77).
18. Hesiod, *Works and Days* 276–81: 'This is the law that Cronus' son has established for human beings: that fish and beasts and winged birds eat one another, since Justice is not among them; but to human beings he has given Justice, which is the best by far.'
19. Aristotle, *Politics* 1253a11-8 (1.1.10). For Aristotle's concept of justice see also *Nicomachean Ethics*, book 5.
20. Animals exist for humans to exploit: Aristotle *Politics* 1256b15–23 (1.3.7). Humans are entitled to wage war on wild animals: Aristotle *Politics* 1256b23–7 (1.3.8) with Newmyer 2017: 77–8.

21. Ancient Greek *oikeioō*, 'to make a person a kinsman', 'to be endeared by nature'. For Zeno see Porphry, *On Abstinence* 3.19, 3.22. For Chrysippus see Porphyry, *On Abstinence* 3.20 and Diogenes Laertius, *Lives of Eminent Philosophers* 7.129 referring to book 1 of Chrysippus' work *On Justice* (with Sorabji 1993: 112–15). On the concept of *oikeiosis*, see Sorabji 1993: 122–33; Zagdoun 2005; Newmyer 2017: 76–106.
22. As reported by Porphyry, *On Abstinence* 3.25.
23. See, e.g., Plutarch, *Beasts Are Rational* 992D; Porphyry, *On Abstinence.*
24. See, e.g., Porphyry, *On Abstinence* 3.25.
25. Newmyer 2017: 90.
26. See Osborne 2009: 138 making the same case for Aelian's telling of the tale.
27. On the denial of animal emotions in ancient philosophy, see, e.g., Diogenes Laertius, *Lives of Eminent Philosophers* 7.110–14 and Newmyer 2017: 121–33 (with further references).
28. Oppian, *On Fishing* 4.172–241.
29. Jealous deer: Aelian, *On Animals* 3.17. Fearful leopards: 6.39. Compassionate mares: 3.8.
30. Arrian, *On Hunting* 5.
31. Aelian, *On Animals* 4.56 and 8.3 respectively.
32. There is also an ancient tradition that depicts certain animals as exemplars of justice. In Sophocles' tragedy *Electra* (1058–65), for example, birds are upheld as models of justice because – unlike the humans in the story – they do not engage in domestic violence.
33. Aelian, *On Animals* 3.21.
34. Pliny, *Natural History* 8.56–60 with Osborne 2009: 135, note 1. Aelian's account of Androclus and the lion concludes with a reference to this story in Pliny.
35. Pliny, *Natural History* 8.57–8.
36. Aelian, *On Animals* 7.48.
37. Pliny, *Natural History* 8.57.
38. Further examples provided by Pliny include a grateful female panther whose litter had fallen into a pit which was saved by human hands, and a snake which, after its release into the wild, recognized its old owner and saved him from an ambush by robbers (Pliny, *Natural History* 8.59–61).
39. On empathy in ancient Greek descriptions and conceptions of human/animal encounters more broadly, see Korhonen and Ruonakoski 2017.
40. This version of the tale seems specific to Gellius. Aelian's telling strictly follows the chronology suggested by the events themselves. Together with the human protagonist we move from Africa to Rome.
41. The identity of Androclus is another way in which Gellius' telling of the tale stands out. Aelian's Androclus is not a slave mistreated by his master but a Roman senator's slave who committed some unspecified offence and runs off to Africa to avoid punishment.
42. In this aspect Gellius' version coheres with Aelian's variant of the story, as pointed out by Osborne 2009: 136.
43. In Aelian's version of the story (*On Animals* 7.48 with Osborne 2009: 136–7), Androclus is able to cook the meat.

44. Aulus Gellius, *Attic Nights* 5.14.26. Aelian (*On Animals* 7.48) has a detail that Gellius does not report: his Androclus decided to return to civilization because of the excessive length of his hair which apparently caused 'a violent itching'.
45. See in detail Osborne 2009: 135–50. See also Smith, S. 2014: 229–33 (comparing Aelian's variant of the story to that of Gellius).
46. Aulus Gellius, *Attic Nights* 5.14.21.
47. Aulus Gellius, *Attic Nights* 5.14.12.
48. Aulus Gellius, *Attic Nights* 5.14.15.
49. As argued by Danta 2018: 64–5. On anthropomorphism and human thinking about the animal, see also de Waal 1999.
50. That the mutual recognition of human and animal is at centre stage for Gellius is also evident from the way in which he summarizes the story in the table of contents to his work. It encompasses 'the account of Apion, a learned man who was surnamed Plistonices, of the mutual recognition, due to old acquaintance, that he had witnessed at Rome between a man and a lion'.
51. I would like to thank Rick Benitez for introducing me to this term.
52. On genre see Vardi 2004. Gellius himself (e.g. at *praefatio* 3) refers to his work as *commentarii* ('notes') indicating that his book started as notes he took from his reading of various Greek and Roman authors.
53. As argued in detail by Morgan 2004.
54. Stevenson 2004: 122. On Gellius as a storyteller, see Anderson, G. 2004. Gellius repeatedly states in the preface to *Attic Nights* (1.23) that the stories are meant to educate and entertain his children.
55. On the *bestiarii* see, e.g., Lindstrøm 2010; Carucci 2019.
56. Here and below see Shelton 2014: 475.
57. On the equation of slaves and animals, see Garnsey 1996: 110–14; Bradley 2000.
58. See Aristotle, *Politics* 1254a17–1254b39 with Bradley 2000: 110.
59. See Aristotle, *Politics* 1253b23–1254a9, as discussed in Bhorat 2022.
60. Aristotle. *Politics* 1256b22–6.
61. Xenophon, *Oeconomicus* 13.9.
62. Cato, *On Agriculture* 2.7.
63. Bradley 2000: 110 speaks of the association between slave and animal as 'a staple aspect of ancient mentality, and one that stretched back to a very early period'.
64. Cicero, *Letters to Friends* 24 (7.1.3).
65. On the association between women and dogs, see in detail Franco 2014.
66. See, e.g., Phaedrus 3.33–50 (on why the genre of the fable was invented). See also Patterson 1991; Lefkowitz 2014: 18–20 (all with further literature). In this point, the ancient human/animal story resonates again with the post-Darwinian animal fable as explored by Danta. Both have the capacity to point to exploitation and injustices in human society as well as their parallels in the human treatment of animals (see Danta 2018: 7–8 on the 'down-to-earthness' of the animal fable).
67. See Forsdyke 2012: in particular 59–73 (with examples).

68. Knight: e.g. Chrétien de Troyes *Yvain, the Knight of the Lion* (ca. 1180); Shepherd: e.g. Jacobus de Voragine *Golden Legend* (ca. 1260); tailor: e.g. George Bernard Shaw *Androclus and the Lion* (1912). On other post-classical variants of this tale, including the famous attribution to Saint Jerome, see Rice 1988: 37–45; Høgel 2021.
69. Aarne-Thompson-Uther (ATU) story type 156.
70. See Gruen 2015 and 2017.
71. Bentham 2007 (1780): 310–11, note 1 (17.4).
72. See Singer 1975: in particular 9–13.
73. See Nussbaum 2006: 325–407.
74. See, e.g., Gruen, L. 2015.
75. The story is told in Rendall 2018 as well as in numerous videos on the online video channel YouTube and in magazine articles.

4 THE CYCLOPS (*CYCLOPS INHOSPITALIS*)

1. See Homer, *Odyssey*, book 9, in particular lines 105–51.
2. As Aguirre and Buxton 2020: 14–16 have rightly pointed out, even though modern commentators generally assume that the Homeric Cyclopes inhabit an island, the Odyssey does not actually say so explicitly. Later sources locate the Homeric Cyclopes on the island of Sicily.
3. Homer, *Odyssey* 9.187–92.
4. As Dougherty 1993: 129 has noted, 'Odysseus and his men arrive at this island unexpectedly and without prior plan or design; instead, in the dark night, the god leads them to it.' See also de Jong 2001: 233 who observes that 'meeting Polyphemus is not . . . a matter of necessity . . . but rather of a curious desire to find out the nature of the inhabitants of the country they first saw from afar, to learn whether they are without justice and god-fearing' (9174–6). The Homeric text itself suggests that it is indeed something like ethnographic curiosity that inspires Odysseus to visit the Cyclopes. As Odysseus says to his comrades 'I . . . will go and make trial of these men, to learn who they are, whether they are cruel and wild, and unjust, or whether they are kind to strangers and fear the gods in their thoughts' (9.172–6).
5. See Homer, *Odyssey* 9.166–8. Prometheus' theft of fire: e.g. Hesiod, *Theogony* 565–9.
6. Homer, *Odyssey* 9.231–5.
7. See Vidal-Naquet 1983: 15–38 on how the encounter between Odysseus and the Cyclops upsets the typical patterns of exchange that normally guide contact between strangers.
8. Homer, *Odyssey* 9.266–71.
9. Homer, *Odyssey* 9.273–6.
10. Homer, *Odyssey* 9.287–93.
11. On the complex relationships between the different kinds of Cyclopes, see Aguirre and Buxton 2020: 28–32.
12. On the meaning of the name of the Cyclopes, see in detail Aguirre and Buxton 2020: 194–205, in particular 195–7. As Bremmer 2021b: 37 has rightly pointed out, not all representations of the ancient Cyclopes feature them with a single eye. Some seem to

have retained two regular eyes (or at least sockets) in addition to the third one. Homer's Cyclops is single-eyed (otherwise the blinding as a surprise ambush would not have worked). Hesiod's *Theogony* 142–4 also mentions a single eye, as does Lucian's *Dialogues to the Sea Gods* 288.

13. Hesiod, *Theogony* 139–46 with Strauss Clay 1993.
14. See, e.g., Pindar fragment 70a6, 169a7 (Maehler); scholium on Euripides, *Orestes* 965; Pausanias, *Description of Greece* 2.16.5; 2.25.8.
15. 'Many-voiced' or 'wordy' is also a possible translation but less likely, given that Polyphemus is not particularly talkative – although he can speak in human language (see below).
16. His encounter with Odysseus is also represented on numerous samples of Greek painted pottery. See, e.g., Touchefeu-Meynier 1997: nos. 1–56. Polyphemus also enjoyed a veritable modern afterlife as the subject of numerous artistic representations both pictorial and literary (on which see now Aguirre and Buxton 2020: 235–375).
17. On scholarly attempts to identify the specific locales of Odysseus' travels, see Romm 1992: 183–96.
18. See Dougherty 2001; Skinner 2012.
19. The ancient Greek word *barbaros* ('non-Greek', 'foreigner') is derived from the unintelligible sounds of non-Greek speakers. At first it had no negative connotations but took these on in the wake of the Persian invasion of Greece during the Persian Wars. See Cartledge 1993: 51–77.
20. Here and below see Skinner 2012. See also Haubold 2014 for the argument that the *Iliad* alludes to an already existing ethnographic tradition. On the traditional view that situates the emergence of ethnographic inquiry more firmly in the late sixth and early fifth centuries BCE, see, e.g., E. Hall 1989; J. Hall 2002.
21. The cumulative and pluralistic sense of early Greek identity: J. Hall 2002.
22. Ancient encounters with other cultures: Gruen 2010. On colonization and Greek ethnicity, see Malkin 1998; J. Hall 2002: 90–124; Dougherty 2001. On travel and knowledge of self and other, see Hartog 2001.
23. As a result scholars now believe that a common Greek identity emerged gradually through such encounters prior to the foundation of visible markers of a joint sense of Greekness (Skinner 2012: 27 names panhellenic festivals, Hellenic genealogies, and the Hellenion at Naucratis, a sanctuary co-founded by several Greek cities together).
24. Ethnography in the *Iliad*: Haubold 2014. In the *Iliad*, Greeks and Trojans do share a common language – and the same set of gods – but they differ in the way they make use of it (see Mackie 1996).
25. On the *Odyssey* and the Greek 'ethnographic imagination', see Dougherty 2001. See also Hartog 1996; Dougherty 1999: 314–19. Homer's *Odyssey* and colonialization: Malkin 1998; Calame 2002.
26. On the Homeric Phoenicians, see Winter 1995; Dougherty 2001: 111–17.
27. Lotus Eaters: Homer, *Odyssey* 9.82–4 with Dougherty 2001: 95–6; Laestrygonians: Homer, *Odyssey* 10.80–3, 10.105–6; 10.118–20; 23.318–20 with Dougherty 2001: 140–2; Phaeacians: e.g. Homer, *Odyssey* 6.1–19 with Dougherty 2001: 102–8, 112–17.

28. See, e.g., Romm 1992, in particular 183–96 on fact and fiction in Odysseus' travels. See also Lenfant 1999: 206–8 on monstrous creatures and the breakdown of human features in distant regions.
29. Herodotus, *Histories* 3.116, 4.13, 4.27. See Karttunen 2002 on the conception of the fringes of the world in Herodotus' *Histories*.
30. See Ctesias, *Fragmente der Griechischen Historiker (FGrHist)* 688 F45.36–43 and 688 F45.50, respectively.
31. Pliny, *Natural History* 7.2.9–11. Some of these creatures were already mentioned by Ctesias.
32. See in detail Dougherty 2001.
33. Odysseus as the 'traveller-observer': Dougherty 2001: 4.
34. See Dougherty 2001: 10, 161–76, Calame 2002: 146–7; Skinner 2012: 49–58; Hartog 2001: 15–21; Malkin 1998: 62–93. As Skinner (2012: 52) put it, in the *Odyssey*, the return home involves 'a return to the – implicit Greek – "self"'.
35. On the Phaeacians see Segal 1994: 12–25.
36. The Cyclopes and the Golden Age: Hernández 2000: 347–50.
37. See Homer, *Odyssey* 7.310–14.
38. On this point see de Romilly 1980: 4. On the use of negations in the Homeric description of the Cyclopes, see Austin 1983: 25–7.
39. On the differences between the Phaeacians and the Greeks, see Hartog 2001: 31–2.
40. Dougherty 2001: 6.
41. On the question of the human in Homer's *Odyssey*, see J. Heath 2005: 39–167.
42. As Charles Segal (1994: 37) has argued, Odysseus' return home is thus not just a return to Hellenicity but also 'a return to humanity in its broadest sense'.
43. See, e.g., Homer, *Odyssey* 9.174, 9.187, 9.214–15, 9.494.
44. Cheese: Homer, *Odyssey* 9.222–7; Wine: Homer, *Odyssey* 9.357–9.
45. Bread-Eaters: Homer, *Odyssey* 9.191.
46. Homer, *Odyssey* 1.71.
47. Von Wilamowitz-Moellendorff 1976, vol. I: 13–14. Wilamowitz here refers to the Cyclops of Euripides' drama (see above), but it is clear that he makes a categorical statement that applies more widely.
48. Hesiod, *Works and Days* 274–80. For a similar link between animals devouring one's own kind and their lack of justice, see also Aelian, *On Animals* 7.19.
49. Later in the history of the ancient world, the Roman author Pliny the Elder acknowledged the fact that some humans do indeed consume human flesh, yet he, too, draws a direct link between this practice and animality. In *Natural History* he states 'when nature implanted in man the wild beasts' habit of devouring human flesh, she also thought fit to implant poisons in the whole of the body, and with some persons in the eyes as well, so that there should be no evil anywhere that was not present in man' (Pliny, *Natural History* 7.2.18). Pliny and Hesiod certainly come to androphagy from opposite ends: the moralizing Hesiod posits its forswearing as a feature distinguishing humans from animals, while Pliny acknowledges the practice. Yet ultimately both

authors end up in the same place. Both associate the consumption of human flesh – and thus those practising it – with wild animals.

50. On the representation of homophagy in Greek literature, see Rawson 1984 (with references).
51. Homer, *Odyssey* 9.291–3.
52. He also does not first offer sacrifice, another marked lack of deference towards the Greek gods.
53. Homer, *Odyssey* 9.296–8.
54. On this point see also Hernández 2000: 353; Aguirre and Buxton 2020: 154–67.
55. The tripartite distinction between gods, humans, and animals in Greek religion: Kindt 2020a.
56. Hernández 2000: 353 describes the Homeric Cyclopes as 'a primitive society of beings who are neither exactly human nor yet inhuman'.
57. Ancient conceptions of the monstrous: Strauss Clay 1993; Atherton 1998; Clare 1998; Lefant 1999; Murgatroyd 2013; Lowe 2015, in particular 6–43 'monster theory'. See also the essays collected by Béthume and Tomasssini 2021.
58. See, e.g., Aristotle, *Generation of Animals* 769b8–30 for a discussion of the monstrous.
59. See, e.g., Homer *Odyssey* 9.187, 9.213–15, 9.494.
60. See, e.g., Glenn 1972; Calame 1977; Mondi 1983; Aguirre and Buxton 2020: 8–14; Bremmer 2021b [1988] (with further literature).
61. On forms of 'proto-racism' (1) in the ancient world, see the landmark study by Isaac 2004.
62. On the history of homophagy in the modern ethnographic imagination, see Lestringant 1997.
63. Arens 1979. See also Obeyesekere 2005.
64. See, e.g., Lee 1950. For scholarly readings of wine as an agricultural product derived from nature through human labour, see, e.g., Austin 1983: 21–2.
65. Cunning intelligence in Odysseus' encounter with the Cyclops: Friedrich 1987.
66. Homer, *Odyssey* 9.364–70. On the role of words in this exchange between Odysseus and the Cyclops, see also Podlecki 1961; Pucci 1993.
67. Homer, *Odyssey* 9.369–70.
68. Homer, *Odyssey* 9.410–2.
69. See in detail J. Heath 2005: 39–167. Haubold 2014: 21 reminds us that despite a few dispersed comments in the *Iliad* and *Odyssey* on foreign people speaking in tongues other than Greek (e.g. *Iliad* 2.867, 4.438), neither poem uses language as a marker of ethnic or cultural difference.
70. J. Heath 2005: 79–84.
71. Homer, *Odyssey* 9.526–35.
72. Hernández 2000: 354 sees the presence of some *logos* in Polyphemus as one of the qualities that distinguishes him from animals.
73. For an image of the Münster's *Cosmographia*, see Campbell 1988: 46.
74. Columbus, *First Voyage*, in Jane 1930: 14 with Aguirre and Buxton 2020: 237.

75. One-eyed figures feature in numerous modern novels and movies. Some allude to the story of Odysseus and Polyphemus, while others do not. See Aguirre and Buxton 2020: 347–75 (with further literature).
76. The figure of the 'wild man': Bernheimer 1952; Bartra 1994, 1997. On the notion of 'savagery', see, e.g., the material discussed in Sheehan 1980; Hulme 1986: 20–2; Pearce 1988; and the essays collected in Sayre 1997. On the 'noble savage', see Ellingson 2001. On references to animal and animality in the Western ethnographic tradition, see Jahoda 2018: 75–96.
77. Darwin 2001: 223.
78. On race in Darwin's oeuvre, see, e.g., the articles collected in Desmond and Moore 2009 and DeSilva 2021.
79. Darwin 2001: 223.
80. Just before his arrival on the shores of the land of the Cyclopes, Odysseus explicitly comments on the fecundity of the nearby goat island, but his description remains tied to the theme that the Cyclopes are unable to reach and exploit it. See Homer, *Odyssey* 9.116–41 with de Jong 2001: 233–5 and Bremmer 1986.
81. See Newton 1983.
82. See Homer, *Odyssey* 9.447–57.
83. The hubristic Odysseus: Friedrich 1991.
84. Barthes 1981.
85. See Barthes 1981: 27.
86. See, e.g., Ram-Prasad 2019 and the conclusion to this book.

5 THE TROJAN HORSE (*EQUUS TROIANUS*)

1. The warning words are spoken by Laocoön, the priest of Neptune (Poseidon) at Troy, and read: 'I am afraid of Greeks, even when they bear gifts' (*timeo Danaos et dona ferentis*, Virgil, *Aeneid* 2.49). Virgil refers to the Greeks as 'Danaans'.
2. See Virgil, *Aeneid* 2.42–9.
3. Virgil, *Aeneid* 2.235–42.
4. Virgil's Aeneas (2.2265) speaks of 'a city buried in wine and sleep'.
5. Accounts of the number of Greek fighters emerging from the horse: e.g. Stesichorus frag. 102 with Davies and Finglass 2014: 420–1 (100 men); Apollodorus *Epitome* 5.14 (naming 50); Quintus Smyrnaeus, *The Fall of Troy* 12.306–33 (names 30 and states that many more entered the horse until it was full); Tzetzes, *Posthomerica*, 641–50 (23 Greek fighters). The *Little Iliad* (according to Apollodorus, *Epitome* 5.14) apparently had 3,000, but (as suggested by West 2003: 133, note 41) this may be a mistake and the actual number given here may actually be 13. On the soldiers hidden inside the horse, see also Austin 1959: 18 (with further evidence).
6. Ever since 1873 when the German businessman and archaeologist Heinrich Schliemann (1822–90), took Homer's *Iliad* and found the remnants of a grand metropolis – now Hisarlik in modern Turkey – the existence of the city itself has been generally accepted as fact. As far as the Trojan War is concerned, there is some evidence that the walls of Troy

VII (what would have been the Troy of King Priam) were damaged around the time the Trojan War would have taken place (see, e.g., Anderson 1970; Rouman and Held 1972). But whether this destruction was the result of warfare or a natural disaster or something else entirely remains unclear. This leaves us with the wooden horse. Was it real, or a symbol for something different, later embellished by storytelling? Did it perhaps represent a siege tower or battering ram? Or a ship carrying Greek soldiers? Or a natural disaster, such as an earthquake, that devastated the ancient city? On such historicizing interpretations, see Strauss 2006: 171–81 (with further references). The problem with such attempts to dismantle the horse is that they seek to preserve the historicity of the war and the iconic narrative of events leading to the city's fall by sacrificing the materiality of the horse. They turn the story of the sack of Troy into an allegorical narrative that corresponds to a historical reality beyond its narrative frame. Others have sought to locate the horse's meaning strictly within the realm of the literary (see, e.g., Austin 1959; Vermeule 1986; Franco 2005/6; Riverlea 2007). These interpretations have yielded invaluable insights about the role of the horse as a literary device. Yet, they resemble the overtly historicizing one in not taking the physical presence of the horse seriously. This is in conflict with the ancient evidence which overwhelmingly seeks to depict the physicality of the horse in realistic terms (see, e.g., Hexter 1990: 117–22; Davies and Finglass 2014: 457).

7. See Faraone 1992: 94–112 on other stories about statues with deadly contents.
8. Here and below see Kelder 2012 (with examples). On the Mycenean evidence for horses and horsemanship, see also Cultrano 2005. Animals in ancient warfare: Mayor 2014.
9. As argued by Kelder 2012: 15.
10. See Greenhalgh 1973: 19–39; Crouwel 1981 (with evidence).
11. For an interpretation of the evidence for the use of Mycenean chariots in battle, see Littauer 1972 (with further literature).
12. See Littauer 1972: 152; Greenhalgh 1973: 11–13.
13. This picture seems to be confirmed by the later Homeric evidence (see, e.g., Greenhalgh 1973: 9 who argues that 'it is the javelin which is the main weapon of the Homeric chariot-borne warrior, and not the long thrusting-spear or the bow, the two weapons which made the chariot so formidable a weapon of war after the revolutionary invention of the light spoke-wheeled chariot in the first half of the second millennium'. On Greek chariot warfare as depicted in Homer and elsewhere, see also Donaghy 2014: 40–51).
14. Homer, *Odyssey* 4.269–89 (Menelaus), 8.492–520 (Demodocus), 11.523–32 (Odysseus) respectively.
15. Homer, *Odyssey* 4.274–9. For further details, see also Apollodorus, *Epitome* 5.19–20, Triphiodorus, *The Sack of Troy* 463–90.
16. As pointed out by Schnapp-Gourbeillon 1981: 169.
17. Homer, *Iliad* 20.156–8.
18. Homer, *Iliad* 2.388–90.
19. On *kleos* see, e.g., Segal 1983.

20. Homer, *Iliad* 2.760–70.
21. In book 16 of the *Iliad*, we learn that Achilles also had a third horse, Pedasus, which was not immortal (see Homer, *Iliad* 16.152–4, 16.866–7). Achilles received it when he killed Eetion, the king of Thebes. He used it as a so-called 'trace horse' together with Xanthus and Balius.
22. Homer, *Iliad* 5.221–3. On these and other special horses in Homer, see Harrison 1991 (in particular on the question why Achilles has supernatural horses but his Trojan sparring partner, Hector, does not).
23. See Homer, *Iliad* 20.221–9.
24. Diomedes winning the chariot race at Patroclus' funeral games: Homer, *Iliad* 23.499–513.
25. See, e.g., Homer, *Iliad* 5.719–77, 13.23–7, 13.34–8.
26. On the links between the Homeric horses and heroes, see also Platte 2017: 36–45.
27. See, e.g., Homer, *Iliad* 2.23, 2.60 (Atreus); 24.804 (Hector); 6.299 (Antenor); 5.781, 5.849, 7.404, 8.194, 9.51, 9.711 (Diomedes); 14.10 (Thrasymedes).
28. Imbrius as 'rich in horses': Homer, *Iliad* 13.171. 'Drivers of horses': e.g. 2.104 (Pelos), 11.93 (Oileius), 4.327 (Menestheus).
29. Argos as 'grazed by horses': Homer, *Iliad* 3.75, 6.152, 19.329 (Argos). Phrygians as 'masters of quick-moving steeds': 3.185.
30. See, e.g., Homer, *Iliad* 2.230, 3.127, 3.131, 3.343, 4.80, 4.333, 4.335, 7.361, 8.71, 8.525, 10.424, 12.440, 17.230, 19.237.
31. See Macurdy 1923: 50 (with evidence).
32. As first pointed out by Macurdy 1923: 50. See also Donaghy 2014: 72–8.
33. See Rouman and Held 1972: 328–9. On Hittite use of chariots, see Donaghy 2014: 36. A thirteenth-century BCE Hittite cult inventory from Sallunatassi in central Anatolia attributes the goddess Maliya (who Hipponax associates with Athena) with the epithet 'of the carpenter'. See Rutherford 2020: 329–34. I would like to thank Jan Bremmer for pointing this out to me.
34. As first noted by J. W. Jones 1975: 245 referring to a private conversation with Edwin Brown.
35. On horses as ancient Greek status symbols, see also Étienne 2005. For a literary study of horses and horsemanship in Greek epic and Lyric poetry, see Platte 2017.
36. Homer, *Iliad* 11.158–62.
37. Homer, *Iliad* 16.466–9.
38. Homer, *Iliad* 16.486.
39. On 'shared mortality' and the general analogy between humans and animals in Homeric epic, see Gottschall 2001, in particular 279–80.
40. See Homer, *Iliad* 17.426–8 (Achilles' horses crying when Patroclus is killed by Hector). Xanthus' speech: Homer, *Iliad* 19.404–17.
41. E.g. Homer, *Iliad* 1.357–8, 8.245–6. See also Monsacré 2018: 159–67 (with further evidence).
42. In particular older scholarship has sought to establish a religious dimension of the Trojan horse by focusing on the god of the sea, Poseidon (see, e.g., Farnell 1896: 4). Yet

the association of the horse with Poseidon remains vague and inconclusive, as it relies on a number of connections between Poseidon and horses that nowhere feature explicitly in the myth about the Trojan horse.

43. See, e.g., Triphiodorus, *The Sack of Troy* 298–9; Apollodorus, *Epitome* 5.15; Virgil, *Aeneid* 2.31 with Horsfall 2008: 71–2.
44. See, e.g., Homer, *Odyssey* 8.493; Stesichorus frag. 100 with Davies and Finglass 2014: 414–19; Triphiodorus, *The Sack of Troy* 2, 57–8; Virgil, *Aeneid* 2.13–16 with Horsfall 2008: 59.
45. Homer's *Odyssey* 8.492–5 refers to 'the horse of wood which Epeius made with Athene's help (*epoiēsen sun Athēnē*)'. See also 8.519–20 for a similar vague phrasing. The passage is also quoted in Polyaenus, *Strategems* 1, preface. The *Little Iliad* (in Proclus' summary) speaks of 'Epeios following an initiative of Athena' (*Epeios kat' Athēnas proaipesin*). The phrasing here is vague enough not to reveal the exact involvement of the goddess.
46. On the question of Athena's input in the making of the horse, see also Horsfall 2008: 59–60 (with further literature).
47. On the problems dating Quintus, see Baumbach and Bär 2007: 1–8; Bär 2009 12–23.
48. Quintus of Smyrna *Fall of Troy* 12.138–48.
49. Quintus of Smyrna *Fall of Troy* 12.108–12.
50. As suggested by Beazley 1963, vol. II: 401–2.
51. The ancient depicting Athena and horses are discussed in Sparkes 1971: 60.
52. See Yalouris 1950: 19–30 (Corinth), 47–64 (Attica). There was also a bronze statue representing the Trojan horse on the Athenian acropolis, on which see Lefkowitz 2020.
53. Detienne 1971.
54. For a detailed view of what sets Virgil's telling of the story apart from other extant ancient authors, see Austin 1959.
55. But see Riverlea 2007 extending the interpretation by Vermeule 1986.
56. As pointed out by Strauss 2006: 173–4.
57. Virgil, *Aeneid* 2.31–2.
58. See Virgil, *Aeneid* 2.57–149. Sinon's intervention is already part of the story in the Trojan Cycle (see *Sack of Ilion,* testimonia 2), but Virgil puts special emphasis on this part of the story. On Sinon as a 'doublet' for Odysseus, see Faraone 1992: 97–8 (with further evidence). On the possible meanings of Sinon's name, see Knox 1950: 390; Hexter 1990: 113–14.
59. Virgil, *Aeneid* 2.114–19.
60. Virgil, *Aeneid* 2.162–94.
61. See, e.g., Oppian, *On Fishing* 3.560–5 (for an example of how to introduce soldiers into a city by stealth) and Krenz 2000 (with further examples). On trickery and deceit in Athenian (political) culture more generally, see Hesk 2000.
62. 'Greek treachery': Virgil, *Aeneid* 2.65. 'Wickedness': Virgil, *Aeneid* 2.10.
63. Virgil, *Aeneid* 2.13–15. On the huge size of the horse, see also Virgil, *Aeneid* 2.32 and Quintus of Smyrna, *The Fall of Troy* 12.566.
64. In the ancient world, monuments commemorating victories in war and other major achievements were a ubiquitous feature. In particular, the famous Greek sanctuaries

like Delphi and Olympia were full of the spoils of war and of other monuments erected to commemorate notable events. On monuments and other representations of the Trojan horse in the Greek world, see D'Agostino 2014: in particular 28–38.

65. E.g. Virgil, *Aeneid* 2.20, 2.52. Aeschylus, *Agamemnon* 825 refers to the fighters as the 'offspring of the horse' (*hippou neossos*), thus also suggesting a mare. The pregnant imagery also features in detail in Triphiodorus, *The Sack of Troy* 200 and 379b–90 (in Cassandra's speech).
66. See Homer, *Odyssey* 8.504–10. See also Stesichorus frag. 103 (with Davies and Finglass 2014 : 421–7). West 2013: 205 states that 'there was not necessarily any such debate in the *Little Iliad*.'
67. Virgil, *Aeneid* 3.537–43 with Horsfall 2007: 379.
68. See Vance 1973: in particular 129–30.
69. Vance (1973: 130) has called this 'the semantics of order and disorder'.
70. On the palladium see, e.g., *Little Iliad* (Proclus' summary) 4; Apollodurus, *Epitome* 5.13; Dionysius of Halicarnassus, *Roman Antiquities* 1.68–9; Ovid, *Fasti* 6.419–54. See also Faraone 1992: 4–7.
71. Palladium at Rome: Dionysus of Halicarnassus, *Roman Antiquities* 2.665–6; Plutarch, *Camillus* 20.
72. On the heroism of Virgil's Aeneas (in contrast to the Homeric heroes), see now Farrell 2021: 196–292.
73. On Mycenean warfare, see Snodgrass 1967: 14–34. Developments in Greek warfare between the Late Bronze Age and the Archaic period are summarized in Snodgrass 1964: 189–212.
74. See, e.g., the examples discussed in Engdahl 2013.
75. See Chase 1902: 84.
76. See Chase 1902: 71 with examples.
77. See Minchin 2001a: 32–4 on the cognitive function of the Homeric similes. See Clarke 1995: 137–8 on the older, dismissive position on the simile taking them as mostly formulaic (with examples) as well as his study of clusters of related simile imagery (138–43).
78. Homer, *Iliad* 13.198–202.
79. See Schnapp-Gourbeillon 1981: 38–64; see also Lonsdale 1990: 39–47 who argues that the typical lion simile is 'modelled on a single type (the marauding lion) involving the confrontation of men and dogs with a wild beast' (39).
80. Homer, *Iliad* 20.403–5.
81. See Homer, *Iliad* 3.28–9.
82. See Clarke 1995: 145–59.
83. See Schnapp-Gourbeillon 1981: 65–94, 95–131 (on Diomedes' association with lions).
84. E.g. Homer, *Iliad* 15.573, 15.579 respectively.
85. Homer, *Iliad* 21.246–8.
86. See, e.g., Homer, *Iliad* 4.331–4, 6.12–4, 14.1–2, 20.283–5. On the battle cry: J. Heath 2005: 126–7.
87. J. Heath 2005: 124. See also K. C. King 1987: 13–28.

88. See, e.g., Homer, *Iliad* 15.348–51, 16.836, 24.406–9 with J. Heath 2005: 134–5.
89. See, e.g., Homer, *Iliad* 22.346–7 with J. Heath 2005: 136–7. On Achilles the man-eater, see also Gottschall 2001: 280.
90. 'Argive beast': Aeschylus, *Agamemnon* 824. 'Trojan leap': Euripides *Andromache* 1139 with Borthwick 1967.

6 THE 'TROJAN' BOAR (*APER TROIANUS OSTENTATOR*)

1. Based on topographical clues in Petronius' *Satyrica*, it is now widely believed that the Roman city of Puteoli, today Pozzuoli in the region of Campania in southern Italy, is the (unnamed) place where the novel is set. See, e.g., Rose 1962; Sullivan 1968: 46–7; Bodel 1984: 224–9; Bodel 1999: 38.
2. See the brilliant study of Trimalchio's milieu by Veyne 1961.
3. See D'Arms 1981: 97–120 on the scholarly debate as to whether Trimalchio's wealth was derived primarily from trade and/or agriculture and usury (with further literature). Based on autobiographical comments by Trimalchio in the text, D'Arms convincingly argues for a diversified economic activity which included concurrent trade, agriculture, and moneylending. On Trimalchio's economic activity, see also Kloft 1994. 5.
4. References to classical Greek and Roman literature in the *Satyrica*: Connors 1998. See also Cameron 1969; Horsfall 1989b; Morgan 2009; Panayotakis 2009 (with further literature); Schmeling 2011: xxxviii–xlviii.
5. See Petronius, *Satyrica* 41–7. The guests use the absence of the host for plenty of 'unsupervised' conversation and speechmaking.
6. Schmeling 1970: 248.
7. The events at Trimalchio's house are narrated by one Encolpius, a fictional character within the *Satyrica*.
8. Petronius, *Satyrica* 40.
9. Petronius, *Satyrica* 40.
10. Petronius, *Satyrica* 40.
11. Petronius, *Satyrica* 40.
12. The place of the *Dinner of Trimalchio* in the larger context of the *Satyrica*: Bodel 1999.
13. The realism of Petronius, *Satyrica/Dinner of Trimalchio*: Veyne 1961; D'Arms 1981: 97–120; Bodel 1999: 41–3.
14. As Bodel 1999: 42 points out, 'in keeping his outlook as an ex-slave, Trimalchio aims for the grandeur of an *eques* ('knight') rather for that of a senator, i.e. not for the highest social rank but for the second-highest, that of the equestrian order, whose members included freedmen notorious for their abundant wealth.'
15. On the origins and suitability of the term *nouveau riche* for Trimalchio and those of his ilk, see D'Arms 1981: 98–9. Bodel 1999: 39 refers to him as a 'social upstart whose culinary extravagances, designed to impress, elicit only scorn from a more sophisticated narrator.'
16. Food as a codified message: Douglas 1972: 61.
17. Douglas 1972.

18. Lévi-Strauss 1969 [1964].
19. See in Garnsey 1999: 1–12, Potter 2004: 12–7; Wilkins and Hill 2006: 4–38 (for an overview), 110–39 (on staple foods), 140–63 (on meat and fish); McInerney 2014.
20. See, e.g., Garnsey 1999, in particular 1–12 and 122–7 vs. Potter 2004: 12–17.
21. On the terminology in Greek and Latin, see Frost 1999: 248–9.
22. See Davies, R. 1971. See also Horsfall 1989a.
23. See White 2015: 132.
24. On regional variations in meat consumption in the Roman world, see King 1999.
25. See Frost 1999; Curtis 2001; Ekroth 2014: 225–6.
26. Strabo 4.3.2.
27. Wilkins and Hill 2006: 54–6, 144–5. On the Greek and Roman consumption of insects, see, e.g., Aristophanes frag. 53 (= Athenaeus 4.133b), *Acharnians* 871; scholium on Aristophanes, *Acharnians* 1130; Theophilus, *Epistles* 14.
28. See, e.g., Herodotus, *Histories* 4.194; Diodorus Siculus 3.21, 3.26; Strabo 16.4.17.
29. Tacitus, *Germania* 31.2.3.
30. Theophrastus, *Characters* 9.4.
31. For an account of slaughter and meat-eating in the Greek ritual context, see Ekroth 2008.
32. See Lynch 2018, 'symposium-feast': 233.
33. On the representation of luxury and its link to the theme of death in the *Satyrica*, see, e.g., Arrowsmith 1966. See D'Arms 1981: 72–96; On Roman feasting, entertaining, and culinary culture, see Gozzini Giacosa 1992; Dunbabin 1996; Dalby 2000: 243–56; Purcell 2003; Dunbabin 2005; Faas 2005; Roller 2006; Nadeau 2010.
34. See, e.g., Plato, *Republic* 404b–c (highlighting the consumption of roast); Euboulos frag. 120.
35. See, e.g., Homer, *Iliad* 1.457–74, 9.5–30, 24.621–27; *Odyssey* 1.139–44, 14.72–84, 20.248–56. See also Bakker 2013: 36–52 (with further examples).
36. Homer, *Iliad* 8.229–34.
37. See McInerney 2014: 249.
38. Pindar frag. 168b (= Athenaeus, *The Learned Banqueters* 10.411d).
39. See, e.g., Callimachus *Hymn to Demeter* 31–6, 96–101; Ovid, *Metamorphoses* 8.751–98.
40. Posidippus, *Epigrams* 120 (= Athenaeus, *The Learned Banqueters* 10.412d–e).
41. Amarantus of Alexandria, *On the Stage* (= Athenaeus, *The Learned Banqueters* 10.414e–15a).
42. Theodorus of Hierapolis, *On Contests*, frag. 1. *Fragmenta Historicorum Graecorum* (*FHG*) 4.514 (= Athenaeus, *The Learned Banqueters* 10e–f).
43. Quintilian, *Institutes of Oratory* 1a.
44. Here and below see Garnsey 1999: 85–91; McInerney 2014: 252–4; Dombrowski 2014. On vegetarianism in the ancient world, see also Haussleiter 1935; Osborne 1995.
45. On the Pythagoreans see Burkert 1972. See also Scarborough 1982; Dombrowski 1984: 35–54; Dombrowski 2014: 536–7.
46. See, e.g., Empedocles frag. B136, 137, 139 (Diels/Kranz); Plato, *Republic* 371E–3E. On Plotinus's vegetarianism see Porphyry, *Life of Plotinus* 2.1–6. For Plutarch see *Beasts Are*

Rational: 985d–992e. Whether these and other ancient philosophers promoting vegetarianism were also themselves practising, it is not always possible to tell with certainty. For an impassionate ancient argument in favour of vegetarianism, see also Ovid, *Metamorphoses* 15.60–477.

47. See Seneca, *Epistles* 108.22.
48. See, e.g., Ovid, *Metamorphoses* 15.60ff.; Plutarch, *On the Eating of Flesh* 993A–6C; Porphyry, *On Abstinence*. Vegetarianism also features in Plutarch's *Beasts Are Rational*, e.g. in 991A and in Theophrastus' (now lost) treatise *On Piety*.
49. In particular, Pythagoras and his followers promulgated the idea of the transmigration of the soul. The Pythagorean position is variously summarized and addressed in Porphyry's treatise *On Abstinence*, e.g. 1.1–36, 2.28, 3.1.
50. Ovid, *Metamorphoses* 15.165–8.
51. Garnsey 1999: 86.
52. Plutarch, *On the Eating of Flesh* 997e–f.
53. The argument is, for example, mentioned in Porphyry, *On Abstinence* 1.19.
54. Ovid, *Metamorphoses* 15.83.
55. Ovid, *Metamorphoses* 15.96–8.
56. Ovid, *Metamorphoses* 15.108–10.
57. How this squares with Plutarch's role as a priest at Delphi (which will have regularly involved the making of blood sacrifices) remains anyone's guess.
58. Plutarch, *On the Eating of Flesh* 993d–4a. For Hyperbius, Prometheus, and the first killing of animals see also Pliny, *Natural History* 7.58.
59. Plutarch, *On the Eating of Flesh* 994a.
60. To prove that humans are not meant by nature to eat animals, Plutarch (*On the Eating of Flesh* 994f–5a) points to the characteristics of human teeth which are even, unlike those of carnivores.
61. See Porphyry, *On Abstinence* 1.27.
62. Porphyry, *On Abstinence* 1.15. On meat-eating, the body, and athletes, see also Plutarch, *On the Eating of Flesh* 995e.
63. Porphyry, *On Abstinence* 1.15.
64. Plutarch, *On the Eating of Flesh* 995e.
65. Plutarch, *On the Eating of Flesh* 995e. Porphyry, *On Abstinence* 1.33.
66. Porphyry, *On Abstinence* 3.1.
67. Ovid, *Metamorphoses* 15.125–9.
68. Plutarch, *On the Eating of Flesh* 994a–b.
69. 'Sanitized' meat: Fiddes 1991: 90.
70. Elias 2000 [1939]: 120.
71. Robust appearance: see above note 9.
72. Petronius, *Satyrica* 40.
73. See in detail Kindt 2021.
74. As evident from the ancient hunting literature, such as Xenophon's *On Hunting*, Arrian's *On Hunting*, and Pseudo-Oppian's *On Hunting*.
75. On initiation see now Bremmer 2021.

76. Xenophon, *On Hunting* 12. Hunting and warfare: Green 1996: 226–7; Barringer 2001: 10–69; MacKinnon 2014: 204.
77. Oppian, *On Fishing* 5.237–71.
78. See C. M. C. Green 1996 on the evidence for hunting in the Roman world from the earliest time onwards (correcting earlier arguments that the Roman hunt was an institution that emerged only late, from the second century BCE onwards). On hunting in the Roman world, see, e.g., J. K. Anderson 1985: 83–100; Hughes 2007; MacKinnon 2014: 207–13.
79. 'Citizens of the middle ranks': C. M. C. Green 1996: 226.
80. Here and below see in detail McKinnon 2014a.
81. See, e.g., Seneca, *Of Clemency* 1.18.2; Columella, *On Agriculture* 8.16.4–5.
82. We do not hear where the boar came from, whether Trimalchio's servants bought it on the market (possibly originating in one of the game parks that were widespread in the Roman Empire) or whether it was hunted specifically for (and perhaps even by) him. Or does it come from the grounds of Trimalchio's own (vast) estates as mentioned in Petronius, *Satyrica* 37, 48, 53)? The suggestion in the story is certainly that it is a wild animal that was hunted for consumption (hence the emphasis of the hunting theme in the presentation of the boar).
83. On the wild boar in the ancient world, see Keller 1912: 389–93.
84. Homer, *Odyssey* 19.428–58.
85. Boar-hunting similes in Homer's *Iliad*: e.g. 11.291–5, 11.324–30, 11.411–20, 12.41–5, 12.146–52, 13.470–6, 16.823–88, 17.281–5, 17.725–30.
86. See, e.g., Bremmer 2021c [1988]: 75–8 showing that in Macedonia boar hunting was a test of manhood which lasted well into historical times.
87. Xenophon, *On Hunting* 10.8.
88. See Pliny, *Natural History* 10.16 with C. M. C. Green 1996: 239. The other animals were wolves, minotaurs, horses, and eagles.
89. Martial, *Epigrams* 1.43.
90. Boar tusks were also enough of a trophy for the Roman emperor Augustus to transfer some famous tusks from the temple of Athena Alea at Tegea – where they had been displayed for centuries – to Rome after the battle of Actium in 31 BCE (see Pausanias, *Description of Greece* 8.46.1 and Bremmer 2021c [1988]: 78). See also the description of the boars' tusks and their peculiar capacity to heat up in Xenophon, *On Hunting* 10.17.
91. The dates are presented as if they are a special delicacy but turn out to be substandard.
92. 'Among the consumed game ... wild boar was perhaps the more popular luxury dish, and a key foodstuff that served to establish social prestige in Roman times' (MacKinnon 2014a: 208).
93. Pliny, *Natural History* 8.78.
94. Here and below see Faas 2005: 76–87 with 87 on Trimalchio's menu.
95. Macrobius, *Saturnalia* 3.13.13 with Schmeling 2011: 157–8. Wild boar is also variously included in Apicius' collection of recipes dating from the first century CE. See Apicius 8.329–38 (Vehling 2012).
96. Macrobius, *Saturnalia* 3.13.13.

97. The *lex Orchia* from 182 BCE, for example, restricted the size of any given banquet by capping the maximum number of guests (see Macrobius, *Saturnalia* 3.17.3). The *lex Fannia* from 161 BCE sought to achieve the same by curbing the sums to be spent on feasting and entertainment (See Pliny, *Natural History* 10.71.1; Macrobius, *Saturnalia* 3.17; Gellius, *Attic Nights* 2.24.1–6, and Zanda 2011: 120–1). It also capped the number of guests, listed specific foodstuffs no longer permitted at private dinner parties, and restricted the budget for individual foodstuffs. The law apparently tried to nudge the Romans towards buying local rather than exotic (imported) foodstuffs. Apparently, these efforts did not produce the desired effect. We know of numerous subsequent laws that were passed to reinforce, strengthen, or amend the existing sumptuary laws. Apparently, it was not merely and perhaps not even primarily moral concerns that prompted the enactment of such laws. The fear that the excessive competition between the members of the ruling classes could ultimately result in a loss of wealth and thus of social influence and political power would also have played a role (see Zanda 2011: 113–28).
98. See, e.g., Athenaeus' description of Caranus' wedding feast in *The Learned Banqueters* 4.128c–30d.
99. See, e.g., Horace, *Satires* 2.2; Juvenal, *Satire* 11.
100. Pliny, *Natural History* 8.6.
101. Chalinus, *Casina* 476 with Green 1996: 243 who argues that the passage mocks the traditional heroic tale, thus satirizing the aristocratic boar hunt.
102. Large estates in the Bay of Naples during the empire: D'Arms 1981: 72–96. The economic and societal place of the freedmen of Puteoli in the Roman Empire: D'Arms 1981: 11–148.
103. Theban dates being inferior: Schmeling 2011: 157 referring to Pliny, *Natural History* 13.47–8 and Statius, *Silvae* 4.9.26.
104. Petronius, *Satyrica* 41.
105. See Schmeling 2011: 157.
106. See MacKendrick 1950: 307.
107. S. Fitzgerald 1998: 33.
108. See, e.g., Fiddes 1991; Rothgerber 2013.

7 THE POLITICAL BEE (*APIS POLITICA*)

1. Seeley 2010: 5.
2. Seeley 2010: 73.
3. See in detail Seeley 2010: 73–145.
4. E.g. Homer, *Iliad* 2.87–93, 12.167–72; Hesiod, *Works and Days* 305–6; Plato, *Republic* 520b, 552a–67d, *Meno* 72a–c; Aristotle, *History of Animals* 488a8–11; Xenophon, *Cyropaedia* 5.124–5; Varro, *On Agriculture* 3.16; Virgil, *Georgics* 4.1–280 (see also 281–314, 548–66); Seneca, *On Clemency* 1.19.1–3; Columella, *On Agriculture* 9.2.1–16.2; Pliny, *Natural History* 11.4–23; Plutarch, *Precepts of Statecraft* 823F; Aelian, *On Animals* 5.10–13.
5. Honeybee monarchy in the ancient world: Carlson 2015: 63–81.

6. The figure of the king bee in ancient thought and literature: Overmeire 2011.
7. See, e.g., Crane 1994 (with further literature); Ransome 2004 [1937]: 75–82 (Greece) and 83–90 (Rome). Urban beekeeping: Rotroff 2002.
8. Several of these texts (e.g. Mago's work on beekeeping) are now lost and only known to us by name. Existing accounts include Varro, *On Agriculture* 3.16; Virgil, *Georgics* 4.1–314; Columella, *On Agriculture* 9; Pliny, *Natural History* 11.4–23, 18.5, 21.41–9.
9. See, e.g., *Pythian Odes* 10.53–4, *Olympian Odes* 10.98/-9.
10. See in detail Ransome 2004 [1937]: 91–111 ('Bees and Honey in Greek and Roman Myths'), 119–32 ('Honey in Greek Religious Rites'), 133–9 ('The Food of the Gods'). See also Elderkin 1939.
11. Here and below see Wilson 2014, in particular 106–39.
12. Honeybees in the ideology of Nazi Germany: Stripf 2019, 247–70.
13. Wilson 2014: 129.
14. Hobbes 1985 [1651]: 225 (part II, ch. 17); Mandeville 2016 [1714]; Marx (1991) [1867–94], vol. I: 284 (chapter 7, section 1). The humanizing and politicizing of honeybees also informed what remains one of the most widely read accounts of honeybee society in the modern area: that of the Belgian dramatist and Nobel laureate Maurice Maeterlinck (1862–1949). In his acclaimed book *The Life of the Bee* (1901), he uses honeybee society as a mirror to speculate extensively on the human condition.
15. Wilson 2014: 109.
16. Bio-politics: e.g. Foucault 1990: 133–60; Agamben 1998: 126–35.
17. The foundational study of socio-biology is Wilson 2000. See Dawkins' influential (but controversial) book from 1976 for the application of socio-biology to human behaviour.
18. Daston and Vidal 2004: 3.
19. In Greco-Roman thought and literature, the normative force of nature was by no means limited to the political workings of honeybees. It is, for example, also at play in Longus' novel *Daphnis and Chloe* (second/early third century CE). This story of the sexual awakening of a boy and girl in a bucolic setting extensively draws on nature in general and the animal realm in particular to set certain models – all heteronormative – for the human sexual encounter that takes place at the end of the novel. But it is striking that the examples of animal-coupling it refers to – above all that of goats and sheep – serve to normalize a form of sexuality that coheres with the patriarchal system of the Greco-Roman world. The novel does not, for example, refer to the sexual practices of the bonobo (one of the great apes) or that of the black widow spider. While the former lives in a matriarchy, the latter receives her name from the fact that she devours her male partner right after the act.
20. Homer, *Iliad* 2.87–93. Not even Homer can claim to have invented the 'genre': the political bee was already buzzing in ancient Egypt where the pictorial sign and the word for bee (*bit*) doubled as that for 'king' and 'Egypt' (see Wilson 2014: 110–11; Carlson 2015: 63).
21. Aristotle, *History of Animals*, *Generation of Animals*, *Parts of Animals*, *Movement of Animals*, and *Progression of Animals*. Animals also variously feature in his other treatises.

22. *Mētēr*: Aristotle, *History of Animals* 553a27–34. *Basileus*: 553b6. *Hēgēmones*: 553a26, 27, 553b6, 553b14–9. 'Worker bees': 553a27 (*chrēstai melittai*, 'productive bees'). 'Drones': 553b5.
23. Aristotle, *History of Animals* 553b15–17.
24. Aristotle, *History of Animals* 553b17–19.
25. 'The balance between productive and reproductive forces': Brill 2020: 168.
26. Aristotle, *History of Animals* 553b19.
27. On the surplus generation of 'queens' and the swarming of honeybees, see Winston 1987: 181–98.
28. *Mesotēs* and 'good measure': e.g. Aristotle, *Nicomachean Ethics* 2.1106a13–9b27.
29. See, e.g., Aristotle, *Generation of Animals* 767a20–35, *Physics* 146b3–20, *Topics* 139b21, 145b7–10.
30. Man as a *zōon politikon*: Depew 1995 (with further references).
31. Aristotle's conception of social animals: Lloyd 1983: 18–26; 2013: 277–93.
32. Aristotle, *History of Animals* 488a8-11.
33. Here and below see Depew 1995; Miller 2017: 189–201.
34. In Aristotle's account, humans and animals come together in the concept of 'shared life'; see Brill 2020.
35. Lloyd 1983: 42.
36. Aristotle, *History of Animals* 624b31–25a4.
37. Productive and destructive forces in the bee hive: Aristotle, *History of Animals* 635a4–33. Factionalism, the robber (*fōr*): Aristotle, *History of Animals* 553b.
38. The difference is that in the realm of human politics, the philosopher/observer takes on responsibility for the good, while in the natural world he does not carry such responsibility. See Aristotle's comments on the division of the sciences in Aristotle, *Topics* 145a15–16, *Physics* 192b8–12; *On the Heavens* 298a27–32, *On the Soul* 403a27–b2, *Metaphysics* 1025b25, 1026a18–19, 1064a16–19, b1–3; *Nicomachean Ethics* 1139a26–8, 1141b29–32 with Bodnar 2018; Falcon 2019. The human model in Aristotle's biological texts: Lloyd 1983: 26–43.
39. More specifically, Aristotle states that humans 'dualise' between being gregarious and solitary beings (Aristotle, *History of Animals* 488a2-7) thus acknowledging the fact that sometimes they are obviously not that great in cooperation. Aristotle's dualizers: Lloyd 1983: 44–53.
40. Aristotle's concept of nature: e.g. Pellegrin 2007: 144–8.
41. On Aristotle's use of analogies, see Hesse 1966: 130–56.
42. See in detail Miller 2017.
43. On this nexus see Frank 2005: 17–53.
44. The politics of honeybee generation: Brill 2020: 161–9.
45. Seneca, *On Clemency* 1.19.1–3.
46. Seneca, *On Clemency* 1.19.3.
47. Aelian, *On Animals* 5.10. See also 1.60.
48. Aelian, *On Animals* 5.10.
49. Aelian, *On Animals* 5.10.

50. Virgil, *Georgics* 4.1–280. Virgil on the rebirth of bees from the carcasses of oxen (*bugonia*): 4.295–314 with Osorio 2020. On the notion of the spontaneous generation of bees from rotten cow carcasses in Virgil and elsewhere in classical literature, see Ransome 2004 [1937]: 112–18; Totelin 2018: 63.
51. See Book 11 of Pliny's *Natural History*. On Pliny see in detail Beagon 1992: 124–58 ('Man and the Animals').
52. Plebeian bees: Pliny, *Natural History* 11.10.26. *Fuci* (drones) as 'imperfect bees': Pliny, *Natural History* 11.11.27, 11.16.46.
53. 'King(s)': e.g. Pliny, *Natural History*, e.g. 11.16.46. 'Imperator(es)': e.g. 11.12.29. 'Leader', e.g. 11.18.56.
54. Size: 11.16.46. Palaces: 11.12.29.
55. Pliny, *Natural History* 11.17.53. Certain *satellites* ('escorts') are also present.
56. Pliny, *Natural History* 11.4.11–12.
57. Pliny, *Natural History* 11.5.14.
58. Pliny, *Natural History* 11.10.22.
59. Pliny, *Natural History* 11.10.25.
60. Pliny, *Natural History* 11.11.27. On the question of whether drones have stingers: 11.11.27 (no stingers), 11.18.57 ('a doubtful point'). In 11.19.60, Pliny repeats the view of some that the worker bees become drones once they have used their sting and no longer produce honey 'as though their strength had been castrated, and they cease at the same time both to hurt and to benefit'.

    Pliny, *Natural History* 11.11.27.
61. Pliny, *Natural History* 11.18.57.
62. See Winston 1987: 199–213, in particular 202.
63. Pliny, *Natural History* 11.17.52.
64. Pliny, *Natural History* 11.17.53.
65. Pliny, *Natural History* 11.17.54.
66. Pliny, *Natural History* 11.20.63.
67. They manifest themselves, for example, in the cycles of life between birth and death.
68. As persuasively shown in the influential contribution to the history of science by Kuhn 1962.
69. This is a recurrent theme in Godfrey-Smith's (2021) introduction to the philosophy of science.
70. See Seeley 2010: 218–31.
71. Seeley 2010: 73.
72. Seeley 2010: 8.
73. Seeley 2010: 25.
74. Seeley 2010: 25.
75. Seeley 2010: 25.
76. Seeley 2010: 199.
77. See, e.g., Anderson, Theraulaz and Denebourg 2002; Tero, Kobayashi, and Nakagaki 2007; Tero et al. 2010; Lutz et al. 2021. See also the bioinspiration research cluster at the University of Melbourne (http://bit.ly/43dKh3T) and the work of my University of Sydney colleague Tanya Latty on ants and traffic jams (https://ab.co/3NNF7Wy).

78. See, e.g., Srinivasan et al. 2011.
79. Seeley 2010: 131.
80. Seeley 2010: 21.
81. Wilson 1971: 5.

8 THE SOCRATIC GADFLY (*HAEMATOPOTA OXYGLOTTA SOCRATIS*)

1. For the wording of the indictment, see Favorinus, frag. 34 Barigazzi (*apud* Diogenes Laertius 2.40). See also Xenophon, *Memorabilia* 1.1.1, *Apology* 10; Plato, *Apology* 24b8–c1, *Euthyphron* 3b; Philodemus, *On Piety* 1696–7 (Obbink); Servius on Virgil, *Aeneid* 8.187. For the charge and the trialm, see Parker 1996: 199–207; Millett 2005: 23–62; Bremmer 2020a [1988]: 1016–20.
2. Plato, *Apology* 30d–e.
3. See Plato, *Apology* 36d–7a.
4. Rhetoric: Plato, *Gorgias*. Love: Plato, *Phaedrus*. Virtue: Plato, *Meno*. Knowledge: Plato, *Theaetetus*. The ancient author Xenophon (430–354 BCE) is another student of Socrates who authored several surviving dialogues featuring his famous teachers (*Apology*, *Memorabilia*, *Symposium*, *Oeconomicus*).
5. See, e.g., Cartledge 2009: 76–90 (with further literature). Socrates was not the only Athenian thinker accused of *asebeia*. On these processes see Cohen 1991: 203–17; Filonik 2013, 2016.
6. See Shear 2011.
7. See Naas 2015 with the argument that the gadfly image works particularly well in American English. On the history of this translation, see Marshall 2017: 163–6.
8. Horse imagery in the *Apology*: e.g. in 25a–b, and 27d. See also Bell 2015.
9. *Myōps* as gadfly/horsefly: e.g. Aeschylus, *Prometheus Bound* 675, *Suppliants* 307; Aristotle, *History of Animals* 528b31, 552a29. *Myōps* as goad or spur: e.g. Theophrastus, *Characters* 2.18; Polybius 11.18.4. *Myōps* as any kind of motivating force: Lucan, *Slander* 14.
10. Xenophon, *On the Art of Horsemanship* 8.5. See also Theophrastus, *Characters* 22.8 (on the character harbouring petty ambition, visiting the marketplace wearing his spurs – presumably a way of showing off).
11. Here and below see Marshall 2017, in particular 168–70. Marshall has pointed out that the metaphors of both horse and spur resonate with a number of other significant words directly adjacent. She further argues that the way in which the *myōps* in its impersonation as a gadfly features elsewhere in Greek thought and literature cannot shed light on its function in Socrates' speech because these supplementary passages depict it in contexts and situations differing fundamentally from that described in the *Apology*.
12. None of the corresponding words and phrases discussed by Marshall excludes the reading of *myōps* as 'gadfly'. Indeed, *proskathizōn* (from *proskathizō*, 'to sit down near', 'to settle'), in Plato, *Apology* 31a, favours the reading of *myōps* as 'gadfly' over 'spur', as Marshall 2017: 170 readily admits but dismisses as irrelevant because outside the *myōps*/horse analogy.

13. Marshall 2017: 165–6 traces the translation of *myōps* into gadfly back to Jowett's translation of the *Apology* in four volumes from 1971 and speculates that he may have preferred the gadfly to other readings 'for personal as well as philological reasons'.
14. On the ambiguity of *kentron*, see Marshall 2017: 172 and notes 19 and 20 below.
15. Plato, *Theaetetus* 143e.
16. See Stavru 2018 with further literature.
17. On Socrates' physiognomy, including his eyes, see Stavru 2018 (with further literature).
18. See also the analogy in Plato's *Republic* 368c–d where a link is made between philosophical investigation and people looking at big letters rather than small script for clear insight.
19. Aristotle, *History of Animals* 596b15.
20. Furnish with a sting: Plato, *Republic* 552d, 555d. Strike with a goad: Herodotus, *Histories* 3.16.
21. Here and below I follow Marshall 2017: 167–8.
22. Oppian, *On Fishing* 2.521–32.
23. The word mostly appears applied to Io, but in Euripides' *Bacchae* it is used to refer to the ecstasy of the Bacchants (Euripides, *Bacchae* 1229). *Oistroplex* and Io: Aeschylus, *Prometheus Bound* 681–2; Sophocles, *Electra* 4–5. Moreover, as Chiara Thumiger (2014: 385) reminds us, '*oistros*, "gadfly", is an established metaphor for a "sting of passion", or even madness in Greek poetic language, with a clear psychological meaning'.
24. Io: Aeschylus, *Prometheus Bound* 669–77, *Suppliants* 307; Apollodorus, *Library* 2.1.3; Ovid, *Metamorphoses* 1.610–67.
25. Homer, *Odyssey* 22.297–9.
26. Plato, *Apology* 30e–31a.
27. See, e.g., Plato, *Apology* 20e–1a. On the Delphic oracles, see Kindt 2016: 87–112.
28. Aristotle, *History of Animals* 596b15. Aelian, *On Animals* 4.51 distinguishes the *myōps* from the *oistros*. He states that the former has a louder buzz and a smaller sting than the latter.
29. Lucian, *The Fly* 5.
30. Homer, *Iliad* 17.569–74.
31. For another (later) example of an ancient story featuring the courage of a bloodsucking insect that ultimately pays for its beneficial contribution to humanity with its life, see also the poem *Culex* ('the gnat') attributed to the Roman poet Virgil (70–10 BCE).
32. Socratic wordplay: e.g. Plato, *Protagoras* 341e, *Symposium* 174b. There is also much wordplay in Plato's *Cratylus*, but scholars disagree on the question of how far this dialogue is Socratic or expresses Plato's own views. The point that *myōps* as gadfly reflects Socratic irony was already made in a commentary on the passage in Stallbaum's edition of the *Apology* from 1827: Stallbaum 1827 with Marshall 2017: 164–5.
33. For a succinct account of the history of this translation in the English-speaking literature, see Marshall 2017: 163–6.
34. Julian Assange as a 'gadfly': https://bit.ly/3D6mqbL. Edward Snowden as a 'gadfly': https://bit.ly/44DB2uS.

35. Diogenes Laertius 2.21.
36. Flea: Aristophanes, *Clouds* 144–7. Gnats: Aristophanes, *Clouds* 156–8. Such jokes are, of course, directed at certain kinds of empirical observations of nature. The play that has come down to us is not the original drama, but a revised version Aristophanes published later.
37. According to Aristotle's *History of Animals* 490a19–21, two-winged, blood-sucking flies use a frontal sting to draw blood, presumably to be then gobbled up with a tongue (*glōtta*) as explained in *History of Animals*, 596b11–15. Such views (if shared by Plato/ Socrates) would provide another opening for a link to Socrates, whose tongue was certainly as sharp as the presumed frontal stinger of the Aristotelian gadfly.
38. Plato, *Apology* 31a.
39. Plato, *Apology* 31a.
40. Ostracism: Forsdyke 2005; Brenne 2018; Kosmin 2018.
41. See Bell 2015: 115: 'Socrates' gadfly-ism is dependent upon and derived from Athens's equinity and vice versa.'
42. Plato mentions that Socrates suggested the monetary fine (*Apology* 38b), while according to Xenophon (*Apology* 23) he refused to suggest any punishment at all.
43. Eighty more judges than those who had found him guilty in the first round of the procedures (280) later voted for the death penalty.
44. On their reception of Socrates, see Villa 2001.
45. See McGowan 1998: 38: 'Her use of the Greeks ... is an attempt to confront modern sensibilities, modern assumptions about the good life, with an alternative orientation to what it means to live amid others.'
46. On this point see, e.g., Arendt 2003 [1971]: 6–8 with Villa 1999: 241–2.
47. In the first volume of *The Life of the Mind*, Arendt explicitly discusses their meaning (see Arendt 1978, vol. I: 172–3). In addition, the three images feature individually and in different combinations in several texts in which she explores the role of Socrates in Athenian politics. This is most evident in her essays 'Philosophy and Politics' (2003 [1971]), and 'Thinking and Moral Considerations' (2005 [1990]), two detailed and explicit investigations of 'the political' in Classical Athens. 'Philosophy and Politics' was later republished as 'Socrates', but I refer to it under its original title.
48. Arendt 2005 [1990]: 174.
49. Arendt 2005 [1990]: 174.
50. Socrates' mother was herself a midwife (see Plato, *Theaetetus* 149a), so presumably he could speak about their experiences with some authority.
51. On the midwife in ancient Greece, see, e.g., Maclachlan 2012: 53–5; Bremmer 2019: 237–8.
52. Here and below see Plato, *Meno* 80a–d.
53. Arendt 2005 [1990]: 174: 'he had nothing to teach, no truth to hand out'.
54. Arendt 2005 [1990]: 175.
55. Arendt 2005 [1990].
56. The midwife as the dominant image of the article: Villa 1999: 244.
57. Arendt 2003 [1971]: 15.

58. Arendt 2003 [1971]: 24.
59. Arendt here merely states the existence of this friction but does not explore it further. This is because the main focus of 'Philosophy and Politics' is to illustrate how philosophy and politics came together in Socrates' teaching – and how they became separated forever in the wake of Plato's response to the trial.
60. Arendt 2005 [1990]: 175 (referring to Xenophon, *Memorabilia* 4.3.14). For a comprehensive comparative discussion of the two articles, see Villa 1999.
61. Arendt 2005 [1990]: 175.
62. See in detail Villa 1999: 247–50.
63. Arendt 2005 [1990]: 40, 189.
64. Arendt on totalitarianism: Arendt 2017 [1951].
65. Here and below Cavarero 2019.
66. Cavarero 2019: 36.
67. Arendt 2017 [1951]: 443.
68. Arendt 2003 [1971]: 176–7.
69. The conflict that Arendt describes helps to define not just the modern gadfly but the Socratic gadfly as well. Without wishing to portray Socrates too strongly as a man of conscience – in the end he did commit himself absolutely to the rule of law when he accepted the death penalty – there were other moments in his life when he did place his conscience over the will of the movers and shakers of the day (see, e.g., Plato, *Apology* 32c–e on Socrates refusing to arrest an innocent man for execution as requested by the Thirty; see also Xenophon, *Hellenica* 1.7.15 and Plato, *Crito* 46b4–7). And yet it would be too simple to see his trial merely as a conflict between individual conscience versus the rule of law. There are several other dimensions to the Socratic gadfly and the particular (historical and cultural) environment it inhabited in Classical Athens. Whatever the real motivations of Socrates' accusers and those citizens who came to condemn him: the way in which the indictment was framed *did* make it look as if the matter was one of individual conscience against the rule of law. So while the reasons for the indictment and ultimate condemnation of Socrates are certainly complex, manifold, and historically specific, the way in which the trial was framed resonates with the kind of conflicts that constitute the environment of the gadfly today.
70. See Villa 2001: 1–58 ('What is Socratic Citizenship?').
71. For a critical account of Western receptions of ancient Greek democracy, see Rhodes 2003.

9 THE MINOTAUR (*HYBRIDA MINOTAURUS*)

1. On Crete see Marinatos and Hirmer 1960; Wallace 2010. Crete and the Minotaur: Evely 1996. On Crete and bulls see also Marinatos 1989; Loughlin 2004. The ancient pictorial record from Crete: Zervos 1956.
2. Minos and Knossos: Pendlebury 2003. Whether Minos was a historical character is contested. There may have been several individual kings with the same name.
3. The Minotaur here carries rocks as a weapon.

4. See, e.g., by Apollodorus, *Library* 3.1.3. On the myth see Siganos 1993.
5. See, e.g., Apollodorus, *Library* 3.3.
6. Pasiphaë was the daughter of the sun god Helios.
7. Apollodorus, *Library* 3.4.
8. 'And by the means of the ingenuity of Daedalus Pasiphaë had intercourse with the bull'. Diodorus of Sicily, *The Library of History* 4.77.3.
9. Some ancient sources also add that the Minotaur's name was Asterios or Asterion. See, e.g., Apollodorus, *Library* 3.4.
10. See, e.g., Pausanias, *Description of Greece* 2.31.1.
11. See, e.g., Pindar fragment 166 (Snell-Maehler).
12. See Antinous' account in Homer, *Odyssey* 21.303.
13. Another example would be the terracotta figures found at the sanctuary of Desponia at Lykosoura featuring a female body with a cow or sheep head, discussed in Aston 2011: 242–4.
14. Plutarch, *Theseus* 15.2.
15. Diodorus of Sicily, *Library of History* 4.77.3.
16. Pausanias, *Description of Greece* 1.24.1.
17. *Biformis*: Virgil, *Aeneid* 6.25; Ovid, *Metamorphoses* 8.166; Seneca, *Phaedra* 1172. *Mixtum*: Virgil, *Aeneid* 6.25. *Geminus*: Ovid, *Metamorphoses* 8.169.
18. For an overview of ancient ideas of generation, see Totelin 2018 (with further literature).
19. Hence its symbolic use in Greek literature (see, e.g., Strong 2010).
20. The donkey in the ancient world: Keller 1909: 259–70; Kitchell 2014: 57–9.
21. Keller 1909: 259.
22. Palladius' poem *On Grafting* includes thirty grafts of which twenty-three are today considered impossible (see Totelin 2018: 65). On grafting in the ancient world more generally, see Hardy and Totelin 2015: 135–41. We also know about some ancient efforts at cross-pollinating individual types of plants. There is, for example, some indication that in the ancient world, date palms were variously cultivated into different varieties (see Roberts 1965: 4–9).
23. Pliny, *Natural History* 15.9.
24. Plutarch, *Table Talk* 2.6.1 (640b).
25. Plutarch, *Table Talk* 2.6.1 (640b).
26. See Hardy and Totelin 2015: 137–9 with further evidence.
27. Theophrastus, *Enquiry into Plants* 2.1.4.
28. Here and below see Totelin 2018: 65 (with further examples).
29. Aelian, *On Animals* 12.16.
30. Aelian, *On Animals* 12.16.
31. And not just the human experience: The ancient sources also record instances of hubris for animals and plants (see Michelini 1978).
32. See Sophocles, *Antigone*.
33. As for example described in Herodotus, *Histories* 7.34–7.
34. See Cohen 1991: 176–80.

35. Plutarch, *Beasts Are Rational* 985d–93e.
36. Plutarch, *Beasts Are Rational* 990e–f.
37. On the 'man-only *topos*' in the ancient world, see Sorabji 1993.
38. Plutarch, *Beasts Are Rational* 991a.
39. Plutarch, *Beasts Are Rational* 991a.
40. On the link between bestiality and sexual transgression (in particular rape) in Greek myth more generally, see Robson 1997.
41. Apollodorus, *Library* 3.15.8. Apparently certain oracles urged Minos to do so (see, e.g., Apollodorus, *Library* 3.1.4). On the (symbolism of the) labyrinth from antiquity to the present, see Hooke 1935; Kerneyi 1950; Matthews 1970; Kern 1982; Hocke 1987; Piper 1987; Schmeling 1987.
42. See, e.g., Apollodorus, *Library* 4.61.3.
43. Apollodorus, *Library* 3.1.4, perhaps quoting Sophocles' *Daedalus*, as suggested by Frazer 1921: 306, note 1.
44. For this part of the story, see Plutarch, *Theseus* 15.19. On Theseus see: Brommer 1982; Calame 1990.
45. See Ziolkowski 2008.
46. See, e.g. Marconi 2017: 109. Even though he never visited Greece, Picasso experienced the ancient world in multiple forms: through the plaster casts of ancient statues he was asked to sketch in his formative years as an artist; through his engagement with the reception of the ancient world in the works of other painters such as Jean-Auguste-Dominique Ingres (1780–1867); and through his inspection of material artefacts from the ancient world in the Louvre (see Ferguson 1962). Most notably, he visited Italy in 1917 for a two-month stay – the one and only trip abroad in his life. Picasso's interest in the ancient world also inspired him to illustrate works of classical literature, such as Ovid's *Metamorphoses* (for which he produced twenty etchings in 1930/1) and Aristophanes' comedy *Lysistrata* (which he illustrated, 1934).
47. See Richardson 2017; 2021, in particular 23–33.
48. The Vollard Suite is named after the French art dealer Ambroise Vollard who commissioned it. The Minotaur features prominently enough in the suite that its later publisher, Hans Bolliger, named two of the seven thematic sections after the ancient figure ('The Minotaur' and 'The Blind Minotaur', see Bolliger 1956). The Minotaur-themed sections are usually published towards the end of the suite, but this is not a convention authorized by the artist himself. On the volatile history of the Vollard Suite, see, e.g., Florman 2002: 70–86.
49. Volume IV of John Richardson's *Life of Picasso* (2021) covering the years between 1933 and 1943 is thus titled *The Minotaur Years.*
50. Picasso lived much of his adult life in France, but as a Spaniard by birth he was familiar with bullfights, attending them even in his later years. Bulls and bullfights as a subject in Picasso: Marrero 1956; Friedewald 2014: 117–35; Richardson 2017.
51. See, e.g., Figures 9.5–8, 9.10–11, and 9.13.
52. On the hybridity of Picasso's Minotaurs, see also Richardson 2017: 145.
53. See e.g. Gedo 1980: 135–68; Gadon 2003; Utley 2017.

54. Souchère 1960: 54, quoted in Ashton 1972: 159.
55. See Rosenblum 1996; Richardson 2021: 3–11.
56. See, e.g., Rosenblum 1996.
57. See Gadon 2003: 24–5.
58. See, e.g., Ferguson 1962.
59. Those commentators who seek to move beyond this perspective do not deny the autobiography of Picasso's works (see, e.g., the brilliant reframing of what is at stake in the autobiographical features included in many of Picasso's works in Clark's 2013: 4–13). But they take issue with the idea that the complexity of Picasso's artistic interventions emerges through the sole focus on the life of the artist who created them. In her interpretation of the Minotaur-themed Vollard etchings, for example, the American art historian Lisa Florman (2002: 71–138 and 140–94 respectively) has drawn attention to the way in which they resonate with other sections of the Vollard Suite, other works of art both contemporary with and pre-dating Picasso, and the writings of the French philosopher Georges Bataille (1897–1962).
60. See, e.g., Clark 2013: 3–21 and 172: 'biography is banality or speculation'. For an early articulation of this criticism, see Barrett 1959: 41–2.
61. The 'celebratory' setting of this etching: FitzGerald 2017: 139.
62. The theme of the sleep-watcher: Steinberg 1972: 93–114 with 101–2 on the sleep-watching Minotaur.
63. I here follow Chris Danta's (2018: 143–51) excellent observations on the significance of the gesture of the open mouth in general (not related to Picasso's Minotaur).
64. The Minotaur with his mouth open also features in a number of other works by Picasso (see, e.g., Figures 9.8 and 9.10). In combination with the raised head, it denotes pain.
65. The scene is strangely reminiscent of the common fairy-tale type 'the bride and the animal groom' in which an animal masquerades as a human until after the wedding night when its real animal nature comes to the fore. On this story type see Danta 2018: 143–51.
66. See, e.g., Bolliger 1956 as pointed out by Florman 2002: 91.
67. FitzGerald 2017: 139–40 speaks of a deeply ambiguous figure.
68. See Utley 2017: 66 on the 'visionary blindness' of Picasso's Minotaur. On the blind Minotaur motif, see also Richardson 2021: 61.
69. See FitzGerald 1996a, 1996b; Léal 1996; Rosenblum 1996; Rubin 1996; Beisiegel 2016.
70. The studio as a subject: FitzGerald 2001; Greely 2006: 159–63; Richardson 2021: 136–7.
71. See, e.g., Vollard Suite, plates 38 (17 March 1933) and 69 (8 April 1933). See also Utley 2017: 62. On the theme of the artist's studio in Picasso's oeuvre, see also FitzGerald 2001.
72. The window as a 'metaphor for works of art': Florman 2002: 122.
73. On Picasso's 'Classical period', which preceded the creation of the Vollard Suite, see Blunt 1968.
74. Zervos 1935: 174; Ashton 1972: 38.
75. On Picasso's portraits of Walter, see Palau i Fabre 2011: 90–104.
76. As discussed in van Hensbergen 2004: 17.

77. The woman as a female matadora: e.g. Richardson 2021: 65. On Picasso's interest in bulls and bullfighting as part of his Spanish heritage, see note 55.
78. Doves and pigeons in Picasso: Friedewald 2014: 9–23. Richardson 2021: 66 takes the birds to be a reference to the pet pigeons of Picasso's father.
79. In addition to the candle, there is a 'Mithraic sun' in the top right-hand corner of the etching as another source of light – a reference to Picasso's interest in the Roman mystery religion of Mithraism.
80. van Hensbergen 2004: 14 identified the figure as a female matadora on the grounds that she seems to hold the sword. See also Barrett 1959: 45.
81. As Ries 1972/3: 144 has pointed out, there is some indication that Picasso at first imagined this Minotaur to carry another head. The contours of an alternative, smaller, and presumably more human head are still visible in the final print of the *Minotauromachy*, just above the torso.
82. The same pose also features in a painting Picasso created in 1936, entitled *Minotaur Carrying a Dead Mare in front of a Cave Facing a Young Girl in Veil* (Picasso National Museum, Paris, MP1163). Picasso created this work in 1936, a year after the *Minotauromachy*. And here, too, the Minotaur features together with the white mare, carrying her limp body in his right arm. In both instances the outstretched arm is directed away from the Minotaur's own line of vision and towards the young woman or women who are looking on. The posture recalls the figure of the blind Minotaur as a motif central to Picasso's oeuvre, which brings out Picasso's concern with (the loss of) vision. It highlights the vulnerable side of a creature which somehow depends on the young girl. But this Minotaur is not asking the young girl for help. Rather, he raises his arm to keep the female onlookers at bay, as if he wards or warns them off while still acknowledging their presence.
83. Autobiographical readings of the *Minotauromachy*: Richardson 2017: 12–16; 2021: 61–7.
84. Picasso's Minotaur and the Spanish Civil War: Richardson 2021: 63.
85. The Spanish Civil War in the work of Picasso (and *Guernica* in particular): Greely 2006: 147–87 (with further references); Utley 2017: 71–2.
86. The link between *Guernica* and the *Minotauromachy*: van Hensbergen 2004: 55.

10 THE SHEARWATERS OF *DIOMEDEA* (*CALONECTRIS DIOMEDEA TRANSFORMATA*)

1. The Scopoli shearwater: Bearman and Madge 1998: 42–72.
2. www.oiseaux-birds.com/card-scopoli-shearwater.html. The calls of the Scopoli shearwater are available here: www.xeno-canto.org/species/Calonectris-diomedea.
3. Virgil, *Aeneid* 11.274 mentions that they 'fill the cliffs with their tearful cries' (*scopulos lacrimosis vocibus implent*).
4. Aelian refers to the bird as an *erōdios*. Usually, the term denotes a heron, but here Aelian is thought to refer to the Scopoli's shearwater. Arnott 2007: 37–8 still has the bird as a Cory's shearwater with which the Scopoli shearwater was long considered to be conspecific. The Roman author Pliny (*Natural History* 10.126) refers to this bird as a *cataracta* ('plunger').

5. Aelian, *On Animals* 1.1.
6. Aelian, *On Animals* 1.1.
7. See, e.g., the depiction of Diomedes in Homer's *Iliad*. Despite his youth, he features as one of the most skilled and experienced fighters. See, in particular, the iconic scenes in Homer, *Iliad* 5.1–114 (Diomedes wounds Aphrodite), 6.119–236 with Harries 1993 (Diomedes' encounter of Glaucus on the battlefield), and 10.150–579 (Diomedes and Rheseus' famous horses). Virgil (*Aeneid* 2.162–8) recounts the famous story in which Diomedes removed the Palladium (a precious sacred statue) from Troy. Several ancient sources also confirm that Diomedes was one of the Greek fighters hiding in the Trojan Horse (see, e.g., Homer, *Odyssey* 4.265–90 (280, Tydeidēs); Hyginus, *Fabulae* 108; Quintus of Smyrna, *Posthomerica* 12.314–35; Tryphiodorus 457–91; Tzetzes, *Posthomerica* 641–50).
8. See, e.g., Homer, *Iliad* 5.297–351. The Greek gods were thought to be immortal but not invulnerable.
9. See, e.g., Ovid, *Metamorphoses* 14.476; Tzetzes on Lycophron 610.
10. The cult of Diomedes as represented in the archaeological and literary evidence: Castiglioni 2008.
11. The story of his comrades' transformation into birds is recounted in several ancient authors. In addition to Aelian, see, for example: Lycos, *Fragmente der Griechischen Historiker* (*FGrHist*): 570, F6; Ps.-Aristotle, *On Marvellous Things Heard* 79; Theophrastus, *History of Plants* 4.5.6; Pomponius Mela, *Chorography* 2.7.114; Virgil, *Aeneid* 11.271–4; Strabo 2.5.20, 5.1.8–9, 6.3.9, 17–22; Ovid, *Metamorphoses* 14.484; Pliny, *Natural History* 3.151, 10.126–7, 12.6; Antonius Liberalis 37.5–6; Solinus 2.45–51; Antigonus Carystius, *Mirabilia* 172; Augustine, *City of God* 18.16; Avien *Orbis descriptio* 646–9; Isidore of Seville, *Etymologies* 12.7.28–9. Smith (2014: 68) points to the Mauretanian king Juba II as a possible source of this story based on the reference in Pliny, *Natural History* 10.16.
12. Thumiger 2014 offers a succinct account of ancient tales of metamorphosis. See Zgoll 2004 on metamorphosis in Augustan poetry; Alexandridis 2009 on iconographic representations.
13. See Buxton 2009.
14. E.g. Homer, *Iliad* 24.614–7; Pausanias, *Description of Greece* 1.21.3. See also Buxton 2009: 201–2.
15. The political dimension of Ovid's *Metamorphoses*: Williams 2009 (with further literature).
16. Ovid, *Metamorphoses* 14.498–503. On this passage see also S. Smith 2014: 69–70 who attributes a 'political edge' to it. He argues that Diomedes' men act like a senate criticizing Venus, 'the ancestral goddess of the Julio-Claudian family', a politicizing of the passage he sees carrying over into Aelian's account.
17. Ovid, *Metamorphoses* 14.504–5. Astonishment and metamorphosis: Buxton 2009: 23–5.
18. Ovid, *Metamorphoses* 14.508–9.
19. As pointed out by Myers 2009: 140.

20. Pliny (*Natural History* 10.126) speculates that it is the fact that these birds also seem to purify the temple of Diomedes by putting water in their beaks and sprinkling it on their wings which gave rise to the story. On animal sounds being turned into human words and utterances, see Bettini 2008: 144–56.
21. On this point see Thumiger 2014: 403–5.
22. Ovid, *Metamorphoses* 1.236–7. For other ancient tellings of the story, see, e.g., Hyginus, *Fabulae* 176; Hyginus, *Astronomy* 2.4.1.1–8; Pausanias, *Description of Greece* 8.2.3; Pseudo-Eratosthenes, *Catasterisms* 8 (and Plato, *Republic* 8.565d–e for an oblique reference).
23. Ovid, *Metamorphoses* 1.233–5.
24. Ovid, *Metamorphoses* 1.236–9.
25. On this point see Thumiger 2014: 404.
26. Metamorphosis and metaphor: Thumiger 2014: 390–1; McLean 2017: 73–87.
27. The *Oxford English Dictionary* (2nd edn.) defines metaphor thus: 'A figure of speech in which a name or descriptive word or phrase is transferred to an object or action different from, but analogous to, that to which it is literally applicable.'
28. Semonides frag. 7.1–2.
29. Semonides frag. 7.2–6.
30. Aristophanes, *Acharnians* 781–3.
31. Apuleius, *Metamorphoses* 1.9.
32. The 'Second Sophistic': Whitmarsh 2005.
33. Here and below, I follow S. Smith 2014: 67–73.
34. S. Smith 2014: 71.
35. On this point see also Zgoll 2004: 218–19; Thumiger 2014: 406. But see, e.g., Aeschylus, *Prometheus Bound* 673 for an example where mind *and* body are claimed to be affected by metamorphosis. See Thumiger 2014 for further examples in which the mind is affected too.
36. Strabo, *Geography* 6.3.9 (284c).
37. Cognitive ethology: e.g. Allen and Bekoff 1997.
38. Homer, *Odyssey* 10.239–40. The erasure of memory in this particular story indicates that memory is frequently a dimension of mind that remains human post-transformation. Its absence in the pigs requires an explanation.
39. On metamorphosis and hybridity, see also Buxton 2009: 76–109.
40. In the ancient world, the ass was regarded as a lowly animal. As a beast of burden, it was not thought to be particularly clever (see, e.g., Plutarch, *Beasts Are Rational* 992c). For the debates about the dating of Apuleius' *Metamorphoses*, see Harrison 2000: 9–10.
41. See in detail Winkler 1985.
42. As argued by Harrison 2000: 238–52 and further substantiated by Murgatroyd 2004.
43. Apuleius, *Metamorphoses* 3.26. Enormous ears (hence improved hearing): Apuleius, *Metamorphoses* 9.15. Gigantic genitals: Apuleius, *Metamorphoses* 3.24.6, 10.22.1.
44. Overburdened: e.g. 3.28, 4.5, 7.18., 8.28, 9.10. Castration: e.g. 7.23. Death: e.g. 8.30, 10.17, 10.34. Beatings: e.g. 3.27, 4.3, 6.25, 7.28, 9.11.
45. Apuleius, *Metamorphoses* 9.13.

46. See, e.g., Apuleius, *Metamorphoses* 8.23. Sold/Traded: e.g. 7.23, 9.10, 9.15, 10.13. Stolen: 9.39, 10.1.
47. See Apuleius, *Metamorphoses* 10.18–22.
48. Apuleius, *Metamorphoses* 6.26.
49. Here and below I follow Bradley 2000. See also Penwill 1975; Bradley 2000;2012: 59–78; Panagotakis and Paschalis 2019.
50. See Bradley 2000, in particular 62–6.
51. Bradley 2000: 65–6.
52. On Lucius' citizenship and social status, see Harrison 2000: 215–20.
53. See Millar 1981 on this novel as a form of social critique.
54. Aristotle, *Politics* 1254b21–7. On the animal analogy in Aristotle's concept of natural slavery, see also N. Smith 1983; M. Heath 2008; Vlassopoulos 2011.
55. Xenophon, *Economics* 13.9; Cato, *On Agriculture* 2.7 with Bradley 2000: 59.
56. Kneebone 2020: 324.
57. Lycophron, *Alexandra* 609–11.
58. Physically, through the need to retrieve the crumbs from the hands of the visiting Greeks.
59. Apuleius, *Metamorphoses* 9.15.
60. Apuleius, *Metamorphoses* 10.13.
61. Darrieussecq 1996: 11.
62. On disgust see Menninghaus 2002. See also Hodson and Costello 2007; Curtis 2011. On disgust in the ancient world, see Lateiner 2017.
63. On the link between feminism and vegetarianism, see the review essay by Gaard 2002.
64. Garnett 1922: 13.
65. See Garnett 1922: 29.
66. See, e.g., Snitow 2015; Fau 2020.
67. Apuleius, *Metamorphoses* 9.2.
68. Apuleius, *Metamorphoses* 4.1.
69. See, e.g., Cicero, *On the Nature of the Gods* 2.140; Galen, *On the Usefulness of Bodily Parts* 3.1. Freud 2002: 41–2 with Danta 2018: 4–12; Kant 2015: 6.
70. On language and humanism in the philosophical tradition, see Osborne 2009: 63–97.
71. Ovid, *Metamorphoses* 1.637–41, 647–50.
72. Apuleius, *Metamorphoses* 3.25.
73. The narrative voice in Apuleius', *Metamorphoses*: W. Smith 1972. See also Slater 2020: 285 who argues that 'Lucius experiences the loss of human speech . . . as one of his greatest deprivations.'
74. Apuleius, *Metamorphoses* 3.29.
75. Kafka 2018: 97 (German orig. 1992b: 58).
76. 'Ungeheures Ungeziefer': Kafka 1992b: 56 (2018: 95 translates it as 'gigantic insect', but this is too neutral a translation.
77. See, e.g., Kafka 1992a: 12–18, 22–4.
78. Kafka 1992a: 22–3. See also: 20, 31, 34.
79. Kafka 1992a: 25–6.

80. Kafka 1992a: 28–9 (cheese).
81. On this point see Robertson 2004: 36.
82. Samsa is hardly the only one transforming in this tale. Other members of the Kafka family, most notably his father and sister, also undergo transformations. Here and below I follow Abraham 2008: 424–6.
83. Beicken 2001: 74.
84. Kurz 1980: 174.
85. Abraham 2008: 426 referring to Beicken 2001: 74, note 22.
86. Abraham 2008: 426 referring to Canetti 1969: 84f. and Sokel 1976: 18.
87. Kafka's verminous bug as a metaphor: Anders 1947; Beicken 2001: 75.
88. On Augustine see the introduction by Chadwick 1986.
89. Augustine, *City of God*, 18.16.
90. Augustine, *City of God* 18.16. See also Pliny, *Natural History* 10.126 for the same information.
91. The claim that animals fall outside of time and thus do not have history does not feature in any explicit sense in the ancient philosophical debate. It is made by Mortimer Adler (1967: 91) who states that 'only man is a historical animal'.
92. Augustine, *City of God* 18.18.
93. In this point, too, the shearwaters of Diomedea are not particular but represent a larger group of transformed creatures who fall outside of time and history at the moment of their transformation.
94. Buxton 2009: 191–209.
95. There is also evidence of such cult activity in Veneto and the Po Delta (see Castiglioni 2008; Parker 2011: 244–6).
96. The literary evidence for the cult of Diomedes is discussed in Castiglioni 2008 (with references).
97. Castiglioni 2008: 10, 15.
98. Localism in ancient Greece: Beck 2020.
99. Ancient criticism of tales of metamorphosis: Buxton 2009: 231–47.
100. Augustine, *City of God* 18.18.
101. See Augustine, *City of God* 18.18. On demons see, e.g., Burkert 1985: 329–32; Sfameni Gasparro 2015.
102. Augustine, *City of God* 18.18.
103. Augustine, *City of God* 18.18.
104. Augustine, *City of God* 18.18.
105. The Myrmidons ('ant-people'), a Thessalian mythological tribe which is said to have descended from Zeus (who had seduced a mortal woman by taking on the form of an ant), can hardly serve as the exception to this rule. Even though they were later turned back from ants into people, their figure is nowhere used to explore how an animal would experience the human existence.
106. See Csordas 2002: 58–87; Gibbs 2005.
107. Wilson and Foglia 2017.

108. Examples in which the transformed creatures experience the world in ways that differ from human experiences are rare. For an example see Plutarch, *Beasts Are Rational* 990a–b (Grunter's superior sense of smell).
109. In his influential essay 'What Is It Like to Be a Bat?', the American philosopher Thomas Nagel argued that it is indeed impossible for humans to experience the world from the point of view of an animal because of our particular kind of human consciousness, which differs from that of bats and other species (1974).

CONCLUSION

1. Gods, humans, and animals in ancient Greek religion: Detienne 1981; Ekroth 2008; Kindt 2021.
2. Berger 1980: 6–9.
3. See Kindt 2020a: 1–2.
4. As suggested by Danta 2018: 64–8 and others.

Bibliography

Abraham, U. (2008) 'Die Verwandlung', in B. von Jagow and O. Jahraus (eds.) *Kafka-Handbuch: Leben – Werk – Wirkung*. Berlin, 421–37.

Adler, M. (1967) *The Difference of Man and the Difference It Makes*. New York.

Agamben, G. (1998) *Homo Sacer: Sovereign Power and Bare Life*, trans. D. Heller-Roazen. Palo Alto, Calif.

Aguirre, M. and R. Buxton (eds.) (2020) *Cyclops: The Myth and Its Cultural History*. Oxford.

Ahrensdorf, P. and T. Pangle (eds.) (2014) *The Theban Plays*. Ithaca, NY.

Akinpelu, J. A. (1967) 'The Stoic *scala naturae*', *Phrontisterion* 5, 7–16.

Alexandridis, A. (2009) 'Shifting Species: Animal and Human Bodies in Attic Vase Painting of the 6th and 5th Centuries B.C.', in T. Fögen and M. Lee (eds.) *Bodies and Boundaries in Greco-Roman Antiquity*. Berlin, 264–84.

Alexandridis, A., M. Wild, and L. Winkler-Horaçek (eds.) (2008) *Mensch und Tier in der Antike: Grenzziehung und Grenzüberschreitung*. Wiesbaden.

Allen, C. and M. Bekoff (1997) *Species of Mind: The Philosophy and Biology of Cognitive Ethology*. Cambridge, Mass.

Anders, G. (1947) *Kafka, Pro und Contra: Die Prozeßunterlagen*. Munich.

Anderson, C., G. Theraulaz, and J. L. Deneubourg (2002) 'Self-Assemblages in Insect Societies', *Insectes Sociaux* 49, 99–110.

Anderson, G. (2004) 'Aulus Gellius as a Storyteller', in L. Holford-Stevens and A. Vardi (eds.) *The Worlds of Aulus Gellius*. Oxford, 105–17.

Anderson, J. K. (1961) *Ancient Greek Horsemanship*. Berkeley, Calif.

(1970) 'The Trojan Horse Again', *Classical Journal* 66, 22–5.

(1985) *Hunting in the Ancient World*. Berkeley, Calif.

Anderson, M. J. (1997) *The Fall of Troy in Early Greek Poetry and Art*. Oxford.

Anderson, S. (2004) *Doctor Dolittle's Delusion: Animals and the Uniqueness of Human Language*. New Haven, Conn.

Arendt, H. (1978) *The Life of the Mind*, 2 vols. New York.

(2003) [1971] 'Thinking and Moral Considerations', in J. Kohn (ed.) *Hannah Arendt: Responsibility and Judgement*. New York, 159–89 (first published in *Social Research* 38 (1971), 417–46).

(2005) [1990] 'Socrates', in J. Kohn (ed.) *Hannah Arendt: The Promise of Politics*. New York, 5–39 (first published as 'Philosophy and Politics', in *Social Research* 57 (1990), 73–103).

(2017) [1951] *The Origins of Totalitarianism.* London.

Arens, W. (1979) *The Man-Eating Myth: Anthropology and Anthropophagy.* Oxford.

Armstrong, R. H. (2005) *A Compulsion for Antiquity: Freud and the Ancient World.* Ithaca, NY.

(2012) 'Freud and the Drama of Oedipal Truth', in K. Ormand (ed.) *A Companion to Sophocles.* Oxford, 477–91.

Arnott, G. (2007) *Birds in the Ancient World from A to Z.* London.

Arrowsmith, W. S. (1966) 'Luxury and Death in the Satyricon', *Arion* 5, 304–31.

Ashton, D. (ed.) (1972) *Picasso on Art: A Selection of Views.* New York.

Aston, E. (2011) *Mixanthropoi: Animal–Human Hybrid Deities in Greek Religion.* Liège.

Atherton, C. (1998) *Monsters and Monstrosity in Greek and Roman Culture.* Bari.

Auguet, R. (1972) *Cruelty and Civilization: The Roman Games.* London.

Austin, J. N. H. (1983) 'Odysseus and the Cyclops: Who is Who', in C. Rubino and C. Shelmerdine (eds.) *Approaches to Homer.* Austin, Texas, 3–37.

Austin, R. G. (1959) 'Virgil and the Wooden Horse', *Journal of Roman Studies* 49, 16–25.

Bär, S. F. (2009) *Quintus Smyrnaeus 'Posthomerica' I: Die Wiedergeburt des Epos aus dem Geiste der Amazonomachie. Mit einem Kommentar zu den Versen 1–219.* Göttingen.

Bakker, E. (2013) *The Meaning of Meat and the Structure of the Odyssey.* Cambridge.

Baldry, H. C. (1952) 'Who Invented the Golden Age?', *Classical Quarterly* 2, 88–92.

Barchiesi, A. (2002) 'Narrative Technique and Narratology in the *Metamorphoses*', in P. Hardy (ed.) *The Cambridge Companion to Ovid.* Cambridge, 180–99.

Barrett, C. (1959) 'The Mystery of Pablo Picasso: Harlequin and the Minotaur', *An Irish Quarterly Review* 189, 37–48.

Barringer, J. (2001) *The Hunt in Ancient Greece.* Baltimore, Md.

Barthes, R. (1981) *Camera Lucida: Reflections on Photography,* trans. R. Howard. London (French orig. 1980).

Bartra, R. (1994) *Wild Men in the Looking Glass: The Mythic Origins of European Otherness.* Ann Abor, Mich.

(1997) *The Artificial Savage: Modern Myths of the Wild Man.* Ann Abor, Mich.

Baumbach, M. and S. Bär (2007) *Quintus Smyrnaeus: Transforming Homer in the Second Sophistic Epic.* London.

Beagon, M. (1992) *Roman Nature: The Thought of Pliny the Elder.* Oxford

Bearman, M. and S. Madge (1998) *The Handbook of Bird Identification: For Europe and the Western Palearctic.* London.

Beavis, I. C. (1988) *Insects and Other Invertebrates in the Classical World.* Exeter.

Beazley, J. (1963) *Attic Red-Figure Vase Painters,* 3 vols. Oxford.

Beck, H. (2020) *Localism and the Ancient Greek City State.* Chicago.

Beicken, P. (2001) *Erläuterungen und Dokumente. Franz Kafka: Die Verwandlung.* Stuttgart.

Beisiegel, K. (2016) *Picasso: The Artist and his Muses.* London

Bell, J. (2015) 'Taming Horses and Desires: Plato's Politics of Care', in J. Bell and M. Naas (eds.) *Plato's Animals: Gadflies, Horses, Swans, and Other Philosophical Beasts.* Bloomington, Ind., 115–30.

Bénatouïl, T. (2002) 'Logos et *scala naturae* dans le stoïcisme de Zénon et Cléanthe', *Elenchos* 23, 297–331.

Bentham, J. (2007) [1780] *Introduction to the Principles of Morals and Legislation.* Mineola, NY.
Berger, R. (1980) 'Why Look at Animals', in J. Berger (ed.) *On Looking.* New York, 1–26.
Bernheimer, R. (1952) *Wild Men in the Middle Ages.* Cambridge, Mass.
Bertrandy, F. (1987) 'Remarques sur le commerce des bêtes sauvages entre l'Afrique du Nord et l'Italie', *Mélanges de l'école française de Rome.* 99, 211–41.
Béthume, S. and P. Tomassini (eds.) (2021) *Fantastic Beasts in Antiquity: Looking for the Monster, Discovering the Human.* Louvain.
Bettini, M. (2008) *Voci: Anthropologia sonora del mondo antico.* Turin.
Bhorat, Z. (2022) 'Automation, Slavery, and Work in Aristotle's Politics, Book 1', *Polis* 279–302.
Bianchi, E., S. Brill, and B. Holmes (eds.) (2019) *Antiquities Beyond Humanism.* Oxford.
Blundell, S. (1986) *The Origins of Civilisation in Greek and Roman Thought.* London.
Blunt, A. (1968) 'Picasso's Classical Period (1917–25)', *The Burlington Magazine* 110, 187–94.
Bodel, J. P. (1984) 'Freedmen in the Satyricon of Petronius'. Dissertation, University of Michigan.
(1999) 'The Cena Trimalchionis', in H. Hofmann (ed.) *Latin Fiction: The Latin Novel in Context.* London, 38–51.
Bodnar, I. (2018) 'Aristotle's Natural Philosophy', in E. N. Zalta (ed.) *The Stanford Encyclopedia of Philosophy* (Spring 2018 Edition). https://plato.stanford.edu/archives/spr2018/entries/aristotle-natphil/.
Bolliger, H. (ed.) (1956) *Suite Vollard.* Stuttgart.
Bologna, C. (1978) 'Il linguaggio del silenzio. L'alterità linguistica nelle religioni del mondo classico', *Studi Storico Religiosi* 2, 305–42.
Borthwick, E. K. (1967) 'Trojan Leap and Pyrrhic Dance in Euripides' *Andromache* 1129–41', *Journal of Hellenic Studies* 87, 18–23.
Boulogne, J. (ed.) (2005) *Les Grecs de l'antiquité et les animaux: Le cas remarquable de Plutarque.* Lille.
Bradley, K. (1994) *Slavery and Society at Rome.* Cambridge.
(2000) 'Animalizing the Slave: The Truth of Fiction', *Journal of Roman Studies* 90, 110–25.
(2012) *Apuleius and Antonine Rome: Historical Essays.* Toronto.
Brassaï, G. (1999) [1964] *Conversations with Picasso.* Chicago, Ill.
Bréchet, C. (2005) 'La Philosophie de Gryllus', in J. Boulogne (ed.) *Les Grecs de l'antiquité et les animaux: Le cas remarquable de Plutarque.* Lille, 43–61.
Bremmer, J. N. (1986) 'A Homeric Goat Island (*Od.* 9.116–41)', *Classical Quarterly* 36, 256–7.
(2019) *The World of Greek Religion and Mythology: Collected Essays II.* Tübingen.
(2020) 'Religion and the Limits of Individualisation in Ancient Athens: Andocides, Socrates and the Fair-breasted Phryne', in M. Fuchs, A. Linkenbach, M. Mulsow, B.-C. Otto, R. B. Parson, and J. Rüpke (eds.) *Religious Individualisation: Historical and Comparative Perspectives.* Berlin, 1009–32.
(2021) *Becoming a Man in Ancient Greece and Rome.* Tübingen

(2021a) [1978] 'Initiation and the Heroes of the Trojan War', in *Becoming a Man in Ancient Greece and Rome.* Tübingen, 3–28.

(2021b) [1988] 'Odysseus versus the Cyclops', in J. N. Bremmer (ed.) *Becoming a Man in Ancient Greece and Rome.* Tübingen, 29–44.

(2021c) [1988] 'The Myth of Meleager in Homer', in J. N. Bremmer (ed.) *Becoming a Man in Ancient Greece and Rome.* Tübingen, 65–79.

(2021d) [1986] 'Oedipus and the Greek Oedipus Complex', in J. N. Bremmer (ed.) *Interpretations of Greek Mythology.* London, 159–74.

Brenne, S. (2018) *Die Ostraka vom Kerameikos.* Wiesbaden.

Brill, S. (2020) *Aristotle and the Concept of Shared Life.* Oxford.

Brommer, F. (1982) *Theseus: Die Taten der griechischen Helden in der antiken Kunst und Literatur.* Darmstadt.

Brown, C. G. (1996) 'In the Cyclops' Cave', *Mnemosyne* 49, 1–29.

Burgess, J. S. (1955) 'Achilles' Heel: The Death of Achilles in Ancient Myth', *Classical Antiquity* 14, 217–44.

(2009) *The Death and Afterlife of Achilles.* Baltimore, Md.

Burkert, W. (1972) *Lore and Science in Ancient Pythagoreanism.* Cambridge, Mass.

(1985) *Greek Religion: Archaic and Classical,* trans. J. Raffan. Cambridge, Mass.

Buxton, R. (ed.) (1999) *From Myth to Reason? Studies in the Development of Greek Thought.* Oxford.

(2009) *Forms of Astonishment: Greek Myths of Metamorphosis.* Oxford.

(2010) 'Metamorphoses of Gods into Animals and Humans', in J. N. Bremmer and A. Erskine (eds.) *The Gods of Ancient Greece: Identity and Transformations.* Edinburgh, 81–91.

Byl, S. (1975) *Recherches sur les grands traités biologiques d'Aristote: Sources écrites et préjugés.* Brussels.

Calame, C. (1977) 'La Légende du Cyclope dans le folklore européen et extra-européen: Un jeu de transformations narratives', *Études de Lettres* 10, 45–79.

(1990) *Thésée et l'imaginaire athénien: Légende et culte en Grèce antique.* Lausanne.

(2002) 'Ulysse, un héros proto-colonial? Un aspect de la question homérique', *L'Homme* 164, 145–54.

Calder, L. (2011) *Cruelty and Sentimentality: Greek Attitudes to Animals, 600–300 BCE.* Oxford.

(2017) 'Pet and Image in the Greek World: The Use of Domesticated Animals in Human Interaction', in T. Fögen and E. Thomas (eds.) I*nteractions between Animals and Humans in Graeco-Roman Antiquity.* London, 61–88.

Cameron, A. (1968) *The Identity of Oedipus the King: Five Essays on the Oedipus Tyrannus.* New York.

(1969) 'Petronius and Plato', *Classical Quarterly* 19, 367–70.

Campbell, G. L. (ed.) (2014) *The Oxford Handbook of Animals in Classical Thought and Life.* Oxford

Campbell, M. (1988) *The Witness and the Other World: Exotic European Travel Writing 400–1600.* Ithaca, NY.

Canetti, E. (1969) *Der andere Prozeß: Kafkas Briefe an Felice.* Munich.

Carlson, R. D. (2015) 'The Honey Bee and Apian Imagery in Classical Literature'. Dissertation, University of Washington.

Cartledge, P. (1993) *The Greeks: A Portrait of Self and Others.* Oxford.

(2009) *Ancient Greek Political Thought in Practice.* Cambridge.

Carucci, M. (2019) 'The Spectacle of Justice in the Roman Empire', in O. Hekster and K. Verboven (eds.) *The Impact of Justice in the Roman Empire: Proceedings of the Thirteenth Workshop of the International Network Impact of Empire (Ghent, June 21–24, 2017).* Leiden, 212–34.

Casanova, A. (2005) 'Il *Grillo* di Plutarco e Omero', in J. Boulonge (ed.) *Les Grecs de l'antiquité et les animaux: Le cas remarquable de Plutarque.* Lille, 97–109.

Cassin, B. (1990) 'Greeks and Romans: Paradigms of the Past in Arendt and Heidegger', *Comparative Civilizations Review* 22, 28–53.

Cassin, B. and J.-L. Labarrière (eds.) (1997) *L'animal dans l'antiquité.* Paris.

Castiglioni, M. P. (2008) 'The Cult of Diomedes in the Adriatic: Complementary Contributions from Literary Sources and Archaeology', in J. Carvalho (ed.) *Bridging the Gaps: Sources, Methodology and Approaches to Religion in History.* Pisa, 9–28.

Castro, E. B. Vivraios de (1992) *From the Enemy's Point of View: Humanity and Divinity in an Amazonian Society.* Chicago.

Cavarero, A. (2019) 'The Human Reconceived: Back to Socrates with Arendt', in E. Bianchi, S. Brill, and B. Holmes (eds.) *Antiquities beyond Humanism.* Oxford, 31–46.

Chadwick, H. (1986) *Augustine: A Very Short Introduction.* Oxford.

Chantraine, P. (1977) 'σφίγγω', in *Dictionnaire étymologique de la langue Grecque,* vol. IV. Paris.

Chase, G. H. (1902) 'The Shield Devices of the Greeks', *Harvard Studies in Classical Philology* 13, 61–127.

Clare, R. (1998) 'Representing Monstrosity: Polyphemus in the *Odyssey*', in C. Atherton (ed.) *Monsters and Monstrosity in Greek and Roman Culture.* Bari, 1–17.

Clark, G. (2000) 'Animal Passions', *Greece & Rome* 47, 88–93.

Clark, R. W. (1980) *Freud: The Man and the Cause.* London.

Clark, T. J. (2013) *Picasso and Truth: From Cubism to Guernica.* Princeton, NJ.

Clarke, M. (1995) 'Between Lions and Men: Images of the Hero in the *Iliad*', *Greek, Roman, and Byzantine Studies* 36, 137–59.

Clay, J. S. (1993) 'The Generation of Monsters in Hesiod', *Classical Philology* 88, 105–16.

(2003) *Hesiod's Cosmos.* Cambridge.

Coche-Zivie, C. (2004) *The Sphinx: History of a Monument,* trans. D. Lorton. Ithaca, NY.

Coetzee, J. M. (1999) *The Lives of Animals.* Princeton, NJ.

Cohen, D. (1991) *Law, Sexuality, and Society: The Enforcement of Morals in Classical Athens.* Cambridge.

Cohn, L. (1894) 'Apion 3', in G. Wissowa (ed.) *Paulys Real-Encyclopädie der Classischen Altertumswissenschaft,* vol. I. Stuttgart, 2803–6.

Coleman, K. M. (1990) 'Fatal Charades: Roman Executions Staged as Mythological Enactments', *Journal of Roman Studies* 80, 44–73.

Columbus, C. (1992) *The Log of Christopher Columbus,* trans. R. Fuson. Camden, Me.

Connors, C. (1998) *Petronius the Poet: Verse and Literary Tradition in the Satyricon.* Cambridge.

Coppel, S. (2012) *Picasso's Prints: The Vollard Suite.* London.
Corey, D. (2005) 'Socratic Citizenship: The Delphic Oracle and Divine Sign', *The Review of Politics* 67, 201–28.
Costa, J. T. (2006) *The Other Insect Societies.* Cambridge, Mass.
Crane, E. (1994) 'Beekeeping in the World of Ancient Rome', *Bee World* 75, 118–34.
Crouwel, J. H. (1981) *Chariots and Other Means of Land Transport in Bronze Age Greece.* Amsterdam.
Csordas, T. J. (2002) *Body/Meaning/Healing: Contemporary Anthropology of Religion.* New York, 58–87.
Cultrano, M. (2005) 'Hunter and Horseman: Glimpses into an Unknown Mycenean Iconography', in A. Gardeisen (ed.) *Les équides dans le monde méditerranéen antique.* Lattes, 289–98.
Curtis, R. I. (2001) *Ancient Food Technology.* Leiden.
Curtis, V. (2011) 'Why Disgust Matters', *Philosophical Transactions of the Royal Society B. Biological Sciences* 366, 3478–90.
D'Agostino, B. (2014) 'The Trojan Horse: Between Athena and Artemis', in A. Moreno and R. Thomas (eds.) *Patterns of the Past: Epitēdeumata in the Greek Tradition.* Oxford, 23–38.
Dalby, A. (2000) *Empire of Pleasures: Luxury and Indulgence in the Roman World.* London.
Damon, C. (1997) *The Mask of the Parasite: A Pathology of Roman Patronage.* Ann Arbor, Mich.
Danta, C. (2018) *Animal Fables after Darwin: Literature, Speciesism, and Metaphor.* Cambridge.
D'Arms, J. H. (1981) *Commerce and Social Standing in Ancient Rome.* Cambridge, Mass.
Darrieussecq, M. (1997) *Pig Tales: A Novel of Lust and Transformation,* trans. L. Coverdale. New York (French orig. 1996).
Darwin, C. (1859) *The Origin of Species by Means of Natural Selection.* London.
(2001) *Charles Darwin's Beagle Diary,* ed. R. D. Keynes. Cambridge.
(2004) [1871] *The Descent of Man and Selection in Relation to Sex.* London.
Daston, L. and F. Vidal (eds.) (2004) *The Moral Authority of Nature.* Chicago, Ill.
Davies, M. (2000) 'Climax and Structure in *Od.* 8.492–520: Further Reflections on Odysseus and the Wooden Horse', *Symbolae Osloenses* 75, 56–61.
Davies, M. and P. J. Finglass (2014) *Stesichorus: The Poems.* Cambridge.
Davies, M. and J. Kathirithamby (1986) *Greek Insects.* London.
Davies, R. (1971) 'The Roman Military Diet', *Britannia* 2, 122–42.
Davies, S. (2016) *Renaissance Ethnography and the Invention of the Human: New Worlds, Maps, and Monsters.* Cambridge.
Dawkins, R. (1976) *The Selfish Gene.* Oxford.
Delcourt, M. (2020a) *Oedipus; or, The Legend of a Conqueror.* Ann Arbor, Mich. (French orig. 1944).
(2020b) 'The Riddle', in M. Delcourt, *Oedipus; or, The Legend of a Conqueror.* Ann Arbor, Mich., 135–45.
(2020c) 'Victory over the Sphinx', in M. Delcourt, *Oedipus; or, The Legend of a Conqueror.* Ann Arbor, Mich., 105–34.

Descola, P. (1994) *In the Society of Nature: A Native Ecology in Amazonia.* Chicago, Ill.

Demisch, H. (1977) *Die Sphinx: Geschichte ihrer Darstellung von den Anfängen bis zur Gegenwart.* Stuttgart.

Depew, D. J. (1995) 'Humans and Other Political Animals in Aristotle's *History of Animals*', *Phronesis* 40, 156–81.

Derrida, J. (2009/2011) [1981] *The Beast and the Sovereign,* trans. G. Bennington, 2 vols. Chicago, Ill.

Descartes, R. (1984–91) *The Philosophical Writings of Descartes,* trans. J. Cottingham, R. Stoothoff, D. Murdoch, and A. Kenny, 3 vols. Cambridge.

DeSilva, J. (ed.) (2021) *A Most Interesting Problem: What Darwin's Descent of Man Got Right and Wrong about Human Evolution.* Princeton, NJ.

Desmond, A. and J. Moore (2009) *Darwin's Sacred Cause: Race, Slavery and the Quest for Human Origins.* London.

Desmond, W. D. (2006) *The Greek Praise of Poverty: The Origins of Ancient Cynicism.* Bloomington, Ind.

Detienne, M. (1971) 'Athena and the Mastery of the Horse' trans. A. B. Werth, *History of Religions* 11, 161–84.

(1981) 'Between Beasts and Gods', in R. Gordon (ed.) *Myth, Religion, and Society: Structuralist Essays by M. Detienne, L. Gernet, J. P. Vernant and P. Vidal-Naquet.* Cambridge, 215–28.

Detienne, M. and J.-P. Vernant (1991) *Cunning Intelligence in Greek Culture and Society,* trans. J. Lloyd. Cambridge.

Dierauer, U. (1977) *Tier und Mensch im Denken der Antike: Studien zur Tierpsychologie, Anthropologie und Ethik.* Amsterdam.

(1988) 'Das Verhältnis von Mensch und Tier im griechisch-römischen Denken', in P. Münch and R. Walz (eds.) *Tiere und Menschen: Geschichte und Aktualität eines prekären Verhältnisses.* Paderborn, 37–85.

Dietrich, B. C. (1962) 'Demeter, Erinys, Artemis', *Hermes* 90, 129–48.

Dillon, J. (1992) 'Plato and the Golden Age', *Hermathena* 153, 21–36.

Dombrowski, D. A. (1984) *The Philosophy of Vegetarianism.* Oxford.

(2014) 'Philosophical Vegetarianism and Animal Entitlements', in G. L. Campbell (ed.) *The Oxford Handbook of Animals in Classical Thought and Life.* Oxford, 535–55.

Donaghy, T. (2014) *Horse Breeds and Horse Breeding in the Greco-Persian World: 1st and 2nd Millennium BC.* Cambridge.

Dougherty, C. (1993) *The Poetics of Colonization: From City to Text in Archaic Greece.* Oxford.

(1999) 'The Double Vision of Euripides' *Cyclops*: An Ethnographic Odyssey on the Satyr Stage', *Comparative Drama* 33, 313–38.

(2001) *The Raft of Odysseus: The Ethnographic Imagination of Homer's Odyssey.* New York.

Douglas, M. (1972) 'Deciphering a Meal', *Daedalus* 101, 61–81.

duBois, P. (1982) *Centaurs and Amazons: Women and the Pre-History of the Great Chain of Being.* Ann Arbor, Mich.

Duchemin, J. (1945) *Le Cyclope d'Euripide.* Paris.

Dunbabin, K. M. D. (1996) 'Convivial Spaces: Dining and Entertainment in the Roman Villa', *Journal of Roman Archaeology* 9, 66–80.

(2005) *The Roman Banquet: Images of Conviviality*. Cambridge.
Edmunds, L. (1981) *The Sphinx in the Oedipus Legend*. Königstein.
(2006) *Oedipus*. London.
Ekroth, G. (2008) 'Meat, Man, God: On the Division of Animal Victims at Greek Sacrifices', in A. P. Matthiou and I. Polinskaya (eds.) *Mikros Hieromnemon: Meletes eis Mnemen Michael H. Jameson*. Athens, 259–88.
(2014) 'A Note on Minced Meat in Ancient Greece', in L. Karlsson, S. Carlsson, and J. B. Kullberg (eds.) *LABRYS: Studies Presented to Pontus Hellström*. Uppsala, 223–35.
Elderkin, G. W. (1939) 'The Bee of Artemis', *American Journal of Philology* 60, 203–13.
Elias, N. (2000) [1939] *The Civilizing Process: Sociogenetic and Psychogenetic Investigations*. Rev. ed. Oxford (German orig. 1939).
Ellingson, T. (2001) *The Myth of the Noble Savage*. Berkeley, Calif.
Endres, N. (2009) 'Trimalchio in West-Egg: The "Satyricon" and "The Great Gatsby"', *The F. Scott Fitzgerald Review* 7, 65–79.
Engdahl, N. G. M. (2013) 'Understanding Shield Emblems on Ancient Athenian Vases: The Case of Geryon's Many Shields', *The Coat of Arms* 226, 67–76.
Étienne, R. (2005) 'Aspects sociaux de l'élevage des chevaux en Grèce', in A. Gardeisen (ed.) *Les équides dans le monde méditerranéen antique*. Lattes, 243–8.
Euben, P. (2000) 'Arendt's Hellenism', in D. Villa (ed.) *The Cambridge Companion to Hannah Arendt*. Cambridge, 151–64.
Evely, D. (1996) *Minotaur and Centaur. Studies in the Archaeology of Crete and Euboea Presented to Mervyn Popham*. Oxford.
Faas, P. (2005) *Around the Table of the Romans: Food and Feasting in Ancient Rome*. Chicago, Ill.
Fagan, P. L. (2001) 'Horses in the Similes of the Iliad: A Case Study'. Dissertation, University of Toronto.
Falcon, A. (2019) 'Aristotle on Causality', in E. N. Zalta (ed.) *The Stanford Encyclopedia of Philosophy* (Spring 2019 Edition). https://plato.stanford.edu/archives/spr2019/entries/aristotle-causality.
Faraone, C. (1992) *Talismans and Trojan Horses: Guardian Statues in Ancient Greek Myth and Ritual*. Oxford.
Farnell, (1896) *Cults of the Greek States*, 5 vols. Oxford.
Farrell, J. (2021) *Juno's Aeneid: A Battle for Heroic Identity*. Princeton, NJ.
Fau, H. (2020) 'Lady into Fox (David Gernett, 1922): Un-weaving a Taylor-Made Gender or Re-Taming the Shrew?', *Gender Studies* 18, 39–47.
Ferguson, J. (1962) 'Picasso and the Classics', *Greece & Rome* 9, 183–92.
Fernández Delago, J.-A. (2000) 'Le Gryllus, une éthopée parodique', in L. van den Stockt (ed.) *Rhetorical Theory and Praxis in Plutarch: Acta of the 4th International Congress of the International Plutarch Society, July 3–6, 1996*. Leuven, 171–81.
Fiddes, N. (1991) *Meat. A Natural Symbol*. London.
Filonik, J. (2013) 'Athenian Impiety Trials: A Reappraisal', *Dike* 16, 11–96.
(2016) 'Impiety Avenged: Rewriting Athenian History', in E. P. Cueva and J. Martínez (eds.) *Splendide Mendax: Rethinking Fakes and Forgeries in Classical, Late Antique, and Early Christian Literature*. Groningen, 25–40.

Finglass, P. J. (2013) 'How Stesichorus Began his Sack of Troy', *Zeitschrift für Papyrologie und Epigraphik* 185, 1–17.
(2015) 'Iliou Persis', in M. Fantuzzi and C. Tsagalis (eds.) *The Greek Epic Cycle and Its Ancient Reception: A Companion*. Cambridge, 344–54.
(2018) *Sophocles: Oedipus the King*. Cambridge.
Finkelpearl, E. (1998) *Metamorphosis of Language in Apuleius*. Ann Arbor, Mich.
FitzGerald, M. (1996a) 'The Modernists' Dilemma: Neoclassicism and the Portrayal of Olga Khokhlova', in W. Rubin (ed.) *Picasso and Portraiture: Representations and Transformation*. New York, 296–335.
(1996b) 'A Triangle of Ambitions: Art, Politics, and Family during the Postwar Years with Francoise Gilot', in W. Rubin (ed.) *Picasso and Portraiture: Representations and Transformation*. New York, 404–45.
(2001) *Picasso: The Artist's Studio*. New York.
(2017) 'Picasso's Alter Egos: Minotaurs, Harlequins, Old Masters, and Other Performers', in J. Richardson (ed.) *Picasso: Minotaurs and Matadors*. London, 138–70.
Fitzgerald, W. (2000) *Slavery and the Roman Literary Imagination*. Cambridge.
Fitzgerald, S. (1998) *The Great Gatsby*. Oxford.
Florman, L. (2002) *Myth and Metamorphosis: Picasso's Classical Prints of the 1930s*. Boston, Mass.
Flower, B. and E. Rosenbaum (1958) *The Roman Cookery Book: A Critical Translation of 'The Art of Cooking' by Apicius for the Use in the Study and the Kitchen*. London.
Forsdyke, S. (2012) *Slaves Tell Tales: And Other Peoples in the Politics of Popular Culture in Ancient Greece*. Princeton, NJ.
Fögen, T. (2007) 'Antike Zeugnisse zu Kommunikationsformen von Tieren', *Antike und Abendland* 53, 39–75.
(2014) 'Animal Communication', in G. L. Campbell (ed.) *The Oxford Handbook of Animals in Classical Thought and Life*. Oxford, 216–33.
(2017) 'Lives in Interaction. Animal "Biographies" in Graeco-Roman Literature?', in T. Fögen and E. Thomas (eds.) *Interactions between Humans and Animals in Graeco-Roman Antiquity*. London, 89–136.
Fögen, T. and E. Thomas (eds.) (2017) *Interactions between Animals and Humans in Graeco-Roman Antiquity*. Berlin.
Forbes Irving, P. M. C. (1990) *Metamorphosis in Greek Myths*. Oxford.
Forsdyke, S. (2005) *Exile, Ostracism, and Democracy: The Politics of Expulsion in Ancient Greece*. Princeton, NJ.
Foster, J. R. (1982) *The Resolution Journal of Johann Reinhold Forster 1772–1775*, vol. IV, ed. M. E. Hoare. London.
Foster, M. D. (2009) *Pandemonium and Parade: Japanese Monsters and the Culture of Yōkai*. London.
Foucault, M. (1990) *The History of Sexuality*, vol. I: *An Introduction*, trans. R. Hurley. New York (French orig. 1976).
Franco, C. (2014) *Shameless: The Canine and the Feminine in Ancient Greece*, trans. M. Fox. Berkeley, Calif.
Frank, J. (2005) *A Democracy of Distinction: Aristotle and the Work of Politics*. Chicago, Ill.
Franklin, J. (1986) 'Aristotle on Species Variation', *Philosophy* 61, 245–52.

Franko, G. F. (2005/6) 'The Trojan Horse at the Close of the *Iliad*', *Classical Journal* 101, 121–3.
Frazer, J. G. (1921) *Apollodorus: The Library, Books 1–3.9.* Cambridge, Mass.
Freud, S. (1886–1982) *The Standard Edition of the Complete Psychological Works of Sigmund Freud*, trans from the German under the general editorship of James Strachey, in collaboration with Anna Freud, assisted by Alix Strachey and Alan Tyson, 24 vols. London.
(2002) *Civilization and Its Discontents*, trans. D. McLintock. London.
Friedewald, B. (2014) *Picasso's Animals.* Munich.
Friedrich, R. (1987) 'Heroic Man and Polymetis: Odysseus in the Cyclopeia', *Greek, Roman and Byzantine Studies* 28, 121–33.
(1991) 'The Hybris of Odysseus', *Journal of Hellenic Studies* 111, 16–28.
Frontisi-Ducroux, F. (2003) *L'homme-cerf et la femme-araignée: Figures greques de la 20etamorphose.* Paris.
Frost, F. (1999) 'Sausage and Meat Preservation in Antiquity', *Greek, Roman and Byzantine Studies* 40, 241–52.
Gaard, G. (2002) 'Vegetarian Ecofeminism: A Review Essay', *Frontiers* 23, 117–46.
Gadon, E. W. (2003) 'Picasso and the Minotaur', *India International Centre Quarterly* 30, 20–9.
Gamwell, L. and R. Wells (eds.) (1989) *Sigmund Freud and Art: His Personal Collection of Antiquities.* London.
Garber, M. (1996) *Dog Love.* New York.
Garnett, D. (1922) *Lady into Fox.* New York
Garnsey, P. (1996) *Ideas of Slavery from Aristotle to Augustine.* Cambridge.
(1999) *Food and Society in Classical Antiquity.* Cambridge.
Gärtner, U. (2020) 'Sua tamen sollertia – "Reden von Tieren" bei Phaedrus', in H. Schmalzgruber (ed.) *Speaking Animals in Ancient Literature.* Heidelberg, 55–79.
Gedo, M. M. (1980) *Picasso: Art as Autobiography.* Chicago, Ill.
Gera, D. L. (2003) *Ancient Greek Ideas on Speech, Language and Civilisation.* Oxford.
Gibbs, R. W. (2005) *Embodiment and Cognitive Science.* Cambridge.
Gilhus, I. (2006) *Animals, Gods, and Humans: Changing Attitudes to Animals, in Greek, Roman, and Early Christian Thought.* London.
Giraud, E. H. (2019) *What Comes after Entanglement? Activism, Anthropocentrism, and an Ethics of Exclusion.* Durham, NC.
Glenn, J. (1972) 'Virgil's Polyphemus', *Greece & Rome* 19, 47–59.
(1978) 'The Polyphemus Myth: Its Origins and Interpretation', *Greece & Rome* 25, 141–55.
Glock, H.-J. (2019) 'Aristotle on the Anthropological Difference and Animal Minds', in G. Keil and N. Kreft (eds.) *Aristotle's Anthropology.* Cambridge, 140–60.
Godfrey-Smith, P. (2018) *Other Minds: The Octopus and the Evolution of Intelligent Life.* London.
(2021) *Theory and Reality: An Introduction to the Philosophy of Science.* Chicago.
Goldhill, S. (1986) *Reading Greek Tragedy.* Cambridge.
(1988) 'Reading Differences: The *Odyssey* and Juxtaposition', *Ramus* 17, 1–31.
(1991) *The Poet's Voice: Essays on Poetics and Greek Literature.* Cambridge.

(2017) 'The Limits of the Case Study: Exemplarity and the Reception of Classical Literature', *New Literary History* 48, 415–35.
(2021) 'Freud, Archaeology and Egypt: Religion, Materiality and the Cultural Critique of Origins', *Arion* 28, 75–104.
Gottschall, J. (2001) 'Homer's Human Animal: Ritual and Combat in the *Iliad*', *Philosophy and Literature* 25, 278–94.
(2013) *The Storytelling Animal: How Stories Make Us Human.* New York.
Gowers, E. (1993) *The Loaded Table: Representations of Food in Roman Literature.* Oxford.
Gozzini Giacosa, I. (1992) *A Taste of Ancient Rome*, trans. A. Herklotz, with a foreword by M. T. Simeti. Chicago, Ill.
Greely, R. A. (2006) *Surrealism and the Spanish Civil War.* New Haven, Conn.
Green, C. M. C. (1996) 'Did the Romans Hunt?', *Classical Antiquity* 15, 222–60.
Green, J. D. (1985) 'Picasso's Visual Metaphors', *Journal of Aesthetic Education* 19, 61–76.
Greenhalgh, P. (1973) *Early Greek Warfare: Horsemen and Chariots in the Homeric and Archaic Ages.* Oxford.
Gruen, E. (2010) *Rethinking the Other in Antiquity.* Princeton, NJ.
Gruen, L. (2015) *Entangled Empathy: An Alternative Ethic for our Relationships with Animals.* Brooklyn, NY.
(2017) 'The Moral Status of Animals', in E. N. Zelta (ed.) *The Stanford Encyclopedia of Philosophy* (Fall 2017 Edition). https://plato.stanford.edu/archives/fall2017/entries/moral-animal/.
Guthrie, W. K. (1993) *Orpheus and Greek Religion.* Princeton, NJ.
Haldane, J. B. S. (1955) 'Aristotle's Account of Bees' "Dances"', *Journal of Hellenic Studies* 75, 24–5.
Hall, E. (1989) *Inventing the Barbarian: Greek Self-Definition through Tragedy.* Oxford.
Hall, J. (2002) *Hellenicity: Between Ethnicity and Culture.* Chicago, Ill.
Ham, J. and M. Senior (1997) *Animal Acts: Configuring the Human in Western History.* New York.
Haraway, D. (2003) *The Companion Species Manifesto: Dogs, People, and Significant Otherness.* Chicago, Ill.
(2007) *When Species Meet.* Minneapolis, Minn.
(2016) *Staying with the Trouble. Making Kin in the Chthulucene.* Durham, NC.
Hardy, G. and L. Totelin (2015) *Ancient Botany.* London.
Harries, B. (1993) '"Strange Meeting": Diomedes and Glaucus in *Iliad* 6', *Greece & Rome* 40, 133–46.
Harris, J. (2018) 'Flies, Wasps, and Gadflies: The Role of Insect Similes in Homer, Aristophanes, and Plato', *Mouseion* 15, 475–500.
Harrison, E. L. (1991) 'Homeric Wonder-Horses', *Hermes* 119, 252–4.
Harrison, P. (1992) 'Descartes on Animals', *The Philosophical Quarterly*, 219–27.
Harrison, S. J. (1996) 'Apuleius' Metamorphoses', in G. L. Schmeling (ed.) *The Novel in the Ancient World.* Leiden, 491–516.
(2000) *Apuleius. A Latin Sophist.* Oxford
Hartog, F. (2001) [1996] *Memories of Odysseus: Frontier Tales from Ancient Greece*, trans. J. Lloyd. Chicago, Ill.

Haubold, J. (2014) 'Ethnography in the *Iliad*', in M. Skempis and I. Ziogas (eds.) *Geography, Topography, Landscape.* London, 19–36.
Haussleiter, J. (1935) *Der Vegetarismus in der Antike.* Berlin.
Hawass, Z. and M. Lehner (1994) 'The Sphinx: Who built It, and Why?', *Archaeology* 47, 30–41.
Hawkins, T. (2017) 'Eloquent Alogia: Animal Narrators in Ancient Greek Literature', *Humanities* 6, 1–15.
Heath, J. (1992) 'The Legacy of Peleus: Death and Divine Gifts in the Iliad', *Hermes* 120, 387–400.
(1999) 'The Serpent and the Sparrows: Homer and Other Animals in Aeschylus' *Agamemnon*', *Classical Quarterly* 49, 396–407.
(2005) *The Talking Greeks: Speech, Animals, and the Other in Homer, Aeschylus, and Plato.* Cambridge.
Heath, M. (2008) 'Aristotle on Natural Slavery', *Phronesis* 53, 243–70.
Hensbergen, G. van (2004) *Guernica: The Biography of a Twentieth Century Icon.* New York.
Herchenroeder, L. (2008) 'Τί γὰρ τοῦτο πρός τὸν λόγον; Plutarch's "Gryllus" and So-Called "Grylloi"', *The American Journal of Archaeology* 129, 347–79.
Hernández, P. N. (2000) 'Back in the Cave of the Cyclops', *American Journal of Philology* 121, 345–66.
Hesk, J. (2000) *Deception and Democracy in Classical Athens.* Cambridge.
Hesse, M. (1966) *Models and Analogies in Science.* New York.
Hexter, R. (1990) 'What Was the Trojan Horse Made Of? Interpreting Vergil's *Aeneid, Yale Journal of Criticism* 3, 109–31.
Hobbes, T. (1985) [1651] *Leviathan.* Ed. with an intro. by C. B. McPherson. London.
Hocke, G. R. (1987) *Die Welt als Labyrinth: Manierismus in der europäischen Kunst und Literatur.* Rev. ed. Hamburg.
Hodson, G. and K. Costello (2007) 'Interpersonal Disgust, Ideological Orientations, and Dehumanization as Predictors of Intergroup Attitudes', *Psychological Science* 18, 691–8.
Høgel, C. (2021) 'St. Sabas among the Lions: The Wild and the Completely Wild in the Writings of Kyrillos of Skythopolis', *Ephemerides Theologicae Lovanienses* 97, 449–68.
Holford-Stevens, L. and A. Vardi (eds.) (2004) *The Worlds of Aulus Gellius.* Oxford.
Holzberg, N. (ed.) (2002) *The Ancient Fable: An Introduction.* Bloomington, Ind.
Hooke, S. H. (1935) *The Labyrinth: Further Studies in the Relation between Myth and Ritual in the Ancient World.* London
Hopwood, N., R. Flemming, and L. Kassell (eds.) (2018) *Reproduction: Antiquity to the Present.* Cambridge.
Horky, P. S. (2017) 'The Spectrum of Animal Rationality in Plutarch', *Apeiron* 50, 103–33.
Horsfall, N. (1989a) 'Atticus Brings Home the Bacon', *Liverpool Classical Monthly* 14, 60–2.
(1989b) 'The Uses of Literacy and the *Cena Trimalchionis*', *Greece & Rome* 36, 74–89, 190–209.
(2008) *Virgil, Aeneid 2: A Commentary.* Leiden.

Howe, T. (2014) 'Domestication and Breeding of Livestock: Horses, Mules, Assess, Cattle, Sheep, Goats and Swine', in G. C. Campbell (ed.) *Animals in Classical Thought and Life*. Oxford, 99–108.

Hudson-Williams, T. (1935) 'King Bees and Queen Bees', *Classical Review* 49, 2–4.

Hughes, J. D. (2007) 'Hunting in the Ancient Mediterranean World', in L. Kalof (ed.) *A Cultural History of Animals in Antiquity*. Oxford, 47–70.

Hulme, P. (1986) *Colonial Encounters: Europe and the Native Caribbean, 1492–1797*. New York.

Isaac, B. (2004) *The Invention of Racism in Classical Antiquity*. Princeton, NJ.

Jahoda, G. (2018) *Images of Savages: Ancient Roots of Modern Prejudice in Western Culture*. London.

Jane, C. (1960) *Journal of Christopher Columbus*. New York.

(1930) *Select Documents Illustrating the Four Voyages of Columbus*. London.

Jazdzewska, K. (2015) 'Tales of Two Lives in Xenophon's *Hiero*, Plutarch's *Gryllos* and Lucian's *Cock*', *Hermes* 143, 141–52.

Johnston, S. I. (1992) 'Xanthus, Hera and the Erinyes (*Iliad* 19.400–418)', *Transactions of the American Philological Association* 122, 85–98.

(2008) *Ancient Greek Divination*. London.

Jones, C. P. (1991) 'Dinner Theater', in W. J. Slater (ed.) *Dining in a Classical Context*. Ann Arbor, Mich., 185–98.

Jones, J. W. (1975) 'The Trojan Horse: *Timeo Danaos et Dona ferentis*', *Classical Journal* 65, 241–7.

Jong, I. de (2001) *A Narratological Commentary on the Odyssey*. Cambridge.

Kafka, F. (1992a) [1915] *Die Verwandlung. Mit einem Kommentar von Vladimir Nabokov*. Frankfurt.

(1992b) *Sämtliche Erzählungen*. Frankfurt.

(2018) *The Complete Stories*, trans. M. Secker. New York.

Kalof, L. (ed.) (2007) *A Cultural History of Animals in Antiquity*. London.

Kant, E. (2015) *Critique of Practical Reason*, trans. M. Gregor. Rev. ed. Cambridge.

Karbowski, J. (2019) 'Political Animals and Human Nature in Aristotle's Politics', in G. Keil and N. Kreft (eds.) *Aristotle's Anthropology*. Cambridge, 221–37.

Karttunen, K. (2002) 'The Ethnography of the Fringes', in E. Bakker, I. de Jong, and H. van Wees (eds.) *Brill's Companion to Herodotus*. Leiden, 457–74.

Keil, G. and N. Kreft (eds.) (2019) *Aristotle's Anthropology*. Cambridge.

(2019a) 'Introduction Aristotle's Anthropology', in *Aristotle's Anthropology*. Cambridge, 1–22.

Kelder, J. M. (2012) 'Horseback Riding and Cavalry in Mycenean Greece', *Ancient West & East* 11, 1–18.

Keller, O. (1909/1912) *Die antike Tierwelt*, 2 vols. Leipzig.

Kerenyi, K. (1950) *Labyrinth-Studien: Labyrinthos als Linienreflex einer mythologischen Idee*, 2nd ed. Zurich.

Kern, H. (1982) *Labyrinthe: Erscheinungsformen und Deutungen. 5000 Jahre Gegenwart eines Urbilds*. Munich.

Khanna, R. (2003) *Dark Continents: Psychoanalysis and Colonialism*. Durham, N.C.

Kietzmann, C. (2019) 'Aristotle on the Definition of What it is to be Human', in G. Keil and N. Kreft (eds) *Aristotle's Anthropology*. Cambridge, 25–43.

Kindt, J. (2016) *Revisiting Delphi: Religion and Storytelling in Ancient Greece.* Cambridge.

(2017) 'Capturing the Ancient Animal: Human/Animal Studies and the Classics', *Journal of Hellenic Studies* 137, 213–25

(2018) 'The Barking Ur-Indo-German Dog: Classicism, Cultural History, Humans, and Animals in Otto Keller's *Die Antike Tierwelt*', *Classical Receptions Journal* 10, 209–28.

(2020a) (ed.) *Animals in Ancient Greek Religion.* London.

(2020b) 'Animals in Ancient Greek Divination: Oracles, Predictions, and Omens', in J. Kindt (ed.) *Animals in Ancient Greek Religion.* London, 197–216.

(2021) *Animals in Ancient Greek Religion.* London.

King, A. (1999) 'Diet in the Roman World: A Regional Inter-Site Comparison of Mammal Bones', *Journal of Roman Archaeology* 12, 168–202.

King, E. (1942) 'Ingres as Classicist', *Journal of the Walters Art Gallery* 5, 68–113.

King, K. C. (1987) *Achilles: Paradigms of the War Hero from Homer to the Middle Ages.* Berkeley, Calif.

Kirby, V. (ed.) (2017) *What If Culture Was Nature All Along?* Edinburgh.

Kitchell, K. F. (1988) 'Virgil's Ballasting Bees', *Vergilius* 34, 36–43.

(2014) *Animals in the Ancient World from A to Z.* London.

(2020) 'Talking Birds and Sobbing Hyenas: Imitative Human Speech in Ancient Animals', in H. Schmalzgruber (ed.) *Speaking Animals in Ancient Literature.* Heidelberg, 447–76.

Kloft, H. (1994) 'Trimalchio als Ökonom: Bemerkungen zur Rolle der Wirtschaft in Petrons *Satyrica*', in R. Günther and S. Rebrenich (eds.) *E fontibus haurire: Beiträge zur römischen Geschichte und zu ihren Hilfswissenschaften.* Paderborn, 117–31.

Kneebone, E. (2020) *Oppian's Halieutica: Charting a Didactic Epic.* Cambridge.

Knox, B. M. W. (1950) 'The Serpent and the Flame: The Imagery of the Second Book of the *Aeneid*', *American Journal of Philology* 71, 379–400.

Konstan, D. (1990) 'An Anthropology of Euripides' *Cyclops*', in J. Winkler and F. Zeitlin (eds.) *Nothing to Do with Dionysos? Athenian Drama in its Social Context.* Princeton, NJ, 207–27.

(2010–11) 'A Pig Convicts Itself of Unreason: The Implicit Argument of Plutarch's "Gryllus"', *Hyperboreus* 16/17, 371–85.

Korhonen, T. and E. Ruonakoski (2017) *Human and Animal in Ancient Greece: Empathy and Encounter in Classical Literature.* London.

Kosmin, P. J. (2018) 'A Phenomenology of Democracy: Ostracism as Political Ritual', *Classical Antiquity* 34: 121–62.

Krauskopf, I. (1994) 'Oidipous', *Lexicon Iconographicum Mythologiae Classicae* 7(1), 1–15.

Krenz, P. (2000) 'Deception in Archaic and Classical Greek Warfare', in H. van Wees (ed.) *War and Violence in Ancient Greece.* London, 167–200.

Kron, G. (2014) 'Animal Husbandry', in C. Campbell (ed.) *Animals in Classical Thought and Life.* Oxford, 109–35.

Kuhn, T. (1962) *The Structure of Scientific Revolutions.* Chicago, Ill.

Kurz, G. (1980) *Traum-Schrecken: Kafkas literarische Existenzanalyse.* Stuttgart.

Lane Fox, R. (1996) 'Ancient Hunting: From Homer to Polybius', in G. Shipley and J. Salmon (eds.) *Human Landscapes in Classical Antiquity: Environment and Culture.* London, 119–54.
Lane, R. D. and K. L. Weihs (2010) 'Feud's Antiquities', *Psychodynamic Practice* 16, 77–8.
Lateiner, D. (2017) *The Ancient Emotion of Disgust.* Oxford.
Lavoie, G. (1970) 'Sur quelques métamorphoses divines dans l'*Iliade*', *L'Antiquite Classique* 39, 5–34.
Léal, B. (1996) '"For Charming Dora": Portraits of Dora Maar', in W. Rubin (ed.) *Picasso and Portraiture: Representations and Transformation.* New York, 384–407.
Lee, A. (1950) 'The Historical Ethnographic Image of the Drinking Peoples of the North', *Folklore* 61, 135–56.
Lefkowitz, J. (2014) 'Aesop and Animal Fable', in G. L. Campbell (ed.) *The Oxford Handbook of Animals in Classical Thought and Life.* Oxford, 1–20.
Lefkowitz, M. (2020) 'The "Wooden" Horse on the Athenian Acropolis', *Hesperia* 89, 581–91.
Lemke, T. (2011) *Biopolitics: An Advanced Introduction,* trans. E. F. Trump. New York.
Lennox, J. G. (2019) 'Is Reason Natural? Aristotle's Zoology of Rational Animals', in G. Keil and N. Kreft (eds.) *Aristotle's Anthropology.* Cambridge, 99–117.
Lenfant, D. (1999) 'Monsters in Greek Ethnography and Society in the Fifth and Fourth Centuries BCE', in R. Buxton (ed.) *From Myth to Reason? Studies in the Development of Greek Thought.* Oxford, 197–214.
Leonard, M. (2013) 'Freud and Tragedy: Oedipus and the Gender of the Universal', *Classical Receptions Journal* 5, 63–83.
(2015) *Tragic Modernities.* Cambridge, Mass.
(2021) 'Freud between Oedipus and the Sphinx', *Arion* 28, 131–55.
Lesky, A. and G. Herbig (1929) 'Sphinx', in A. Pauly and G. Wissowa (eds.) Paulys *Realencyclopädie der classischen Altertumswissenschaft* 2.6. Berlin, 1703–49.
Lestringant F. (1997) *Cannibals. The Discovery and Representation of the Cannibal from Columbus to Jules Verne,* trans. R. Morris. Berkeley, Calif.
Lévi-Strauss, C. (1969) *The Raw and the Cooked: Mythologiques,* vol. I. Chicago (French orig. 1964).
(1990) *The Origin of Table Manners: Mythologiques,* vol. III. Chicago (French orig. 1968).
(2020) [1962] *Wild Thought,* trans. J. Mehlmann and J. Leavitt. Chicago, Ill.
Levin, L. (2015) 'Bees and Wasps as Shield Devices in Greek Vase-Painting', in C. Lang-Auinger and E. Trinkl (eds.) *Corpus Vasorum Antiquorum,* Beiheft 2, 81–5.
Lewis, S. and L. Llewellyn-Jones (2018) *The Culture of Animals in Antiquity: A Sourcebook with Commentary.* London.
Lilja, S. (1976) *Dogs in Ancient Greek Poetry.* Helsinki.
Lindstrøm, T. C. (2010) 'The Animals of the Arena: How and Why Could their Destruction and Death be Endured and Enjoyed?', *World Archaeology* 42, 310–23.

Lissarargue, F. (2000) 'Aesop, Between Man and Beast: Ancient Portraits and Illustrations', in B. Cohen (ed.) *Not the Classical Ideal: Athens and the Construction of the Other in Greek Art.* Leiden, 132–49.

Littauer, M. (1972) 'The Military Use of the Chariot in the Aegean and Late Bronze Age', *American Journal of Archaeology* 76, 145–57.

Lloyd, G. E. R. (1983) *Science, Folklore, and Ideology: Studies in the Life Sciences in Ancient Greece.* Cambridge.

(1991) 'Aristotle's Zoology and his Metaphysics: The Status Quaestionis – A Critical Review of Some Recent Theories', in D. Devereux and P. Pellegrin (eds.) *Biologie, logique, et métaphysique chez Aristote.* Paris, 7–36.

(2013) 'Aristotle on the Natural Sociability, Skills and Intelligence', in V. Harte and M. Lane (eds.) *Politeia in Greek and Roman Philosophy.* Cambridge, 277–93.

Lonsdale, S. H. (1990) *Creatures of Speech: Lion, Herding, and Hunting Similes in the Iliad.* Stuttgart.

Loughlin, E. (2004) 'Grasping the Bull by the Horns: Minoan Bull Sports', in S. Bell and G. Davies (eds.) *Games and Festivals in Classical Antiquity.* Oxford, 1–8.

Lovejoy, A. O. (2001) [1936] *The Great Chain of Being: A Study of the History of an Idea.* Cambridge, Mass.

Lowe, D. (2015) *Monsters and Monstrosity in Augustan Poetry.* Ann Arbor, Mich.

Lutz, M. J., C. R. Reid, C. J. Lustri, A. B. Kao, S. Garnier, and I. D. Couzin. (2021) 'Individual Error Correction Drives Responsive Self-Assembly of Army Ant Scaffolds', *Proceedings of the National Academy of Sciences of the United States of America* 118(17), 1–8. https://doi.org/10.1073/pnas.2013741118.

Lynch, K. (2018) 'The Hellenistic Symposium as Feast', in F. van den Eijnde, J. Blok, and R. Strootman (eds.) *Feasting and Polis Institutions.* Leiden, 233–56.

Mackay, L. A. (1946) 'The Earthquake Horse', *Classical Philology* 41, 150–4.

MacKendrick, P. L. (1950) 'The Great Gatsby and Trimalchio', *Classical Journal* 45, 307–14.

Mackie, H. (1996) *Talking Trojan: Speech and Community in the Iliad.* London.

MacKinnon, M. (2004) *Production and Consumption of Animals in Roman Italy: Integrating the Zooarchaeological and Textual Evidence.* Portsmouth.

(2006) 'Supplying Exotic Animals for the Roman Amphitheatre Games', *Mouseion* 6, 137–61.

(2014a) 'Hunting', in G. L. Campbell (ed.) *The Oxford Handbook of Animals in Classical Thought and Life.* Oxford, 203–15.

(2014b) 'Pets', in G. L. Campbell (ed.) *The Oxford Handbook of Animals in Classical Thought and Life.* Oxford, 269–81.

MacLachlan, B. (2012) *Women in Ancient Greece: A Sourcebook.* London.

Marconi, C. (2017) 'Picasso and the Minotaur: A Chapter in Modern Mythmaking', in J. Richardson (ed.) *Picasso: Minotaurs and Matadors.* London, 88–110.

Macurdy, G. (1923) 'The Horse-Taming Trojans', *Classical Quarterly* 17, 50–2.

Maeterlinck, M. (2006) [1901] *The Life of the Bee*, trans. A. Sutro. New York.

Malkin, I. (1998) *The Returns of Odysseus: Colonisation and Ethnicity.* Berkeley, Calif.

Mallen, H. (2014) 'Pablo Picasso and the Truth of Greek Art', *Athens Journal of Humanities & Arts* 1, 283–98.
Mandeville, B. (2016) [1714] *The Fable of the Bees: Or, Private Vices, Public Benefits.* Oxford.
Marcovich, M. (1976) 'Pythagoras as Cock', *American Journal of Philology* 97, 331–5.
Marinatos, N. (1989) 'The Bull as Adversary: Some Observations on Bull-Hunting and Bull-Leaping', *Ariadne* 5, 23–32.
Marinatos, S. and M. Hirmer (1960) *Crete and Mycenae.* London.
Marquis, É. (2020) 'Philosophy in the Farmyard: The Speaking Cock in Lucian's *Gallus sive Somnium*', in H. Schmalzgruber (ed.) *Speaking Animals in Ancient Literature.* Heidelberg, 359–75.
Marrero, V. (1956) *Picasso and the Bull,* trans. A. Kerrigan. Chicago, Ill.
Marsh, D. (1998) *Lucian and the Latins: Humor and Humanism in the Early Renaissance.* Ann Abor, Mich.
Marshall, L. A. (2017) 'Gadfly or Spur? The Meaning of ΜΎΩΨ in Plato's *Apology of Socrates*', *Journal of Hellenic Studies* 137, 163–74.
Marx, K. (1991) [1867–94] *The Capital,* trans. P. Fowkes, 3 vols. London.
Matthews, W. H. (1970) *Mazes and Labyrinths: Their History and Development.* New York.
Mayhew, R. (1999) 'King-Bees and Mother-Wasps: A Note on Ideology and Gender in Aristotle's Entomology', *Phronesis* 44, 127–34.
Mayor, A. (2014) 'Animals in Warfare', in G. L. Campbell (ed.) *The Oxford Handbook of Animals in Classical Thought and Life.* Oxford, 282–93.
McLean, S. (2017) *Encounters and Fabulations at the Edges of the Human.* Minneapolis, Minn.
McCready-Flora, I. C. (2019) 'Speech and the Rational Soul', in G. Keil and N. Kreft (eds.) *Aristotle's Anthropology.* Cambridge, 44–59.
McGowan, J. (1998) *Hannah Arendt: An Introduction.* Minneapolis, Minn.
McInerney, J. (2010) *The Cattle of the Sun: Cows and Culture in the World of the Ancient Greeks.* Princeton, NJ.
(2014) 'Civilization, Gastronomy, and Meat-eating', in G. L. Campbell (ed.) *The Oxford Handbook of Animals in Classical Thought and Life.* Oxford, 248–68.
(2020) 'The Entanglement Between Gods, Humans, and Animals', in J. Kindt (ed.) *Animals in Ancient Greek Religion.* London, 17–40.
Menninghaus, W. (2002) *Ekel: Theorie und Geschichte einer starken Empfindung.* Stuttgart.
Michelini, A. (1978) 'HYBRIS and Plants', *Harvard Studies in Classical Philology* 82, 35–44.
Miguélez Cavero, L. (2013) *Triphiodorus, the Sack of Troy. A General Study and Commentary.* Berlin.
Mill, J. S. (2007) [1859] 'On Liberty', in M. Philip and F. Rosen (eds.) *Utilitarianism and Other Essays.* Oxford, 78–9.
Millar, F. G. B. (1981) 'The World of the Golden Ass', *Journal of Roman Studies* 58, 126–34.
Miller, F. D. (2011) *Nature, Justice, and Rights in Aristotle's Politics.* Oxford.
(2017) 'Aristotle's Political Theory', in E. N. Zalta (ed.) *The Stanford Encyclopedia of Philosophy* (Winter 2017 Edition). https://plato.stanford.edu/entries/aristotle-politics/.

Millett, P. (2005) 'The Trial of Socrates Revisited,' *European Review of History* 12, 23–62.

Minchin, E. (2001a) 'Similes in Homer: Image, Mind's Eye, and Memory', in J. Watson (ed.) *Speaking Volumes: Orality and Literacy in the Greek and Roman World.* Leiden, 25–52.

(2001b) *Homer and the Resources of Memory: Some Applications of Cognitive Theory to the Iliad and Odyssey.* Oxford.

Mitchell, J. (1974) *Psychoanalysis and Feminism.* London.

Mitchell, R. W., N. S. Thompson, and H. L. Miles (eds.) (1997) *Anthropomorphism, Anecdotes, and Animals.* New York.

Mondi, R. (1983) 'The Homeric Cyclopes: Folktale, Tradition, and Theme', *Transactions of the American Philological Association* 113, 17–38.

Mongan, A. (1947) 'Ingres and the Antique', *Journal of the Warburg and Courtauld Institutes* 10, 1–13.

Monsacré, H. (2018) *The Tears of Achilles,* trans. N. J. Snead. Washington, DC.

Moore, K. (1980) 'The Beauty of the Beast: Presence/Absence and the Vicissitudes of the Sphinx in Sophocles' Oedipus Rex and Oedipus at Colony's', *Boundary* 2, 1–18.

Mordeglia, C. and P. Gatti (eds.) (2017/2020) *Animali Parlanti,* 2 vols. Florence.

Moret, J.-M. (1984) *Oedipe, la Sphinx et les Thébains: Essai de mythologie iconographique.* Rome.

Morgan, J. R. (2009) 'Petronius and Greek Literature', in J. Prag and I. Repath (eds.) *Petronius: A Handbook.* London, 16–31.

Morgan, T. (2004) 'Educational Values', in L. Holford-Stevens and A. Vardi (eds.) *The Worlds of Aulus Gellius.* Oxford, 187–205.

Morley, N. (2007) 'Civil War and Succession Crisis in Roman Beekeeping', *Historia* 56, 462–70.

Mossmann, J. and F. Titcher (2011) 'Bitch is Not a Four-Letter Word: Animal Reason and Human Passion in Plutarch', in G. Roskam and L. van der Stockt (eds.) *Virtues for the People. Aspects of Plutarchan Ethics.* Leuven, 273–96.

Moulton, C. (1977) *Similes in the Homeric Poems.* Göttingen.

Mundis, H. (1976) *No He's Not a Monkey: He's an Ape and He's my Son.* New York.

Murgatroyd, P. (2004) 'The Ending of Apuleius' Metamorphoses', *Classical Quarterly* 54, 319–21.

Müller, G. (2019) 'Spot the Differences! The Hidden Philosophical Anthropology in Aristotle's Biological Writings', in G. Keil and N. Kreft (eds.) *Aristotle's Anthropology.* Cambridge, 118–39.

Murphy, L. (2017) 'Horses, Ships, and Earthquakes: The Trojan Horse in Myth and Art', *Iris* 30, 18–36.

Murthy, K. (1985) *Mythical Animals in Indian Art.* New Delhi.

Murgatroyd, P. (2013) *Mythical Monsters in Classical Literature.* London.

Myers, S. (2009) *Ovid: Metamorphoses,* book XIV. Cambridge.

Naas, M. (2015) 'American Gadfly: Plato and the Problem of Metaphor', in J. Bell and M. Naas (eds.) *Plato's Animals. Gadflies, Horses, Swans, and Other Philosophical Beasts.* Bloomington, Ind., 43–59.

Naddaf, G. (2006) *The Greek Concept of Nature.* New York.

Nadeau, R. (2010) *Les manières de table dans le monde Greco-romain: Tables des hommes*. Rennes.

Nagel, T. (1974) 'What Is It Like to Be a Bat?', *The Philosophical Review* 83, 435–50.

Nelson, S. (1997) 'The Justice of Zeus in Hesiod's Fable of the Hawk and the Nightingale', *Classical Journal* 92, 235–47.

Newman, J. K. (2003) 'Ovid's Epic, Picasso's Art', *Latomus* 62, 362–72.

Newmyer, S. T. (1995) 'Plutarch on the Moral Grounds for Vegetarianism', *Classical Outlook* 72, 41–3.

(1996) 'Of Pigs and People: Plutarch and the French Beast Fable', *Ploutarkhos* 13, 15–22.

(1997) 'Just Beasts? Plutarch and Modern Science: On the Sense of Fair Play in Animals', *Classical Outlook* 74, 85–8.

(1999) 'Speaking of Beasts: The Stoics and Plutarch on Animal Reason and the Modern Case against Animals', *Quaderni Urbinati di Cultura Classica* 63, 99–110

(2006) *Animals, Rights, and Reason in Plutarch and Modern Ethics*. London.

(2007) 'Animals in Ancient Philosophy: Conceptions and Misconceptions', in L. Kalof (ed.) *A Cultural History of Animals in Antiquity*. London, 151–74.

(2014) 'Being One and Becoming the Other: Animals in Ancient Philosophical Schools', in G. L. Campbell (ed.) *The Oxford Handbook of Animals in Classical Thought and Life*. Oxford, 507–34.

(2017) *The Animal and the Human in Ancient and Modern Thought: The 'Man Alone of Animals' Concept*. London.

(2021) *Plutarch's Three Treatises on Animals: A Translation with Introductions and Commentary*. London.

Newton, R. (1983) 'Poor Polyphemus: Emotional Ambivalence in *Odyssey* 9 and 12', *Classical World* 76, 137–42.

Norris, M. (1985) *Beasts of the Modern Imagination: Darwin, Nietzsche, Kafka, Ernst, and Lawrence*. Baltimore, Md.

Nussbaum, M. (2006) *Frontiers of Justice: Disability, Nationality, Species Membership*. Cambridge, Mass.

Obeyesekere, G. (2005) *Cannibal Talk: The Man-Eating Myth and Human Sacrifice in the South Seas*. Berkeley, Calif.

Osborne, C. (1995) 'Ancient Vegetarianism', in J. Wilkins, D. Harvey, and M. J. Dobson (eds.) *Food in Antiquity*. Exeter, 214–24.

(2009) *Dumb Beasts and Dead Philosophers: Humanity and the Humane in Ancient Philosophy and Literature*. Oxford.

Osorio, P. (2020) 'Virgil's Physics of Bugonia in Georgics 4', *Classical Philology* 115, 27–46.

Overmeire, S. van (2011) 'The Perfect King Bee: Visions of Kingship in Classical Antiquity', *Akroterion* 56, 31–46.

Pabst, A. (2020) 'Wenn Tiere reden könnten – Vom *Logos*-Gebrauch der Wesen ohne *logos* bei Plutarch', in H. Schmalzgruber (ed.) *Speaking Animals in Ancient Literature*. Heidelberg, 333–57.

Padgett, J. M. (2003) *The Centaur's Smile: The Human Animal in Early Greek Art*. New Haven, Conn.

Pakkanen, P. (2000/1) 'The Relationship between Continuity and Change in Dark Age Greek Religion: A Methodological Study', *Opuscula Atheniensia* 25/26, 71–88.

Palau i Fabre, J. (2011) *Picasso: Del Minotauro al Guernica (1927–1939).* Barcelona.

Palmatier, R. A. (1995) *Speaking of Animals: A Dictionary of Animal Metaphors.* Westport, Conn.

Panagotakis, S. and M. Paschalis (eds.) (2019) *Slaves and Masters in the Ancient Novel.* Groningen.

Panayotakis, C. (1995) *Theatrum Arbitri: Theatrical Elements in the Satyrica of Petronius.* Leiden.

(2009) 'Petronius and the Roman Literary Tradition', in J. Prag and I. Repath (eds.) *Petronius: A Handbook.* London, 48–64.

Parker, R. (1983) *Miasma: Pollution and Purification in Early Greek Religion.* Oxford.

(1996) *Athenian Religion. A History.* Oxford.

(2011) *On Greek Religion.* Oxford.

Patterson, A. (1991) *Fables of Power: Aesopian Writing and Political History.* Durham, NC.

Payne, M. (2010) *The Animal Part: Human and Other Animals in the Poetic Imagination.* Chicago, Ill.

Pearce, R. H. (1988) *Savagism and Civilization: A Study of the Indian and the American Mind.* Berkeley, Calif.

Pellegrin, P. (1982) *Aristotle's Classification of Animals: Biology and the Conceptual Unity of the Aristotelian Corpus,* trans. A. Preus. Berkeley, Calif.

(2007) *Dictionnaire Aristote.* Paris.

Pendlebury, J. D. S. (2003) [1954] *A Handbook to the Palace of Minos at Knossos with its Dependencies.* Oxford.

Penwill, J. L. (1975) 'Slavish Pleasures and Profitless Curiosity: Fall and Redemption in Apuleius' Metamorphoses', *Ramus* 4, 49–82.

Perry, B. (1952) *Aesopica: A Series of Texts Relating to Aesop or Ascribed to Him or Closely Connected with the Literary Tradition That Bears His Name,* vol. I: *Greek and Latin Texts.* Urbana, Ill.

Piper, J. (1987) *Das Labyrinthische: Über die Idee des Verborgenen, Rätselhaften, Schwierigen in der Geschichte der Architektur.* Braunschweig.

Platte, R. (2017) *Equine Poetics.* Washington, DC.

Podlecki, A. J. (1961) 'Guest-Gifts and Nobodies in "Odyssey 9"', *Phoenix* 15, 125–33.

Pollard, J. (1977) *Birds in Greek Life and Myth.* London.

Porphyry (2000) *On Abstinence from Killing Animals,* trans. G. Clark. London.

Posèq, A. W. G. (2001) 'Ingres's Oedipal "Oedipus and the Sphinx"', *Notes in the History of Art* 21, 24–32.

Potter, D. S. (2004) *The Roman Empire at Bay, AD 180–395.* London.

Pucci, P. (1993) 'L'io e l'altro nel racconto di Odisseo sui Ciclopi', *Studi Italiani di Filologia Classica* 11, 26–46.

Puetz, B. (2014) 'Good to Laugh With': Animals in Comedy', in G. L. Campbell (ed.) *The Oxford Handbook of Animals in Classical Thought and Life.* Oxford, 212–45.

Purcell, N. (2003) 'The Way We Used to Eat: Diet, Community, and History at Rome', *American Journal of Philology* 124, 329–58.

Raaflaub, K. (1997) 'Homeric Society', in I. Morris and B. Powell (eds.) *A New Companion to Homer.* Leiden, 624–48.

(1998) 'A Historian's Headache: How to Read 'Homeric Society?'', in N. Fisher and H. van Wees (eds.) *Archaic Greece. New Approaches and New Evidence.* Cardiff, 169–93.

(1998) 'Homer, the Trojan War, and History', *Classical World* 91, 386–403.

Ram-Prasad, K. (2019) 'Reclaiming the Ancient World: Towards a Decolonised Classics', *Eidolon.* https://eidolon.pub/reclaiming-the-ancient-world-c481fc19c0e.

Rand, H. (2015) 'What Was the Trojan Horse?', *Vulcan* 3, 1–18.

Ransome, H. (2004) [1937] *The Sacred Bee in Ancient Times and Folklore.* New York.

Raphael-Leff, J. (2007) 'Freud's "Dark Continent"', *Parallax* 13, 41–55.

Rawson, C. J. (1984) 'Narrative and the Proscribed Act: Homer, Euripides and the Literature of Cannibalism', *Literary Theory and Criticism* 2, 1159–97.

Redfield, J. (1994) *Nature and Culture in the Iliad: The Tragedy of Hector.* Durham, NC.

Rendall, J. (2018) *Christian the Lion: The Illustrated Legacy.* Guilford, Conn.

Renger, A.-B. (2013) *Oedipus and the Sphinx: The Threshold Myth from Sophocles through Freud to Cocteau.* Chicago, Ill.

Rhodes, P. J. (2003) *Ancient Democracy and Modern Ideology.* London.

Rice, E. F. (1988) *Saint Jerome and the Renaissance.* Baltimore, Md.

Richardson, J. (ed.) (2017) *Picasso: Minotaurs and Matadors.* London.

(2021) *A Life of Picasso* (4 vols.), vol. IV: *The Minotaur Years: 1933–1943.* London.

Ries, M. (1972–3) 'Picasso and the Myth of the Minotaur', *Art Journal* 32, 142–5.

Ristau, C. A. (ed.) (1991) *Cognitive Ethology: The Minds of Other Animals. Essays in Honor of Donald R. Griffin.* Hillsdale, NJ.

Riverlea, M. (2007) 'The Making of the Wooden Horse', *Iris* 20, 5–12.

Roberts, H. F. (1965) *Plant Hybridization Before Mendel.* New York.

Robertson, R. (2004) *Kafka: A Very Short Introduction.* Oxford.

Robson, J. E. (1997) 'Bestiality and Bestial Rape in Greek Myth', in S. Deacy and K. F. Pierce (eds.) *Rape in Antiquity.* London, 65–96.

Rohde-Dachser, C. (2003) *Expedition in den dunklen Kontinent: Weiblichkeit im Diskurs der Psychoanalyse.* Gießen.

Roller, M. B. (2006) *Dining Posture in Ancient Rome: Bodies, Values, and Status.* Princeton, NJ.

Romilly, J. de (1980) 'Docility and Civilization in Ancient Greece', *Diogenes* 28, 1–19.

Romm, J. S. (1992) *The Edges of the Earth in Ancient Thought: Geography, Exploration, and Fiction.* Princeton, NJ.

Rory, E. (2014) 'Insects', in G. L. Campbell (ed.) *The Oxford Handbook of Animals in Classical Thought and Life.* Oxford, 180–92.

Rose, K. (1962) 'Time and Place in the Satyricon', *Transactions of the American Philological Association* 93, 402–09

Rosenblum, R. (1996) 'Picasso's Blond Muse: The Reign of Marie-Thérèse Walter', in W. Rubin (ed.) *Picasso and Portraiture: Representations and Transformation.* New York, 337–83.

Rosivach, V. T. (2006) 'The Lex Fannia Sumptuaria of 161 BCE', *Classical Journal* 102, 1–15.

Rothgerber, H. (2013) 'Real Men Don't Eat (Vegetable) Quiche: Masculinity and the Justification of Meat Consumption', *Psychology of Men & Masculinities* 14, 363–75.

Rothwell, K. S. (2007) *Nature, Culture, and the Origins of Greek Comedy: A Study of Animal Choruses.* Oxford.

Rotroff, S. (2002) 'Urban Bees'. *American Journal of Archaeology* 106, 297.

Rouman, J. C. and W. H. Held (1972) 'More Still on the Trojan Horse', *Classical Journal* 67, 327–30.

Rubin, W. (1996) 'The Jacqueline Portraits in the Pattern of Picasso's Art', in W. Rubin (ed.) *Picasso and Portraiture: Representations and Transformation.* New York, 446–81.

Rudnytsky, P. (1987) *Freud and Oedipus.* New York.

Rutherford, I. (2020) 'Athene, Maliya and the Carpenter', in G. Battista et al. (eds.) *Il potere della parola: Studi di letteratura greca per Maria Cannatà Fera.* Alessandria.

Said, E. (2003) *Freud and the Non-European.* London.

Sayre, G. M. (1997) *Les Sauvages Américaines: Representations of Native Americans in French and English Colonial Literature.* Chapel Hill, NC.

Scarborough, J. (1982) 'Beans, Pythagoras, Taboos, and Ancient Dietetics', *Classical World* 75, 355–8.

Schmalzgruber, H. (ed.) (2020) *Speaking Animals in Ancient Literature.* Heidelberg.

Schmeling, G. (1970) 'Trimalchio's Menue and Wine List', *Classical Philology* 65, 248–51.

(2011) *A Commentary on the Satyrica of Petronius* (with the collaboration of A. Setaioli). Oxford.

Schmeling, M. (1987) *Der labyrinthische Diskurs: Vom Mythos zum Erzählmodell.* Frankfurt.

Schnapp-Gourbeillon, A. (1981) Li*ons, héros, masques: Les représentations de l'animal chez Homère.* Paris.

Scobie, A. (1977) 'Some Folktales in Graeco-Roman and Far Eastern Sources', *Philologus* 121, 1–23.

Scopoli, G. A. (1769) *Annus I. Historico-naturalis.* Leipzig.

Seeley, T. D. (2010) *Honeybee Democracy.* Princeton, NJ.

Segal, C. (1981) *Tragedy and Civilization: An Interpretation of Sophocles.* Cambridge.

(1983) 'Kleos and its Ironies in the *Odyssey*', *L'antiquité classique* 52, 22–47.

(1994) *Singers, Heroes, and Gods in the Odyssey.* Ithaca, NY.

(1995) *Sophocles' Tragic World: Divinity, Nature, Society.* Cambridge, Mass.

(2001) *Oedipus Tyrannus: Tragic Heroism and the Limits of Knowledge.* Oxford.

Segal, W. K. (1989) *Orpheus: The Myth of the Poet.* Baltimore, Md.

Sfameni Gasparro, G. (2015) 'Daimonic Power', in E. Eidinow and J. Kindt (eds.) *The Oxford Handbook of Ancient Greek Religion.* Oxford, 413–27.

Shear, J. (2011) *Polis and Revolution: Responding to Oligarchy in Classical Athens.* Cambridge.

Sheehan, B. (1980) *Savagism and Civility: Indians and Englishmen in Colonial Virginia.* Cambridge.

Shelton, J.-A. (2014) 'Spectacles of Animal Abuse', in G. L. Campbell (ed.) *The Oxford Handbook of Animals in Classical Thought and Life.* Oxford, 461–77.

Sherratt, S. (2010) 'The Trojan War: History or Bricolage?', *Bulletin of the Institute of Classical Studies* 53, 1–18.
Shettleworth, S. J. (2001) 'Animal Cognition and Animal Behaviour', *Animal Behaviour* 61, 277–86.
Siegfried, S. (2009) *Ingres: Painting Reimagined.* New Haven, Conn.
Siganos, A. (1993) *Le Minotaure et son mythe.* Paris.
Simpson, T. (2006) 'Who are our Contemporary Gadflies?', *Journal of Thought* 41, 3–8.
Singer, P. (1975) *Animal Liberation: A New Ethics for Our Treatment of Animals.* New York.
Skinner, J. E. (2012) *The Invention of Greek Ethnography: From Homer to Herodotus.* Oxford.
Slater, N. W. (2020) 'Animal Speech and Animal Silence in the World of Apuleius's *Golden Ass*', in H. Schmalzgruber (ed.) *Speaking Animals in Ancient Literature.* Heidelberg, 285–312.
Smith, N. D. (1983) 'Aristotle's Theory of Natural Slavery', *Phoenix* 37, 109–22.
Smith, S. D. (2014) *Man and Animal in Severan Rome: The Literary Imagination of Claudius Aelianus.* Cambridge.
Smith, W. S. (1972) 'The Narrative Voice in Apuleius' Metamorphoses', *Transactions and Proceedings of the American Philological Association* 103, 513–34.
Snitow, A. (2015) 'The Beast Within: *Lady into Fox and a Man in the Zoo*, in *The Feminism of Uncertainty: A Gender Diary.* Durham, NC, 153–6.
Snodgrass, A. M. (1964) *Early Greek Armory and Weapons: From the End of the Bronze Age to 600 BCE.* Edinburgh.
(1967) *Arms and Armour of the Greeks.* London.
Sokel, W. (1976) *Franz Kafka: Tragik und Ironie: Zur Struktur seiner Kunst.* Frankfurt.
Sorabji, R. (1993) *Animal Minds and Human Morals: The Origins of a Western Debate.* Ithaca, NY.
Soriano, A. M. (2019) 'Making Images Talk: Picasso's Minotauromachy', *Philosophy and Society* 30, 1–28.
Souchère, R. D. de la (1960) *Picasso in Antibes: Official Catalogue of the Musée d'Antibes known as the Musée Picasso.* New York.
Sparkes, B. A. (1971) 'The Trojan Horse in Classical Art', *Greece & Rome* 18, 54–70.
Srinivasan, M. V. (2011) 'Honeybees as a Model for the Study of Visually Guided Flight, Navigation, and Biologically Inspired Robotics', *Physiological Reviews* 91, 413–60.
Srinivasan, M. V., R. J. Moore, S. Thurrowgood, D. Soccol, D. Bland, and M. Knight (2013) 'Vision and Navigation in Insects, and Applications to Aircraft Guidance', in J. S. Werner and L. M. Chalupa (eds.) *The New Visual Neuroscience.* Cambridge, Mass., 1219–29.
Stallbaum, G. (1827) *Platonis Dialogos Selectos.* Gotha.
Stavru, A. (2018) 'Socrates' Physiognomy: Plato and Xenophon in Comparison', in G. Danzig, D. Johnson, and D. Morrison (eds.) *Plato and Xenophon: Comparative Studies.* Leiden, 208–51.
Steinberg, L. (1972) *Other Criteria: Confrontations with Twentieth-Century Art.* Oxford.

Steiner, G. (2005) *Anthropocentrism and Its Discontents: The Moral Status of Animals in the History of Western Philosophy*. Pittsburgh, Penn.

(2008) 'Das Tier bei Aristoteles und den Stoikern: Evolution eines kosmischen Prinzips', in A. Alexandridis, M. Winkler and L. Winkler-Horaček (eds.) *Mensch und Tier in der Antike: Grenzziehung und Grenzüberschreitung*. Wiesbaden, 27–46.

Stevenson, A. J. (2004) 'Gellius and the Roman Antiquarian Tradition', in L. Holford-Stevens and A. Vardi (eds.) *The Worlds of Aulus Gellius*. Oxford, 118–55.

Strauss, B. (2006) *The Trojan War: A New History*. New York.

Strauss Clay, J. (1974) 'Demas and Aude: The Nature of Divine Transformation in Homer', *Hermes* 2, 129–36.

Stripf, R. (2019) Honig für das Volk: Geschichte der Imkerei in Deutschland. Leiden.

Strong, A. (2010) 'Mules in Herodotus: The Destiny of Half-Breeds', *Classical World* 103, 455–64.

Suen, A. (2015) *The Speaking Animal: Ethics, Language and the Human–Animal Divide*. London.

Sullivan, J. P. (1968) *The Satyricon of Petronius: A Literary Study*. Bloomington, Ind.

Suzuki, T. N. (2021) 'Animal Linguistics: Exploring Referentiality and Compositionality in Bird Calls', *Ecological Research* 36, 221–31.

Taylor, N. and R. Twine (eds.) (2014) *The Rise of Critical Animal Studies: From the Margins to the Centre*. London.

Temerlin, M. K. (1975) *Lucy: Growing Up Human: A Chimpanzee Daughter in a Psychotherapist's Family*. Palo Alto, Calif.

Tero, A., et al. (2010) 'Rules for Biologically-inspired Adaptive Network Design', *Science* 327, 439–42.

Tero, A., R. Kobayashi, and T. Nakagaki (2007) 'A Mathematical Model for Adaptive Transport Network in Path Finding by True Slime Mold', *Journal of Theoretical Biology* 244, 553–64.

Thompson, D. P. (2004) *The Trojan War: Literature and Legends from the Bronze Age to the Present*. Jefferson, Mo.

Thompson, S. (1989) *Motif-Index of Folk-Literature: A Classification of Narrative Elements in Folktales, Ballads, Myths, Fables, Mediaeval Romances, Example, Fabliaux, Jest-Books and Local Legends*. Revised and enlarged edition, vol. I. Bloomington, Ind.

Thumiger, C. (2014) 'Metamorphosis: Humans into Animals', in G. L. Campbell (ed.) *The Oxford Handbook of Animals in Classical Thought and Life*. Oxford, 384–413.

Tilg, S. (2014) *Apuleius' Metamorphoses: A Study in Roman Fiction*. Oxford.

Totelin, L. M. (2018) 'Animal and Plant Generation in Classical Antiquity', in N. Hopwood, R. Flemming, and L. Kassell (eds.) *Reproduction: Antiquity to the Presesnt*. Cambridge, 53–66.

Touchefeu-Meynier, O. (1997) 'Polyphemos I', *Lexicon Iconographicum Mythologiae Classicae* 8(1), 1011–19.

Trustram, M. (2011) 'Response to "Freud's Antiquities" by Richard D. Lane and Karen L. Weihs', *Psychodynamic Practice* 17, 73–9.

Utley, G. R. (2017) 'Picasso and the Minotaur: A Self-Revealing Diary of a Most Painful Period', in J. Richardson (ed.) *Picasso: Minotaurs and Matadors.* London, 60–72.

Vance, E. (1973) 'Warfare and the Structure of Thought in Virgil's *Aeneid*', *Quaderni Urbinati di Cultura Classica* 15, 111–62.

Vardi, A. (2004) 'Genre, Conventions, and Cultural Programme in Gellius' *Noctes Atticae*', in L. Holford-Stevens and A. Vardi (eds.) *The Worlds of Aulus Gellius.* Oxford, 159–86.

Vehling, J. D. (2012) *Apicius. Cookery and Dining in Imperial Rome.* New York.

Vermeule, E. (1986) ''Priam's Castle Blazing': A Thousand Years of Trojan Memories', in M. Mellink (ed.) *Troy and the Trojan War: A Symposium Held at Bryn Mawr College October 1984.* Bryn Mawr, Penn., 77–79.

Vernant, J.-P. (1990a) 'Oedipus without the Complex', in J.-P. Vernant and P. Vidal-Naquet (eds.) *Myth and Tragedy in Ancient Greece.* New York, 85–111.

(1990b) 'Ambiguity and Reversal: On the Enigmatic Structure of Oedipus Rex', in J.-P. Vernant and P. Vidal-Naquet (eds.) *Myth and Tragedy in Ancient Greece,* trans. J. Lloyd. New York, 113–40.

(1990c) *Myth and Society in Ancient Greece,* trans. J. Lloyd. New York.

(1991) *Mortals and Immortals: Collected Essays,* ed. F. Zeitlin. Princeton, NJ.

Veyne, P. (1961) 'Vie de Trimalcion', *Annales: Economies, Sociétés, Civilisations* 16, 213–47.

Vidal-Naquet, P. (ed.) (1983) *The Black Hunter: Forms of Thought and Forms of Society in the Greek World,* trans. A. Szegedy-Maszak. Baltimore, Md.

Villa, D. (1999) 'Arendt and Socrates', *Revue Internationale de Philosophie* 208, 241–57.

(2001) *Socratic Citizenship.* Princeton, NJ.

Vlassopoulos, K. (2011) 'Greek Slavery: From Domination to Property and Back Again', *Journal of Hellenic Studies* 131, 115–30.

Vlastos, G. (1991) *Socrates: Ironist and Moral Philosopher.* Ithaca, NY.

Vogt, R. (1996) *Psychoanalyse zwischen Mythos und Aufklärung oder das Rätsel der Sphinx.* Frankfurt.

Waal, F. B. M. de (1999) 'Anthropomorphism and Anthropodenial: Consistency in Our Thinking about Humans and Other Animals', *Philosophical Topics* 27, 255–80.

(2016) *Are We Smart Enough to Know How Smart Animals Are?* New York.

Wächli, P. (2003) *Studien zu den literarischen Beziehungen zwischen Plutarch und Lukian.* Leipzig.

Waldau, P. (2013) *Animal Studies: An Introduction.* Oxford.

Wallace, S. (2010) *Ancient Crete: From Successful Collapse to Democracy's Alternatives, Twelfth to Fifth Centuries BC.* Cambridge.

West, M. (ed. and trans.) (2003) *Greek Epic Fragments.* Cambridge, Mass.

(2013) *The Epic Cycle: A Commentary on the Lost Troy Epics.* Oxford.

White, J. F. (2015) *The Roman Emperor Aurelian: Restorer of the World.* Barnsley.

Whitmarsh, T. (2005) *The Second Sophistic.* Cambridge.

Wilamowitz-Moellendorff, U. von (1976) [1931/32] *Der Glaube der Hellenen,* 2 vols. Berlin.

Wildberger, J. (2008) 'Beast or God? – The Intermediate Status of Humans and the Physical Basis of the Stoic *scala naturae*', in A. Alexandridis, M. Winkler, and L. Winkler-Horaček (eds.) *Mensch und Tier in der Antike: Grenzziehung und Grenzüberschreitung.* Wiesbaden, 47–70.

Wilkins, J. and S. Hill (2006) *Food in the Ancient World.* London.

Willey, H. (2021) 'Gods and Heroes, Humans and Animals in Ancient Greek Myth', in J. Kindt (ed.) *Animals in Ancient Greek Religion.* London, 82–101.

Williams, G. D. (2009) 'The Metamorphoses: Politics and Narrative', in P. E. Knox (ed.) *A Companion to Ovid.* London, 154–69.

Wilson, B. (2014) *The Hive: The Story of the Honeybee and Us.* London.

Wilson, E. O. (1971) *The Insect Societies.* Cambridge, Mass.

(2000) *Sociobiology. The New Synthesis.* Twenty-Fifth Anniversary Edition. Cambridge, Mass.

Wilson, R. A. and L. Foglia (2017) 'Embodied Cognition', in E. N. Zalta (ed.) *The Stanford Encyclopedia of Philosophy* (Spring 2017 Edition). https://plato.stanford.edu/archives/spr2017/entries/embodied-cognition/.

Winkler, J. (1985) *Auctor and Actor: A Narratological Reading of Apuleius' The Golden Ass.* Berkeley, Calif.

Winston, M. L. (1987) *The Biology of the Honey Bee.* Cambridge, Mass.

Winter, I. (1995) 'Homer's Phoenicians: History, Ethnography, or Literary Trope?', in J. B. Cater and S. P. Morris (eds.) *The Ages of Homer.* Austin, Texas, 247–71.

Wolfe, C. (ed.) (2003) *Zoontologies: The Question of the Animal.* Minneapolis, Minn.

(2009) *What is Posthumanism?* Minneapolis, Minn.

Wolff, F. (1997) 'L'animal et le dieu: Deux modèles pour l'homme: Remarques pouvant servir à comprendre l'invention de l'animal', in B. Cassin and J.-L. Labarrière (eds.) *L'animal dans l'antiquité.* Paris, 157–80.

Wood, M. (2015) *In Search of the Trojan War.* London.

Yalouris, N. (1950) 'Athena als Herrin der Pferde', *Museum Helveticum* 7, 19–64.

Young-Bruehl, E. (1990) *Freud on Women: A Reader.* New York.

Zagdoun, M. A. (2005) 'Problèmes concernant l'oikeiosis stoicienne', in J.-B. Gourinat (ed.) *Les Stoïciens.* Paris, 319–34.

Zak, W. F. (1995) *The Polis and the Divine Order. The Oresteia, Sophocles and the Defence of Democracy.* Lewisburg.

Zanda, E. (2011) *Fighting Hydra-Like Luxury in the Roman Republic.* Bristol.

Zatta, C. (2021) *Aristotle and the Animals: The Logos of Life Itself.* London.

Zervos, C. (1935) 'Conversation avec Picasso', *Cahiers d'Art* 10, 173–78.

(1956) *L'art de la Crète. Néolithique et minoenne.* Paris.

Zgoll, C. (2004) *Phänomenologie der Metamorphose: Verwandlungen und Verwandtes in der Augusteischen Dichtung.* Tübingen.

Ziegler, K. (1939) 'Orpheus', in *Realencyclopädie der classischen Altertumswissenschaft* 18, 1200–316.

Ziolkowski, T. (2008) *Minos and the Moderns: Cretan Myth in Twentieth-Century Art and Literature.* Oxford.

Index